# WILLIAM GILPIN
*Western Nationalist*

X

# WILLIAM GILPIN

## Western Nationalist

by

THOMAS L. KARNES

UNIVERSITY OF TEXAS PRESS

AUSTIN AND LONDON

Standard Book Number 292-70003-2
Library of Congress Catalog Number 77-105398
Copyright © 1970 by Thomas L. Karnes
All rights reserved

Type set by G&S Typesetters, Austin
Printed by Capital Printing Company, Austin
Bound by Universal Bookbindery, Inc., San Antonio

TO
SHELLY AND STEVE

# Contents

# Illustrations

*Following page 150*

# Acknowledgements

Because William Gilpin traveled so widely and pursued such varied activities in his long life, I found it necessary to call upon a large number of persons and agencies for help in research as well as understanding. I would like first to thank a number of historians, some of whom I have never met, for their careful reading of chapters which they are particularly well qualified to comment on. Lewis Atherton, Gerald M. Capers, Norman Graebner, LeRoy R. Hafen, the late Edwin C. McReynolds, Max Moorhead, and John E. Sunder all performed this task with courtesy and dispatch. Nyle H. Miller of the Kansas State Historical Society, Maurice Georges of Portland, Oregon, and Professor G. Malcolm Lewis of the University of Sheffield each lent insight into technical matters of Gilpin's career in letters exchanged with me. The footnotes and bibliography indicate my reliance upon a number of libraries and archives, but I want especially to thank Mrs. Laura Ekstrom of the State Historical Society of Colorado, Mrs. Frances H. Stadler of the Missouri Historical Society, and and the staff of the Tulane University Library for extraordinary ingenuity and assistance. Mrs. Reba N. Herman of the Tulane History Department typed several drafts and significantly added breadth to the manuscript by her real interest. I am indebted to the American Philosophical Society and the Tulane University Council on Research for grants that made summer research possible. To my wife, Virginia, and our daughter, Shelly, and son, Steve, goes my deep appreciation for having made easier thousands of miles of manuscript hunting and for contributing their sour good humor to the task of endless proofreading.

# WILLIAM GILPIN
*Western Nationalist*

# Prologue

William Gilpin achieved a measure of fame and success through participation in the nineteenth-century westward movement of the United States and, more particularly, in the early history of Missouri and Colorado. But on the national scale he became most closely identified with his message, delivered to the American people in flamboyant prose, that the West was a glorious place in which to live and that only by exploiting that region could the nation fulfill its God-given role. More sweeping than the language of Manifest Destiny, Gilpin's vision was of an America that would link Europe and Asia in ideas and commerce, and spread the dream of self-government around the world. To his contemporaries he was prophet, speculator, or charlatan, depending upon their own fortunes; today, exaggerations and distortions cast aside, he is most clearly revealed as America's first geopolitician.[1]

In most other regards William Gilpin was representative of an American type; every western territory had its share of Gilpins, some failing to leave a mark on the scene, others acquiring dominant local importance or even achieving brief national significance. This book is a biography of one man, but it reflects a belief that a study of William Gilpin will help Americans understand the lives of a large number of our nineteenth-century western politicians and entrepreneurs who contributed markedly to America's growth. These leaders of the West were easternborn, of comfortably situ-

[1] Bernard De Voto, "Geopolitics with the Dew on It," *Harper's Magazine*, CLXXXVIII (March, 1944), 313–323.

ated and often important families (still anchored in the East), educated a great deal more than the average American of the time, and always alert to grasp the next opportunity. Consequently, meeting the needs of the environment peculiar to the frontier, they usually pursued several distinct careers. William Gilpin plunged into a substantial share of these, failing as often as he succeeded, and accepting either conclusion with equal jauntiness. He was an inept farmer with no real heart for turning the soil. He was a soldier and a good one, rising as far as a nonprofessional could go, honored by his men and superiors alike. He was a lawyer with no briefs, using the bar as a means to other ends. He was a fearless editor, fighting for the common man with brilliant pen and little judgment (he probably would not have stayed long in that business without being shot). He was a politician, laughable as a campaigner, able as an administrator. He was a speculator and promoter specializing in the near miss—except once, when he made himself rich. Surpassing all these—and certainly most important in his own mind—he was a writer, speaker, publicist, and exhorter for the West, a field in which he was without equal.

William Gilpin enjoyed with other pioneers that restless energy which almost by definition characterized the frontiersman. In Gilpin's own words the pioneer army moved twenty-four miles each year, planted a crop, threw up a shanty good enough for one harvest season, and then sold out in order to push west again. Horace Greeley reported the same phenomenon and was appalled by it: "To see a man squatted on a corner-section in a cabin which would make a fair hog-pen . . . living from hand to mouth by a little of this and a little of that, with hardly an acre of prairie broken . . . waiting for someone to come along and buy out his 'claim' and let him move on to repeat the operation somewhere else—this is enough to give a cheerful man the horrors."[2]

Greeley and Gilpin were talking about the dirt-farmer pioneer, however, who was not usually a member of the class of territorial leadership that Gilpin represented, although even the politicians took a turn at farming when other choices were scarce. The territorial leaders expressed their restlessness in long, dramatic jumps to the newest opportunity and considered as part of the job the

[2] Horace Greeley, *An Overland Journey*, p. 52. Greeley also noted the easy shifting of vocations by the pioneers that he met.

surprisingly frequent trips to New York for capital or to Washington for favor. Gilpin must have traveled scores of thousands of miles in his lifetime on temporary business, and he made several permanent moves that covered hundreds of miles each.

When statehood was considered, these imported territorial officials were often repudiated by the dirt-farmer pioneer, who was more inclined to choose one of his own kind, or at least a man with more obvious roots in that community. But the Gilpin type accepted unquestioningly the boasted frontier democracy, in almost every sense of the word. His titles of "governor" and "colonel" rested lightly on his shoulders, for smaller men demonstrated how easily they could be obtained. Not infrequently a man became a high territorial official merely by knowing one congressman; and many westerners, after serving in a militia a very short time and moving on into new territory, promoted themselves retroactively. Gilpin enjoyed life's comforts and cultivated society; he loved books and—between domestic brawls—indulged his wife's tastes for music and art. But he was just as happy riding with "Peg-Leg" Smith, sleeping off a drunken fandango on the dirt floor of a peon's shack, or talking to his little ponies on lonesome mountain trails.

Political democracy to Gilpin meant only one thing—direct participation in government by all of the country's male citizens—and he regularly exulted that eleven million people all stopped on the same day to tell the government what to do. Holding this point of view and possessing such occupational mobility and restlessness, Gilpin was necessarily closely involved in almost every issue facing the American people in his lifetime, with the exception of post-Civil War reconstruction. His eccentric character probably kept him from playing many major roles; but always regionally, and often nationally, he was the "furious partisan." Not tied for long to any party line, he frequently embarrassed his chieftains with his activities.

Since William Gilpin held public office for only about three years, it was not vote-seeking that forced him to announce these opinions. It was rather the typical behavior of the western leader, active and informed, who saw clearly his region's stake in the future. For Gilpin's attitudes were always those of a westerner, not a Democrat or Republican, farmer, or businessman.

In broader terms Gilpin was a western nationalist, the most

vocal if not the most influential of a noisy breed. Perhaps only rarely did these men think in terms of some western nation arising by way of secession, but they believed that they were speaking for a region too vast for local or state government, a region that was, in fact, a sub-nation. In practice, this meant a bypassing of local government and a reaching to Washington, the founder of territories and the government responsible for sending most of these men into the West. The men of the sub-nation went to Washington for transportation, for water, for land charters, for grazing and mineral rights. Thus Independence, Denver, Santa Fe, Cheyenne, and the others could never be great cities because they never made great decisions.

It was in this environment, with its constant change and attendant excitement, that William Gilpin built and boasted and found his triumphs and defeats.

CHAPTER ONE

# The Brandywine Gilpins

*Background and School Days*

William Gilpin was born into a post-Revolutionary home that was comfortable, cultured, almost self-sufficient, and constantly stimulated and enriched by close family and commercial ties with the Old World.

The Gilpins were old enough in English history so that genealogy was a family hobby. Extended visits to the British Isles and government or commercial tours of duty made by various eighteenth- and nineteenth-century Gilpins refreshed the traditions and helped transplant a good deal of Englishness to America.

The family traced itself to the Norman name De Gaylpin or Guylpin, with the first accurate records referring to a certain Richard who about 1206 received an estate in Westmoreland from the Earl of Kendal. One story has it that Richard killed a wild boar that had injured a number of people. At any rate the family coat of arms included a boar.

Eleven successive generations resided at the estate of Kentmere, until the Gilpins temporarily lost it during the civil wars. Several Gilpins played significant roles supporting Elizabeth and later

Cromwell. One of these officers, Thomas Gilpin, joined the Society of Friends after the battle of Worcester in 1651. He and his family seem to have suffered sufficient persecution for this step that one son, Joseph, determined to leave for America. His father-in-law ceded his own Pennsylvania land grant to Joseph and his wife to help make their settlement possible.

The young couple reached America in 1696 and took up their land in Chester County, Pennslyvania, so impoverished that their home that first winter was a cave hollowed out of the dry, white clay. But the farm they started did well; their home soon became a log cabin and finally a frame house. Fifteen of their children married; and, since most of the early American Gilpins had large families, their descendants number in the thousands. They gradually scattered throughout Pennslyvania, Maryland, Delaware, and Virginia, but William's immediate ancestors clung closely to the region between Philadelphia and Wilmington.

It was in this area that William's grandfather, Thomas, expanded the developing family fortune. He inherited a large farm on the Susquehanna and, more important, land on the Chester River in Maryland and on the Brandywine in Delaware. Thomas visited Great Britain in 1752 to arrange for marketing of his wheat, tobacco, and corn, but being a man of versatility and scientific interests, he gained ideas for expansion into a variety of businesses. When he returned home he established a marketing village at the head of the Chester River in Maryland and named it Gilpinton (now Millington). Self-educated, he nevertheless published articles on the wheat fly, American locusts, coal, shells, and marine life. Thomas was one of the first members of the American Philosophical Society and in this manner became closely associated with Benjamin Franklin.

In 1764 Thomas married Lydia Fisher. The marriage could be considered advantageous, for Lydia's father, Joshua Fisher, was a cartographer and wealthy merchant of Philadelphia. The Fishers were also an old American Quaker family, and their business interests soon merged with those of the Gilpins as the Gilpin activities broadened.[1] Thomas gave a good deal of money to help found

[1] Information about Thomas Gilpin, 1727–1778, and his ancestors came from Myron L. Lazarus, "Joshua Gilpin, Esq.," (M.A. thesis), *passim*; Carl and Jessica Bridenbaugh, *Rebels and Gentlemen*, pp. 345–349; Dard Hunter, *Papermak-*

Wilmington Academy as a college preparatory school and regularly aided in its administration. But given Thomas' scientific aptitudes and the families' wide commercial activities, one development seems to have been inevitable—the desire to achieve the fullest utilization of the waterways which abounded in the Philadelphia-Wilmington area.

To exploit his businesses and landholdings and bring rapid growth to the entire region, Gilpin, from the 1750's on, urged businessmen and assemblymen to support a canal from the Delaware River to Chesapeake Bay. Thomas was propagandist, fundraiser, surveyor, and draftsman and even considered organizing his own canal company. He was perhaps ahead of his time; in any case, the outbreak of the American Revolution postponed all plans, and the canal had to await two subsequent generations of Gilpins.

Thomas Gilpin also wanted to make productive the shallow, swift waters of the Brandywine. Using property inherited from his uncle, Thomas operated a dam, race, and several mills, with some financial assistance from the Fishers.

These thriving and growing investments suddenly became the concern of the Gilpin family when in September, 1777, Thomas, with several other prominent Quakers, was arrested by officers of the state of Pennsylvania. The latter, fearing the strong British ties of these businessmen, demanded written oaths that the men would not, among other things, do anything injurious to the United States. Thomas declared that he would not assist the British cause in any way, but to take the oath demanded would violate his religious principles. The other men maintained similar positions, and they were hauled by wagon to Winchester, Virginia, where they were imprisoned with a number of German mercenaries. The Pennsylvania government soon reconsidered its action and early in 1778 asked for the release of the prisoners. But the internment had been too much for Thomas' health; he died that winter in Virginia.

Thomas and Lydia Gilpin had five children. Only two lived to adulthood, Joshua, William's father, born in Philadelphia in 1765,

*ing in Pioneer America*, pp. 82–83; *William Gilpin*, MS, P-L330, Bancroft Library; and Thomas Gilpin, "Memoirs of Thomas Sr.," *Pennsylvania Magazine of History and Biography*, XLIX (1925), 289–328.

and the younger Thomas, born in 1776. Both young men were tutored at home to fill in the gaps in their education left by the Wilmington Academy. At very early ages they assumed responsibility for the family's diverse business interests. Joshua was businessman, landlord, scholar; Thomas was inventor, scientist, mechanic. When they needed additional funds for their expansions they turned to the Fishers, who were content to be silent partners.

The most important consequence of this cooperation was a series of experiments in paper manufacturing. The shift into this activity came about logically in the 1780's. The Brandywine was increasingly bordered by mills, giving evidence of its power. It provided relatively pure water and the many growing towns along its banks were the source of large quantities of rag, cheaply transported. With Uncle Miers Fisher the two Gilpins in 1787 founded the first paper mill in Delaware. Receiving advice from Franklin and from various Europeans earlier visited by the elder Thomas, the firm prospered immediately and a French traveler said that the paper equaled France's best and was much simpler to make.[2]

The brothers and the manager of the mills alternated in studying European machinery. The Gilpins regularly put the consistent profits back into the mills, and, by 1817, owned the first mill in America that could manufacture an endless sheet of paper.[3] This product was of high quality and became very popular among users of fine paper. For many years this business was the center of the Gilpins' financial world. The mills, reported to be worth $300,000 to $400,000, employed around eighty people (most of whom lived in cottages on Gilpin land) and produced some $60,000 annually, according to Joshua. But the Gilpin commercial and industrial interests were not circumscribed by paper. Joshua and his neighbor E. I. du Pont (whose operations were much smaller than the Gilpins' in 1820) were officers of the Society for the Promotion of American Manufacture. Joshua continued marketing Maryland and Delaware grains in Philadelphia; he managed widely scattered family property that brought thousands of dollars in rent each year; and he seriously considered investing in—and perhaps did

[2] Hunter, *Papermaking*, p. 83.

[3] Lazarus, "Joshua Gilpin," p. 23; Elizabeth Montgomery, *Reminiscences of Wilmington*, pp. 32–38.

invest in—such activities as mining, iron manufacture, insurance, and banking.

This diversification was most fortunate for the family because ultimately the paper business declined. Competitors bribed Gilpin employees and stole plans and soon made rather public the Gilpins' manufacturing secrets. Much equipment and even part of the dam were washed away in catastrophic floods of the Brandywine in 1822 and 1838, and a fire in 1825 consumed a major building.[4] The mills were gradually converted to the manufacture of cotton between 1835 and 1840. The Gilpins sold the mills during that period.

In the midst of this fever of business activity Joshua Gilpin established a cultivated family life that was to surround William from his birth. Joshua was in Europe from 1795 to 1801 and in July, 1800, while in England, he married Mary Dilworth, of another of the transatlantic families with whom the Gilpins did business.

They made their home in Philadelphia, and several of their children were born there. In time, however, Joshua decided to move to the Brandywine to be nearer the mills. The estate on which the Gilpins settled was called "Kentmere," after the ancestral home in England. The house overlooked the mills about two miles north of Wilmington in a wooded, hilly section subsequently absorbed into the city.

Evidently both Thomas and Joshua reduced some of their Philadelphia interests and became increasingly tied to the Brandywine home. Theirs was a good and gracious life. Most of the important Americans of the turn of the century were friends of the Gilpins', from George Washington to Andrew Jackson. Visitors—du Ponts, Reads, Bayards, McLanes, Rodneys, Latrobes, Dickinson, and Jefferson—made life stimulating.[5] Joshua and Mary copied English country living even to the gardens, the furniture, and the superb library, the copying made easier by surprisingly regular and prolonged visits to Britain.

The several descriptions of Kentmere life agree in their extravagant praise of a home that combined the best of the idyllic and the

[4] Lazarus, "Joshua Gilpin," pp. 31–32; Henry Simpson, *The Lives of Eminent Philadelphians*, pp. 409–412.

[5] Lazarus, "Joshua Gilpin," p. 50; Gilpin MS, P–L330, Bancroft Library.

urban. Time could even be found for writing poetry, business tracts, histories, and travel accounts. All of his writing forms reveal much about Joshua, but his travel journals best foreshadow the interests of William with one significant difference: William lacked money sense. Joshua recorded every penny that he spent on his journeys to Bethlehem or Pittsburgh, or those to inspect western lands for speculation. Poet and businessman combine as Joshua describes the beautiful countryside in one paragraph and the prospects for its exploitation in the next. Joshua provided an interesting as well as comfortable home for his family.[6]

Of Mary Dilworth Gilpin, Joshua's wife and William's mother, far less information is available. She was an English-American Quaker whose father was a very successful banker in Lancaster, England. William's written praise of his mother is genuine, if overly sentimental. As a young man his letters to his father were direct and often businesslike in a youthful fashion. But writing to his mother or sisters brought a different tone from William; he included little news and no business but concentrated on lavish descriptions of the nature that so intrigued him. Perhaps he wrote what he thought his parents wanted to read. But William's love for the wilderness reached his pen most vividly when he wrote to his mother.

She and Joshua evidently remained in England from their marriage in July of 1800 until shortly after the birth of Henry on April 14, 1801. In the next fourteen years Mary gave birth to seven more children. Of the four girls only Elizabeth married.[7] Jane is never mentioned in William's family correspondence and must have died very early. It is possible that she and Thomas, the third Thomas in three consecutive generations, were twins. Sarah, Elizabeth, and Mary Sophia all lived until very late in the nineteenth century.

6 Simpson, *Lives*, p. 400; Lazarus, "Joshua Gilpin," *passim*; Joshua Gilpin, "Journey to Bethlehem," *Pennsylvania Magazine of History and Biography*, XLVI (1922), 122–153; Jennie Field, "The Story of Kentmere," Edward Gilpin Papers, Historical Society of Delaware; *Journal Every Evening* (Wilmington, Del.), September 12, 1914.

7 Elizabeth, 1804–1892, married James Maury, consul to England for several decades, and a cousin to Captain Matthew Maury, the brilliant naval scientist and oceanographer (Gilpin MS, P–L330, Bancroft Library). Lazarus (p. 57) is mistaken in calling Elizabeth *Matthew's* wife.

William's three brothers deserve some attention. Henry Dilworth Gilpin, the eldest child, was without question the closest to Joshua. He early took on a great share of the family business, generally directing affairs from Philadelphia, where he read for the bar with Joseph Ingersoll. He was admitted in 1822 at the age of 21. An ardent Jacksonian, he was for a time a government director of the Bank of the United States. Jackson's unsuccessful attempt to appoint him governor of Michigan Territory brought some unhappiness to the Gilpins and a great deal of party strife in Washington. President Martin Van Buren, a close friend, named him to the posts of solicitor of the Treasury and, in 1840, Attorney General of the United States. He retired from public office at the end of Van Buren's term.[8]

In the nonpolitical realm Henry's life was also significant. He edited Madison's papers, wrote a life of Van Buren, and edited *The Atlantic Souvenir* magazine for several years; he was director of the Pennsylvania Academy of Fine Arts, vice president of the Historical Society of Pennsylvania, a very active member of the American Philosophical Society, trustee of the University of Pennsylvania, and director of Girard College. As a young man he was secretary-treasurer of the Chesapeake and Delaware Canal Company, the old dream of his grandfather and his father; led by Mathew Carey and Henry, and frequently advised by Joshua, the corporation pushed the canal through to completion in 1829.

Henry Gilpin's position and achievements must be mentioned in a study of the career of his brother, William. Fourteen years younger, William looked as much to Henry for help as to his father. In his first twenty-five years William turned to the two older

---

[8] "Henry Dilwood Gilpin" in *The National Cyclopædia of American Biography*, Vol. VI. This article carries the wrong middle name for Henry.

Henry Gilpin's career can be examined with great profit as one element in the Bank war literature. Although he feared the Whigs' power over the Bank, he saw the necessity of a national banking system. Most Jacksonians hated the Bank. Henry's close friends included George Dallas, Charles Ingersoll, James Buchanan, Martin Van Buren, Benjamin Butler, and Amos Kendall. To imply as Arthur M. Schlesinger, Jr. (*The Age of Jackson*, p. 203) does that Henry was a traitor to his class is to misinterpret Philadelphia society of that era. The many well-to-do families along the Delaware were socially very close but of mixed party allegiance. Joshua and Henry were politically Jeffersonians before they heard of Andrew Jackson.

men for financial assistance, aid in securing military posts, and last-ditch security when his own variety of plans went wrong. Henry's clear successes were never begrudged by William; he presumed them and used them until the day came in his late twenties when he decided to stand alone.

William's other two brothers are not so well known. Thomas, 1806–1848, spent many years in Europe, first as a clerk of American business houses, then as a Jackson-appointed consul at Belfast. Thomas kept an eye on the Gilpins' British interests and his home served as a rendezvous point for the various Gilpins touring or going to school in the British Isles. Richard, 1812–1887, presumably born in England, owned a Chester County, Pennsylvania, farm for many years, according to most records, but family correspondence locates him also as a draftsman in England and an engineer in Illinois for brief periods.

This large Quaker family on the Brandywine stands out in retrospect as one full of love for and interest in one another, a family of comfort and achievement, a family of culture and diversity. As a group they suffered little: the one premature death in the family was rare for the times, and their variety of business interests kept up a good income even when depressions critically hurt some investments. Within this unit William was to be spoiled a little, but the Gilpin paternalism would prevent serious mistakes. The logic would have been for William to follow Henry in law and business and live his days out in Philadelphia or on the Brandywine. But William very early in life became intoxicated with the successive American Wests, and once he followed the western lure, he never again made his home in the East.

William's birthplace and birth date are both subject to a confusion partly fostered by Gilpin himself. In his later years he repeatedly told friends that he was born October 4, 1822, on Brandywine battlefield. He gave the same account to Hubert Howe Bancroft for the brief subsidized sketch of his life included in Bancroft's *Chronicles of the Kings,* and sensibly enough most writers mentioning Gilpin have assumed that the date was correct.[9]

It is not. A brief comparison with his school and military rec-

[9] William Gilpin, "A Pioneer in 1842," P–L28, October 18, 1884, Bancroft Library; Hubert Howe Bancroft, *History of the Life of William Gilpin.*

ords indicates that he could not have been born so late as 1822. No birth certificate exists, but a safe conclusion can be reached from two other public records. The United States Military Academy records declare that Gilpin entered West Point "July 1834, age 18 years 9 months." This would date his birth in the autumn of 1815, varying a few days with the accuracy of the "9 months." Gilpin's Mexican war pension records give October 4, 1815, as his birth date, information evidently gained from Gilpin when he filed in 1887. Whether his memory was failing when he talked to Bancroft or whether he deliberately decided to gain a few years one can only guess; October 4, 1815, is almost certainly the right birth date.[10]

The problem of a birthplace is more involved. Gilpin frequently asserted that he was born on the Brandywine *battlefield*, which, of course, is in Pennsylvania. All public records state that he was from New Castle County in Delaware or "Kentmere near Wilmington." Lazarus' biography of Gilpin's father has the wife and family in Liverpool in September, 1815, and landing at Marcus Hook on the Delaware in November. If all dates are correct then William was born aboard ship. However, this is too dramatic an event not to have been chronicled by his family and recounted by William many, many times in the future. The dates of the voyage are probably wrong. A reasonable guess is that young William grew up on the large estate on the Brandywine and was told that the important revolutionary battle was fought nearby. He then appropriated the actual scene of combat—only a few miles away—as his birthplace.[11]

William's family enjoyed, as we have seen, the life of English country squires, and there is no reason to believe that William did not make the most of his environment. He had very little formal schooling until he was at least ten or eleven years old. He was tutored by his father in the family tradition, but growing up among

[10] United States Military Academy, letter to author, July 31, 1958; Gilpin File, Mexican War Records, National Archives. *The Dictionary of American Biography* lists the birthdate as October 4, 1813.

[11] Christopher L. Ward, *The Delaware Continentals*, pp. 195–211. Another red herring drawn by Gilpin is that he lived on land in which Mason and Dixon's line marked the junction of three counties, Cecil, New Castle, and Delaware. Again he is almost right. There is such a common point if one substitutes Chester County, Pennsylvania for Cecil County, Maryland. That point is about four miles from Brandywine battlefield and on the Brandywine River.

du Ponts and other French exiles, he learned their language, fluently according to his own testimony. Even for young children life along the Brandywine and Delaware meant much visiting with the large families and hospitable friends. William claimed a good deal of importance for these people: nine signers of the Declaration of Independence lived nearby and three or four married into the Gilpin family.[12] Even discounting William's exaggerations it is clear that the Gilpin family was welcomed in many, many homes in those days of leisurely entertainment.

One childhood recollection of William's can be authenticated, at least in part. He recalled seeing, as a young boy on a horse behind his father, the triumphal return of the Marquis de Lafayette to the Brandywine country. Lafayette visited the United States in 1824 and 1825. In July, 1825, he traveled from Philadelphia to the du Pont home and then out to Chadds Ford (Brandywine battlefield). He accepted the greeting of several committees and then paid his respects to old Gideon Gilpin, a distant cousin to William's father, confined to bed in his home, which had been Lafayette's headquarters in September of 1777.[13] The prayers, the dinners, the toasts, and the other ceremonies provided a few memorable days for old-timers, and one can scarcely doubt that Joshua would have taken William along.

The informal education that Joshua provided William was not enough. When the boy was about thirteen, Joshua decided to send him to England for a period of schooling. In the care of the ship's captain William sailed on the *Montezuma* for Liverpool. Tom, Dick, and one sister were already in England and met him after a voyage of some three weeks. Tom, a Jackson appointee as consul at Belfast, arranged for quarters and a school.

The school, dating from the sixteenth century, was at Settle in Yorkshire, not far from the Gilpins' ancestral home. It was a small place of only sixty boys, liberal enough to tolerate Americans and Quakers. But evidently it did not meet American notions of proficiency in mathematics, for in the winter William left Settle tempo-

[12] Gilpin MS, P–L330, Bancroft Library.

[13] Gideon died at age eighty-seven shortly after their visit. J. Bennett Nolan, *Lafayette in America Day by Day*, p. 297.

rarily for Liverpool and special mathematics tutoring arranged by Tom.[14]

The school days must have been pleasant enough. William's letters to his family have no complaints in them. He enjoyed ice skating in Liverpool and passing holidays with his brother and many cousins in the British Isles. By 1830 he had left Settle permanently and begun a roundabout trip home. In January, 1831, he journeyed to Liverpool. With some friends he waited twenty minutes to see the train from Manchester come through a tunnel, "its rapid, regular, and even motion exceeding anything of the sort I ever saw."[15] It was a very memorable day for young William Gilpin, whose adult life was so often to be involved with the development of steam locomotion. He said good-by to Tom as they toured Belfast and were impressed by the northern lights. He returned to the United States on board the *Martha* after a tedious and uncomfortable forty-six–day voyage.[16]

The immediate occasion for his return was his father's decision to advance William's education at the University of Pennsylvania. But there was a problem with the faculty, Quakers and friends of Joshua though they were. Richard, in London, thought that he knew the reason for their reluctance to admit William. He commented to Henry that when his father wrote that William's "mathematics had been so much neglected in this country that the College gentry would not admit him to an advanced class I was much surprised and it struck me that I might in some measure be the cause and that my lack-lustre career might have taught them a lesson."[17]

But the faculty told William what he needed to do, and he immediately commenced to cram. Through the entire summer of 1831 William lived in Philadelphia at the home of his brother Henry. The latter hired one Hugh Hawthorne as a tutor who put

[14] Gilpin MS, P–L330, Bancroft Library.

[15] William to Henry D. Gilpin, February 4, 1831, Gilpin Collection, Historical Society of Pennsylvania (hereafter cited as Gilpin Collection, HSP). See also William to Joshua Gilpin, January 5, 1831, in the same collection.

[16] Richard Gilpin to Joshua, April 4, 1831; William to Henry D., April 6, 1831, Gilpin Collection, HSP.

[17] Richard to Henry, July 27, 1831, Gilpin Collection, HSP.

William through an "enormous number" of books in his "appalling" course of study.[18]

On September 16 the faculty of the University of Pennsylvania began an examination of William which lasted three days. According to Henry the tests were very strict and designed to see if William had the thorough knowledge needed for work at the University and had not simply prepared himself to pass an examination. To the elation of all the Gilpin family William passed in such fashion that he was admitted to the University that autumn as a junior.[19]

William seems to have had no problems at the University. He joined the Zelosophic Society; he visited Kentmere frequently, enjoyed the busy social groups that surrounded Henry, and began to take interest in national and world affairs as he learned of them through the many notable Democrats who dined and partied with his brother. Henry by this time had done a good deal of editing and literary work and in 1832 he became United States district attorney in Philadelphia. Henry's progress stirred William, and he began thinking and talking of commencing a legal career after he finished school.

Henry's reputation brought to the Gilpin door two eminent young travelers in 1831, who also were to leave a mark upon William. Alexis de Tocqueville and his friend Gustave de Beaumont were sent by the government of Louis Philippe to study American prison systems. In a nine month period they visited widely scat-

[18] In later years Gilpin somehow converted Hugh into Nathaniel Hawthorne and so reported the name of his tutor to Bancroft and several interviewers. It should be again pointed out that *Henry* Gilpin supervised William, hired the tutor, and generally fathered him. Joshua was at Kentmere, not far from Philadelphia, but got his news of William through his almost daily correspondence with Henry. Henry to Joshua, May 10, July 23, and July 29, 1831, Gilpin Collection, HSP.

[19] Henry to Joshua, September 17 and 22, 1831, Gilpin Collection, HSP. William's own account (Bancroft, *William Gilpin*, p. 8) adds a recollection that the faculty would not consider the unusual request at all until Joshua threatened to send him to Princeton and reminded the professors that Gilpins were as important as Franklins at Pennslyvania. Since no one wanted to lose a student, William was permitted to take the exam. I find no evidence of this story elsewhere. At any rate he did have to take a comprehensive examination to get in.

tered sections of the United States, recording their impressions that were to result in the foremost foreign interpretation of America's institutions.

Seeking a thorough understanding of the Pennsylvania judiciary system, Tocqueville was told that the best authority was Henry Gilpin. On November 15 the two young men (Alexis was twenty-six, Henry thirty) spent more than four hours discussing America's common law heritage, Pennsylvania's code, and, in particular, the jury system.

Tocqueville makes no mention of sixteen-year-old William, but they must have met, probably at Henry's home.[20] William later reported, "another [influence] was my association with De [sic] Tocqueville, the French writer, who visited this country, whom I assisted in collecting data in the libraries at Washington. He taught me the importance and value of statistics and how to look into the future with a good deal of reliability from the data the present affords."[21]

The two Frenchmen soon left Philadelphia for the frontier, then returned to Washington in January, 1832. Tocqueville records the efforts of members of Jackson's Administration to provide him with public documents and other material. What is more likely than his use of a favored college boy to run errands and perhaps engage in friendly discourse in French?

Until his graduation William seems to have resided at Henry's sociable bachelor quarters on Walnut Street. He received his A.B. degree in 1833 at the age of seventeen.[22]

William now gave serious consideration to studying law and commenced some reading, but he was looking for something more exciting. Several of the visitors to the Walnut Street home were army men, and, if we can believe William, the General himself, President Andrew Jackson, passing through Philadelphia, stopped off to see Henry and William. The idea of a military career became uppermost in William's mind. He begged his father and his brother to use their rather substantial political friendships to get him a

[20] George Wilson Pierson, *Tocqueville and Beaumont in America*, pp. 529–535, 663–678; Alexis de Tocqueville, *Journey to America*, pp. 277–287.

[21] *Rocky Mountain Herald* (Denver), January 14, 1913.

[22] University of Pennsylvania Alumni Records, letter to author, July 7, 1964.

place at West Point. Within the Jackson cabinet of 1833–1834 almost all of the men were friends of the Gilpins, but the active agent for securing the appointment was Secretary of State Louis McLane from Delaware. In spite of Joshua's own initial reluctance, he and Henry sought the assistance of McLane and others to get to Jackson, and William was made a cadet at the United States Military Academy effective July 1, 1834.[23]

Several reports of William Gilpin's life have him graduating from West Point—and at a very early age. These are all false and are probably based upon his own wishful recollections. At the Academy William was very unhappy from the start. He studied French and mathematics, not tactics and strategy, and reported to his father that they had no military or any other kind of exercise but remained "cooped up" all that winter.

After some six months, to the family's substantial embarrassment, William suddenly sought his release from the Academy. The reason that he gave to his parents was the boredom and inactivity of West Point. His father and mother were discovering an increasing restlessness and impetuosity in William that they did not know how to meet.

But Joshua was secretly pleased with the prospect of William's coming home. He thought that the awkward situation might teach William a lesson, and it confirmed Joshua's belief that West Point was not very military. He and Henry discussed the proper way to get William out of school and concluded unhappily that they must use the same means that got him in. Some visits and letters to prominent Democrats smoothed the path homeward; Joshua fibbed slightly to the War Department when he wrote that "my age and infirmities render it so extremely desirable and useful to myself and family to have him near me."[24] Joshua and Mary had no reason to think that William would return to Kentmere. He left West

[23] Joshua to Henry Gilpin, January 12, 1835, Gilpin Folder, Historical Society of Delaware (hereafter cited as Gilpin Folder, HSD); Gilpin MS, P–L330, Bancroft Library; letter U.S.M.A. to author July 31, 1958. He was pushed ahead of 1,750 applicants. I see little evidence that the Gilpins objected to a military career on religious grounds. Joshua seems to have felt that William was young and unstable and to have wanted him still within reach of the family.

[24] Joshua to Henry, January 12, 1835, Gilpin Folder, HSD.

Point, with his resignation effective February 15, 1835, and promptly moved back to Philadelphia and Henry's quarters.

William's one term at West Point was not time wasted. He did reasonably well academically—his rank in a class of sixty-seven was twenty-ninth in mathematics and twenty-fifth in French.[25] He had time to read widely; he became acquainted with two upper classmates, Montgomery Blair and George Meade, who tutored him and inadvertently inspired him to copy them later by taking part in the Seminole War. The former became William's introduction to the influential Blair family, later to be important in William's career. And for the rest of his life William classified himself as a West Pointer, a statement accepted by his friends and enemies and useful to both groups.

Back in Henry's home William began to read law once again. Without his realizing it, however, his world was about to change decisively and he could be neither Philadelphia lawyer nor Brandywine squire.

Henry's life suddenly was in a turmoil, and he had little time to consider the problems of his youngest brother. Henry had become one of the government directors of the Bank of the United States in the heat of the struggle between Jackson and Nicholas Biddle over the very existence of that institution. Biddle looked upon Gilpin as something of a government spy and carefully excluded him from important committee positions while keeping him in the dark on most Bank matters. On the other hand Gilpin was, like Van Buren, much more moderate than other Jackson advisors on the Bank—Amos Kendall, Francis Blair, Roger Taney, and Thomas Hart Benton—who urged the Bank's destruction.

But Henry Gilpin's loyalty to the President was firm, and it was reciprocated. Jackson reappointed him to the Bank for 1834; when the Senate rejected the nomination twice, Jackson sought a less controversial reward for Gilpin and designated him for the position of governor of Michigan Territory.[26] For many weeks Henry was

[25] Brig. Gen. C. Gratiot to Joshua Gilpin, January 28, 1835, Gilpin Papers, Missouri Historical Society (hereafter cited as Gilpin Papers, MHS).

[26] Thomas P. Govan, *Nicholas Biddle, passim*; Ralph C. H. Catterall, *The Second Bank of the United States*, pp. 308–309; Henry to Joshua, January 14, 1835, Gilpin Folder, HSD.

in doubt as to whether the Senate would permit him to be sent to Michigan, and unfortunately for William's peace of mind he had moved from West Point to live once again with Henry at precisely the period of greatest uncertainty. In the end a Senate dominated by anti-Jacksonians rejected Henry's appointment and he resumed his Philadelphia way of life.[27]

But not quite. Henry had fallen in love during the months of his political wars, and this event meant a drastic change in William's life. The lady was Eliza Sibley Johnston of Louisiana, widow of Josiah Stoddard Johnston, senator from Louisiana, killed in 1833 when the *Lioness* blew up in the Red River. Johnston had been in the Senate for many years and the grieving Eliza visited old friends in Washington and Philadelphia after the tragedy. She already knew, or now met, Henry in Philadelphia, and they agreed upon a marriage to take place during the summer of 1835.[28]

Eliza and William had no quarrel with one another, and she told William that after her marriage he could stay on in the back room studying law. But William knew that the good old days were over. The parties, the fine bachelor dinners, the friendship of a protective brother would all draw to a close. Perhaps it was time.[29]

Several ideas worried one another in William's head. He

[27] Also wounded in the Senate's angry barrage was the career of Henry's friend, Roger Taney. Jackson had selected him as interim Secretary of the Treasury in 1833 during the deposits crisis, but in January, 1834, the Senate refused to confirm his appointment. A year later Jackson appointed him Associate Justice of the Supreme Court. Once again the Senate defeated Jackson, and Taney's appointment was thrown out at about the same time as Henry's appointment was rejected, and by the same groups (Leonard D. White, *The Jacksonians*, p. 110). Within a year Taney became Chief Justice with the blessings of a new Senate.

[28] William Preston Johnston, *The Johnstons of Salisbury*, pp. 63–73. Johnston and Gilpin were opponents on matters of the Bank of the United States and Andrew Jackson, even if they could agree about Eliza.

[29] The Johnstons had one child, William Stoddard Johnston. He was about the same age as William Gilpin, and the two young men both stayed with Henry for awhile before Henry's marriage. William Johnston then moved to Alexandria, Louisiana, and became a lawyer and parish judge. From time to time he encountered William Gilpin in their travels; they seem to have been good friends. Johnston married Maria Williams, also of Louisiana, about 1837. He had survived the explosion that killed his father, having been blown from his

could study law with Henry, perhaps boarding out, but he was tired of books. He could go to Kentmere, but that seemed dull. A worried Joshua wanted him home and upbraided Henry for interfering with this plan by setting William such an exciting example of non-Quaker living. Henry denied the unfair charge and told both men that William must become more independent, an idea that William was already nurturing.

To pass the long evenings just prior to his marriage, Henry had been doing more entertaining than usual and happened to meet a number of army and navy officers. Some had just returned from the frontier and talked with Henry and William of the Pawnees and the Osages. One officer, Captain Clifton Wharton, had been commander of the Santa Fe caravan escort of sixty dragoons just the year before, "the first American cavalry to see the plains." Wharton described another expedition of the same summer (three hundred more dragoons to impress and treat with the Comanches) and told how these men were struck down by malaria and how their commander, General Henry Leavenworth, died.[30]

This was the kind of military career William craved; he had had enough of sitting in staff rooms studying French and reading Kent's *Commentaries*. Records do not exist that help explain the next few weeks of his life; William appears to have had an argument with Henry—very unusual in that family—just about the time of Henry's marriage to Eliza in the summer of 1835. Henry wrote to Joshua that "it is a subject too painful to write about and one in which it is difficult to know what is to be done" and instead sent an explanation to Kentmere orally by means of Uncle Tom who was passing through.

The quarrel could easily have been over family matters, perhaps concerning the new bride. But more likely the problem was

---

stateroom into the river and hospitalized for several weeks, but could not escape the southern fevers and died in 1839. A child, William S. Johnston, Jr., was born posthumously to Maria, who gave him for adoption to his grandmother Eliza Gilpin. This William grew up in the Gilpin home, fought with the Confederate army, and spent most of his life in business in Philadelphia (Johnston, *The Johnstons*, pp. 73–74, 155–156).

[30] David Lavender, *Bent's Fort*, pp. 154–157; Henry to Joshua, February 7, 11, and 14, 1835, Gilpin Folder, HSD.

William's immediate future, for Henry discussed the argument with Charles Ingersoll, a very close friend, who had taken an interest in William's law reading. Whatever the issue, nineteen-year-old William moved out of his brother's home and left no word, then returned to get his clothing and some books while Henry and Eliza were traveling in New York.[31] Confused and undecided he lived alone in Philadelphia for a short time. He talked of continuing school, applying for admission to the bar, or traveling west, perhaps to Indiana. His father agreed to continue his quarterly allowance of $100, on Henry's suggestion, and to permit him to use it as he saw fit. He obtained letters of introduction to various people in the Mississippi Valley and led his friends to believe that it was his destination.[32]

Suddenly, with no message to his family in Philadelphia or Kentmere, he boarded ship for Liverpool. Getting word of the voyage through friends, the Gilpins hoped William planned to join his brother Tom, but Henry wryly commented that that would not necessarily mean that they would know much more because Tom never wrote either.

But William was looking for adventure and had gone to England to serve in the British Foreign Legion, then being formed to fight for Isabella II in the Spanish Carlist War. William wanted a commission, however, and the British officials would not give him one; his first dream of military glory ended quickly.[33] He remained in

[31] Henry to Joshua, September 23 and 29, and October 10, 1835, Gilpin Folder, HSD. Henry and Eliza encountered huge crowds in New York swelling the hotels and boarding houses. They were saved by Ben Butler, who had left town to visit Martin Van Buren at Kinderhook and gave the Gilpins his room. Thirty-two persons left visiting cards at the Gilpins' home during their brief absence, which was probably a delayed honeymoon. In the summer and fall of 1835 the Vice President, the Secretary of State, the Attorney General, and the Postmaster General all visited Henry in Philadelphia. The Delaware and Pennsylvania congressmen were frequent guests.

[32] Henry to Joshua, October 14 and 21, November 1, 2, and 14, 1835, Gilpin Folder, HSD.

[33] Bancroft, *William Gilpin*, p. 9; Eliza Johnston Gilpin to Joshua, November 16, 1835, and Henry to Joshua, November 28, December 1 and 12, 1835, Gilpin Folder, HSD; Ferril interview in *Rocky Mountain Herald* (Denver), January 4, 1913.

Great Britain throughout the winter until word reached him of a new war. Breaking transatlantic speed records the *Toronto* arrived at Southampton with the news that on December 28, 1835, the Seminoles had massacred a detachment of American soldiers and that war had broken out in Florida.[34]

[34] John E. Hicks interview, *Kansas City Star*, June 14, 1950. University of Pennsylvania records have Gilpin receiving a master of arts degree in 1836 (University of Pennsylvania Records Center, letter to author, September 21, 1960). This is most unlikely since by family correspondence he was reported in England from November, 1835, until March, 1836.

CHAPTER TWO

# Prairies and Everglades

*Lieutenant in the Seminole War, 1836–1838*

William Gilpin served in four wars during his lifetime, in three as an officer before he reached the age of thirty-five, in the fourth as governor and commander-in-chief of Colorado Territory. None of these conflicts was shabbier than the Second Seminole War, William's earliest experience with combat.

The Seminoles were originally Creeks from Georgia who, in the late eighteenth century, because of family disputes, moved in several small contingents into Spanish Florida. The word *Seminole* is, in fact, one version of the Creek word for *runaway*. Both the Spanish government and English agents found the Seminoles useful tools against the young United States. Andrew Jackson fought them in 1812 and 1818 and separated them from the Creeks. The United States acquired Florida from Spain in 1821 and made it into a territory, a form of government that gave the Seminoles a bit of temporary federal protection not available to the Creeks, Choctaws, Cherokees, and Chickasaws in the neighboring southern states. While white men were demanding the expulsion of these other tribes, the Seminoles received the protection of the Treaty of Camp Moultrie.

This agreement, signed in 1823 by Colonel James Gadsden and thirty-two Seminole chiefs, provided a number of benefits and annuities for twenty years if the Indians would consent to remain in a large area of central Florida. Within a few years both parties considered renegotiation; the Indians were faced with a drought and near starvation, while the United States was pressed by local whites to put an end to an asylum that was proving most attractive to runaway slaves.

In 1832 another treaty, Payne's Landing, was concluded, which provided that the Seminoles would give up their Florida home, would merge with the Creeks in lands west of the Mississippi, and would receive cash for their animals, plus certain unlavish gifts. This agreement was contingent upon seven chiefs visiting the lands and declaring them suitable—or so the Indians were led to believe. Instead, the seven (under shadowy circumstances) signed an agreement which the United States declared bound the entire Seminole tribe to move to Arkansas Territory. Most of the Seminoles believed that they had been tricked and flatly refused the demand that they leave Florida within three years.[1]

Ill will increased on both sides. White settlers moving into Florida wanted Seminole lands. Stock stealing became the practice of whites, and Indians retaliated by burnings and an occasional killing. Seminole slaves, numbering about eight hundred, were a crucial issue. According to the treaty they could not go to the new lands but would be sold to whites in Florida and Georgia. Fearing the end of a tranquil if not a very good existence, the slaves encouraged the Indians to rebel. Above all, the Seminoles probably feared the consequences of being absorbed once more into the Creek nation.

Some of the lower-ranked chiefs believed that the old leaders were too timid and were not protecting their rights. Among these newcomers Powell, variously called Oseola, Osceola, and Assiola, the son of an English trader and an Indian woman, quickly took the

[1] Although some of the chiefs were not above cheating the tribe, the Seminoles generally get sympathetic treatment from historians. Full accounts can be found in John T. Sprague, *The Origin, Progress and Conclusion of the Florida War*; Woodburne Potter, *The War in Florida*. Sprague and Potter were United States army officers who served in the war. The basic study of this tribe is by Edwin C. McReynolds, *The Seminoles*.

lead in opposing migration. After several incidents in which unidentified Seminoles killed their agent, a messenger, and a chief
who favored migration, the United States army began to reinforce
certain Florida posts. On December 28, 1835, two companies of
troops traveling from Fort Brooke to Fort King were attacked from
ambush by a body of Seminoles. Out of Major Francis Dade's detachment of 110 men, only 3 escaped, and they were wounded.[2]
The Second Florida War had begun in earnest; this was the report
that reached William Gilpin in England and sent him hurrying
home.

Back on the Brandywine in the spring of 1836 William once
again sought and obtained his family's considerable influence to
gain a military favor. He told Henry that he had seen everyone
to help get a "prospect." He approached former senator George M.
Dallas, later to be Vice President of the United States; Secretary of
War Lewis Cass (William called him Governor) intimated that
some appointments to the army would soon be made; President
Jackson told him that he would choose "staunch fellows . . . highly
indignant as he was at the failures in Florida."[3] Delayed in Baltimore by an "old complaint" of earache, headache, and sore throat,
he missed seeing his senator, James Buchanan, but wrote him a
plea from Philadelphia to urge Jackson to act in his behalf. Gilpin's
spokesmen were powerful, and on June 8, 1836, Buchanan wrote
him that "The Senate have this moment confirmed your nomination as Second Lieutenant of the regiment of Dragoons. You stand
first in the list of second lieutenants."[4]

While waiting for his active duty orders, William began negotiations to be admitted to the Pennsylvania bar, presuming that his
military status might hasten proceedings. It did not, but his orders
soon came. He was assigned to the Second Dragoons, taking his
oath of allegiance in Philadelphia, June 13.

[2] Sprague, *Florida War*, pp. 88–90; Potter, *War in Florida*, pp. 102–108.

[3] William to Henry, May 23, 1836, Gilpin Collection, HSP. See also Buchanan to William, June 8, 1836, Gilpin Papers, MHS.

[4] Buchanan to William, June 8, 1836, Gilpin Papers, MHS. See also William
to James Buchanan, May 27, 1836, Gilpin Collection, HSP; Dallas to A.G.O.,
May 12, 1836, G109, Gilpin File, Letters Received, 1836–1837, Adjutant General's Office, National Archives (hereafter cited as Gilpin File, Letters Received,
A.G.O., National Archives).

The record does not show whether William requested to be in the Dragoons or whether his assignment to a new unit of the very organization of whose exploits he had heard one winter's night at Henry's home was merely coincidental. The Dragoons' history was brief. In 1832 the Congress created a battalion called the Mounted Rangers for service in the Black Hawk War. Its commander was Major Henry Dodge. The next year the unit was expanded to a regiment called the First Dragoons and Dodge was made a colonel, with Lieutenant Colonel Stephen Watts Kearny as his executive officer. In 1834 they made their first expedition to the plains; William had heard of this through Captain Wharton. Dodge was replaced by General Henry Leavenworth but soon resumed command when Leavenworth died on the prairie from fever and the consequences of being thrown by his horse.[5]

During the Florida War the First Dragoons were needed on the western frontier, except for two companies; but Congress and the War Department concluded that an identical regiment would be useful against the Seminoles.

In June, 1836, the Second Regiment of Dragoons was established, with Colonel David E. Twiggs of Georgia commanding and William S. Harney as the executive officer with the rank of lieutenant colonel. Twiggs had a reputation for toughness in a career that began in the War of 1812. Harney had nearly twenty years' service, including recent action in the Black Hawk War. Second Lieutenant William Gilpin was assigned to "E" Company; his two immediate superior officers were Captain Jonathan Bean and First Lieutenant James Hamilton.[6] To fill the ranks and train the men as rapidly as possible the officers were divided into small groups, with some ten men under Harney dispatched "west of the mountains" to do their recruiting. As one of these officers, William was thus separated from "E" Company, which was organized and trained in the East and sent to Florida in December, 1836.

William's road to the Florida campaign was a long and devious journey of eighteen months. At times restive and frustrated over the delay, William, nevertheless, found the trip excitingly educa-

[5] John K. Herr, *The Story of the United States Cavalry*, pp. 24–26.

[6] *Army and Navy Chronicle* (Washington, D.C.), June 16 and 23, 1836. William stated in his oath that he was a citizen of Pennsylvania; his active duty orders classified him as being from Delaware.

tional, for his wanderings on government recruiting service opened up a whole new United States to him. He saw the American frontier for the first time, and he was never again the same man.

Early in July William made his preparations to leave Philadelphia. He visited friends including some in New York, received a going-away gift of $25 from his father, paid some bills for him, and got his mother to send up some clothing from Kentmere. Minor complications prevented one last trip home, but he left a letter for his mother at New Castle as he sailed down the Delaware on the first leg of his journey to the West. He reached Baltimore by way of the Chesapeake and Delaware Canal, so important in his family's history. The next morning he climbed aboard a train and arrived in Frederick at 1:00 P.M. after a very slow journey.

One can feel young William's excitement as he described to his family his impressions of the ever-new country now opening to him. From Frederick he took a "nine inside coach."

This night, the following day and night were . . . [spent] amongst the mountains in crossing ridge after ridge, all equally beautiful along the national road which is very good being macadamized and beautifully smooth—the salubrious air of this high country is very remarkable and pleasant. The high cliffs of limestone rock on both sides of Mill's Creek along which the road passes just after leaving Cumberland reminds me strongly of the scenery around Giggleswick [his English school town].[7]

William was delighted by his first crossing of the Alleghenies. The Cumberland and National Road, partly the work of surveyor George Washington, had been opened to Wheeling in 1818. Earlier (and for years afterward) the degree of federal participation in the construction, maintenance, and extension of this highway was a major issue in the United States. The road reached its terminus in Vandalia, Illinois, in 1852. Today, of course, as U.S. 40, it is one of the best known American highways. But even in Gilpin's time it was well and solidly built, and thousands of Americans, like William, first traveled to their new homes in the Mississippi Valley along its course.

Two days' ride from Frederick, William left Maryland for southwestern Pennsylvania; he crossed the swollen Monongahela on a

---

[7] William to Joshua, July 14, 1836, Gilpin Papers, MHS.

ferry because the bridge had been flooded out; and at noon the next day he was in Wheeling "on the western waters." Here he became a passenger on a river steamer and sailed down the Ohio. Stopping briefly at Cincinnati he met General and Mrs. William Ashley of St. Louis. The companionship was mutually agreeable and they traveled the rest of the river trip together.[8] The General was in Congress now but had spent thirty years in the West. For hours as their steamer *Roanoke* bore them down the Ohio, Ashley told young William of the plains and the Rockies beyond, of the two great rivers he had yet to see; of the Indians, the soil, and the minerals. Then they left the Ohio and turned up the Mississippi for St. Louis, and William wrote his family ecstatically that the "working of a high pressure engine to overcome the turbid current of the Mississippi makes so great a motion in the vessel as almost to prevent writing."[9]

William immediately began his efforts to recruit dragoons for Florida. He found "prospects dim." Wages were high and land was cheap in St. Louis; the young men were not interested in fighting Seminoles. Whether Captain Bean traveled at all with William is not known. Probably they first met in St. Louis, where the two officers received instructions from Colonel Harney. William and Bean were to operate recruiting stations at Franklin and Boonville on the Missouri, Potosi in Washington County, and Palmyra up from St. Louis on the Mississippi.

William spent only three days in St. Louis; he thought it to be about the same size as Washington and growing very rapidly. He prowled the waterfront, looking at the stores and warehouses, the

[8] Ashley (*c.* 1778–1838), was one of the most important early figures in the West. He had been a Virginia militia officer, and moved to Missouri to manufacture gunpowder. He and Andrew Henry entered the fur trade together and in spite of many mistakes, did very well. He conceived of the rendezvous system and substituted overland pack trains for the Missouri River route to speed deliveries of supplies. Introducing to the fur trade many of its most famous figures, he sold the Rocky Mountain Fur Company in 1826 to Jackson, Smith, and Sublette and retired a wealthy man. Ashley did not fit the modern historian's pat groupings: a Democrat and Jacksonian, he favored internal improvements at federal expense, rechartering of the Bank of the United States, and a protective tariff. On this platform he was elected to the House of Representatives from Missouri three times (John E. Sunder, *Bill Sublette, Mountain Man*, p. 101).

[9] William to his father, July 14, 1836, Gilpin Papers, MHS.

dozens of "large steamboats with continual arrivals and departures." In the short time that he remained in St. Louis William had a vision of its future. Not yet twenty-one, he outlined for his mother the first of his many predictions of America's growth. In years to come he was to make the same prophecy again and again for ever more westerly cities (and villages), and he was to gain increasingly large audiences whose interest was directly related to their investments.

But in 1836 he adopted the Mississippi Valley as his own on sight. He exclaimed to his mother,

Just look at her [St. Louis'] position on the map of North America— Exactly in the *centre* of the territory of the Union, where the navigable arteries unite. This will be, one day not far off, the seat of government and the great Heart of the Great Valley—I had thought of giving you a description of the Ohio and Mississippi; but I find it too rash an undertaking . . . if you would wish to appreciate the scale of sublimity on which all nature is here arranged, come and see it.[10]

Cities in the wilderness were not William's only energizer. Captain Bean assigned the Potosi and Palmyra districts to William. He rented a horse and set out to spend nearly a month with the former village as his headquarters. William was encountering firsthand one of America's biggest speculative eras. Easy credit and limitless land, large expenditures on internal improvements, and heavy migration westward inflated Missouri's economy and turned recruiting into a hunt. William had an office, but no one came to seek him. Instead he rode over the countryside hoping to find idle young men who would listen to him. He did an honest job and found a few recruits, but from the view of economic history he was a year too early.

He enjoyed himself immensely. Each night he spent at a different farm house or mining camp. He rode one entire day with the owner of a large farm who also was a circuit rider; they talked for hours of religious doctrine and politics. William thought that the theory of "democratic republicanism" was successfully practiced on the frontier, and he more than once dreamed of making a home for himself there when his tour of duty ended.

[10] William to his mother, August 18, 1836, Gilpin Papers, MHS.

Then he reached the St. François Mountains in the northern extreme of the Ozarks and saw Iron Mountain, one of the "curiosities which nature has made perfect . . . [and which] ranks with Niagara or before it." Incredibly the mountain was for sale—$300, "but I had it not, and it has since been bought."[11] Iron Mountain was to give up millions of tons of ore in Gilpin's lifetime, but he did not know for some years what a fortune he had missed. It was his first experience with the possibilities of mineral riches in America—an idea he was to propound again and again in his publicist years.

The beauty of the wilderness also impressed Gilpin. He wrote his mother to tell his sister, the younger Mary, that the woods were full of fine turkeys and deer, frequently breaking across his path. The crisscrossing limestone ridges created many small valleys, very fertile and bordered by streams. Farms abounded in the region, "but there are still millions of acres for emigrants at $1.25 per acre."

The Potosi area included broad varieties of people, but William noticed two frontier types in particular—old soldiers of the Revolution and "that class of men who still keep on the border in advance of civilization." In the latter category in Missouri were the hunters and miners, and William chanced on one of these men who might have been a personal and political friend had they met back East. He was a man in his mid-sixties, an older brother of the new Chief Justice of the United States, Roger Taney. Known in family records as Michael VI, this brother had disappeared about the same time that a family feud had driven the father (Michael V) and Roger from Maryland to Virginia. Michael ("wild in his youth," according to William, who used that identical expression to describe himself to biographers decades later) gradually moved ahead of settlements until he reached Missouri. While he was Secretary of the Treasury, Roger offered his brother a government job. "He mounted a horse and rode to Selma on the Mississippi, where reflecting on the change an acceptance would bring over him he finally turned his horse's head and returned to the diggings . . . he

---

[11] *Ibid.* A low knob about five hundred acres in area with some of the purest iron ore in the United States.

lives in a log cabin, digs all day in a hole and swears that all the powers of earth shall not draw him thence—yet he is poor and without the ambition to be rich."[12]

Michael Taney VI might have had reasons to lose himself on the frontier; at any rate, he and the Revolutionary veterans were not receptive to William's persuasion. After nearly a month in southeast Missouri, the unsuccessful recruiter was ordered to St. Louis and then northward to Palmyra with only a small share of his quota filled. In St. Louis he received letters from home, from Joshua and Henry. He hoped that his mother would send newspapers; the local press was unreliable and the cafes too dirty to sit in and chat. He was elated to learn that Martin Van Buren was likely to be elected President of the United States. A full-scale military man by now, he wrote to his family of rumors about the places that his unit might be sent that fall, and he wondered if his Uncle Tom, the Quaker, had forgiven him for becoming a soldier.

By all present standards, Palmyra is small, but it had large hopes in the 1830's. It was Missouri's chief town near the upper Mississippi and was on the edge of the prairie. It was the county seat as well, and William was impressed by its potential to expand into a large city. But Palmyra was too far from the river for significant growth, a fact that William did not yet understand. He even suggested to town builders that they were laying out neighboring Marion City too close to the river considering the danger of floods. A few years later, remembering the incident, William placed his Gilpintown-Centropolis too far from the Missouri, and progress passed it by for a rival on the water's edge, Kansas City.

Increasingly, William was becoming a student of American geography. He had traveled widely; in Missouri his journey was leisurely and alone. Somewhere he had become familiar with the writings of Alexander von Humboldt, and they caused him to consider the relationship of climate to geography. Just west of Palmyra William saw land that differed as sharply from the north-

---

[12] William to Elizabeth, October 4, 1836, Gilpin Papers, MHS. William thus stumbled upon the answer to one of the minor mysteries of American history. See Carl Brent Swisher, *Roger B. Taney*, pp. 102–104; Walker Lewis, *Without Fear or Favor: A Biography of Chief Justice Roger Brooke Taney*. Roger Taney evidently helped support his brother (Roger Taney to James Mason Campbell, January 23, 1845, copy of MS courtesy of Walker Lewis, Washington, D.C.).

ern Ozarks he had just left as it did from the river bottoms. For the first time he was on the prairies. To many people, then as now, the word *prairie* conjured up no romantic visions; it was merely land to be farmed or not to be farmed. But not to William. Not yet ready to deliver his message to the farmer, the town builder, or the politician, he was talking as one nature lover to another when he wrote to his sister, Elizabeth, that she must get out Mitchell's map and find the irregular ridge that runs from St. Charles north-westerly between the waters that flow into the Mississippi and the Missouri. "This is the 'Grand Prairie' or 'Divide'. . . . On its crest you may journey a thousand miles on a dead level—its beauty cannot be excelled, free from timber or shrubs of any sort, and covered with most luxuriant grass, it is so gently rolling as to be effectually drained yet not break its perfect smoothness." Beyond Missouri the prairie widens, "passes the Missouri and extends south to Texas—lying between these states and the Rocky Mts. . . . extends 600 miles, being in many parts only a sandy waste, but near the rivers which traverse it, fertile and covered with herds of buffalo, timber being seen only along the water courses."

How did William Gilpin, age 21, fit into this grandeur? He was still a soldier, destined for the Seminole War.

Florida finished (should no stray bullet or yellow jacket prevent it), from thence . . . to Fort Leavenworth . . . the great Prairies of Buffalo, Indians and wild horses and

> "The clouds beyond them to the White *Rocks* lend
> And *I* must pierce them to their summits where
> The earth to his entrance compels the powers of air."

These mountains passed, the Columbia River must be descended and the Pacific reached—I often think . . . that the part of the Valley which lies on the Mississippi and *West* of it must one day surpass aught now existing or which has existed in all that constitutes national resources —hence my strong desire to see and learn all I can—indeed one who has not seen the Valley of the Mi'ppi can hardly be said to have been in America—he knows not what a *heart* and *sinews* she has.[13]

Three days in St. Louis had been enough for William to claim it as his own and to predict its future as the hub of the "Great

13 William to Elizabeth, October 4, 1836, Gilpin Papers, MHS.

Valley." Now two days in Palmyra gave him a glimpse of something beyond the Valley. The Valley was still his to proclaim to America, but if he "pierced the White Rocks" he might have a grander song to sing. Ashley and Humboldt had taught him much, but he had to see for himself.

As Humbolt had done, William filled his saddlebags with mineral and floral specimens; then he threw them away. He had no room; moreover, collections tied one down and kept one from finding more specimens to examine and throw away. It was the same with his ideas as he moved throughout the "Great Valley" seeking soldiers.

Colonel Harney felt that the men had pretty well exhausted the supply of recruits in Missouri, and in October he sent William to Kentucky, using Louisville as a temporary headquarters.

To William the Kentucky visit was a pleasant interlude. It kept him away from his new-found prairies, but he enjoyed himself and behaved like most young men given the circumstances. The people were fine—"their generous qualities were a reflection of the country from which they drew their subsistence." He began to meet old friends; in St. Louis he had encountered none, while at Palmyra a few Pennsylvania friends were trying to start a college; but in Louisville the society was stimulating. He met several of the Johnstons and Prestons, so well known in Kentucky history, and distantly related to William through Eliza and Henry Gilpin. Albert Sidney Johnston was Eliza's brother-in-law and to William he was a friend with an exciting career underway. Johnston had recently left Louisville for New Orleans and Texas, and William regretted missing him.

For the first time William, who celebrated his twenty-first birthday in Louisville, took some interest in the ladies. He now associated with "merchants here [who] form the *elite*; add a few briefless lawyers—a female circle numerous, *rich* and hansome [*sic*]—indeed an admirable place for an officer (officers are *prime favorites*) to enjoy the frivolities of society and choose a wife . . ." He received word from the Adjutant General that he had been promoted in October to first lieutenant. This was rapid progress, but he had never been in combat and felt that he needed the experience. "What man can seek important employments until he has developed a capacity to discharge them with energy? How can that development be made unless opportunity and trial be found? Where is a military man to find them but in Florida?"[14]

On November 14, 1836, he wrote to the War Department asking for active duty in the Seminole campaign; what he did not know was that the tour was coming without his prompting.[15] Being farther from the pull of Texas, Kentucky produced more volunteers than did Missouri, according to William, and the ranks were nearly filled. The War Department was ready to move them.

Before leaving Louisville William gave more thought to using his knowledge of the frontier for profit. His father and his uncle had done some successful speculating years before, and the boy wanted to show what he had learned. He wrote to Joshua that the western farmer made little money on his crops but improved his holdings primarily for resale. The land was too rich for many purposes—he had never seen a spadeful of manure used—but at $1.25 an acre no one could lose by speculating. Slavery in Missouri ("declining") had driven Eastern capital into Illinois, Michigan, and Wisconsin, hence the public domain of Missouri included wonderful farm and mining lands open for entry. He had some plans, but no capital and no time.

Wondering who would be at Kentmere for Christmas (he now had missed three in a row there), he left Louisville December 23 with a detachment of recruits on the *Henry Clay* (the name an anathema to the Gilpins) and reached New Orleans on December 30, 1836. One man had jumped ship at Natchez; the remaining thirty-seven were ready for winter training at New Barracks.[16]

For a change William learned something factual about the Second Dragoons and the Second Seminole War. Along the coast recruiting had gone swiftly; Colonel Harney had gathered five companies of dragoons under his command at Charleston, South Carolina, and they were en route to Florida. Bean and Hamilton,

---

[14] William to Joshua, October 6, 1836, and December 4, 1836, Gilpin Papers, MHS. See also Charles K. Gardner, *A Dictionary of All Officers in the Army of the United States*, p. 192.

[15] William Gilpin to B. F. Butler, Secretary of War, November 4, 1836, G 293, Gilpin File, Letters Received, A.G.O., National Archives.

[16] Francis P. Prucha (ed.), *Army Life on the Western Frontier*, p. xxxiv; Gilpin to Adjutant General, January 6, 1837, G 12, Gilpin File, Letters Received, A.G.O., National Archives.

Gilpin's associates on the frontier detail, had joined Harney. About February 6, 1837, this detachment amounting to about half the projected regimental strength, reached Lake Monroe in Florida.

They were attacked by three to four hundred Seminoles the next day. One officer was killed and about fifteen enlisted men wounded. Harney and several of his officers were commended by eyewitnesses for their bravery. As was their fashion the Seminoles disappeared into the hammock lands and lost their pursuers. The incident was typical of the Seminole War.

Much of the military failure in Florida was due to divided and confused command. Before the war ended ten generals had served in Florida, and none had added any luster to some otherwise able careers. Just before the Second Dragoons arrived, the federal government had put an end to the military efforts of Florida's Governor Richard Call, and had appointed Major General Thomas S. Jesup as commanding general. With the largest force yet assembled in Florida, some eight thousand, Jesup pursued the Seminoles vigorously, got some chiefs to accept removal, and by March thought he had ended the war.[17] A number of volunteers and militia were prematurely mustered out of service as many of the Seminoles were being concentrated by the army at the staging areas before shipment west.

The rumor of peace reached those dragoons still training in New Orleans, where William, now assistant commissary of subsistence, found that his foraging tasks gave him time to see something of the South and visit with old friends and new.[18]

Early in February, while in Mobile, he wrote to his family expressing the northerner's inevitable surprise at the early spring on the Gulf coast. His father's health was a family concern, and William hoped that soon Joshua could get out into the garden among the peas and the asparagus just as the people of Alabama were now doing. He returned to New Orleans and promptly contracted the measles (an epidemic hit both Seminoles and army that winter). Health conditions in the Crescent City were a matter of regular concern for himself as well as for his confined trainees;

[17] McReynolds, *Seminoles*, pp. 164–168.
[18] William Gilpin to Joel R. Poinsett, Secretary of War, May 15, 1837, G 116, Gilpin File, Letters Received, A.G.O., National Archives.

New Orleans for William was "neither very healthy nor agreeable," and it was not easy to leave the post for the town.[19]

The French language and a "French Air" predominated, he said, but the "Anglo-Saxon is pushing aside the Frenchman and eating him up. The big steamers . . . are Anglo-Saxon, the huge stores and warehouses into which [goods] are piled have an Anglo-Saxon look and an Anglo-Saxon ship bears them hence. [Of] all the new part of the city, the only decent part is English."[20]

He did not care for the French and Spanish people. ". . . *passion* overmasters judgement and a restive temperament, always ready to take offense easily does so, which destroys social intercourse." He was getting more sure of himself as he wrote to his father to tell Henry to "go *West* and not turn *South*," a bit of interesting and presumptuous advice from a raw youth to a district attorney, counsel of the Bank of the United States, and close friend of the new President, Martin Van Buren, who was about to name him solicitor of the Treasury.[21] But this was the wonderful enthusiasm of a youth who had discovered something!

William remembered his other relatives, too, although he failed to write to Uncle Tom because the old Quaker could not forgive a lawyer's turning soldier. A ship from Belfast was in port and William made a point of visiting the captain. Of course, the man knew brother Tom, had seen him in November, "always arunning after his business," and he, the captain, would be glad to bring word from William to his Anglicized brother.

Richard, back at Kentmere, was tired of farming, had some knowledge of engineering, and wanted a job in the West. William solicited for him but so far had found nothing.

The sprawling, tragedy-prone Johnston side of the family kept close contact with William as they migrated variously from Kentucky to Louisiana homes. He attended the funeral in New Orleans of Eliza's sister-in-law, Mrs. John Harris Johnston, married but six years to Judge Johnston, who survived her only some eighteen months. When the Judge died, his North Louisiana bench went to William Johnston, his nephew, who was Eliza's son and William Gilpin's best friend in the South.

19 William to Joshua, February 18, 1837, Gilpin Papers, MHS.
20 *Ibid.*
21 William to Joshua, March 30, 1837, Gilpin Papers, MHS.

Another brother-in-law to Eliza was Albert Sidney Johnston, also an occasional friend of William Gilpin. Johnston was in Texas, but William located the surgeon who recently had extracted the ball with which General Felix Huston had wounded his friend. Then William had to break the news to Eliza that her own father, Dr. John Sibley of Natchitoches, had just died.[22] Frontier menaces included fevers and exploding steamboats, and William was the wandering agent who informed his widespread family of the tragedies reported to him.[23]

Better news was that William had seen Eliza Griffin of Louisville. She was on her way east to school, and he encouraged her to visit the Gilpins. William expressed more interest in her than in any girl so far: "If you see her you will forthwith love her for who can be more beautiful and of a temper so gentle and attractive?"[24] But just a year and a half before, Albert's first wife had died, and soon Eliza Griffin was to be fiancée and bride to Colonel Albert Sidney Johnston, and later she would be widow of General Johnston, C.S.A.

In this age of travel William was pleased but not too surprised to encounter another good friend in New Orleans. Mr. J. J. Audubon came by to see him, "strolled from a schooner in which he was going to the Sabine. You [father] have seen him? He looks more animated and complacent than when I saw him thirteen years ago in Philadelphia painting his birds . . ."[25]

William also was developing a new interest; as yet casual, it was one day to become a very important factor in his life. Railroad fever was striking the South and William had a slight touch of it. He studied the new methods for track-laying and interested himself in the progress of the New Orleans and Nashville through the swamps. But it was now 1837; the money market was changing and railroad financing was getting tighter. William thought that the situation in Missouri might be more favorable, but he wanted a tour of combat duty before he planned anything of a speculative turn.

His immediate future was settled by the War Department.

[22] William to Eliza, April 18, 1837, Gilpin Papers, MHS.
[23] William Preston Johnston, *The Johnstons of Salisbury.*
[24] William to Eliza, April 18, 1837, Gilpin Papers, MHS.
[25] William to Joshua, March 30, 1837, Gilpin Papers, MHS.

Colonel Twiggs came to New Orleans in April with instructions to reassemble the Second Dragoons at Jefferson Barracks, Missouri, for training while the Seminole situation was straightened out. William had not yet seen any Seminoles, but some seven hundred Creeks passed through New Barracks on their "Trail of Tears" to the West, and he spent time among them, impressed as much by their dignity and reserve as by their "tall athletic forms." Then, with about four hundred recruits, William and other officers of the Second moved back to St. Louis in May, 1837.[26]

Headquarters of the Second Dragoons was now set up at Jefferson Barracks. Apparently the reason for the selection of this site was the exceptional facilities for training horsemen. Both men and animals of the Second Dragoons were new to the military world, and the Barracks had the large area needed to get them to function together. Colonel Twiggs now had more than twenty-five years of service, including his Florida experience. "A martinet of the old type—arbitrary and capricious at times—he moulded the new organization with an iron hand, originating certain regimental characteristics and customs of service, and establishing an *esprit de corps* admirable as it was lasting."[27] Most of his officers of a year before were still with him, giving the regiment a combat-tried cadre. William was relieved of his subsistence responsibilities on June 1, 1837, and returned to full-time training duty, to his pleasure.[28]

The Jefferson Barracks program of training was a happy circumstance for the War Department. Early in June General Jesup informed the Adjutant General that the emigration plan had failed. Very few Indians had been deported, and most of them were Creeks, not Seminoles. The aggressive leaders of the Seminoles, Powell, Arpeika (Sam Jones), and Cloud, had taken over from Jumper and Micanopy who had signed the capitulations. Micanopy was believed to be a prisoner of his tribe. A renewal of hostilities was imminent as some seven hundred Indians fled back to the swamps.

[26] William to Joshua, February 18, 1837, Gilpin Papers, MHS.

[27] Theo. F. Rodenbough, *From Everglade to Cañon with the Second Dragoons,* p. 19.

[28] Gilpin to General Jones, June 3, 1837, G 134, Gilpin File, Letters Received, A.G.O., National Archives.

In a military sense Jesup had succeeded, as he pointed out to Joel Poinsett, Secretary of War. Northern Florida was safe. But the problems left were enormous. Speculators were "soonering" on Seminole lands; officers were seizing Seminole slaves and keeping or selling them for personal profit; the concentrated Indians were naked and underfed through poor administration, from Washington down. The Negroes themselves were very anxious to resume the war, knowing too well the consequences of peace. Jesup believed that the transfer of the Indians to the West was impossible and the only result could be an even fuller war leading to the death of the Seminole nation. He concluded that the best solution was to guarantee the Seminoles a smaller section of southern Florida where they would be protected if they promised peace. Jesup meanwhile (failing to get the release from active duty that he sought) resumed the attack as ordered by the War Department. For this campaign the Second Dragoons were to be ready.[29]

William enjoyed his part of the task. Jefferson Barracks was a tonic to him. "Escaped from the fiery sun of Louisiana, I breathe again amongst the hills of Missouri, at this post the most beautiful and pleasant army station in the West." Richard was in the West, too. They had just missed each other in St. Louis, but Richard came back in mid-June for a brief visit. He was working as an engineer out of Belleville, Illinois, forty miles away. They could not see each other very often, but it made William happy to talk with his brother and to hear directly of the others.

The young first lieutenant was "trying to convert 70 'Virginia boys' from their native elasticity to the carriage and discipline of soldiers." When that was accomplished he would have more "leisure" for his chief interest, the turning "to account the valuable possibilities of the surrounding country."

The money panic had hit Missouri. Jackson's Specie Circular, in effect nearly a year now, had pricked the speculative bubble. Already land prices had sagged, William noted. "The troubled state of the times makes the chances more favorable than a year ago, of securing very rich lands for a very small sum." William asked his father's help to borrow $10,000 to put into some of Mis-

29 McReynolds, *Seminoles*, p. 178; Sprague, *Florida War*, pp. 188–201.

souri's rich mineral lands. He expected to triple the investment quickly.

Curiously, in his plea, William stressed the fact that *he* could procure specie (necessary for land purchases since the Circular) while others could not. He did not elaborate to his father. Conceivably he could use his military position for access to some "gray market," but at the time of writing he was no longer a subsistence or recruiting officer and, therefore, was less likely to have access to official specie. Nor was William likely to suggest anything illicit to his Quaker father, who, worse, always told Henry what he had heard from William. The question must go unanswered just as the "golden opportunity [passed] unimproved."[30]

But "dear father" could not suggest any plan by which William "would become the temporary possessor of $10,000," and William's dreams of a fortune disappeared still another time.

Suddenly tired of training, late in July, William asked for and received three weeks leave of absence to go to Washington and obtain a discharge. His excuse was a trip to Europe with relatives. His real reason is obscure. The leave was granted, he went to Washington, changed his plans, and reported to the Adjutant General for reassignment.[31]

Twiggs' command left Jefferson Barracks September 5 and marched to Florida by way of Shawneetown, Illinois, through Kentucky to Nashville, across the Cumberland Mountains, Lookout Mountain, then central Georgia by way of Milledgeville, and finally reached Jacksonville, Florida, on October 31, 1837—a solid accomplishment of twelve hundred miles covered in fifty-five days by four companies.[32]

But William was not with Twiggs' detachment. Anxious for combat, he was elated to be offered immediate duty in Florida. He went on to Jacksonville alone and on reporting for duty, learned that his former superior officer, Captain Jonathan Bean, had re-

[30] William to Joshua, June 4, 1837, Gilpin Papers, MHS.

[31] Gilpin to Twiggs, Twiggs to General E. P. Gaines, Gaines to A.G.O.; all July 30, 1837, and Gilpin to A.G.O., August 21, 1837, G189 and 199, Gilpin File Letters Received, A.G.O., National Archives.

[32] Rodenbough, *Second Dragoons*, p. 28.

signed after recruiting a few-score Indians, who were still at Jef-
erson Barracks.[33]

Although still holding the rank of first lieutenant, William was
given Bean's position as commander of "H" Company early in
October, 1837.[34] He and his unit were stationed a few miles from
St. Augustine with other elements of the Second Dragoons augmented by an artillery detachment all under Brigadier General
Joseph Hernandez, one-time delegate to Congress from Florida,
now commander of all the troops east of the St. John's River.

Hernandez' brigade captured two chiefs and enough men and
slaves to persuade the Seminoles to discuss a truce; on October 21,
1837, Powell and seventy warriors came to Hernandez' camp at
Fort Peyton, seven miles from St. Augustine, to arrange terms. In
spite of the white flag, Powell and his men were seized by Hernandez, under General Jesup's orders, and placed in confinement by
the two hundred dragoons at the site. "H" Company, under Lieutenant William Gilpin, was one of five units taking part.[35] No gun
was fired.

There has been much discussion, then and since, over the degree
of deception perpetrated by the troops, and Jesup has been subject
to a great deal of criticism.[36] But the war was far from over, guile
or not. Coacoochee and Sam Jones now became the chief leaders
for resistance to migration, and the struggle continued throughout
the winter.

William's experiences were in the nature of scouting expeditions
that often turned into skirmishes, limited to a small scale by the
grass lakes and cypress swamps. From time to time little groups of
Seminoles would surrender and accept the plan for migration.
Many Negroes, slaves and free, were captured at the same time,
and argument ensued over their future. Most preferred to remain
with the Seminoles; many were alleged to be the rightful property
of Florida or Georgia planters and subject to capture; some were
seized by officers and retained or sold; some fell into the hands of

[33] *Army and Navy Chronicle* (Washington, D.C.), October 19, 1837.

[34] Gilpin to A.G.O., November 1, 1837, G303, Gilpin File, Letters Received,
A.G.O., National Archives.

[35] Rodenbough, *Second Dragoons*, p. 26; U.S. House of Representatives, *Executive Document No. 327*, 25th Cong., 2nd Sess., 1838.

[36] Grant Foreman, *Indian Removal*, p. 351.

Creek mercenaries who had been promised booty. Meanwhile, much of the army was engaged in guarding both Indians and Negroes.[37]

This new duty was onerous to William. His company was now dismounted (probably because the horses were of dubious value in the swamp country), he was not getting enough excitement guarding slaves and horses, and he did not like Twiggs. In later years he maintained that his chief objection was that the whole war turned into a movement to strengthen the "slave power," but no such comment is in his contemporary correspondence. Whatever the reason, on April 30, 1838, First Lieutenant William Gilpin, Second Dragoons, resigned from the service.[38]

William had no feeling of a job unfinished. Technically the Seminole War had no ending; generals came and went after short tours, and militia were being mustered out during every stage of the war. William had been in the service just under two years; left undone was only the dreary task of negotiating and removing, feeding and protecting. He wanted to move on.

Needless to say, William Gilpin became the observant tourist again as he left the Second Dragoons. His goal was St. Louis, his route a carefree ramble. He left Florida on May 1 for Charleston, where he received word that his resignation was official. A stage carried him to Augusta in one day, then on to Milledgeville, Macon, and Columbus. Central Georgia reminded him of northern Delaware, except for the general poverty in the former state. In Milledgeville he observed the opening shots of the next congressional

[37] U.S., House of Representatives, *Executive Document No. 225*, 25th Cong., 3rd Sess., 1839.

[38] *Army and Navy Chronicle* (Washington, D.C.), June 28, 1838; William to Joshua, June 9, 1838, Gilpin Papers, MHS. The Seminole War went on unchanged for many months after Gilpin's departure. But in 1840 Colonel Harney, who lost three-fourths of his small detachment in a surprise attack the year before, hit the Seminoles hard by following the Miami River into the Everglades and capturing some key leaders. Resistance ended by 1842. At a cost of at least fifteen hundred men and $50,000,000 the United States had worn out the Seminoles. Most (about three thousand) of them moved to what was to become Oklahoma. A few hundred managed to stay in Florida. "The only ones who could be said to have profited from this dismal affair were the contractors supplying the troops, and those militiamen whose active duty against the Seminoles might be considered an early form of W.P.A." (William T. Hagan, *American Indians*, p. 77.)

campaign being fired by Union Party candidates. In Montgomery he boarded the *Jefferson,* "a noble steamer," bound for Mobile. The Alabama River delighted him, deep and clear, passing through rich cotton and corn lands. Of course, he met and made friends. He spent five days in New Orleans, chiefly with army officers of his acquaintance. Temporarily at New Barracks were also fifteen hundred Seminoles, en route, like William, from Florida to the West. On June 1, 1838, just a month from Fort Peyton, William reached St. Louis, his new home.

CHAPTER THREE

# Fierce in the Good Cause

*Missouri Editor, 1838–1841*

During his tour of duty with the Second Dragoons William Gilpin concluded that the most desirable spot for his postwar home would be Missouri. He ignored opportunities in several of the family businesses, and did not even return to Kentmere for a visit.

He would have taken new military duty if offered, but having made his escape from the miserable Florida War, he would accept only a post on the western frontier.[1] Since none was available, he became, in 1838, a civilian in St. Louis.[2]

William believed that rich prospects awaited him in that city. Earlier he had seen frenzied land speculation with its easy profits. Now he correctly envisioned solid development. St. Louis tripled in population in the 1830's and, including suburbs, numbered thirty thousand people by the time William returned. In spite of

[1] Hubert Howe Bancroft, *History of the Life of William Gilpin*, p. 13. I find no evidence to support Bancroft's statement that William went to see President Van Buren for a western command.

[2] The government's indecision about the future of the army bothered William, also.

the absence of manufacturing, wages were good and employment rates high. The burgeoning economy was based upon commerce of wide variety, directed at the rich agriculture of Missouri and Illinois and the young pioneer communities of the upper Mississippi and Missouri rivers. But the expansion of this trade had been hampered by physical conditions—shifting river channels, snags, and unmarked little islands in the Mississippi, and poor and insufficient docking facilities.

The town's location had demanded its early growth; anything further was the problem of its citizens, and William's arrival coincided with the first community effort to create a city. Engineers were clearing the river; ships tied up almost bow-to-stern might unload in mud one day and upon firm macadam the next. Local clay and marble were being utilized for the first time and in 1838 some three hundred new brick stores, offices, and warehouses were constructed.

Cautious banking procedures, based in part upon Mexican silver, minimized the impact of Jackson's Bank war and the nationwide depression that had begun in 1837. William's interest was especially piqued by the fact that land values were still slowly rising. Litigation over city real estate was spirited, for land titles, often inherited from Spanish days, were troublesome and even fraudulent. Matters were complicated by the sales, beginning in 1836, of several thousand acres of "commons," lands earlier set aside by the town fathers for future schools. At the time of William's arrival speculators were taking second looks at their expensive purchases, averaging $150 an acre, and often forfeiting down payments or demanding their money back from the city.

William concluded that the situation offered unlimited opportunities for St. Louis lawyers and he applied to the state supreme court for admission to the bar.[3] During part of the short waiting period he was confined to his room because of bad teeth and some disease contracted in Florida. But he soon recovered and, using the long arm of brother Henry's influence, he obtained from the United States district attorney, Arthur Magenis, the use of office space and law books until he could get established. Books were too expensive

[3] John Thomas Scharf, *History of St. Louis City and County*, II, *passim*; William to Joshua, June 9, 1838, Gilpin Papers, MHS.

in St. Louis, so William wrote to Henry in Philadelphia asking for duplicates to augment his library.

Before the month was out William was licensed to practice law in Missouri. He had saved $500 which he considered a small sum but "many have started under less propitious auspices." Joshua had evidently cut off William's allowance while he was an officer (not a punitive measure, but simply because, for the first time, William had a regular salary). Now as a young, underemployed attorney, he frequently wrote home of his determination to get along without financial assistance of any kind. Yet, if Joshua or Henry had any business which they wanted to commit to his care, he would be extremely grateful.

William hoped to engage in a practice that would avoid the political feuds which he saw as ruinous to some careers and to give especial attention to land and mineral questions. This would be the way to develop his own fortune, for he felt that Missouri's resources must some day yield up their remaining undisclosed secrets. William had some knowledge of Pennsylvania's legal procedure (he probably was admitted but never practiced in that state), and he noted the difference in procedure on the frontier. In Missouri small jury cases were tried before justices of the peace who had much broader jurisdiction than those of Pennsylvania. William hoped to concentrate on these petty cases; he noticed that most attorneys shunned them, yet the business was reasonably lucrative.

He did take one small squint at politics—he attended a "Barbecue." Candidates of both parties came to address the voters. He enjoyed the speeches but noticed reprovingly that many guests, especially the wives and daughters, spent the time dancing, not listening. The Democrats were strong in the state, and William concluded that they would continue to be, with Thomas Hart Benton and Lewis Linn in the Senate and the Blair family taking some interest in the *Missouri Argus*.[4]

So William became an attorney. He received books from home and particularly requested that Henry send him documents published by Congress on Missouri or the "territories up the river." His special interest was material on "geological deposits, etc." He also

[4] William to Henry, June 6, 1838, Gilpin Collection, HSP; William to Henry, June 15, 1838, Gilpin Papers, MHS.

received the eastern newspapers so that he could see how they treated his friend, Martin Van Buren. To stimulate his practice he got Joshua to prepare some cards and circulars endorsed by important men of the family's acquaintance. One card read:

William Gilpin, late of Philadelphia, now of St. Louis, in the State of Missouri, takes this method to inform his friends that he has settled in the practice of law at St. Louis, and will attend to all professional business committed to him in the State of Missouri, and to the collection of debts, and settlement of Bounty and Pre-Emption Land claims, in the States of Missouri and Illinois.

Letters post-paid will be punctually attended to, and reference is given to his father, Joshua Gilpin at Wilmington, Delaware, and his Brother Henry D. Gilpin, Solicitor of the Treasury, Washington and to the following gentlemen:—

March 1st, 1839

| | |
|---|---|
| Horace Binney | Benjamin F. Butler |
| Charles Chauncey | C. C. Cambreleng |
| Joseph R. Ingersoll | Stephen Cambreleng |
| Robert Hare, Jr. | M. R. Maury, N. York |
| Charles Macalester | J. A. Bayard, Wilm'n, D. |
| Henry Toland, Philadelphia | Jon Meredith, Baltim' |

The advertising was distributed in Philadelphia and Washington as well as St. Louis, for the age was one of tangled land claims, and William correctly assumed that he might locate some contesting owners in the East.[5] But William did not find much business; the frontier was full of young lawyers, many better known in Missouri than William and some having equally influential families. Montgomery Blair, William's one-time classmate at West Point, was an example. Two years older than William, he had graduated from the Academy, fought in Florida, resigned to study law, and preceded William to St. Louis and the Missouri bar by a year. He, too, had good references and one day would argue a case concerning one Dred Scott. In Washington his father edited the *Globe*, mouthpiece of the Jackson and Van Buren administrations—a powerful man and a powerful paper. The Blair and Gilpin families were

[5] Broadside, HSD; Joshua to Henry, February 27, 1839, Gilpin Collection, HSP.

15450

close in Washington as well as in St. Louis, but their respective western scions were having trouble building clientels from the same groups.

William's shingle was hanging in St. Louis when his brother, Richard, asked him to look at some land that he had just entered in Southern Illinois. They met at Jonesboro in April, 1839. Richard had 560 acres, four miles from the Ohio and directly on the route of the Central Railroad (the future Illinois Central). He wanted William's help in securing title and perhaps some advice on the best way to exploit the land. In years to come William, the publicist, would have turned to the public and told them of the great future of the area and the opportunities for investment. But the young William still confined these ideas to his family, earnestly believing that if his father and Henry would help the two younger boys a bit now, they all would profit enormously in the near future.

William now discovered Cairo as two years before he had discovered St. Louis. "Cairo *will soon become* an immense city— During one day which I spent there last week 17 large steamboats passed going to different points along the Mpi, Mo, Ohio, Wbash, Tennessee, Cumberland, etc etc—for all of which trade and much more Cairo will soon become the Central Depot." With the gift of hindsight one could point out a difference in William's comments about St. Louis and those of Cairo: in the former town he had counted three or four dozen ships *at* the docks; in Cairo he saw a lesser number of ships, and more important, they were *passing* Cairo on their way to other towns. William missed this point, for he thought in terms of geopolitics, not business.

Cairo is the highest point of Mippi accessible to large vessels throughout the year . . . [while] Chicago is the head of the valley of the St. Lawrence and the avenue from the Atlantic to the Lakes—the Central Railroad of Ill's connects these two points [Cairo and Chicago], having branches to St. Louis and Louisville—A railroad is constructing from Cairo thro' Nashville to Charleston, S.C. which will have a branch to Mobile—The Ohio River joins the Mippi at Cairo—the Missouri River at St. Louis 200 miles above—The Illinois River (flowing almost from Lake Michigan) 18 miles above [St. Louis]—Thus you see Cairo is right in the navel of North America to which the avenues of commerce natural and artificial concentrate—viz from Canada & the North

and South Atlantic States—from the central states and the Gulf of
Mexico and from the upper Mississippi, Missouri and Arkansas countries.[6]

What could the Gilpins do to take advantage of this brilliant
future? William had a plan based on Joshua's frequently made suggestion that he would divide his western holdings among the three
sons (Thomas, in England, was never considered in these divisions,
presumably because Joshua felt that he neded no assistance and
would be in no position to participate in any of the transactions).
Joshua's frontier land—6,000 acres in Indiana County, Pennsylvania, a smaller undisclosed parcel in Luzerne County (near
Wilkes-Barre) Pennsylvania, and some 10,000 acres in Lincoln
County in central Kentucky—produced no income, and William
thought that the speculative era had passed them by.

William recommended selling these lands (the best would bring
five dollars an acre, he believed) and using the proceeds to invest,
at the government price, in land along the Ohio and Mississippi. He
suggested especially the Cairo region which

> equals in fertility and excellence of position any lands in the West,
> and is covered with oak timber scarcely inferior for naval purposes to
> the live oak of the South, of a size and beauty not often rivalled . . .
> [the lands] are composed of calcareous alluvion being in fact naturally
> perfect manure—The climate delightful and perfectly healthy . . .
> tracts may be purchased at $1.25 per acre, which like Gov. Cass' farm
> at Detroit will in ten years produce $125 per acre.

Above all William recommended Illinois because the legislature
had just approved a two-year extension of its internal improvement
system, an absolute necessity for the exploitation of frontier lands.

By coincidence William and Richard were minor participants
and eyewitnesses of an early struggle for the control of Illinois;
yet they were in no position (or lacked the political acumen) to
understand the forces at work. They could not foresee that the

6 William to Joshua, no month, 1839, Gilpin Folder, HSD. William never had
occasion to visit Chicago (about five years old at this time), a fact which perhaps explains his enthusiasm for Cairo, and his missing the significance of his
own comments about Chicago. Commerce passing through Chicago had to
change carriers, and so the city grew. Commerce found no reason to stop at
Cairo, and so it is a small town.

Illinois Central would not be open until 1856, and then with a new depot, Chicago, which would draw the state's commerce northward and eastward, leaving Cairo in the backwash. It would take two decades of powerful political action, huge outside investment and labor, and 2,500,000 acres of federal land grants to make the line possible. None of these elements was present in 1838 when William and Richard looked upon Cairo.[7]

In the 1830's many of the states had begun expensive programs of road, canal, and river improvement; the states either provided much of the credit or did the work themselves. The demands were great, as practically all Westerners could agree on the philosophy of improving communications (if not on how to pay for them). The financing was accomplished by heavy borrowing against the anticipated profits.

Stimulating the boom was the generally cheap price collected by the federal government for its sales of land. In Illinois the situation was irritated when farmers found that the absence of small streams made impossible the shipment of their corn and pork. Thousands of these farmers asked for a system of communications that would end their commercial isolation; the result was Illinois' first internal improvement program, loaded with ambitious projects that could not yet be supported.

One of these projects was the Central (or later, the Illinois Central) Railroad, chartered in 1836 to link the Ohio-Mississippi at Cairo to Galena in northwestern Illinois. To get the measure through the state legislature the line was routed through several prairie villages and around some larger towns like Springfield and Peoria. The road was originally a promotion of speculators with holdings near Cairo who hoped to tap the state for its agricultural produce as well as the lead from Galena. When their own plan for a railroad failed (Charles Dickens was one of the unfortunate investors), they joined with the Illinois Central group.

Financing the line during the long depression following 1837 proved impossible. The state by 1840 had acquired an enormous debt, high taxes, and a bad credit rating to accompany forty miles of embankment (no track), running north from Cairo.

[7] Paul W. Gates, *The Illinois Central Railroad and Its Colonization Work*, pp. 21–43; Carlton J. Corliss, *Main Line of Mid-America*, p. 11.

The plan (which also included four east-and-west links) was simply too vast for a young, nonindustrialized state. Unwittingly Richard had invested, and William was trying to persuade his father to invest, in a land boom of already declining promise. The young men might have been alerted by Richard's visit to the state capital concerning the future of his job as engineer. In February he went to Vandalia and watched the legislature in session. He had never before seen a legislative body in action except for the British Parliament, and he was shocked at the members' behavior. Abraham Lincoln and his "Long Nine" from Sangamore County had just succeeded in getting the capital moved to Springfield by conceding to other towns' measures in the Internal Improvements Program.[8] "The plan of operation is what they call 'log-rolling'— which is neither more nor less than bribery and corruption—so unless a 'quid' is given for a 'quo' there is no possibility of getting anything done." The legislature had juggled jobs, titles, and salaries but Richard was protected by his district commissioner and was now resident engineer on the Shawneetown and Alton Railroad.[9]

Perhaps the fact that Richard's job was secured by the legislature kept the brothers from seeing the danger in their reckless enthusiasm for the improvements program. The two concurred in a proposal for the land swap and sent it to Joshua. Richard went to Equality for his new engineering post, and William returned to St. Louis.

Joshua agreed in principle to the transfer of his lands, and William plunged into the task of clearing titles. He got some information from home, but probably made a quick visit to Kentucky to obtain the details of ownership. William ran the titles back to the original grant in 1784 when one John Garland entered and surveyed 20,313 acres on the Green River in Lincoln County, Kentucky. Governor Patrick Henry of Virginia issued the patent to Garland in 1786. The property quickly changed hands twice and was divided; by 1806 Joshua and Thomas Gilpin held about 10,000 acres. The other half was shared by a General John Brown, since

8 Corliss, *Main Line*, p. 8.

9 Richard to Joshua, April 16, 1839, Gilpin Folder, HSD. Richard mentioned William's recent "delightful journey to the East" but gave no details. Possibly he went home for Christmas, 1838, but more likely he visited Kentucky to investigate his father's land titles in that state.

deceased, and Thomas Leiper of Philadelphia. Leiper was a friend of Henry's, and William believed that he would sell his share back to the Gilpins. The heirs of General Brown had not yet been located, and this was proving a nuisance. William asked his father how much further to proceed.[10]

William did not realize the condition of his father's health. Joshua had spent a very uncomfortable winter and thought that it might be his last. Thinking it time to clean up some of his tangled business possessions, he turned, as usual, to Henry for advice. Henry was too comfortably fixed in Washington to want his portion of the lands, and he shared with his father a concern for the two western Gilpins who seemed generally short of cash. He drew up a deed for Joshua and Mary to sign, carefully following Kentucky form and in this fashion, turned 5,000 acres of central Kentucky land over to Richard and William. Henry told Joshua how to deal with the Leiper family and suggested that Joshua ask his brother, Tom, to turn his 5,000 acres over to his nephews also.[11]

It was to the good fortune of William and Richard that the Gilpin holdings were so encumbered that months passed before anything could be done to further the plan of buying or trading for lands "down in Egypt." A mercurial personality like William's needed action that could not be supplied by searching land titles and badgering heirs; he soon gave up the idea of trading his Kentucky lands and bought eighty acres of his own through the Kaskaskia land office in Illinois.[12]

Probably through Montgomery Blair, William became acquainted with the owners of the *Missouri Argus*, St. Louis' only Democratic paper of the time. When William first returned to St. Louis after the Seminole War, the paper was campaigning for the reelection of Senator Thomas Hart Benton, and it may have received some financial help from the Blair family and the *Globe* in Washington (at least William made one cryptic comment to that effect). Sometime late in 1839 the *Argus* acquired a new publisher, Andrew Jackson Davis, and lost a steady advertiser, "William Gilpin,

[10] William to Joshua, April 16, 1839, Gilpin Folder, HSD.

[11] Joshua to Henry, May 7, 1839, Gilpin Collection, HSP; Henry to Joshua, May 14, 1839, Gilpin Folder, HSD.

[12] Land Certificate No. 6263, signed by President Martin Van Buren, October 10, 1840, Gilpin Folder, HSD.

Attorney and Counsellor at Law, Office on Pine Street one door W of Second." For counsellor Gilpin was now editor of the *Missouri Daily Argus*.

As an old man Gilpin stated that the *Argus* was at that moment campaigning for Benton and Missouri's other senator, Lewis F. Linn—another instance of his telescoping memory. While the *Argus* was ardent in its support of these two Democrats, neither was up for re-election while William was editor, both having been safely sent back to Washington by the Missouri legislature before William became associated with the paper.

Now William was clearly a new cog in the Benton machine: Magenis, who lent him an office, Montgomery Blair, who got him a job, and Abel Rathbone Corbin, William's predecessor at the *Argus*, were all strong Benton men—at least most of the time. To an advanced degree the *Argus*, before and during William's editorship, copied the attitudes of Francis Blair's *Globe*. Old editions of the paper make quite clear the issues of the day and where William stood upon them. Repeatedly the paper discussed the coming presidential election. The *Argus*, of course, strongly favored Van Buren's re-election against William Henry Harrison, whom he had defeated in 1836. Linn was not mentioned often—well liked in Washington and Missouri, he never aroused the emotions that the senior senator could inspire. Andrew Jackson, whose cloak the Democrats hoped would fit Van Buren, was also one of William's heroes and received much adulation in the editorials. Curiously, William rarely attacked Harrison and his rather blank political record, but fired his long-range artillery at Henry Clay and Daniel Webster as the real leaders of their party. William refused to call them Whigs, but—shades of the Hartford Convention, perhaps—classified all his opponents as Federalists. Not too surprisingly he also condemned New England and the Bank of the United States and anyone who suggested its re-establishment.[13]

In Missouri William looked upon his party as the truly democratic one (he usually called it the Democracy), and his anti-Whig editorials were generally along class lines as he attacked paper money and property qualifications for voters. Federalists (Whigs)

[13] Bancroft, *William Gilpin*, p. 14, has William attacking Webster in the *Argus* when the latter came to St. Louis. This could not have happened, as the visit took place in 1837.

were cold-blooded merchants, avaricious, remorseless, and opposed to labor—the real producers. He was especially upset because the Whig's ticket of William Henry Harrison and John Tyler used a log cabin as a symbol, for it was Benton who took the lead in aiding the real pioneer. At the same time Gilpin accused the "Federalists" of being abolitionists who would seek to take away one's property.

During his editorship, William was chosen secretary of the Young Men's Democratic State Convention (of 1840) probably because of his strong anti-Whig position. While he fired away at Clay, the immediate canvass that spring was for mayor of St. Louis. The *Argus* appears to have been the only paper supporting James J. Purdy for the post; William claimed that he fought four Federalist papers that trumpeted for John Darby, three times mayor.

One writer on Missouri's economic history concludes that Gilpin's views "were of more than ordinary importance." His philosophy

was a curious mixture of positive and negative attitudes toward the role of government in the economy, but was consistently equalitarian. The "true Aristocracy," according to the young editor, was to be found in the ranks of industry, among the productive classes. The object of his editorial labors was simply to obtain for them the controls of the government. They asked ". . . no privileges not common to all, but only protection in their lawful pursuits and property—in a word to be let alone!" . . . Despite this statement of principles, with its overtones of hostility to positive government, the *Argus* continued its firm support of the state bank and various specific proposals for the promotion of prosperity by state action . . . an editorial denounced "corporations, banks, insurance companies and monopolies of every kind and quality" because they contained ". . . the embryo of the reduction of the government into the hands of a few."

On the other hand, democracy "established universal suffrage and raised the mass of the people to a share in government. With equal political rights, government would produce equality of social condition, and equality of wealth, comfort and happiness."[14]

The St. Louis voters must have concluded that the community

[14] James N. Primm, *Economic Policy in the Development of a Western State, Missouri*, pp. 43–44. Reprinted by permission of Harvard University Press.

had enough equality, for Darby was victorious by a slight majority. William evidently was not surprised by this defeat, but it made him pause to take stock once more. The best evidence of his feelings in the spring of 1840 is a letter in which he unburdened himself—as usual—to Henry.

The job was becoming too much for him; six days a week he worked from nine in the morning until midnight, much of the time reading exchange papers and selecting items from them for printing. He was not sure that he had made the right choice of jobs. "I assumed the editorial chair as much from a caprice of the moment as any other reason and after about five minutes reflection. It was the entering wedge of Col. Benton and several other prominent men in this state who have been my predecessors." But he was not sure that the paper would carry him forward if he were always fighting for losing causes. All of the merchants were against him, he said, supporting five daily Federalist papers, with the *Argus* the only Democratic daily paper west of Louisville. Furthermore, his party's organization was fundamentally weak because of the peculiar nature of St. Louis. Much of the working-class element was made up of groups too heterogeneous for him to manage.[15] He got along well with the Irish—he was the special guest of the Hibernian Society on St. Patrick's Day and of the "several dozen" toasts, only William's was recorded for posterity: "The Green Isle of Erin—a little body with a mighty heart. We welcome her brave, generous and enthusiastic sons to our free republic."[16]

But the other groups—"Canadian-French, Rocky Mountain fur hunters, simple, primitive, bigoted people, skinflint Yankee and southern merchants come here to repair their fortunes"—William could not unite in the Democratic cause, especially now that the party lacked the personality of a Jackson.

For the future William urged Henry to continue his financial aid to the *Argus* and to visit the West during the summer and campaign for Van Buren. The President would need help. Meanwhile the old restlessness was showing—could Henry get him a military or a diplomatic post, perhaps secretary to one of the Florida territories. "A new state is the best for a beginner."[17]

[15] William to Henry, May 22, 1840, Gilpin Collection, HSP.
[16] *Missouri Daily Argus*, March 19, 1840.
[17] William to Henry, May 22, 1840, Gilpin Collection, HSP.

Henry had nothing to offer, and William continued in St. Louis throughout most of 1840. Occasionally he saw Richard, who reported home that William *was* working very hard and was "fierce in the good cause." But Richard was worried about frontier life on two scores: log-rolling in the treacherous Illinois financial scene and the bitterness of the St. Louis newspaper war. The first problem came quickly to a head. Richard's job was eliminated in March, and he decided to leave Equality and to move back home to help with his father's farm.[18]

Richard's concern for William also proved justified but not so rapidly; before leaving Illinois Richard felt that William had "silenced the howling pack of rival editors."[19] But the political battle was getting more personal. One paper accused William of following in the footsteps of his fathers who were Quakers in Delaware and "during the Revolution sided with the Britishers. This accounts for his being so bitter against Harrison and Tyler."[20] The reference, of course, was to William's grandfather who had been confined in Virginia, not for aiding the British but for refusing to swear that he would not.

With the close of the mayoralty campaign St. Louis had a respite from vitriol for a few weeks and William had time to concern himself with new matters. No one of his nature could live long in St. Louis and not hear wondrous stories of the next frontier, the Oregon country. From the days when he first met General Ashley on an Ohio River steamer William had dreamed of the new land and what it must be like. Too involved in Missouri's affairs to consider a visit, he already had visions of Oregon's resources and future. His political ties were perfect for publicizing these qualities. Senator Benton had long been a spokesman for the West, most of whose commerce passed through Missouri; in 1833 the other senator, Alexander Buckner, had died and had been replaced by Dr. Lewis F. Linn, another Jacksonian. Linn and Benton were friends

[18] Joshua to Henry, March 10, 1840, Gilpin Collection, HSP. As so often before, Joshua was concerned that he did not hear from William often, especially since "the adoption of his new plan of life."

[19] Richard to Henry, January 12, 1840, Gilpin Collection, HSP.

[20] The argument was a useful defense against Democratic charges that the Federalists were traitors in the War of 1812. Richard to Henry, February 22, 1840, Gilpin Collection, HSP.

and in close harmony on most issues during the decade that Linn served.

Elected in 1836 in his own right, Linn two years later was chairman of the Committee on Territories. In this capacity he first introduced the Linn Bill for the protection, occupation, and settlement of Oregon. The generally accepted definition of Oregon in the 1830's was that vast region west of South Pass and the Bitter Root Mountains running to the Pacific between the 42nd parallel and 54°40'. Ownership of much (but not all) of this region was disputed by Great Britain and the United States, from the time of the treaty of joint occupation in 1818. This ten-year compact was renewed in 1827, with the understanding that either nation might withdraw from the agreement with one year's notice. Through the activities of the Hudson's Bay Company the British claim was firmly based. Mountain men and promoters alike failed to take Oregon for the U.S. or even whittle at the Company's power, but the job was accomplished by other agents. In answer to a fanciful call from some Indians a frenzied missionary movement began. In 1834 Jason Lee and the Methodist mission settled in the Willamette Valley. The next year Samuel Parker and Marcus Whitman, representing the American Board, made their initial visit to Oregon and established plans for a mission among the Indians near Fort Walla Walla. The first Catholic mission was established in the Willamette Valley late in 1838.

Whatever the influence of these groups upon the Indians (and it was not great), their ventures widely advertised Oregon to other Americans. Looking for free, good land, a commercial opportunity on the coast, or merely a way to block Great Britain, the American pioneer was destined to be the conqueror of Oregon.

Linn's bill in 1838 anticipated the great Oregon rush. Based on letters, reports, and official surveys, the bill provided for military occupation of parts of Oregon, a liberal land policy, and the establishment of territorial government. To justify these acts the bill included annexes tracing American claims to the area and showing the current extent of occupation. The bill stirred a great deal of debate in Congress and much enthusiasm outside, but it did not pass. Reintroduced by Linn the measure came to William Gilpin's attention for the first time in 1840.

William was "much taken by the plan." He asked Henry for

detailed information about it and printed the replies in the *Argus* to meet popular demand.[21] Linn's proposal interested no state more than Missouri. That region would obviously flourish as the pioneers followed the rivers upstream to the north and west. The merchants could sell wagons, teams, tools, and food; unemployed and roust-abouts might catch on with the trains; retired mountain men would be needed as guides. In the days of the "Van Buren depression," few Missourians could lack interest in the Linn Bill.

Four years earlier William had described for his sister the mag-nitude and wealth of the great plains—a region he had just touched upon. Now with a public audience for the first time, he assumed the task of describing a West he had never seen. He had known William Ashley and lesser trappers who could tell him of Oregon, but he also relied on his friend William Sublette, mountain man extraordinary, who, with Jedediah Smith and David Jackson, bought out Ashley in 1826 and became the leading business figure of the Rocky Mountain Fur Company. For fifteen years Sublette had studied the Trans-Mississippi West. He knew the country well enough to manage the first wagons into the Rocky Mountains (1830), and he knew it well enough to make it pay him.[22]

Drawing upon this collection of sources, William used the pages of the *Argus* to describe Oregon and the continent to which it belonged. In Gilpin's books and speeches of later years he had his descriptions fairly fixed, but as a twenty-five-year-old editor he had to feel his way. He wrote that North America had two chains of mountains, the "Andes" and the Alleghenies. The countries out-side these were on the "rind of the continent." The interior of this "circumjacent rim of mountains" is in three divisions, the most important of which is the Mississippi Valley. This valley, with St. Louis as the center (since he did not buy Cairo land he had moved the continent's center back to St. Louis), covers 1,500,000 square miles, the most sublime of the earth's subdivisions. But the United States needed colonies on the Pacific coast to trade with Asia's high civilizations. The climate was excellent, editorialized Gilpin, and the Rockies (Andes) were no more difficult to cross than the Alle-

---

21 Richard to Henry, January 12, 1840, Gilpin Collection, HSP.

22 William to Henry, December 1, 1841, Sublette Papers, Missouri Historical Society (hereafter cited as Sublette Papers, MHS); John E. Sunder, *Bill Sub-lette, Mountain Man*, pp. 84–89.

ghenies. And in the event that the *Argus* had any eastern readers, the articles bore a warning for them. With the passage of the Linn Bill and its 640 acres per family, there would grow up "a body of western oceanic states . . . possessing greater natural and commercial advantages than those which now wield a predominant influence in the National Councils."[23] This, incidentally, was William's declaration of war on the Atlantic community—considering his heritage, a very odd development. The regional issue pops into his thinking very frequently thereafter and can probably best be explained by his very bitter feud of that same hour with the Whigs, whom he looked upon as New England Federalists.

As self-appointed champion of Oregon, William tolerated no criticism of that area. In his "irksome labor" of copying exchanges he encountered "eastern journals" that quoted another authority to the effect that Oregon was a cold, dreary desert, almost uninhabitable for agricultural purposes. Such opinions were all wrong, William proclaimed: travelers' first impressions were often poor (some people did not even like Washington when they first viewed it), he reminded his readers. But the Far West had a wonderful future; one day many states would exist "on the Oregon." William was so shocked by the desert theory that he wondered if the writer were not in the pay of the British like those other critical travelers, Frederick Marryat and Frances Trollope.[24]

The writer of the articles was *not* in British pay. Like William, he was merely intrigued with Oregon. He was Thomas Jefferson Farnham, from Illinois, who had been inspired to visit Oregon in 1838 when Jason Lee spoke in Peoria about the wonders of the Willamette Valley. With a militant little group of young Illini called the "Oregon Dragoons," Farnham marched to the coast, saw Oregon, California, and Hawaii, and returned home to write a book about his journey.[25]

Although Farnham's book had not yet been published, extracts from his journal were already appearing in print. It is impossible to determine, therefore, whether the various editors were selecting

[23] *Missouri Daily Argus* (St. Louis), March 21, 1840.

[24] *Ibid.*, June 26, 1840. Their biographers make no assertion that these writers were in British pay. See, for example, Eileen Bigland, *The Indomitable Mrs. Trollope*, and David Hannay, *Life of Frederick Marryat*.

[25] Le Roy R. Hafen and Carl Coke Rister, *Western America*, p. 237.

from Farnham those bits that criticized Oregon or whether William himself used that device. The truth was that Farnham's description of much of Oregon, as later published in full, was quite accurate (as Bill Sublette could have told William); and it was also true that Farnham was anxious to advertise Oregon. In some portions of the book he described the region as glowingly as did William in the *Argus*. Thus, two of the first and most fanatical writers on Oregon early spilled printer's ink over the endless question of what is the Great American Desert.

William's attack on Farnham came to nothing. Oregon was getting publicity, accurate or not, and the American people slowly realized that they might lose their stake if they did not counteract the British influence. William could not know it yet, but he would have an opportunity to fight for Oregon in person. His editing days were numbered.

After the election of John Darby as mayor in April, 1840, some of the political heat had cooled in St. Louis, but by late May the Whigs and the Democrats were at one another again as they argued the case of Harrison versus Van Buren. The mayoralty and presidential campaigns in Missouri were both bitterly fought but the personalism of the struggle can be better explained in terms of a battle for economic control of the state. Party lines were not always important, but economic positions were.

Within Missouri the question of the existence of a national bank and its corollary problem of hard or soft money was probably more intensely debated than in any other state. The presence of "Old Bullion" Benton was in itself enough to keep the questions before the public; Benton played the key role in the destruction of the Bank of the United States, in the issuance of the Specie Circular, and in the drive toward a national currency that would minimize bank paper. Throughout the 1830's Benton fought in Congress for these measures, partly on constitutional grounds, partly because he believed that he spoke for the farmer, the artisan, and the laborer. In frontier communities these people shared alike unhappy experiences with the vagaries of shifting credit and declining paper money values.

The business community in Philadelphia, New York, Washington—even in St. Louis—fought Benton for a decade. They believed that a national banking system would eliminate wildcat practices, and they believed that in an era of rapid expansion bullionism was impossible. Benton's thirty years in the Senate proved the popularity of his beliefs, in Missouri, at least, but he was fighting a losing battle. Missouri, abstaining from the wild promotion schemes of her neighbor states and benefitting from the silver of the Santa Fe trade, remained singularly debt-free and solvent until about 1840. In time, the depression following the panic of 1837 was to strike Missouri as well, and the Benton machine was to lose favor among workers who saw in the hard money philosophy no relief for their problems.[26]

But the sharpest and ablest opposition to the Bentonites came from St. Louis' business interests. The Benton philosophy had them trapped by virtue of its protagonist's control of the state legislature. In 1836 the Bank of the State of Missouri was chartered, a mixed-enterprise monopoly that at first satisfied both "Hards" and "Softs." But the Bank operated conservatively and much of St. Louis' business was transacted with notes from Illinois and other states. The Bank directors feared the redeemability of the out-of-state notes; and late in 1839 they announced that they would accept no more of them.

In retaliation angry businessmen withdrew their deposits from the Bank and placed them with various chartered utility companies which acted additionally as banks, beyond the powers granted to them by the state of Missouri.[27] The issue was now joined: the Benton faction, whose most important editor in the state, and only editor in St. Louis, was William Gilpin, battled with Whigs and a significantly growing group of Democrats for the economic control of the state. In a sense the war was between St. Louis and the rest of the state, at least many contemporaries oversimplified their analysis to that degree. The *Argus* in these terms was something of a fifth-column for the farmers and all others opposed to privilege. But politics is never that simple, and many Democrats felt that Missouri could grow only if investors might

[26] This account draws heavily upon Primm, *Economic Policy*; Elbert B. Smith, *Magnificent Missourian*; and William N. Chambers, *Old Bullion Benton*. These three authors are in substantial agreement on Benton and Missouri's economic structure of the 1830's and 1840's.

[27] Primm, *Economic Policy*, pp. 40–43; John R. Cable, *The Bank of the State of Missouri*, pp. 179–188.

have freer hands and some of the advantages of monopoly. (For example, Abel Rathbone Corbin, William's predecessor *and* successor as editor of the *Argus*, a job he owed to Benton, gradually turned against Benton about 1841 because of Benton's opposition to chartering a state railroad.)[28]

The governor, Thomas Reynolds, a Benton man, was more moderate than some Democrats; he did not oppose all corporations but said that he would use the power of the state to correct and enforce the charters, rather than revoke them. Other Democrats in the legislature went so far as to oppose all corporations, even charitable ones. The problem headed for a showdown in November of 1840 when the eleventh General Assembly was to meet.

William, meanwhile, became a central figure in the most violent reflection of the state war. Late in May he wrote a scathing editorial against the Whigs for putting James J. Purdy on their committee to establish the national bank (Purdy was the *Argus'* recently defeated candidate for mayor). Purdy told the *Argus* that the action was taken without his knowledge or permission, and that he wanted nothing to do with such a bank.

William's language was rough but representative of the time. He snarled that the trick was the type the "Dung hill breed of the federalists and toadies made use of to play off the game." One of the Whigs concerned was William P. Darnes who wanted to know if the editorial applied to him; he addressed his question to publisher Davis as responsible because the "editor's standing in my opinion for moral integrity and veracity forbid that I should have any communication with him."

Calling Darnes a "jackass," "toady," and a "half-witted drone," William replied that he wrote all of the editorials and did mean Darnes in his attack. Two days later the enraged Darnes met Davis on Market Street. The two argued until, encouraged by one Thornton Grimsley, Darnes struck Davis in the jaw, then bludgeoned him over the head with an iron cane that demolished Davis' protective umbrella. Davis' skull was fractured and he was in serious condition.[29]

---

[28] Chambers, *Old Bullion*, pp. 260–261.

[29] *Missouri Daily Argus*, June 2, 1840. Some of the "Liberty of the Cudgel" is described in William H. Lyon's *The Pioneer Editor in Missouri, 1808–1860*, pp. 73–84. Lyon calls Gilpin "one of the most vehement of all the pioneer editors."

A week later, June 8 at six in the evening, Davis died. The *Argus* repeated the story of the beating in columns edged in black. The twenty-four-year-old lawyer turned publisher, a resident of Missouri for only four years, was buried the next day in the Presbyterian burial ground. One of the pallbearers was another young newcomer, Montgomery Blair.

Davis' death forced a change in Williams' career that he had been considering for some time. The sale of the *Argus* became a matter for the county court which ruled out a purchaser who would have kept William on. The danger arose that the paper might be sold to a Whig. While William continued on an interim basis, Davis' heirs tried to sell "The Leading organ of the Administration in Missouri."³⁰

Finally, in August, 1840, and undoubtedly with pressure from Benton, the paper was sold to Abel Corbin, who had established it in 1835. Corbin's first issue announced that Gilpin had been persuaded to "battle in his present station until, at least," the general elections in November, "when if he persists in his original intention of not becoming a permanent member of the corps editorial, other arrangements will be made."³¹

William's remaining few months in St. Louis were active, even exciting to a young man. He was secretary of the Young Men's Democratic State Convention which met in October at Jefferson City;³² the 750 delegates heard a two-hour address by Senator Benton in which, according to a Whig paper, Old Bullion "set his teeth hard whenever he mentioned St. Louis, Banks, or Merchants."³³

The killer of Davis had not yet been tried but soon would be. Gilpin meanwhile sharpened his pen on Darnes' accomplice, Thornton Grimsley. Grimsley had been in St. Louis nearly twenty years as saddler and outfitter to fur companies and western explorers.³⁴ He had been alderman, state legislator, state senator, and a

---

Oddly, Davis and Darnes had been very close personal and political friends until the attacks in the press.

³⁰ *Missouri Daily Argus*, June 12, 13, and 17, July 8, 1840.

³¹ *Ibid.*, August 17, 1840. William was usually, but probably not always editor during this period.

³² *Ibid.*, October 16, 1840.

³³ Chambers, *Old Bullion*, p. 245.

³⁴ "Colonel Grimsley's Proposed Expedition to Oregon in 1841," *Oregon His-*

promoter of the state internal improvements program. In 1839 he was Whig nominee to the United States Congress, but lost the election partly through the efforts of Gilpin and the *Argus*. Needless to say he was anti-Benton and anti-Gilpin even before the assault on Davis.

William accused Grimsley of inflaming Darnes against Davis. Grimsley now commenced a literary attack upon the *Argus* but as Darnes had done before, he ignored editor Gilpin and condemned the publisher. Corbin, knowing too well his predecessor's fate, wrote an editorial making very clear where he stood. He, too, accused Grimsley of being accessory to murder, but admitted that he was no fighter; he would battle Grimsley with a pen, but if that were insufficient, Gilpin was available. "As Mr. Gilpin handles the weapons of death quite as well as Mr. Grimsley pretends to do, I assume" that is why Grimsley passed Gilpin by.[35] This was too much of a challenge for Grimsley, who must have been very conscious of Darnes' position. On Friday the 13th of November, however, Darnes was brought to trial, found guilty only of fourth-degree manslaughter the next day, and fined $500. The Democrats were incensed and Grimsley was inspired.[36]

Meanwhile, although the Whigs had won the presidency with Harrison on a log-cabin platform, they lost the three westernmost states to Van Buren, the allegedly aristocratic easterner. The pop-

---

*torical Quarterly*, XXIV (December, 1923), 434–447. Grimsley offered his services to the new Whig government to conquer Oregon. He knew that Secretary of War John Bell preferred West Pointers, but Grimsley was sure "that with two months reference to the Tactic of the country, I can drill a company of horse, a squadron or regiment, equal to any man in the Army."

[35] *Missouri Daily Argus*, October 26, 1840.

[36] *Ibid.*, November 16, 1840; a significant factor in the mild punishment meted to Darnes was the fact that while three physicians swore that Davis died of the blows, three others maintained that an unnecessary trephine operation brought fatal consequences. The chief attorney for the defense was Henry S. Geyer, the Whig who was to defeat Benton for his seat in the Senate in 1851 (Richard Edwards and M. Hopewell, *The Great West*, pp. 370–371). The trial was a great social event in St. Louis with the court so crowded that the judge gave up his bench to some of the ladies. Geyer played upon the professional jealousies of other doctors to convince the jury that there was reasonable doubt as to the cause of the death. The whole affair is ably described in Cynthia De Haven Pitcock's article, "The Darnes-Davis Case of 1840," *Missouri Historical Review*, LVIII (October, 1964), 31–45.

ular vote was extremely close in some states, and a switch of a few thousand votes would have given Van Buren his re-election. The Democrats, who carried Missouri for Van Buren, cried fraud for a week, then settled down to state affairs.

The General Assembly convened at Jefferson City on November 16. The Democrats included in their ranks the new governor, Thomas Reynolds, and Sterling Price as speaker of the house. William Gilpin defeated J. Gordon of Boone for chief clerk, William's reward for his "furious partisanship." He now left the *Argus* permanently and Corbin resumed as editor.[37]

In Jefferson City William was reasonably safe from physical attack, but he did commence going about armed. His enemies in St. Louis attempted to prefer charges against him, but Governor Reynolds assured him that he could protect him from the courts.[38] One day, however, William read a copy of a notice that had been posted on the St. Louis courthouse to the effect that Thornton Grimsley would attack him on sight if he returned to St. Louis. At the close of the legislative assembly Gilpin took the new laws to Cape Girardeau for printing, traveling by way of St. Louis, where he was waylaid by Grimsley. Evidently each man had a club, but Grimsley was forty-two and William twenty-five, a wiry six-footer in good shape. Gilpin won the brief encounter, breaking his hickory stick over his opponent's head as the blood ran.[39] That seems to have ended the feud and, according to Gilpin, Grimsley lived an exemplary life ever after; he was not seriously injured.

With the close of the eleventh General Assembly in May, 1841, William was unemployed. He had had enough of the newspaper business and never returned to it. The Whigs were in Washington, and William's usual family connections were weakened.

[37] Primm discusses the *Argus* during this session as if it had been in Gilpin's hands, attacking charters and corporations and the misuse of state power. William subscribed to these beliefs at this stage of his life, but probably did not write the editorials. They are doubtless Corbin's (*Missouri Daily Argus* [St. Louis], November 9, 1840; Primm, *Economic Policy*, p. 45).

[38] Governor Reynolds told William, "Give yourself no uneasiness on that score, for whatever they do I have always your pardon written out" (Bancroft, *William Gilpin*, p. 15).

[39] I do not doubt that a fight occurred, but the only evidence we have is William's own account to Bancroft (*William Gilpin*, pp. 15–16), who calls the bully "Grimsey."

Henry left the office of Attorney General with Harrison's inauguration and returned to his Philadelphia law practice. Father Joshua was critically ill and finally passed away August 24, 1841. William may have gone home at this time but he left no record of such a trip.[40]

Within a month of his inauguration Harrison was dead; his successor, John Tyler, was something of a Democrat but of the wrong branch for the Gilpins. Even his record shuffling of cabinet posts was to bring none of the Gilpin family sponsors to the Washington scene. William could get no military command.[41]

For the moment William's political dreams were gone from Missouri as well. No longer an editor, he would not be likely to get the legislative clerkship again from the state Democratic machine, and he did not feel firmly enough established to run for local office, even with the unquestioned Benton blessing. If he had political aims, he did not at this time record them. Perhaps he was momentarily tired of battles; he was ready again to move on.

Three years in St. Louis had brought great changes in William. His father's death and the termination of Henry's political career meant an end of family patronage. His correspondence home almost completely ceased after 1840. Always physically active, he was summoned more and more by the wilderness of the West he had grown to love. It was a time of schooling for him, as he saw firsthand the configuration of the American continent and began to form his notions of geopolitics. St. Louis, as it has been with so many men, was his gateway to the West.

In St. Louis, also, William first framed his ideas on the political and economic problems of the day. That he would be a Democrat was ordained by heritage. Jackson, Van Buren, and Buchanan were family friends, and evidently very good family friends. People of that era bitten by the Jackson bug rarely recovered; William was

[40] I have found no record that William returned home during 1841 but he could have easily accomplished the trip between the dates that I can place him in Missouri.

[41] The Missouri Whigs wanted all Democrats out of national positions that concerned the West. See, for example, Grimsley's attempt to have the Harrison-Tyler Administration remove Joshua Pilcher from the post of Superintendent of Indian Affairs, a position he had just assumed in 1839 on the death of William Clark (Chambers, *Old Bullion*, p. 233; "Colonel Grimsley's Proposed Expedition," *Oregon Historical Quarterly*, XXIV, 434–436).

no exception. On moving to St. Louis he had attached himself to the
local Democrats as Henry had worked through the party machinery
to foster his law career. A friend of the Blairs from West Point days,
William thus was doubly pushed into the Benton organization.
This all fitted a predictable pattern. The oddity is William's enormous enthusiasm for Bentonian ideas, then being eroded by the new
wave of Democratic economics. Loyalty to Benton was proper, but
William's editorials for the *Argus*—referring here only to those
which *William* unquestionably wrote—have a ring of personal
endorsement. Within a few years William was to run for office on
a similar platform at a time when Benton's ideas were in greatest
disrepute.

This philosophy was inconsistent with William's background.
The Delaware Gilpins were but incidentally farmers; they were
inventors, manufacturers, merchants, and small-scale financiers.
They knew the advantage of and could use a protective tariff;
they sought charters and monopolies as exemplified by the Chesapeake and Delaware Canal Company, in which activity, incidentally, they were partners of Mathew Carey, one of the earliest of
America's economic nationalists. They fought the Bank of the
United States only when they found it beyond their control. In
short, the elder Gilpins neatly fitted the measurements of the
"Democrat by trade."

Where does William belong? Clearly, not with his family. He
could support Van Buren, and did, most energetically, but on local
matters he adopted enough Benton philosophy to permit only a single state bank and limited state action on developmental programs.
William believed that individuals must be free to do whatever was
not unconstitutional, but corporations were not individuals and
would have to be closely guarded. This was the role of *all* of the
people (hence his campaign for manhood suffrage), acting through
the state legislature. In an equalitarian society William saw no
room for privilege. The growers and the workingmen were the
equals of the bankers and the stockholders, and they would remain
equal so long as the state served to guard against privilege. William,
like Benton, was a "Democrat in principle."

Only twenty-four years old when he became a St. Louis editor,
William previously could have given but little attention to these
issues as he wandered through the forests looking for recruits and

later led those recruits through the Everglades. Probably no conflict between his newly developed philosophy and that of his father ever entered his mind. He liked the farmer and the immigrant laborer in Missouri, and he quickly embraced the Benton philosophy that was aimed at their support. In some senses it was the point of view of a states' rights southerner, but it was at heart, more a response to the needs of the less-privileged westerner. An anti-abolitionist in the 1840's, he was in time to see his inconsistency and to turn against the privilege of slavery as well.

Probably too hot-headed in his arguments, William, the editor, believed deeply in the common man and free land. Another young man had been killed defending William's statement of this ideology. William wanted to test his beliefs in a new country where privilege did not yet exist and where he could start fresh. The true frontier, he decided, was four hundred miles west, where the Missouri River came in from the north before it made its broad sweep across the state.[42] Banks and charters and railroads would not matter here; here would be home.

[42] The distance across Missouri is less than three hundred miles by road; following the river the distance is four hundred miles. His statement may mean that he took the steamer to Independence, although a coach was available much of the way.

CHAPTER FOUR

# What a Heart and Sinews She Has!

*Oregon Pioneer, 1841–1843*

Late in the summer of 1841 William Gilpin finished his chores for the state legislature, turned his back on St. Louis and Jefferson City, and began his long ride to the next frontier. After some reflection he had decided, as had so many before him, that the best opportunities for a young man lay in new lands. Increasingly was he being driven to see all of America, to advertise her to her people, and to hasten the achievement of the nation's destiny. But he also had to make a living. He was nearly twenty-six years old, his father was dead, and William could be a financial burden to Henry or their mother no longer. Nothing detained him in St. Louis so he journeyed west across the rolling Missouri prairies to Independence, his new home.

For several years after the Louisiana Purchase, Americans had remained ignorant of the nature of that bargain in those areas not reached by the expedition of Lewis and Clark. Something of a corollary to the work of that expedition was the secretive journey in 1806–1807 of Lieutenant Zebulon Pike into the Southwest. Allegedly lost, Pike and his men were arrested by Spanish troops in New Mexico and taken as prisoners to Chihuahua. Released shortly thereafter, Pike returned to the United States and in 1810 published his journal of the region he had seen. His *Account* revealed that centered around Santa Fe was a possible market for American goods of great significance, with New Mexicans able and willing to pay for these goods with gold, silver, and furs. This almost untapped purchasing power existed because the New Mexican area was simply too far from Chihuahua, the region that by Spanish policy, was supposed to supply the northern frontier of the Empire. Delivery was difficult and unpredictable, and goods were sold in Santa Fe at exhorbitant prices. Pike's publication even included schedules of the prices that the northern Mexicans were paying.[1]

The result of the news was a series of attempts by Americans to break into this commerce in spite of Spain's mercantile practices. Until about 1821 when Mexico became independent from Spain and adopted a policy of welcoming the American merchant, most of these efforts failed.

In the first few years these prairie salesmen left the States from a variety of frontier locations but gradually they settled upon western Missouri as a point of departure. The ease with which St. Louis received goods from the eastern seaboard (and even Europe), the cheap transportation across Missouri by river, and Missouri's early statehood (1821), all played key parts in dictating the route to Santa Fe. In 1822 William Becknell first demonstrated that wagons could be driven to Santa Fe, greatly expanding the quantity and variety of goods that could be delivered, and on the same journey he found a new route that followed the Arkansas River from the Missouri settlements, then cut off southwestward to avoid Ratón Pass in the Colorado Rockies.

This then became the Santa Fe trail. Becknell used Franklin, Missouri, as his base, primarily because it was his own town, but merchants found it advantageous to use the Missouri River to the greatest extent possible and gradually moved their staging area farther west to the boundary of Missouri. Independence was founded about 1827 after a river shift badly damaged Franklin,

1 Max L. Moorhead, *New Mexico's Royal Road*, pp. 57–59.

and, throughout most of the trail's history, Independence was considered the chief depot.[2]

And so William Gilpin had chosen America's farthest frontier settlement to be his new home town. He had never seen it, but Independence did not disappoint him. Probably Ashley and Sublette had told him of the place and even Senator Benton might have given his protégé advice on selecting a new town, for none knew Missouri better than Old Bullion. But no matter, Independence was on the edge of the frontier, and that was where William wanted to be.

He built a cabin (renting a room for himself while the work went on) in the area between the Missouri and the older section of Independence where most of its 125 settlers lived.[3] William had brought his law books with him and again hung out his shingle. Independence was the county seat of Jackson County, and William hoped he could once more find a living by specializing in land claims. Always tucked away in his mind was the conviction that he would strike it rich one day by some real estate promotion if only he had the resources for the initial investment.

The records for his first years in Independence are very skimpy. He appears to have had little money and probably had not yet received anything from his father's estate. Late in 1840 he had finally bought eighty acres of federal land through the Kaskaskia, Illinois, land office, probably thus using most of his ready cash. He may have sold the land (on Crab Orchard Creek near present-day Carbondale) when he left for Independence, but this at best would have meant only a few hundred dollars and considering the state of the Illinois economy then, perhaps only the government price of $1.25 per acre. Rumors of a later era were that William inherited a good deal of land; nothing of his behavior prior to the mid-1840's would indicate that he had yet received this gift.

William made a quick visit to Philadelphia early in 1842. He

[2] Moorhead points out that no single highway ever existed. Caravans left Missouri where they saw fit and used whatever route they wished. Some drivers deliberately sought different routes to obtain grass and water more easily or to avoid the ruts and dust created by predecessors (*New Mexico's Royal Road*, p. 96).

[3] The figure is Gilpin's. The sixth Census of the United States lists about 7,600 people for Jackson County. My guess is that Gilpin's figure is too low.

saw his family and was at Henry's home during a visit of ex-President Van Buren. If William transacted business of any kind, he left no record of it.[4] Soon he was back in Independence, and in his own words he was a struggling young lawyer doing a little farming on the side.[5]

As the months wore on William saw more and more evidence that his adopted home was the gateway to the West. Wagons bound for Santa Fe, and pack mules returning from that mysterious place laden with literally untold wealth, passed by his little cabin each spring and autumn. But Santa Fe belonged to Mexico, and no one yet questioned that fact. Oregon was something else, and an increasing number of Americans were willing to gamble that that region would never be British. These Americans, too, passed William's front door—for the first forty miles from Independence, in fact, the two trails were one. In the winter Independence was still, her residents doing what they could to make a living, but each spring the same excitement arose as the trails lost their snow and ice, the grass gradually turned green, and caravan leaders completed their many transactions before the departure date.

William knew or met most of the key frontier figures of that time—Kit Carson, the Bents, the Sublettes, and many a lesser name. He wrote a letter of introduction for his good friend, Bill Sublette, to Henry, asking for the family hospitality when Sublette next went east.[6] And William shortly was to make more important friends.

In May of 1842 the settlements around Independence were stirred by the massing of Oregon-bound immigrants. This was to be the caravan of 1842 which according to Ghent "really begins the epic of the settlement of Oregon and the acquisition of the whole region by the United States."[7] The group was led by Reverend Elijah White who had gone to Oregon in 1837 to assist Jason Lee with the Willamette missions and returned to the states in

[4] Henry D. Gilpin to Martin Van Buren, January 6, 1844, Martin Van Buren, Papers, Manuscript Division, Library of Congress.

[5] Hubert Howe Bancroft, *History of the Life of William Gilpin*, p. 17.

[6] William described Sublette as a "rich acquaintance" and the "hero of Washington Irving's Rocky Mountain Sketches," William Gilpin to Henry D. Gilpin, December 1, 1841, Sublette Paper, MHS.

[7] W. J. Ghent, *The Road to Oregon*, p. 58.

1840 because of an argument. Now White was organizing a party
to go back, but this time he bore the title of United States Indian
agent to the Oregon country. The party had over one hundred
members; White was elected captain in the manner of the rough
democracy of the trail, which meant that White could be (and was)
replaced along the way. Besides White, the leadership included
Lansford Hastings (who helped destroy the Donner party), Asa
Lovejoy (whose loss of a coin flip a year later meant that Oregon's
chief city was to be called Portland and not Boston), and Stephen
Meek, all to be famous in Oregon history.[8]

On May 16 this first migration left the Missouri for Oregon.
Into their wake moved another party, equally important for the
history of Oregon and the United States. It was a small group of
men, under orders from the chief of the Corps of Topographical
Engineers and led by Second Lieutenant John C. Frémont, whom
the War Department had ordered to explore and report upon the
region of the Rocky Mountains' South Pass. This expedition had
been a pet project of Senator Benton, who in October of 1841 acquired Frémont as a son-in-law. As Benton and the departing
Democratic administration planned it, however, the expedition's
secret mission was much more important than that announced—
the giving of assistance to the Oregon emigration movement.

President-elect William Henry Harrison concurred in the con-
tinuation of the program, and let it be known that the leader
would be Joseph N. Nicollet, a French scientist residing in St.
Louis, who had already accomplished considerable exploratory
work in the Mississippi Valley. On two of these occasions Frémont
had been Nicollet's assistant. When Nicollet became ill, command
of the proposed mission passed to Frémont. According to Frémont
the death of Harrison almost ended any concern for Oregon, but the
Benton authority in Congress was enough to guarantee that the
expedition could continue, however reduced in support.

Frémont and his men settled down at Chouteau's Landing near
the mouth of the Kansas River while awaiting the animals and
supplies that he had purchased. Nearly three weeks were passed
completing these arrangements, while the men entertained themselves in the surrounding villages.

[8] Le Roy R. Hafen and Carl Coke Rister, *Western America*, pp. 601–602.

William Gilpin and John C. Frémont must have first met at this time, for a year later Frémont was to describe William as a friend and accept him in his second expedition. Granted William's absorbing interest in the West he would certainly have visited this 1842 encampment and talked with the men and their leader. Gilpin and Frémont had much in common—as young officers each had been assigned duty among the southeastern tribes, each owed a great debt to Tom Benton, and in later years William sometimes said that Frémont had beaten him to the hand of the beautiful, brown-eyed Jessie. But, above all, the men shared a devotion to the wilderness, not as mountain men loving the land solely for itself and regretting the inevitable change they helped to bring about, but as explorers, publicists, exploiters, looking to future greatness for themselves through the land.

Possibly William asked Frémont's permission to go along on this first expedition. If so, it was not granted. More likely William had matters to attend to that summer and resolved to be ready when the next occasion arose. A probable obstacle was state politics, which was attracting William's renewed interest. William's friend, Montgomery Blair, was running for mayor of St. Louis. The census of 1840 now gave Missouri five congressional seats, and the Benton machine was being attacked for them as much by other Democrats as by Whigs. Furthermore, Senator Linn was up for re-election, and William was most anxious that the kindly doctor be continued in office. So in that summer the Bentonites were busy all over the state, and in remote Jackson County William could make his contribution.

Like other frontier counties Jackson viewed with enthusiasm the pending legislation in Washington which would require each state to divide itself into as many congressional districts as it had representatives in Washington. On this issue Benton dragged his heels, for most of his lieutenants lived in the central portion and might all be in the same district. Gilpin was named by the county Democratic machinery to attend the party's state convention in June to help campaign for frontier county's rights. Just about the time of Frémont's arrival in Independence William withdrew from the convention. He did so in the interests of harmony, feeling that reconciling Jackson County and Benton views on the districting question was impossible. In August, 1842, the Democrats elected at large all five congressmen and suspended until 1844 implementing this "federal interference in state affairs."[9] These local matters must have proven too engrossing; William was not to go up the Platte this summer.

Besides Frémont, the waiting party included several others of interest or importance to Gilpin, with whom he could talk. Chief hunter was Lucien Maxwell from Illinois, but more lately, Taos, New Mexico, and Fort St. Vrain, a close friend of Kit Carson and one day to be engaged in an enormous land transaction with William Gilpin. Assistant cartographer was Charles Preuss, a grouchy German map maker of great skill who had sought out Frémont in Washington, looking for work. Preuss was to accompany Frémont on the second and fourth expeditions also, and drew some of the finest western maps of the time. In 1843 he and William Gilpin were to be companions for several weeks on Frémont's second venture.

Frémont's guide was supposed to have been Andrew Drips, one of the earliest of the mountain men. But the ship that brought Frémont from St. Louis to Kansas Landing included a broad-shouldered, unassuming frontiersman who impressed Frémont immediately. His name was Kit Carson, and his manner and new reputation caused Frémont to forget Drips. Carson had been to St. Louis to enter his part-Arapaho daughter into a St. Louis convent. In St. Louis Carson probably learned of the expedition and made himself available by taking the same ship west as Frémont did.[10]

Then there was nineteen-year-old Henry Brant and twelve-year-old Randolph Benton, who, in St. Louis, had teased their way into parental permission to accompany Frémont. The Brants were kin to the Bentons-Frémonts and Randolph, of course, was the Senator's son. The boys were going only to Fort Laramie, but they were excited with the prospects.

The labor of the expedition was to be provided by twenty-two

[9] Clarence H. McClure, *Opposition in Missouri to Thomas Hart Benton*, pp. 27–30; *Jefferson Inquirer* (Jefferson City, Mo.), February 24, 1853; William N. Chambers, *Old Bullion Benton*, p. 260.

[10] Frémont says they met by accident on the ship (John C. Frémont, *Memoirs of My Life*, pp. 73–74; David Lavender, *Bent's Fort*, pp. 211–212). Frémont paid Carson the astonishing wage of $100 a month.

French Creole and Canadian voyageurs whom Frémont located in St. Louis.

By June 10 the matériel was complete, the weather had cleared, the grass was green enough, and the expedition left the Missouri for the prairies. Throughout that summer small groups straggled back to Independence with progress reports of White and his emigrants and Frémont and his wonderful paraphernalia—of men collecting flowers and snakes, drawing maps, measuring peaks and inflating a smelly, rubber boat for the shallow streams. On the tenth of October Frémont was back at the mouth of the Kansas; he did not linger here to tell his story for he had a more significant audience in Washington. But William could see the success on Frémont's face and the cockiness in the bearing of the two boys even though they had had to spend the most exciting days at Fort Laramie instead of on the Wind River with their captain-kin. William vowed that next year he too would "pierce the White Rocks to their summit."

The winter of 1842–1843 turned bitter. Two men were racing from the Walla Walla country through the Rockies to Taos, the Santa Fe Trail, and the East. The desperate journey was to save a small dream. Elijah White, leading the Oregon emigrants, had delivered a note from the officers of the American (Mission) Board to Marcus Whitman, ordering a sharp retrenchment in the Oregon Indian missionary program. To protest, Whitman headed east, accompanied only by Asa Lovejoy, who for some unknown reason was in this fashion willing to delay for a year his homesteading on the Willamette. The men were warned of Sioux on the Oregon Trail (Jim Bridger had told Frémont the same story, and Kit Carson had made his will), and Lovejoy prevailed upon Marcus to go home by way of New Mexico. In spite of powdery blizzards that once held them fast for a week, the men reached Taos in two months—their last diet being mule and dog meat.

The missionary and his friend rested briefly in the warmth of the Taos winter sun, but as quickly as possible they obtained the services of a guide and set out from Taos for Bent's Fort up the Santa Fe Trail. Learning that a party of mountain men were leaving the fort for Independence, Whitman hurried ahead of his two companions to catch the other group. Later, he blamed himself

for traveling on Sunday. Whatever the reason, he became lost and
Lovejoy beat him to Bent's. He prevailed upon the trappers to wait
until Whitman showed up, done in, but with the same Whitman
spirit. The next day, January 7, 1843, Marcus departed for Missouri. Lovejoy, exhausted, spent the rest of the winter at the fort
and met Whitman and the Great Migration at Fort Laramie the
next summer.

In mid-February Whitman was at the Kansas Landing. Before
taking the steamer for Boston he spent a week at Westport, a dozen
miles from Independence. Possibly his delay was enforced, undoubtedly he needed rest. Nevertheless, Whitman curiously spent
the week publishing a pamphlet and in other ways telling local
citizens of the glories of Oregon.[11]

Once again William Gilpin was on the scene to get a firsthand
account of that wonderful country.

Just as Whitman safely reached Missouri, a well-to-do Mexican
merchant, Antonio José Chávez, moved out of Santa Fé also bound
for Independence, with five servants, two wagons, fifty-five mules,
some furs and gold and silver varyingly reported as worth $10,000
to $32,000. It should have been a routine trip for Chávez, but his
luck ran out this time. The same terrible winter that had punished
Whitman and Lovejoy had not yet let go of the southern plains;
a March freeze killed all but five of Chávez' mules and forced him
to consolidate what goods he could in one wagon. By April he was
well within United States territory when he was suddenly attacked
by a stray band of fifteen men who called themselves Texans.
They were probably en route to join a larger body under Colonel
Charles Warfield, one of several groups licensed by the republic
of Texas to weaken New Mexico through attacks on its Missouri
commerce. The detachment that held up Chávez was under "Captain" John McDaniel. They had been recruited illegally among
Missourians by Warfield (some of the men were from Independence) and probably had far more interest in booty than in Texas
expansion. Seven of the fifteen bandits took some $400 to $500
each from Chávez and headed back for Independence on foot, because of a stampede among their horses. The other men, including

[11] Opal S. Allen, *Narcissa Whitman*, pp. 257–270; Lavender, *Bent's Fort*, pp.
215–216.

McDaniel and his brother, held their prisoner for two days, drew lots, and four of them shot the unfortunate Mexican and dumped his body in the ravine. Finding the rest of the gold, they, too, returned to the settlements.

Under vague circumstances the robbery was reported and some of the first detachment were arrested in Independence. The border townspeople, whose existence depended upon the functioning of the Trail, went into action. William Gilpin was selected to lead the posse because of his military background.

He immediately set out for his first venture on the Santa Fe Trail to try to locate the remaining McDaniel gang. Gilpin commanded about twenty men, reported to the press as dragoons (surely a Gilpin term), and they scoured the Trail for a distance of one hundred or more miles. Gilpin said they went as far as present-day Dodge City. Whatever the distance, McDaniel doubled around the dragoons and appears to have been captured back at Independence. Ultimately all fifteen were taken, tried in St. Louis and found guilty. The McDaniels and two others were sentenced to be hanged; the others were fined and imprisoned.[12]

This minor incident on the frontier created only a momentary flurry of excitement as one element in the Texas versus New Mexico struggle. But William was in his glory—his first command on the Great Plains!

By coincidence William's brief absence on the Trail caused him to miss an old family friend who was passing through Independence. One of the first up the Missouri in 1843, the great year of migration, was John James Audubon. He took the *Omega* from St. Louis on April 25th with plans to visit the northern Rockies.

Audubon had lived no sheltered career, but even he was sur-

---

[12] Josiah Gregg, *Commerce of the Prairies*, pp. 227–229; William C. Binkley, *The Expansionist Movement in Texas, 1836–1850*, p. 110; *Niles' National Register* (Baltimore), May 13, 1843, pp. 163, 195, 234–235; *Daily Picayune* (New Orleans), May 21, 1843. The government of Texas disavowed McDaniel. According to Gilpin, Chávez' servants reported the robbery and set the expedition under way. Only Chávez' hair was found, wolves having reached the body before the posse did (Bancroft, *William Gilpin*, p. 17). A presidential pardon commuted the death penalty for the younger McDaniel and one other man (*St. Louis Democrat*, June 17, and August 17, 1844). A slightly different version has Gilpin and his men capturing John McDaniel and one other man (William L. Webb, *The Centennial History of Independence, Missouri*, p. 230.

prised by some of the enterprise of frontiersmen. At Glasgow townspeople fired guns at the *Omega* for not stopping, and at another town the *Omega* lost a race to the *John Auld* for the only firewood. On May 2 he reached Independence; the ship left freight for the wondrous junket of William Drummond Stewart, already being rumored around the frontier, and Audubon found that his friend Gilpin was leading his dragoons after the Chávez murderers. Early the next morning the *Omega* got up steam for Fort Leavenworth, and Audubon was on his way to the Yellowstone country.[13]

Audubon, with free and easy passage to the mountains, was thus to be weeks ahead of the many other western-bound groups. When William Gilpin returned to Independence he found the entire riverfront area, from his home to Westport Landing, swarming with migrants, their wagons, their animals, their equipment. Surely it was the most exciting spring in the region's history as Independence turned into a small scale melting-pot. Scientists (Sublette called them "Bugg-Ketchers"), cartographers, military men, trappers, priests, royalty—all were present at least this once, to join the more typical pioneer on the Oregon Trail.

Probably William, young, experienced in the wilderness, an officer, and glib of tongue, could have accompanied any of the many units that moved West during May and June. Audubon, for example, could have found room on the *Omega*, but he was not going to the Columbia and that was William's goal.

Another expedition, forming a bit farther west near Shawnee Mission was the circus-like party of Sir William Drummond Stewart. As a retired captain in the British army, Stewart had first come to America from his native Scotland in 1832. He had wandered alone to St. Louis where he acquired the friendship of many of the famous and wealthy and, in particular, of Bill Sublette. With Sublette, Stewart first attended a Rocky Mountain fur rendezvous. He lived in St. Louis and New Orleans for several years and made a number of trips into the Rockies. Stewart returned to Scotland for

[13] The *Omega* belonged to Pierre Chouteau and Co. which made the ship available to Audubon. Audubon's *Journals*, incidentally, were often printed on the famous Gilpin paper. (*Niles' National Register* [Baltimore], May 13, 1843; Maria R. Audubon, *Audubon and His Journals*, I, 460–468). Audubon did see Father Pierre Jean de Smet briefly in Independence.

three years after learning of his inheritance of a baronetcy and vast lands and income.

Now Sir William, in May of 1843, was back in Missouri, ready for his last trip to the mountains. He planned no trapping, little trading. This was to be a sporting tour with comforts and good company abounding.

The river from St. Louis to Independence was crowded that year and an expedition could scarcely be in ignorance of the many others. So the coincidence was slight that Sir William invited Audubon to join the grand tour, but Audubon declined. He was nearly sixty-three, and the deck of the *Omega* looked far more comfortable to the painter than did a saddle. Conceivably, too, the size of Stewart's party (around fifty) would have been a handicap to the old man's work.[14]

As it was, Sir William's band was interesting enough. Bill Sublette was leader; one of the hunters was Batiste Charboneau, son of the famous Sacajawea of the Lewis and Clark expedition; another member of Stewart's party was a son of that same Clark. His shock of red hair resembled his father's so much that he startled some of the Indians who had known the father a generation earlier. Two Jesuits went along, taking leave of Father Pierre de Smet who had to journey to Europe instead. Some men were brought for their utility—Steadman Tilghman, M.D., as well as a number of servants, for example. Some were merely young men of means looking for a good time roughing it. But four men were eminent botanists from Europe with fine equipment paid for by Stewart. Perhaps most useful to later generations was Matthew C. Field, whose feature articles sent back to the New Orleans *Picayune* provide a prime source of information about the grand tour.[15]

On or about May 22 Stewart and most of the caravan left the Missouri settlements and headed up the Oregon Trail, traveling a bit north of it to avoid (and bypass) most of the emigrants. On the 27th Sublette and the rear-guard set out and overtook Sir William in about three days, easily locating the superb crimson tent on the green prairie.

[14] Edward Harris, *Up the Missouri with Audubon*, p. 15.
[15] William Clark Kennerly, *Persimmon Hill*, pp. 143–167; Mae Reed Porter and Odessa Davenport, *Scotsman in Buckskin*, pp. 213–225.

This was the last that William Gilpin could have seen of the Stewart expedition. Well-mounted, with abundant carts and wagons, they soon passed everyone on the Oregon Trail, including Jason Lee and Marcus Whitman.[16] They were to have a maximum of entertainment and a minimum of trouble, spending several weeks in Wyoming before leaving for Missouri in late August. Some ill will arose over Stewart's surprisingly (to the young socialites) military discipline, but all was settled by the time they reached St. Louis.

The possibility exists that William Gilpin was briefly a member of Stewart's party, and this possibility introduces one of the small mysteries of William's life. In one of his own accounts he mentions starting for Oregon and having his pack-mule break loose and toss off all of the equipment to the hilarity of his friends. The accident necessitated a second start but the intervals between departures is not specified.[17]

At approximately the same time, Matt Field told the *Picayune* that a member of the Stewart group had been thrown by a refractory, bare-backed mule and that Dr. Tilghman had set the dislocated shoulder of this man. The temptation is great to identify these events and present William Gilpin leaving for Oregon two days later with Frémont because his shoulder was too sore to let him accompany Stewart. No story names the unhappy mule rider; since William also had a horse, one would assume that he would not mount the mule, but the same assumption must go for all of Stewart's command.[18]

The Bancroft version is that William desperately wanted to go to Oregon but completely lacked funds. He sold his library and other items, borrowed additional money, bought a horse for $95, a rifle, and camping outfit and left Independence for Oregon. The first thirty miles—to Lone Elm—he was accompanied by his

[16] Misses Porter and Davenport compare the expedition to an ancient Mongolian caravan laden with ivory and jade—except for the muleteers' language. I would enter a mild demurrer that we are unsure of the ancients' language (*Scotsman in Buckskin*, p. 227). Among other people they encountered along the way was our earlier acquaintance, Asa Lovejoy, waiting at Fort Laramie for an Oregon-bound caravan.

[17] Bancroft, *William Gilpin*, p. 18.

[18] *Daily Picayune* (New Orleans), May 30, June 1, June 3, 1843.

creditor, David Waldo. From that point on he intended to journey alone. But that first night he ran into Frémont, and the famous explorer convinced Gilpin that for his own protection he should throw in with him.[19]

Frémont's version is restrained: ". . . we encamped at Elm Grove, in company with several emigrant wagons . . . under the direction of Mr. J. B. Childs, of Missouri. . . . We were joined here by Mr. William Gilpin, of Missouri, who intending this year to visit the settlements in Oregon, had been invited to accompany us, and proved a useful and agreeable addition to the party."[20]

More detail was added by Gilpin himself to a friend, Will Ferril, many years later in Denver. According to Ferril, Gilpin explained:

I sold my twelve law books to Congressman Matt Hughes of North Missouri for $60 and borrowed $100 from David Waldo of Independence. I remember the money was silver, and in an old-fashioned money bag. Waldo had made a good deal of money in his trade with New Mexico and could easily spare the money. And then I think he was very glad to let me have the money to get me out of the country, as we were both in love with the same girl. I was her sweetheart, but she did not claim me as hers. . . . With this money and what was due me that I could collect, I purchased an outfit. A part of that outfit was old Flash, a horse that I bought from a farmer named Ross, who resided about four miles from Independence, paying $90 for him. Old Flash was a fine horse. He crossed the great continental divide three times, the first two carrying me, and Frémont the third.[21]

[19] Bancroft, *William Gilpin*, p. 18.

[20] Frémont, *Memoirs*, p. 170. Frémont meant Joseph B. Chiles.

[21] Probably the key to the little puzzle lies in Frémont's words that William "had been invited." In other words, the invitation existed before they met at Elm Grove. In fact, it was almost the practice of traveling parties to move in separate echelons for the first few days as they performed shake-down operations.

The exasperating aspect of William Gilpin's memories is reflected in his story of "Old Flash." Of course, I can not trace the truth of the three crossings, but in his memoirs of his third expedition (the next one after this crossing with Gilpin), Frémont rejoices that he can use horses "hardened by the previous journey and thoroughly rested . . ." (*Memoirs*, p. 424). Since this march of Frémont merges with his Mexican War career the odds are strongly against his returning to the East with the same animals that he took from Missouri. Hence Gilpin's assertion that Flash made three trips? Let us hope "Old Flash" was not lost—along with so many others—to Frémont's horse-thief Indians, who were always hungry.

I well remember the crowd that gathered around me that June morning at Independence in 1843, and the people of that little town and some of the farmers near there were present to wish me good luck, but they seemed to think I was off on a wild, reckless trip . . . I had just $2.50 in my pocket when I started. I camped the first night at the old elm tree, about forty miles out. Soon after, a crowd of campers came up, also to spend the night. A man with military bearing and appearance soon approached to where I stood. He was Frémont. "Hello, Gilpin, exclaimed Frémont, extending his hand, what the d-l are you doing here?" "On my way to the Columbia," I replied. "You will never get one-hundredth part of the way alone," he added, "and so turn your pack animals in with mine and go along with me." I did so, and that was the way I joined Frémont.[22]

Thus the Frémont second expedition, with its "agreeable addition," sore shoulder or no, set out for Oregon. Frémont was the man in the field for the activist element in Washington concerning the dispute with Great Britain over the whole Oregon territory. President John Tyler, literally read out of the Whig party, had much eastern support, nevertheless, for a policy of not provoking the British people or government over a wilderness that would probably be American in time, no matter what the President did.

Opposed to this possibility were many westerners and other expansionists of both parties who late in the winter of 1843, had put the Linn Bill through the Senate, but not the House. The bill's purpose was to assure American supremacy in Oregon by urging settlement through cheap homesteads protected by forts. Unquestionably the Americans moving west that year assumed that this partial passage of the bill foretold a strong government policy in Oregon. The feeling was reinforced by Frémont's presence in Missouri; no one needed to be told that he was Benton's son-in-law, and that Old Bullion was the most expansionist-minded man in Washington.

Frémont's orders from a divided War Department, prodded by a tight congressional clique, required him to approach the Rockies from a different route than in 1842, link with it at South Pass (his

[22] *Rocky Mountain Herald* (Denver), January 4, 1913, Ferril interview. Elm Grove had been reduced to a single tree by 1843 because of demands for firewood.

previous terminus) so that "the two expeditions would give a connected survey of the interior and western half of the continent.[23]

For this reason Frémont planned to vary his route from that of 1842, following generally the Kansas and Republican rivers rather than the Little Blue and the Platte, the usual Oregon route. He would thus add to his geographical information and at the same time avoid the heavy traffic. The expedition got under way from Elm Grove on June 1 and for only about three days followed the traditional road to Oregon.

The composition of the party varied as some individuals left to run errands and others were added from time to time, but forty was probably the average. Most of these were Creoles and French Canadians, some of whom had accompanied Frémont in 1842. Two Delawares served as hunters; Tom Fitzpatrick was guide. The German, Charles Preuss, was back as head cartographer. Lucien Maxwell, another 1842 returnee, planned to travel part way with them. Besides Gilpin, two other "gentlemen" were going west—Frederick Dwight, who was trying to get to China from Massachusetts, and Theodore Talbot, assigned to Frémont by order of Colonel Abert, Frémont's chief.

A final member of the party must be mentioned for its everlasting fame, and that is Frémont's howitzer. That he had the howitzer with him was no mere chance. He had persuaded Colonel Stephen Watts Kearny, commander of the Third Military Division, to issue him the piece from the St. Louis Arsenal. Frémont, meanwhile, enlisted Louis Zindel, a Prussian artillerist, to be the gun captain.

While completing the outfitting of his company along the Kansas-Missouri border, Lieutenant Frémont suddenly received from his wife, Jessie, a letter urging him to leave the settlement immediately and to wait at Bent's Fort, if necessary, until there was sufficient grass for his stock. In his *Memoirs* he denied having knowledge of any reason for her warning, but when he returned to St. Louis he got a clearer, if incomplete, version. By his instructions Mrs. Frémont had opened all of his mail while he was away; one letter was an order from Colonel Abert to postpone or cancel the mission, return the howitzer, and travel to Washington to ex-

[23] Frémont, *Memoirs*, p. 165.

plain to the War Department why a scientific expedition was so
heavily armed.

Jessie concluded, as did her husband later, that the order was a
pretext to put an end to the expedition for the political reasons of
the many enemies of Benton and Frémont in the government. Subsequently, Benton sought an investigation of the order but received
no explanation from the government.

Thus Frémont, his friends, and his howitzer continued to move
slowly westward once he concluded that no one was likely to overtake him. Because the expedition was primarily scientific it carried a variety of equipment requiring carts and wagons as well as
great care in packing. Coddling this baggage and making daily
readings meant that the company would not travel rapidly; the
occasional sneer then, and since, that women and children reached
Oregon before Frémont that year, is hardly fair.

The first few hundred miles were monotonous. The men arose
daily at four, Frémont and Preuss doing the calculating, with William Gilpin the best trained man to lend an occasional hand. The
other members got the meals, packed the dozen carts, hitched up
the mules, and saddled their horses for the long day ahead.

They found that their route was much more broken than that
of the year before because of the numerous small streams that
required bridging. They saw Kansas and Delaware Indians during
the first week, but these were peaceful tribes. The first risky encounter with Indians took place on June 6. Much to Frémont's
annoyance, Dwight's horse had broken loose and headed for home,
saddle and all. Maxwell, searching for the animal, was surprised
by a band of the pesky Osages, who followed him in hot pursuit
to the camp. Not catching Maxwell, they consoled themselves by
running off a number of Frémont's horses. The animals were recovered but only after a long, hard chase that did considerable
damage to the party's mounts.

Soon they reached the well-timbered Republican, gathering
place for considerably more game. High water here meant slow
progress, and in mid-June Frémont split his party in the interest
of speed; he, with fifteen men, the howitzer and one wagon of instruments, moved ahead, leaving Fitzpatrick, assisted by Gilpin, in
command of some twenty-five men to bring up the heavy baggage.
They were to meet again at St. Vrain's Fort, on the South Platte,

near the present Greeley, Colorado. Just before the two sections parted they made the first test of the howitzer. At one quarter mile range a shell struck the target, a four-foot post; Frémont was satisfied that it was worth dragging with the advanced echelon.[24]

The variation in speed of the two units can be calculated fairly well. Gilpin's outfit (traveling twenty to twenty-eight miles a day) ran out of timber for fuel on June 28. During the morning of the 26th Frémont found that the nature of the country had suddenly changed; his detachment was now surrounded by bare sand hills and only in the distance could they see one or two groves of trees. The express unit had gained about two days in twelve of travel on the baggage train following the same route. But men of both parties who had gone to Oregon the year before concluded that the usual route clinging to the South Platte was some ten days faster and much easier than their present road.

The high plains that they were now crossing overwhelmed William with their vast distances and shimmering mirages that fooled even Tom Fitzpatrick. Impressed by campfire stories and this first limited experience, William declared that "millions of aboriginal cattle" fattened on this barren land, and he concluded that the short grass could provide rich nourishment for domestic livestock and make possible the rapid exploitation of the land by ranchers.

Gilpin's notion was then, and still is, unacceptable to most pioneers and farmers who knew the land as the Great American Desert, but within three years he was to start a bombardment of an interested public with his pamphlets, articles, and government documents designed to sell his thesis and populate the land. On several future occasions William's propaganda was intended to enrich himself by speculation; so far, however, his motives were quite impersonal, for he had not invested a dollar in the plains country. Rather was he pushing his early geopolitical beliefs that he had found America's heartland and must overcome much natural prejudice to persuade a nation of the need for its settlement.

That they had neared the limits of the Great Plains (a name probably introduced to the public by Gilpin) became clear on the

---

[24] Theodore Talbot, *The Journals of Theodore Talbot*, p. 13; I have to rely heavily on Frémont's *Memoirs* (pp. 166–172) here and for what follows. It is possible that Talbot was a War Department "spy" against Frémont.

tenth day of July when they first noticed a haze to the west, breaking up into individual peaks as the sun set.

Meanwhile, Frémont's contingent had reached Fort St. Vrain on the 4th of July and enjoyed a feast given them by the owner, Marcellin St. Vrain, one of the many Missouri French who had become traders. The usually generous St. Vrain had no animals or provisions for Frémont. While the latter could hunt for food, he could not go on without mules and horses. He left word that Fitzpatrick's men should remain at St. Vrain's and he set out for the south. The destination was the junction of Fountain Creek with the Arkansas River, where they would await Maxwell already hastening on to Taos, New Mexico, for the mules.

Their route southward was the South Platte, following it upstream to its three sources. At Fort Lupton Frémont had to sit out a wild thunderstorm, probably the same one that struck William Gilpin's party some two hundred miles to the northeast. The latter reached St. Vrain's on the 14th of July and did little for a week but poke about the fort, awaiting Frémont's return.

On that same day the advanced element camped at the mouth of Fountain Creek (Fontaine-qui-bouit, the trappers called it, for its bubbling appearance) and worried about Maxwell who with his mules had probably run into a wandering band of Utes, known to be near. Maxwell was also in danger from a Pueblo uprising that had driven a number of Americans out of Taos.

The entire expedition was now in jeopardy because of the scarcity of mules, when to Frémont's delight Kit Carson came into the camp. The encounter had not been planned officially. Carson had hoped to work for Frémont again but had been delayed that spring. He had stumbled into Taos in the midst of the anti-foreign rioting, taken steps to protect his family and friends' families, and left Taos only when the town quieted down.[25] His purpose was to seek military help at Bent's Fort for the people of New Mexico who

[25] Lavender, *Bent's Fort*, pp. 223–226. The details of the tumult are vague. Native New Mexicans apparently feared that Americans were aiding the Texan attacks on the province; at the same time they plotted an overthrow of the Mexican governor. G. Malcolm Lewis, "William Gilpin and the Concept of the Great Plains Region," *Annals of the Association of American Geographers*, LVI, No. 1 (March, 1966), 33–51. Lewis appears to be the first writer giving Gilpin credit for conceiving of, and publicizing, a Great Plains region.

were expecting another attack from a force of Texans.[26] By the time Carson got to the Fort, American dragoons under Captain Philip St. George Cooke had intercepted, disarmed, and broken up the Texans' expedition. With New Mexico safe once more, Carson was footloose; he rushed back up the Arkansas and hired out to Frémont.

That officer had concluded that Maxwell could not return and promptly dispatched Carson down the Arkansas again to Bent's Fort to purchase mules and to take them loaded with supplies directly to Fort St. Vrain. Frémont left a note for Maxwell to meet him at St. Vrain's and began a relatively meandering journey back north once more.[27]

On July 23 Frémont rode into St. Vrain's and found that Carson and ten heavily laden mules had preceded his arrival by three days; Fitzpatrick and Gilpin had journeyed as far as the site of the future Denver, then met Carson at Fort Lupton, and returned with him to the main body.[28]

After a brief rest the entire expedition moved out of St. Vrain's on July 26—Frémont and Carson seeking a new route on a "beeline" across the mountains to Fort Hall (in Idaho), Fitzpatrick and William Gilpin moving nearly due north into Wyoming to link

[26] The McDaniel gang, whom William Gilpin pursued for the Chávez murder, had expected to join the Texan force.

[27] Frémont expressed confidence that Maxwell was all right although mountain men visiting camp (present-day Pueblo, Colorado) were convinced Maxwell was dead. Maxwell lived to join Frémont during the Mexican War in California and to become holder of an enormous estate in New Mexico. Lavender makes a good case for Carson and Maxwell meeting in the mountains north of Taos.

[28] Gilpin's dates are clearly wrong. He could easily have camped at the site of the future capital; during the week that he and Fitzpatrick waited for Frémont he had time to travel to the mouth of Cherry Creek and back. Talbot, *Journals*, p. 27; William Gilpin, "A Pioneer of 1842," MS, P–L28, October 18, 1884, Bancroft Library. On July 26, 1843, William wrote from the "South Fork of Platte" to the editor of the *Western Expositor*, "I drop you a line by a couple of Shawnee Indians, who are going to return to Mo. from this place. We are about halfway to Ft. Hall, here, and I expect to reach the mouth of the Col. by the first of October. The emigrants are all ahead of us, and have, by this time, reached the South Pass through the mountains." This was quoted in the New Orleans *Picayune*, September 16, 1843 (*Oregon Historical Quarterly*, II [June, 1901], 192).

up with the Oregon Trail and eventually to rejoin Frémont at Fort Hall by way of South Pass.

William Gilpin was to lose contact with Frémont for several weeks; the "bee-line" proved impossible for humans, and Frémont, beaten by rain, mosquitoes, and the necessity of crossing the swollen North Fork of the Poudre eight or nine times in one day, abandoned the Colorado Rockies for the even terrain of Wyoming.[29] They marched north along the Laramie River, the North Platte, and then to the Sweetwater and the old Oregon Trail, a few days ahead of William and Fitzpatrick.

The expedition had already proven that the easiest way to Oregon was the road through Wyoming in use by the white man since 1812. Vehicles would have to wait for modern engineering before they could cross the Colorado Rockies.

On August 2 William Gilpin spent some time in an Oglala camp. The Indians lamented that fifteen hundred whites had already passed on to Oregon that summer and asked him if any remained back east. The Oglalas thus missed an opportunity to reduce the westward flow, for within two years William was to be one of the most vocal and renown exhorters of migration in the United States.

About the 16th or 17th of August William had his first sight of the best-known landmark on the Oregon Trail. Just west of the present Casper, Wyoming, the men reached the junction of the Sweetwater with the North Platte, and that night they camped at Rock Independence—or, to modern writers, Independence Rock. This single pile of granite standing out vividly in open country, had been a source of much interest to a generation of travelers who, as early as 1824, began carving their names on it. Preuss called it a miserable rock, but to de Smet and nearly all migrants it was the "Register of the Desert."

Estimated by Frémont the year before at 650 yards in length, the vast sway-backed pile squeezed the trail on the north bank of the Sweetwater down to a few yards in width. Perhaps 40,000 names, including many of the most famous, were once recorded on its sides.

The pioneers of 1843 made no exception to this custom and announced in carved letters that the "Oregon Co. arrived July 26

[29] Gertrude Barnes, "Following Frémont's Trail through Northern Colorado," *Colorado Magazine*, XIX (September, 1942), 185–189. *Niles' National Register* (Baltimore), September 30, 1843.

'43." As William read this publicity, he noticed other items of interest. Tom Fitzpatrick had recorded his name several times before but was anxious to do it again. Bill Sublette had gone by a few weeks earlier with the Stewart hunting party and had hacked out his name; thus an early American prestige item had turned into competition between two of the oldest mountain men. William put his name alongside Old Broken Hand's.

But William saw an item that was a challenge to him. Someone with Stewart had on July 22 printed "HENRY CLAY" in bold letters. William snorted and went to work with his knife. Directly above "Henry Clay," in letters three times as large, he dug out "MARTIN VAN BUREN BY WILLIAM GILPIN." About two weeks later, some of Stewart's men moving down the Sweetwater for home observed William's work, and Matt Field made mention of it in a dispatch to the New Orleans *Picayune*. Wrote Field,

Gilpin was some two or three years since editor of the St. Louis *Argus*, a furious partisan print, and followed us out in company with young Lieut. Frémont, the topographical engineer. Finding the name of Clay on the rock, he determined not to be outdone in advancing the interests of his party, and up went Martin Van Buren, in mammoth capitals, over the head of Henry Clay.[30]

Curiously this episode on a remote frontier reached the eastern press, just beginning to take interest in Oregon. Back in Philadelphia one wing of the Democratic Party was warming up for the election of 1844. On January 6, 1844, Henry Gilpin, managing the Van Buren forces in Pennsylvania, wrote to his chief:

I do not know whether you have come across the anecdote which I have cut from a newspaper of my brother William's exploit at "Rock

---

[30] Mathew C. Field, *Prairie and Mountain Sketches*, pp. 117, 175. See also Robert S. Ellison, *Independence Rock, passim*. The Natrona County Historical Society and the Casper Chamber of Commerce have identified perhaps six hundred names still legible, the majority dating from the 1850's. Thousands of names have disappeared or are beyond reading. In 1842 Frémont tried unsuccessfully to photograph the rock with a daguerreotype camera, probably the first effort ever made to photograph a phase of any exploration. Preuss naturally blamed Frémont for the failure (Charles Preuss, *Exploring with Frémont*, p. 32). On July 4, 1847, a party of nearly one thousand celebrated at the Rock en route to Oregon. Their liberal use of gunpowder defaced many names that might otherwise have remained legible (letter from Natrona County Historical Society [Wyoming], October 15, 1964).

Independence." We have not seen him since he was with us when you were here two years ago. I do not think it quite fair to call him a *furious* partizan editor, for I believe he was mild in that vocation, as in his whole deportment, ———— [till?] he had to show he would defend his opinions even at the risk of his life among the Federalists of St. Louis. A democrat however is always furious, a Federalist never![31]

Perhaps too much should not be made of this incident, but a chain of events should be noted. Oregon fever was already high among masses of people, especially in the West. It was a deaf politician who would not soon hear the clamor for a vigorous position in Oregon against Great Britain. Yet Congress had not taken such a position, nor had the ex-president, Martin Van Buren, who had presumed his re-election in 1844. By spring of that year the *Congressional Globe*, published by the Gilpins' close friend, Francis P. Blair, was demanding of an inactive Congress that it stand up to Great Britain over Oregon as it was facing Mexico over Texas.[32] At the same time Henry nagged Van Buren again. "Have your sentiments been made up on the Oregon question? To me it seems one of vital importance and that the whole west must feel it so; they justly look to a decided stand being taken on that question, and this I think Mr. Clay will not do. He cares too much for what the merchants and brokers, in the Atlantic cities, may say."[33]

When William commenced his writing in the 1850's he regularly blamed "salt water" politicians for holding back western development. If it is fair to conclude that he borrowed some of his ideas from Henry, perhaps it is also fair to conclude that Henry borrowed some of his enthusiasm for the West from William.

Leaving Independence Rock, William and his friends moved slowly up the Sweetwater, leaving it only to detour around Devil's Gate, a sharp, deep cut in a ridge through which the river raced. Beyond the gate the road became a broad valley gradually climbing to the South Pass at an altitude of 7,550 feet.[34] On August 21, eight days behind Frémont, William reached South (or "Frémont's")

[31] Henry D. Gilpin to Martin Van Buren, January 6, 1844, Van Buren Papers. The letter includes information on the Van Buren campaign strategy.

[32] William E. Smith, *The Francis Preston Blair Family in Politics*, I, 165.

[33] Henry D. Gilpin to Martin Van Buren, March 1, 1844, Van Buren Papers.

[34] Frémont estimated the Pass at 7,000 feet in 1842 and 7,490 in 1843, using his barometer.

Pass and observed, as had so many before and since, that it was no narrow defile, but a wide saddle, nearly twenty miles across and already containing several roads. That night water froze in the storage buckets.

For the first time William had crossed the Divide, or as he had promised his mother seven years before, he had pierced the "White Rocks." Soon he was on the banks of the Little Sandy, the first stream that he encountered whose waters flowed into the Pacific.

The detachment had several alternative routes here but stayed closely to the one most heavily traveled.[35] They followed the Little Sandy to the broad, crystal Green, until it swung east, at which point they cut overland to Black's Fork. On August 30 they reached the site that was gradually to be known as Fort Bridger, formally opened earlier that year by the partnership of Louis Vasquez and Jim Bridger.

This post, probably more famous than useful to frontiersmen, had been established by the two trappers so as to provide the Oregonians with "Horses, Provisions, Smith work, etc." in exchange for the "ready cash" with which the migrants were "generally well supplied." They also hoped to trade with Indians for beaver.[36]

When William Gilpin reached the buildings they were deserted. Bridger was off to the Wind River with a brigade of trappers, and Vasquez returned with another party later that very day—"dashing into camp at full speed"—the usual manner of the mountain men.

Vasquez told them that Cheyennes had recently swept through the valley stealing the horses of the fort as well as those of some neighboring Snakes. The Cheyennes had also helped reduce the already small quantity of game. All of the parties of that summer were getting low on food at the same time that livestock forage was beginning to burn up, explaining why nearly all of the travelers of 1843 made the long detour by way of Black's Fort and Bridger's instead of taking the even drier short cuts due west of South Pass.

In 1846 a new road would be tried from Bridger's Fort due west, for Californians who wanted to avoid the extensive northward

[35] Between South Pass and Fort Bridger the returning Stewart-Sublette party must have met the Gilpin-Fitzpatrick party, yet no diarist mentions the event.
[36] The Mormons burned the fort in the "Mormon War" of 1857 (J. Cecil Alter, *Jim Bridger*, pp. 207–210, 280).

swing to Fort Hall that the Oregonians preferred. But in 1843 this tragic alternative had not yet been dared, for everyone was bound for Oregon. Out of Fort Bridger William, Talbot, and Fitzpatrick made their way northwest; now the water supply was abundant, the grass nearly adequate. Everywhere they saw signs of the pioneer families, graves along the road (two that summer), trashy campsites, stray cattle that needed milking, and a determined ox headed for Missouri (or an Indian barbecue) all by itself.

On September 7 they crossed a high hill, the "greatest impediment" from the United States to Fort Hall. They now dropped down into the valley of the Bear River and on September 9 camped at Soda Springs (variously called Beer or Bear Springs), a spot very popular with Oregon trains for rest and recreation.[37] The temptation to linger was broken by the weather; the fine autumn days were now being interrupted by squalls, and water left outside the tents in shallow containers froze nearly every night.

They needed four days to reach Fort Hall, in modern Idaho, another landmark of the Oregon Trail. Built in 1834 by Nathaniel Wyeth as a trading post on the Snake River, the fort had too much competition, and in 1837 Wyeth sold out to the Hudson's Bay Company. Here Gilpin learned that Frémont was farther south exploring the Great Salt Lake and would probably return as soon as Carson reached him with supplies from the post.[38]

All of the men were impressed by the location. The upland sage country was beginning to grow beautiful in their eyes, broken as it was by the Bannock, Port Neuf, Roseaux, and other pleasant streams, feeding numerous clusters of aspen and service berry. Talbot and William did not care for the fort itself. It was too small and poorly constructed in their minds, and Captain Richard Grant, the Hudson's Bay Company's resident agent, impressed them unfavorably. Grant looked upon himself as something of a viceroy. He talked of the entire Oregon country as British without question, and the Indians in the area were serfs owing allegiance to the Crown. The fort was swarming with the last of the season's mi-

---

[37] In 1835 Captain Benjamin Bonneville's men became so exhilarated drinking from the springs that they convinced themselves it was a better drink than beer (Washington Irving, *The Adventures of Captain Bonneville, U.S.A.*, pp. 277–278).

[38] Carey, *Journals*, pp. 44–47.

grants, and for some reason Grant refused to sell them any more food. By the crimson light of a night prairie fire Talbot and William argued with Grant and convinced him at last to sell the food to the pioneers.

Probably Grant had little choice, for the persons concerned were tougher than the average Oregonian. They were the so-called Chiles (erroneously given as Childs in some accounts) party—a motley group of twenty or so English, Scotch, Spanish, and Canadians, led by Joseph Chiles of Missouri. Chiles had been to California in 1841 and now was returning with wagons bearing two girls and machinery for a mill. This group knew where it was going and how rugged the road would be.

To strengthen the tight group even further they had picked up Joe Walker at Fort Laramie. Walker, one-time sheriff of Jackson County, Missouri, had roamed the prairies for more than twenty years, had guided Bonneville a dozen years before the great migration and probably knew the trans-Rocky area better than any living American. Now at Fort Hall, Chiles split his party; he, taking command of only a handful, went on to Fort Boise, meaning to turn southwest across the Oregon desert to reach California.

Walker, with the girls, the wagons, the mill, and most of the men, prepared to move south and went to the Humboldt River.[39] Joe was perhaps the first of California's public relations men and tried for two or three days to persuade some of the Oregon-bound that the lands to the south were superior, but not a single person changed his mind—and direction.

About the time that the Californians departed, Frémont received his relief supplies and at Fort Hall his whole party gloried in a breakfast that included flour and butter brought by Old Broken Hand. The "saved" then fooled, or thought they fooled, the "savior" by feeding him horsemeat and calling it elk.[40] The weather turned miserable, cloudy, rainy, just above freezing—and then snow be-

[39] Frémont, *Memoirs*, p. 245–246; Talbot, *Journals*, pp. 47–49. Grant probably demonstrated the Crown's new fear that vast American migration could capture Oregon more readily than diplomacy or war. Customarily the British were generous to the Americans and charged prices that were no worse than those demanded by American frontier merchants like Bridger and Whitman.

[40] Preuss, *Exploring with Frémont*, p. 90. The mountain men's slogan was "Meat's meat." Fitzpatrick probably knew and did not care what he was getting.

gan to fall. It was a time for adjustment. Eleven men accepted Frémont's option to return home, carrying mail with them; none of the eleven was one of the "gentlemen," Gilpin, Talbot, Dwight, or Preuss.[41]

Frémont bought some good oxen and sorry horses from Grant; the party checked their clothing and equipment and once more was ready to move. The entire company—now about thirty in number—left Fort Hall September 22 in a driving rainstorm, the trail generally following the Snake River across present Idaho. Once again they were on a heavily traveled road, but made very slow by mud. Attempting a detour Frémont followed for a number of miles the ruts of a small train before he discovered that its path was swinging south. The Pathfinder was mistakenly following Walker into California!

The error was promptly corrected with the loss of only a half day; Preuss was so distressed by rain, snow, wet boots, and suffocating smoke in the tent that he lacked enthusiasm for giving Frémont, Carson, and Fitzpatrick their proper excoriation in his diary.

Campsites were proving more difficult to locate and so the commander decided to divide the company again. He and ten, including Carson and Preuss, went ahead. Gilpin and Talbot, as before under Fitzpatrick, brought up the baggage and the rear echelon.

The weather now improved, becoming clear and moderately warm. At times the Snake passed through narrow canyons of black rock, forcing the trail away at some distance. On these occasions grass and water were very scarce and the animals had to be led down steep cliffs to graze after the normal day's chores were done. It was bold, striking country and many of the falls were beautiful.

Everywhere the men encountered Indians, probably of the Shoshone family. Peaceful people, they lived off salmon, then swapped fish for the Oregonian's extra clothing. Many of the Indians, too sophisticated to exchange salmon for trinkets, wore shirts or trousers obtained in this fashion.

Gradually dropping back again, William and Talbot did some sight-seeing. They visited Shoshone lodges and deplored the deep poverty. They also observed that the tribes were "diggers," root-

[41] Frémont's original plan was an eight month expedition. Now he told the men that they would be gone all winter.

eaters, in spite of the great abundance of salmon. Preuss had found the Indians "insolent and arrogant."

For a few days William noted how the country had been influenced by volcanic action, then in mid-October he began to see trees again and finally substantial groves as the party entered the well-watered Boise River region. On the 14th he reached the Hudson's Bay Company post, Fort Boise, four days behind Frémont.[42]

Fort Boise had been the end of the line for Marcus Whitman's wagons back in 1836, and the emigrants of 1843, ignoring Grant's warning had brought their vehicles to this point on the urging of Whitman, their guide. The fort, built first in 1834, had like most western forts, been meanwhile moved, and it was now located near the junction of the Snake and the Boise. It was a single building commanded by an ex-trapper, stout, jovial, François Payette. His staff was one man, a Canadian. Payette was a more open-handed man than Grant and happily shared with the Americans his supply of butter, home-grown vegetables, and the inevitable salmon.[43]

The Indians were a miserable collection of Shoshone, often nearly naked, but surprisingly fat, probably from the salmon, Preuss surmised. Yet they suffered in the winter, according to Payette. He had never been able to convince them that they should store up food for the lean months, and in the winter they huddled in their tents eating ants and lizards. Rumor had it they were even given to cannibalism.[44]

Frémont did not wait at this post for Gilpin and the baggage but set out immediately for Whitman's missions on the Walla Walla. William's heavily loaded detachment needed more than two weeks to make the journey from Fort Boise to Fort Walla Walla, the next Hudson's Bay Company post.

[42] Talbot, *Journal*, pp. 53–58; Frémont, *Memoirs*, pp. 246–257; Preuss, *Exploring with Frémont*, pp. 91–93. Talbot's *Journal* for 1843 ends at Fort Boise. Dwight left Frémont here and caught up with a group of Oregon-bound pioneers (John Boardman, "The Journal of John Boardman," *Utah Historical Quarterly*, II [October, 1929], 99–121).

[43] "The farther we go from the States, the more unpretentious the trading posts become," noted Narcissa Whitman in 1836 (Allen, *Narcissa Whitman*, p. 139).

[44] Frémont, *Memoirs*, pp. 259–267; Preuss, *Exploring with Frémont*, pp. 93–95.

In some regards this stretch of the Oregon Trail was the most difficult. Too often the migrants figured that their troubles ended at South Pass, and that henceforth the trip was downhill. But within a day or two from Boise the pioneers all swung west to avoid the impassible canyons that the Snake carved out for itself to a depth of more than a mile. Hell's Canyon was created by the river as it raced to its meeting with the Columbia; it would one day form a convenient state boundary, but it was no means of transportation. To get to Oregon another range of mountains had to be crossed—the Blues—but before that came the Burnt River Canyon.

The river was about thirty feet across, twisting through its deep gorge in such fashion that men and horses spent hours crossing and recrossing the water. At times only the stream could pass through its gorges and the pioneers had to detour over the lowest nearby mountain. Frémont had never seen anything called a road that was so bad. Yet Narcissa Whitman and Eliza Spalding had made the trip side-saddle seven years before, and now in 1843 the great migration was preceding the Pathfinder through this maze.

One reason for the huge party's success was Marcus Whitman, who after a year's feverish travel and bitter argument with his Board, had returned with the 1843 migration, and at Fort Hall had become its guide. Against all expert advice Whitman convinced his wavering flock that they could drag their wagons to Oregon. In September following Whitman's light wagon, they hacked and forded and cursed their way through the Burnt River Canyon. Beautiful country everyone agreed, but why should spirits be so tormented this close to their new homes.

William, with his friends, Talbot and Fitzpatrick, probably the last people to reach Oregon that year, saw overturned wagons, and wheels and axles as silent evidence of the struggle. Leaving the Burnt the men continued north through evener ground. A lone pine, a tall beacon advising travelers of the trail (if they followed Payette's advice), was lying on the ground even before Frémont's arrival.

October had passed when William first saw and dropped down into Oregon's lovely Grande Ronde—a flat, round, valley some twenty miles in diameter. He could see where the migrants had gone out of their way to pass through this valley en route to the Blue Mountains, and he could not blame them. The surrounding hills and mountains were thick with conifers of all sorts giving a bluish cast to the sharp, autumn air. The Indians had lately burned the grass and the men were surprised to see new, green shoots creeping through the morning frosts.

Having crossed the Grande Ronde, the trail led to the foot of the Blue Mountains. Frémont concluded that the wagon train had taken an unnecessarily difficult ascent, and he detoured a few miles to the east of that path. It is not clear what choice Fitzpatrick made, but soon his group also reached the summit of the Blues. Due west, white and dramatic, stood Mount Hood. At his feet Gilpin could see unrolling west and north an enormous dry plain through which he knew (but could not see) twisted the majestic Columbia. Another day's travel through firs and ponderosas, reaching 150 to 200 feet in height, brought them to a good road descending to the Walla Walla plain. All of the parties of 1843 viewed this region with elation except perhaps Preuss. His day was ruined by the report (not too inaccurate!) that once they reached the Columbia, they would experience nothing but rain from November until March.

The road down from the summit of the Blues was good, and clear of trees by the time William reached it. Within two days he was at Fort Walla Walla, principal British trading post for the Nez Percé, at the junction of the Walla Walla and the Columbia. He had covered some six hundred miles from Fort Hall in about six weeks, moving steadily with Fitzpatrick's well-disciplined baggage train.

William had no reason to linger at the Whitman Waiilatpu mission, some twenty-five miles east of the fort. He missed Marcus who had gone down the river on business; emigrants in large number were still there when Frémont arrived, and together they cleaned the mission out of everything edible except potatoes— which everyone found unusually good. Frémont left a mule in payment and resumed his march along the banks of the Columbia, while many of the emigrants broke up their wagons to make rafts.

The emigrants had been split into two groups months before, back in Kansas. The issue was cattle, with the owners of none, or very few, feeling no necessity to help guard the property of those families that owned large numbers. The original leader (Peter Burnett, later governor of California) resigned over the problem as factions formed. The solution was division into two (later four) sections, with the livestock or "Cow Column" bringing up the rear.

The leader of the Cow Column was Jesse Applegate, ever after famous in Oregon history for his diary as well as his achievements. At Fort Walla Walla a new shuffling took place. Some families with small herds went overland along the Columbia to the point where they faced the inevitable and terrible necessity of going around Mount Hood.

Applegate and friends swapped their cattle at Fort Walla Walla for inferior California stock to be received at Fort Vancouver. This uneconomic trade had the virtue of freeing the migrants from the responsibility of being drovers and made possible the quick descent of the Columbia by raft.[45]

Some of these people paddled past Frémont in late October and early November before William Gilpin reached the Fort. Still other emigrants by the score rested and reorganized themselves for the final plunge. The last lap of the long race from Independence thus brought the many trail parties into close contact for the first time.

Applegate, for example, remembered seeing Frémont only once —at Soda Springs—where he noted the lieutenant's men having such a hilarious time drinking the water that he suspected the addition of liquor to the party. He recalled that the men sobered quickly when one of the migrants pulled a huge frog out of the springs. And he saw and touched the cannon.[46]

Now, in sadness, Frémont noticed Applegate. At The Dalles—a deep, narrow trough through which the Columbia churns in a series of eddies—one of the Applegate rafts hit a rock and overturned, throwing all of its pasengers into the river.

The trail at this point was at water's level, and Frémont's party and Lindsay Applegate stood helplessly on the bank watching a tragedy too swift to be averted. One old man and two ten-year-old

[45] The emigrants could deal with McKinlay of the Hudson's Bay Company or Whitman. The pioneers generally felt that they were cheated. One wrote: "Whitman lied like hell. He wanted my cattle, and told me the grass was burnt off between his place and The Dalles. The first night out I found the finest grass I ever saw, and it was good every night" (Hubert Howe Bancroft, *The Works,* XXIX, 405 n.); Daniel Waldo, "Critique," MS, P–A74, Bancroft Library.

[46] Maude A. Rucker, *The Oregon Trail and Some of Its Blazers,* pp. 117–118.

cousins, Warren and Edward, sons of Lindsay and Jesse, drowned in the grey Columbia, eighty miles from the end of the Oregon Trail.[47]

As far as Frémont was concerned The Dalles was now the destination for much of his party. From that point to the Bay Company's Fort Vancouver there was no cart road, and he saw no reason to make the effort to reach the fort with his heavier instruments and (especially?) with the howitzer.

So he set up camp near the Methodist mission at The Dalles and wrote Tom Fitzpatrick to leave his carts at Fort Walla Walla and build pack saddles to carry the supplies down to The Dalles. Frémont, Preuss, and two others went by Indian canoe downriver to Fort Vancouver, leaving Kit Carson in charge.

With an Indian crew Frémont reached Fort Vancouver quickly, where he received the unfailing consideration of Dr. John McLoughlin, Hudson's Bay Company's executive for the Pacific Northwest. For nearly two decades this white-haired giant had ruled the region with a firm paternalism noted by all who entered his domain. Probably none knew better than he that his power was weakened daily by the arrival of the tough men and women— especially the women—who had walked from Independence. The beaver, main reason for the company's existence in Oregon, was already disappearing coincidental with the decline of the popularity of the beaver hat. Most of the migrants of that year, significantly, noted the absence of any game between Fort Hall and Walla Walla where the British had mined beaver so thoroughly. McLoughlin made no effort to stop the flow of American migration, and on Frémont's arrival was providing food, shelter, and animals for hundreds of foreigners who would soon be his neighbors up the Willamette River.

Frémont purchased supplies from the fort, encountering but one problem: Preuss refused to shave before having dinner with McLoughlin. Preuss's wife later wrote that he and Frémont almost had a duel over the matter. Each man was too useful to the other, however, and Preuss, cursing the weather, the boats, and his captain, ate in the tent with the Indians.[48]

When Preuss and Frémont got back to The Dalles with their

[47] David Lavender, *Westward Vision*, p. 381; Rucker, *Oregon Trail*, p. 250.
[48] Preuss, *Exploring with Frémont*, pp. 97–98.

winter supplies, they found that Carson had moved the camp away from the river to better grazing. Fitzpatrick had not yet come down from Fort Walla Walla (he arrived three days later, November 21), but William Gilpin was there with Kit Carson.

William had been eager to go on from Walla Walla and made a trade with the factor, Archibald McKinlay. William exchanged his mule for a canoe, potatoes, horse meat, and once-used green tea. Leaving his horse with McKinlay, William and an Indian guide paddled down to Carson's camp near The Dalles. He had been there about three days when Frémont reached that spot on his way back from Fort Vancouver.

Frémont tried to prevail upon his friend to accompany him on his return to the states by way of California, but William had yet to reach his goal and declined. The next morning on finding that his canoe had been stolen during the night, William accepted the use of Frémont's boats, to return them to McLoughlin at Fort Vancouver.

William and his friends parted company on November 19, 1843, after a journey of six months and two thousand miles. Always looked upon as a guest, William shared equally with the others the chores, the fun, and the dangers. With no personal responsibilities he could look upon the expedition as pure adventure. He was accepted by mountain man and "gentleman" alike. He had learned a great deal that summer. Two of the ablest frontiersmen and America's premier scientific explorers were his companions and teachers. Moreover, during much of the journey they crossed land that was new to all of them. Frémont's immense curiosity and breadth of interest rubbed off on William and stimulated an already active mind.

Still, the influence of the explorers on William must be considered secondary to a far stronger influence. Probably his obsession developed slowly, but he was beginning to formulate ideas about those unknown pioneers in whose wake he had crossed the prairies and passes. To William they were the advance guard of an army that would soon sweep the continent to carry out America's "untransacted destiny." They needed a spokesman in the press and in the halls of Congress to help bring them the roads, the forts, the mail service, the government. William decided that this would be his job.

CHAPTER FIVE

# The Untransacted Destiny of the American People

*Western Expansionist, 1843–1846*

Late in November of 1843 William pushed Frémont's string of borrowed canoes into the Columbia and left the expedition for the last time. Frémont was headed south, for California and a large place in history. William was to see many of these men again in his western travels and in time was to engage in a significant and official argument with Tom Fitzpatrick over methods of fighting the Indian. But on this grey, drizzly day William thought first of completing his journey and discharging his obligations to Frémont and himself.

Below The Dalles the Columbia broadened, and as he paddled easily downstream William could sweep his eyes from shore to shore, catching an occasional view of the magnificent white cone of Mount Hood on the left in contrast with the low brown hills that rolled away from the right bank.

He saw Indians, generally fishing lazily in the back pools of the river, and in later years convinced himself that they were dangerous.[1] Increasingly he encountered signs of a considerable settlement, grazing livestock, cultivated fields, screeching saw mills, permanent evidence that the two Anglo-Saxon peoples had jumped two thousand miles of prairies, mountains, and basins to plant a society looking out on the Pacific world.

John Jacob Astor's Pacific Fur Company had given the United States a slight head start in the battle to control Oregon, by building Astoria at the Columbia's mouth in 1811. The North West Company bought the post in 1813 and retained it as Fort George for some years, even though it was technically retransferred to American control after the War of 1812. In 1824, fearing President James Monroe's recommendation for a colony at that site, the Hudson's Bay Company (which in 1821 merged with the North West Company) abandoned Fort George and began construction of a new post on the north bank of the Columbia just above its junction with the Willamette. Fort Vancouver, so called to emphasize the discoveries of Vancouver as a claim to Oregon, was formally opened in 1825.[2] For twenty years it gave the British Crown a formidable advantage in the nonviolent struggle for the Oregon country. The British and American governments had agreed in 1818 upon a joint occupation of Oregon, but the Bay Company and Crown both seemed to assume that the Columbia River would almost certainly be the boundary. Hence, in the 1830's as the fur business declined, John McLoughlin, in charge of Fort Vancouver, encouraged British development of stock raising and agriculture in the region that is now southern Washington, and almost completely prevented American settlement north of the river.

From the arrival of the first American missions in the 1830's McLoughlin had pursued another effective policy, that of assisting the new migrants in getting located along the Willamette River. The soft climate, the soil, the long growing season, and the beauty of the valley lured the midwesterners into making their homes where McLoughlin dictated, south of the Columbia. This comfor-

[1] They might have been. One group of Indians threatened a party as it arrived at Fort Vancouver, crying, "It is good for us to kill these Bostons!" McLoughlin quickly ended the disturbance (Richard G. Montgomery, *The White-Headed Eagle*, p. 300).

[2] John S. Galbraith, *The Hudson's Bay Company as an Imperial Factor, 1821–1869*, pp. 79–80, 182–183.

table trap even succeeded to the extent that several missions grew up along the Willamette in spite of Indian requests and mother-church intentions that they be placed in the barren lands hundreds of miles to the east.

As the large migration of 1843, now broken into scores of family and other groups, moved on Fort Vancouver, the kindly McLoughlin continued his program. He lent feed, seed, tools, and even food and clothing to many of the new settlers in return for labor around the fort or simple promises to pay when they could. Doubtless McLoughlin made some bad investments, and he violated company policy when he extended credit, but he calculated well. McLoughlin wanted friends, not trouble, for the Company, and he clearly saw that the wave of 1843 was merely a beginning. Nothing the Company could do would stop the flow or divert it to California as many British officials hoped.

William's leisurely pace across America had made him one of the last arrivals of 1843 at Fort Vancouver. Neither he nor Mc-Loughlin recorded the date that they met for the first time, but it was around the first of December. William returned the canoes that Frémont had borrowed and presented himself to the fort's chief factor.

McLoughlin, now aged fifty-nine, was as imposing in appearance as in reputation. A full six feet four inches tall, broad and heavy set, he added a touch of the dramatic by keeping his white hair at shoulder length, and wearing on formal occasions a long, dark blue cape. The Chinooks called him the White-Headed Eagle, and history has called him the Father of Oregon. To William Gilpin he was the supreme commander of the Oregon country, an affable, generous and honest man, but an enemy because in Oregon he was the British government.

William, more than thirty years younger, described by a contemporary as about six feet tall, 150 pounds, and "ramrod straight," was instantly popular with the old man. They could talk knowledgeably about their travels, about England, about affairs in Washington, and, most dangerous for McLoughlin, about the massing of pioneers in the lower Missouri Valley. McLoughlin was never isolated at Vancouver; he met educated and informed men there or during sessions with London stockholders, but these were his business associates, critical, looking for greater profits.

William, on the other hand, was a cultivated American, constantly questioning McLoughlin about the country or diverting the older man with tales of Missouri politics. The result of the friendship was that William was given the hospitality of Fort Vancouver for more than two months that winter with little to do but dine and hunt and prowl the countryside. The great men of the Company passed through the forest during those days and William found them all congenial. James Douglas, McLoughlin's executive officer for the past dozen years and one day to be governor of Vancouver Island and British Columbia, was one. Another was Peter Skene Ogden, from a Loyalist family, an early brigade leader and clerk with the North West Company, remembered by the Indians for his big belly, his profanity, and his ability to terrorize them. Ogden was chief trader and had spent years in charge of operations in the Snake and the Fraser river countries. Ogden, McLoughlin's successor in 1845, generally was credited with the plan for making a fur "desert" out of the eastern Oregon region so that it would be unattractive to Americans.[3]

William dined regularly with these and other officials in McLoughlin's or Douglas' quarters and learned as much as he could of the country, its resources, and the affairs of the Company. William might have been merely entertaining himself and enjoying the easy living of the fort, but McLoughlin began to think otherwise. This young man who had attended West Point, who boasted of his friendships in Washington, his attachment to Benton and Frémont, was very possibly in Oregon as a spy.

Whether he actually was or not, we shall never know. The best evidence is one of William's cryptic comments written four decades later. In a brief autobiographical sketch, he declared, "Senator Linn, Gov. Reynolds of Mo. and Col. (Bill) Sublette were the only three men who knew the object I had in going there."[4]

No satisfactory explanation of this statement has been found. The three men named were all Missourians of note in the 1830's and 1840's; they were all Benton Democrats and permanently so, an important alignment during the years when the Missouri De-

---

[3] Galbraith, *Hudson's Bay*, p. 90. A favorite Ogden joke was to order all the Oregon midwives suddenly to call upon his mother.

[4] William Gilpin, "A Pioneer of 1842," MS, P–L28, October 8, 1884, Bancroft Library.

mocracy was rapidly splitting; all were political and personal friends of William. An additional, and striking, coincidence is the timing of their deaths. Lewis Linn, after predicting his own death, died October 3, 1843. Thomas Reynolds, suffering much abuse from Whigs and Soft Democrats, committed suicide in the governor's mansion on February 9, 1844. Sublette died of tuberculosis on July 23, 1845. The first two of these men died while William was in Oregon, and he probably did not learn of any of the tragedies until he returned to Missouri in 1844. The early passing of three men might also explain why no record exists to explain William's comment that only that trio knew the reason for his overland journey.

Whatever may have been the real reasons for William's activities, McLoughlin now decided to get William out of Oregon, offering him free passage to Hawaii first, then on to London. The delights of the islands were held before William along with letters of introduction to the powerful Baron John Henry Pelly, governor of the Hudson's Bay Company and of the Bank of England. But William was not interested in returning to England, and the company officials decided to shanghai him. He and a friend named Campbell whom he had met at Fort Walla Walla, were invited to reside on board a British ship lying in the river. They were dined in glorious fashion and generously supplied with wine and brandy. William, nevertheless, did not succumb, but breakfasted on tender, roast duckling, and moved jauntily back to the post—to the great annoyance of the officials.[5]

William now left the fort and journeyed up the Willamette River to visit the American settlements around Oregon City. The first permanent American colony had been located in the valley in 1834, established by the Methodists as a mission. It grew very slowly and in 1838 could count only some sixty persons, about twenty of whom were Canadians formerly employed by the Hud-

---

[5] Hubert Howe Bancroft, *History of the Life of William Gilpin*, pp. 20–21. I wish I knew how much truth is in the story. Evidently the conspirators did not ply our young hero with the local beverage, "Blue Ruin." Bancroft calls the Governor Sir Hugh Pelley, but doubtless, it is the same man (Galbraith, *Hudson's Bay*, pp. 14–16). This Campbell will have to remain unidentified. The name was very common in Missouri and Oregon, and several Campbells were associated in business with Bill Sublette.

son's Bay Company. But the colony was prospering and producing surpluses of wheat and livestock that they sold to the Company.

One of the missionaries was Dr. Elijah White who, after four years in Oregon, quarreled with other members of the mission and left for the states. After some months he visited Washington in the hope that he might be appointed governor of Oregon Territory. He talked with Senator Linn and Secretary of War John C. Spencer as well as President John Tyler. They concluded that given the boundary issue with Great Britain, no governor could be appointed, and instead made White a sub-Indian agent for the Oregon country.

In this role White recruited the emigration of 1842, stressing the themes of Indian souls to save and good soil to sow. Somewhere in excess of one hundred people left Independence for Oregon with White that summer. Many of these settlers clustered around the falls of the Willamette, a few miles south of Fort Vancouver, and this became Oregon City, the chief American settlement in Oregon, in spite of a loss to California of about one-third of the recent arrivals.[6]

The Willamette Valley from Fort Vancouver to Salem bustled with newcomers in the winter of 1843–1844 as William Gilpin made his new home at Oregon City. The power of the Methodist and Catholic missions, even like that of the Hudson's Bay Company, was already under the attack of the hundreds of new families. At the moment these people were better inclined toward McLoughlin than toward the missions, for the latter were reluctant to give up any of the land that they had monopolized for a decade.

The migrants of 1843 were thus deeply concerned about the nature of government in Oregon, about what rights they could expect, and particularly about the status of their new land claims. Oregon, of course, had no government in the usual sense. English and Canadian unquestioningly obeyed the Company so long as they were in its employ; most Americans looked upon the mission councils as law until early in 1843 when the settlers drew up a loose, provisional government. The Canadians who lived south of

[6] Hubert Howe Bancroft, *The Works*, XXIX, 265. It will be recalled that William saw White's party form in Independence in the spring of 1842.

the Columbia took no part in these proceedings, at the urging of Father Francis Blanchet, head of the Catholic mission.

The newcomers of 1843 were aggressive and land-hungry, and made bolder by their numbers and the belief that the Linn Bill would soon be law. Many of these pioneers were Methodists, and this helped soften some of the animosity between the American groups. But the majority of migrants were from the Middle West and were annoyed by the rigidity of that class of New Englander who controlled the missions.[7]

Now, early in 1844, the Canadians seem to have become concerned with their position in the new Oregon and petitioned an "Address" to the Americans to consider certain requests. To reconcile the views of the two nationalities and at the same time to clarify the Oregonians' relationship to the United States, a meeting was held at Champoeg on March 4, 1844.[8]

At about the time of the Champoeg meeting—perhaps the same day—occurred the so-called "Cockstock incident," a very confusing affair in which an Indian named Cockstock and two or three white Americans were killed. The murders very probably reduced public interest in the political purposes of the Champoeg meeting and possibly could explain the absence of more written records.[9] William Gilpin's construction of the Champoeg meeting is the most complete available; since it tends to emphasize his participation,

[7] "The American Missionaries done no good here. They made the Indians worse." According to Waldo they received $200,000 from the eastern boards and converted one Indian girl. She said she had been converted by *all* of the missionary men. Waldo, "Critique," MS, P–A74, Bancroft Library.

[8] Robert C. Clark, "How British and American Subjects Unite in a Common Government for Oregon in 1844," *Oregon Historical Quarterly*, XIII (June, 1912), 140–159; E. E. Rich, *The Hudson's Bay Company, 1670–1870*, II, 702. Much of early Oregon history is uncertain including William Gilpin's part in it. Prior to 1912 most historians knew nothing of this Champoeg meeting.

[9] It has been suggested that these killings caused people to forget the meeting earlier that day, explaining why its importance went unrecognized for so long (J. Neilson Barry, "The Champoeg Meeting of March 4, 1844," *Oregon Historical Quarterly*, XXXVIII [December, 1937], 425–432). McLoughlin confirms that a meeting was held that day to petition the United States Congress to extend its jurisdiction over the Oregon settlers (Katherine B. Judson, "Letter of Doctor John McLoughlin to Sir George Simpson, March 20, 1844," *Oregon Historical Quarterly*, XVII [September, 1916], 215–239).

its reliability can be questioned, yet no evidence has been found disproving any portion of his account.[10] Using Joe Meek as a guide, William visited settlers throughout the Willamette Valley urging them to attend the meeting. Since Elijah White, who was unpopular with many of the Americans, had called the meeting, the American attendance was not large, and the Canadians were in a majority. The Hudson's Bay Company officers also abstained from any participation, in spite of William's urging.

According to William, 123 persons were present that day at Champoeg—"sailors, whalemen, Canadians, outcasts, emigrants . . . We set a trap American style." Sidney ("Blubber" or "Blubbermouth") Smith was president and two illiterate French Canadians were vice presidents.

A proposal was made that they petition the United States Congress for a territorial government. Smith ruled the motion out on the ground that the meeting was not called to favor one nationality or the other. Nevertheless, William drew up a memorial, asking Congress to establish a Territory of Oregon; survey the Willamette and other Oregon areas; put into effect the land provisions of the Linn Bill; establish naval yards on the Columbia and "Fugitt's" Sound; provide regular mail between Independence and Oregon City; give adequate Indian protection; and enforce certain commercial regulations. The Canadians, who had believed Smith's statement that only local affairs would be on the agenda, signed or marked the petition because none could read well enough to understand its contents. William was given the responsibility of delivering the memorial to Congress, and the meeting was adjourned.

The long-range aim of the Champoeg session was to get from Congress a settlement for the Oregon question, and this was the task of William Gilpin. It is clear, however, that to most of the people represented at Champoeg their immediate needs were more important. That the "address" of the Canadians was signed by the same men who were officers at the meeting is something of a puzzle unless one accepts Gilpin's premise that the Americans were entrapping them. Nevertheless, the Canadians also got their wishes,

<hr>

[10] *New York Daily Tribune*, March 22, 1879, p. 3; Bancroft, *William Gilpin*, pp. 21–23.

for changes later in 1844 concerning land laws, taxation, and other local matters resulted from the Canadians' first participation (including voting) in Willamette Valley affairs.[11]

William thus played an important part in managing a closer tie between English and Americans in Oregon, just as he was destined to bring the Oregon story to a national audience as soon as he could return home.

Active as this remarkable man was in Oregon's behalf, it was his misfortune always to associate himself with schemes that failed to ripen. This, together with the fact of his brief association with Oregon's development, has prevented his name from being enshrined in Oregon history. But whatever his worldly misfortunes may have been, let us remember that he had an idea. In his opinion it was the "untransacted destiny of the American people . . . to subdue the continent—to rush over the vast field to the Pacific Ocean . . ." Oregon's statehood is a product of this destiny. Both Oregon's settlers and the American people who annexed Oregon believed in this destiny. It is the writer's considered opinion that Gilpin's greatest contribution to Oregon was the clear and magnificent development of the idea of the Manifest Destiny of our state and our nation.[12]

[11] In studying the Canadians' "address," McLoughlin correspondence, and other scattered materials of 1843–1844 I get a strong feeling that the inevitability of United States' acquisition of much of Oregon was accepted by most residents of the Columbia country. See Clark, "How British and American Subjects Unite," *Oregon Historical Quarterly*, XIII, 157.

[12] Maurice O. Georges, "A Suggested Revision of the Role of a Pioneer Political Scientist," *Reed College Bulletin*, XXV (April, 1947), 67–84. I am heavily indebted to Maurice Georges, of Portland, Oregon, whose Reed College prize-winning essay first built the case for Gilpin's work in Oregon. I am in agreement with Mr. Georges that Gilpin knew too much about the meeting to have made up his story, and that there is no evidence that contradicts any of William's claims. Subsequent to my correspondence with Georges I encountered the following in the *Jefferson Inquirer* (Jefferson City, Missouri), February 24, 1853: "A Member of the Convention [State Democratic] of 1842" was nominating Gilpin for Congress using these words, "he penned upon the banks of the Willamette, in 1844, the document from which sprung the first American government on the shores of the Pacific." Even granting the possibility that William wrote or prompted this article, I can see little point in his fabricating the whole experience. Similar in content is a letter in the Ladd-Deady correspondence: "While I was in Philadelphia I met Gov Gilpin of Colorado Ty who is a very intelligent gentleman and was in Oregon in '43 and took quite an active part in the organization of the provisional Govt. etc. . . .

William was not quite ready to go home with his memorial. Some personal business could be completed while the snows melted between him and the east.

The '43 migration included some of the usual frontier real estate speculators. A few of these men concluded that near the confluence of the Columbia and the Willamette was a strategic location for a city. Honoring Oregon's patron saint, two or more sites were named Linnton. One of these was abandoned during that winter of 1843–1844 because none of the newcomers would purchase lots. Conceivably, present-day Portland is on one of the early Linnton plots, but information is sketchy. No one's memoirs connect William with any of these land booms, but an old Denver friend reported many years later that William helped to found Portland but gave it the name of Linnton. (Most Oregon histories agree that Portland was founded in 1845 by Lovejoy and Pettygrove; William is normally not mentioned in connection with either town.) Given William's great speculative interest and empty purse, it is likely that he talked with these various town fathers, gave his unsolicited advice, and invested nothing. He would have violated his most basic principles if he had not observed the surveys with much enthusiasm.

William now thought it time to transact some of his own destiny. Back in Independence he had promised himself that he would go to the Pacific. The last segment of his journey must be completed before he could return home. He borrowed a jerry-built catboat with a bedsheet for a sail and persuaded a young sailor, a Missourian, and a veteran mountain man, Robert "Doc" Newell, to accompany him.[13]

They sailed down the Willamette and into the Columbia, soon

----

He knew all of the old Hudson Bay men Had quite an interesting time with him He said the name was Indian and spelt 'Wallamat' or 'it' . . . but said was the same as Walla Walla in pronunciation." (W. S. Ladd to M. P. Deady, Papers, F39, 1–24, January 29, 1875, Oregon Historical Society).

[13] A classic example of William's unsophisticated name-dropping. With a dozen years in the fur trade Ohio-born "Doc" Newell was well known to trappers then and historians today, for he kept a journal. Newell moved to a Willamette farm about 1841 and later became a sub-Indian agent. He was a commissioner appointed to prevent an expansion of the so-called Cayuse War that followed the Whitman massacre (Robert Newell, *Robert Newell's Memoranda*).

pausing when it was obvious that they were making no headway. William suggested tying in at the shore until the tide changed. The power of the current frightened Doc. "When I find myself in a country where water runs up stream, I want to get out of it; it is no place for an Ohio man." William tried to force Newell to remain with the boat but gave up and replaced him with a passing Nez Percé.[14] The little crew finally battled their way through the wind and choppy water until they reached Astoria. The tiny British settlement at Fort George, which had watched the arrival for several hours, received them generously. The crew stayed at the post, until William engaged a young Indian girl to guide them the remaining distance to the ocean. Briefly lost, they camped one night in the brush and stumbled on to the beach the next morning near the point where Lewis and Clark spent the winter of 1805–1806. They examined the forty-five foot skeleton of a whale and William took his symbolic dip in the cold Pacific. The mission completed, they returned to Astoria and Fort Vancouver.

One final matter remained to be settled. McLoughlin had come to look upon William as an honest man who would be impartial if the interests of the United States were not at stake. The old man appealed to William to help settle one of the ever-present land disputes that upset every frontier.

Before the arrival of any of the American missionaries in Oregon, McLoughlin had seen the value of a Bay Company site at the falls of the Willamette, a few miles south of Fort Vancouver. Whether he wanted a homestead for himself or acted as agent for the Company is not clear, but he staked several claims in the valley; and with the introduction of the Linn Bill he laid claim to an additional 640 acres authorized by that measure to all white males in Oregon and built a home for himself. (That the Linn Bill did not pass is of little significance to the McLoughlin case because other homesteaders made the same faulty assumption.)

The Methodists settled at the falls about 1840. The Reverend Alvin F. Waller, Jason Lee's assistant, claimed a square mile of land including some that McLoughlin had pre-empted. Waller declared that he had no intention of seizing the land but wanted first choice in the event that the United States took that part of

---

14 Newell's *Memoranda* does not mention the Columbia River episode.

Oregon and invalidated McLoughlin's title because of his foreign citizenship.

Meanwhile, Sir George Simpson, overseas governor and Mc-Loughlin's supervisor, ordered him to hold fast to the land for the Company and sent him a great mill to be assembled at the falls. The extent of Company participation in the land question is thus confused; probably McLoughlin, frequently at odds with Simpson, was planning for his own future, away from the British flag. Simpson assumed McLoughlin's loyalty and believed that any Oregon provisional government would be more liberal to the White-Headed Eagle than to the Company.

The first land laws of the Oregon "government" of 1843 were clearly aimed at the Company and McLoughlin; Waller now pushed his claim against McLoughlin; several of McLoughlin's friends, including Douglas, urged him to make a settlement with Waller before it was too late. Waller hired an itinerant lawyer who publicly declared that McLoughlin was only an agent and had no land rights at all south of the Columbia.

At this point McLoughlin turned to William Gilpin for help.[15] An arbitration committee, composed of Gilpin, Douglas, and White, was set up; two missionaries, Waller and Leslie, represented Methodist interests.[16] William and White felt that Waller's demands were excessive, but Douglas recommended prompt settlement "to have done with it," and Gilpin agreed. McLoughlin reluctantly paid Waller $500 for his claim, deeded him five acres clear and gave the Mission fourteen lots in Oregon City.

This ended William's part in Oregon's first great land suit, but there was a postscript. Jason Lee had recently been replaced as head of the Methodist Mission, and his successor decided to sell the holdings at the falls. McLoughlin bought the property back at prices high enough to anger him in spite of the ten years allowed for payment. In 1849 he retired from the Company and became a United States citizen.[17]

[15] Bancroft, *Works*, XXIX, 223.

[16] Frances F. Victor, *The River of the West*, p. 360. Oddly Gilpin, Douglas, and White composed the same group that planned the Champoeg meeting a few weeks earlier.

[17] I have followed the narrative of the Waller affair as told in Rich, *Hudson's Bay Company*, II, 705–710. Bancroft's *Works*, XXIX, has much more detail, but

For William the time had come to return to the states. He called on Daniel Waldo, who had reached Oregon in 1843, and asked, "What shall I say for you, to your brother in Missouri?" Daniel, an acid-tongued and positive Missourian, replied, "Tell him I would not give the bare idea of owning a section of land in Oregon for all I own in Missouri," (two sections that he could not sell) "and that I would not give a section of land here for the whole state of Missouri."[18] Waldo was already doing well and could forget the autumn before when he had called Whitman a liar and cheat and worried about cattle prices.[19]

Similar prosperity was touching most of the Americans in Oregon. Only adequate clothing was in short supply; with McLoughlin's help they were eating enough and had made promising starts on buildings and lands. Through fear or kindliness the Hudson's Bay Company made sure that no one starved as the population of Oregon doubled that season.

Much, of course, remained to be done, and many immigrants were dissatisfied. They were midwesterners who wanted "hog and hominy and whiskey" and were not so industrious and moral as the New Englanders, according to one view. But the worst of these people would cause no trouble, for California was proving a "safety valve to let off these uneasy spirits."[20]

William was, withal, elated with the story that he could take home. He would carry to Washington the message of the "pioneer army"; the government must know their needs and supply them, and Oregon would be American all of the way to "Fugitt's" Sound.[21]

---

lacks Rich's recent research as well as objectivity. The shoddy treatment that McLoughlin subsequently received from Oregonians is reported by many eye-witnesses.

[18] William Henry Gray, *A History of Oregon*, p. 377.

[19] Waldo, "Critique," MS, Bancroft Library; F. W. Pettygrove, MS, 1878, P–A60, Bancroft Library. Waldo left Missouri with 108 cattle and reached Oregon with 68. Oregon prices were double those of the states until 1849 when the California demands multiplied the difference. Waldo moved west for his health; he reported that he could make as much money in Missouri.

[20] *Niles' National Register* (Baltimore), April 13, 1844.

[21] I see little evidence that the pioneer wanted 54°40′. The *wagons* of the "pioneer army" bothered McLoughlin and the Company for they meant permanence. He once declared, "The devil is in the Americans . . . They will turn

More than two years were to elapse before the Oregon boundary issue was settled with Great Britain—two years of diplomatic and political discussion, popular argument, and rumors of war. But the hundreds of people who went west with William in 1843 had already rendered the final verdict.

William found no one who was planning to return to the states so he sought company and assistance wherever he could. In taking leave of McLoughlin for the last time he borrowed five Indians, a canoe, and some provisions, departing April 10, 1844. Loaded with pioneers' letters for home, he paddled up to The Dalles where he exchanged his company for one Indian and five horses, proceeding from The Dalles along the Columbia Valley road back to Fort Walla Walla. "Old Flash" was still at the post and well rested for the trip home. The long road to Fort Hall was considered too dangerous for the solitary traveler so William waited for companionship.

By chance, the Hudson's Bay Company fur brigade soon reached Walla Walla, and William and "Old Flash" cut into the party. The leader was Fort Hall's commander and Chief Trader, Richard Grant, with whom William had argued the summer before about selling supplies to the pioneers. Grant still was not happy about Americans, for they were competing with the Company for the Indian trade, and he sensed that he might be presiding over the end of a part of the Company's kingdom.[22]

He welcomed William, nevertheless, and they journeyed with little incident to Fort Hall where Grant and his men stopped. Again looking for a partner, William was pleased to meet Thomas "Peg-Leg" Smith, momentarily at Fort Hall for supplies. Smith was headed south to Fort Bridger, and the two men agreed to travel together for the next link of William's trip home.

Whether Grant was concealing his larder, or whether he was in short supply William could not tell, but once again it was almost impossible to obtain food at Fort Hall. William and Smith left without meat. They found a ground hog easier to kill than to digest and were nearly starved before they shot an antelope near Soda

---

their oxen and waggons down to the mouth of Columbia and go over into Japan next." J. L. Parrish, MS, 1839, P–A60, Bancroft Library.

   [22] Galbraith, *Hudson's Bay*, p. 108.

Springs. Here they celebrated the Fourth of July with soda water and fresh meat and then moved on.

Peg-Leg informed William of the origin of his nickname. Like most mountain men he had several versions of his autobiography, and no one today knows which was correct. He told William that he had been thrown from a heavily laden supply wagon which passed over his leg just below the knee. Fearing poisoning, and in the absence of any physician, Smith had performed an amputation on himself with a butcher knife; he completed the operation by searing the cut with a red-hot wagon bolt.[23]

On the nineteenth of August the two men reached Bridger's Fort, Gilpin found a young Mexican willing to be his guide for the next lap, and took leave of the tough old cripple. At this point William departed from the Oregon Trail. Like many another tourist he had no wish to return by the same path that he had come, and he was thus pleased to find someone who knew the Mexican lands to the south. The change in direction meant that William met only a few of the Oregon-bound immigrants that summer.

This was an even larger mass movement than the one in 1843 that William had trailed. The Platte Valley spring had been very wet, streams were high, and the muck slowed the wagons dangerously. The pioneers had traveled scarcely one hundred miles the first month. The entire expedition was behind schedule with many wagons not reaching Bridger's (the half-way point) until September. William saw only thirty of the summer's army before he left Fort Bridger, disappointed that he was unable to give firsthand trail advice to the new groups of potential listeners.[24]

William and his guide rode south from the Fort into the Uinta Mountains—easily crossed from this direction—probably following the Uinta or one of the other small streams that feed the Green. They continued along the Green in present-day Utah and at some point intersected the trail made by Frémont bound home from California a few weeks before. The Pathfinder had reached St. Louis in August, then moved to Washington to prepare his report for the government.

[23] Bancroft, *William Gilpin*, p. 25; Lavender has Milt Sublette finishing the surgery after Peg-Leg passed out (*Bent's Fort*, pp. 74–76).
[24] Bancroft, *Works*, XXIX, 448–452; *Niles' National Register* (Baltimore), Nov. 16, 1844; J. Cecil Alter, *Jim Bridger*, pp. 213–214.

William and his companion traveled along the Green until they encountered the old Spanish Trail, swinging widely northward from Santa Fe to Los Angeles. Here they turned east from the Green, crossed the Rockies-born Colorado River and entered present-day Colorado.

The journey must have been difficult but generally safe enough. William's own story is that only once were the two men in danger. The Ute Indians gave them some concern so that they often traveled days at a time without firing a gun or building a fire, but one evening William's horses ran off with those of a band of Indians, probably Utes. Coolly and patiently William negotiated for hours with the Indians, recovering the horses by exchanging some trinkets.

William's route across Colorado can be approximated. He followed the Colorado upstream to its junction with the Gunnison. Near the mouth of this river the men encountered a Mexican trading post, the only settlement for hundreds of miles. At some point the travelers left the Gunnison and crossed the Divide at Cochetopa Pass, somewhat to the southward. They left the mountains, passed through the San Luis Valley, crossed the Sangre de Cristo Range and emerged on the plains below, near the Arkansas River.[25]

Summer was ending when William and his anonymous friend reached Bent's Fort, high up the Arkansas. No longer needing a guide, William must have dismissed the Mexican at the Fort, with what payment we do not know. William had picked up something that looked like gold back in the San Juans; he quizzed George Bent about minerals and the huge Spanish land grants that cross-hatched the maps of that region and tucked this information in the back of his mind for future use. Frémont, he learned, had passed through the Fort on the 1st of July. It was time for William to get his message to the nation, too.[26]

On September 22, accompanied by several others, he left Bent's Fort for Independence. One month later he reached the Missouri border.[27] He had been gone nearly seventeen months and had traveled at least 4,500 miles.

[25] Bancroft, *William Gilpin*, p. 26; *Gunnison Review* (Gunnison, Colo.), May 15, 1880.

[26] Lavender, *Bent's Fort*, p. 230.

[27] *St. Louis Reveille*, Nov. 1, 1844.

Some of the excitement over his homecoming was diluted by the fact that it was election day. Missouri state officers had been selected in August, but now, out on this distant frontier, the citizens were helping to choose the President of the United States. William rode "Old Flash" up to the post office known as "Little Santa Fe" to learn what the excitement was about. While listening to the clamor, he spent one dollar (half his remaining funds) for a bushel of corn for his horse. "Old Flash" had not tasted this luxury in so many months that William had to persuade him that it was edible. Then "Flash" ate the entire bushel, and according to the westerner's code, William could go about his business.

In greasy, ragged buckskin he was not recognized by any of the judges, and they contested his right to vote. Finally one old farmer remembered him. "Well, I'll be damned if that isn't Gilpin . . . He used to live in Missouri and has been nowhere since."[28]

The matter of his residence having been settled by this technicality, William voted. Naturally the Whigs had nominated the hated Henry Clay; but to William's chagrin Martin Van Buren was not a candidate. William knew little about James Polk, the Democrats' nominee, but Polk was for Oregon and that was sufficient inducement to secure William's vote.

Although his journey was completed, William felt considerable unrest. No one in Independence was awaiting his return, and he had no job. As well as possible he distributed the heavy mail that he had brought from Oregon to friends and relatives anxious to hear from the pioneers on the coast. He told the recipients that the caravans had undergone "great hardships" but all were settled and the present year's migration should be nearly to the Columbia by now. He calculated that Oregon had about 2,000 American settlers with their farms and new towns, a dozen lumber and flour mills, numerous schools and churches, and a college.[29] Oregon could be saved for America, but the government would have to act quickly to carry out the proposals that he had brought from the Willamette.

William did not remain long at Independence, concluding that he might get some political post if he once again were available to the Benton faction. That battered political organization had been

28 *Rocky Mountain Herald* (Denver), Jan. 4, 1913.
29 *Niles' National Register* (Baltimore), Nov. 16, 1844; *Oregon Historical Quarterly*, IV (September, 1903), 271–272.

struggling for its life for at least a year, for the deaths of Senator Linn and Governor Reynolds deprived Benton of two of his most trusted followers. To fill out Linn's term David R. Atchison, a Soft Democrat, was named senator; the governor, just elected in August, was John C. Edwards, a friend of Benton, but an opponent on several significant issues.

Benton himself was in trouble. The hard-soft currency issue continued to split the Democrats in Missouri, and the Whigs expected to lure some of the Softs into their camp when the Senatorial election was held in November. Benton had also lost some votes on the Texas question; he opposed Tyler's annexation treaty on the grounds that it would lead to war with Mexico—a prospect that disturbed most westerners not at all. Benton, however, feared that war would mean an end to the flow of Mexican silver and gold into Missouri and the consequent destruction of his hard-currency program. To compensate he drafted a treaty of his own which he declared would make possible Texas' annexation without war. His enemies, nevertheless, could make the charge that he was anti-expansionist, and Benton's long residence in the Senate was threatened.

By the time that the state legislature convened in Jefferson City, however, the Hards had once more got control of the Democratic party machinery, and a number of Softs temporarily pledged their allegiance in order to defeat the Whigs. The legislature met on November 18 and promptly chose two Benton men for important positions. Claiborne F. Jackson was elected speaker of the house (probably a reward for not running against Benton for senator).[30] William Gilpin, just arrived from the West, was chosen chief clerk.[31]

The next day the battle for the Senate began, and by a narrow

---

[30] Jackson continued to be important in Missouri affairs and served as a pro-Confederacy governor in the early months of the Civil War. The story was told that Jackson married successively five sisters. When he went to "ask the old gentleman's consent to marry the last one, the venerable father is reported to have said, "yes, Claib, you can have her; you have now got them all. For goodness' sake, don't ask me for the old woman!" John F. Darby, *Personal Recollections*, p. 465.

[31] Walter Davis and Daniel S. Durrie, *History of Missouri*, p. 126.

margin Benton was victorious once again.[32] What part, if any, William played is not known. He was a fierce competitor, and his most recent return from Oregon gave him a new reputation as an authority on the West. His reward as chief clerk, paid before Benton's re-election, would indicate that he performed unusual services for his boss.

William remained in Jefferson City throughout the winter of 1844–1845, receiving the handsome allowance of $18 per day for the hundred-day session. For the first time in months he was solvent, and he planned to resume his journey to Washington when his task with the Assembly would end.[33]

Now back in his beloved Mississippi Valley, he returned also to his promotional schemes. In December he wrote to his brother Richard, living in Philadelphia with Henry, reporting that the state of Missouri held 500,000 acres of land donated by the federal Congress for internal improvements. He guessed that the Missouri legislature would use the income from the sale of these lands for improving the Osage River. An engineer with Richard's skill could find employment helping the legislative committee make "judicious application" of the funds.

Wrote William: "The Osage waters one of the richest countries in all the Mississippi Valley, and near its mouth passes through an immense formation of 'Cannel' coal. Still further down it grazes the mineral region which we visited together some years ago."

As before, however, William warned Richard not to give up anything worth while just to come west. Not much money had yet been realized from land sales, and jealousies might prevent the consummation of the plan that William described. Richard decided that the gamble was too great and remained at home, and William was to see none of his family until the spring of 1845.[34]

William would have been greatly surprised to learn that a different Gilpin had wandered out to Missouri during his absence. Uncle Tom, a bachelor, age sixty-eight, the same Quaker who objected so to William's military career, had a sudden notion to tour western

[32] Clarence H. McClure, *Opposition in Missouri to Thomas Hart Benton*, pp. 94–95.

[33] *New York Daily Tribune*, March 22, 1879.

[34] William to Richard, December 1, 1844, Gilpin Folder, HSD.

Pennsylvania alone. So taken was he with the country that he boarded an Ohio River steamer and traveled as far as St. Louis. By coincidence Uncle Tom had met Frémont in that city, and the Pathfinder could assure the Gilpins that William was in good health and would be back "in November with the larger part of the expedition."[35] Since the "larger part" was for a time Peg-Leg Smith and for a time an unnamed Mexican, and the true larger part was with Frémont, one can puzzle why this message was delivered to the family. But Frémont knew that they had not received word from William for more than a year, and he could understand a mother's worry; he may have made up a story and hoped that William would have the same good fortune returning from Oregon as he had on his way out.

William was anxious to go home soon and see his mother. His father had been dead three years now, and though theirs was a large and busy family, Mary and William (her youngest) had always been very close. His youthful letters and his later articles and books make obvious his compulsion to describe America's magnificence to those who lacked his opportunities. Now back from Oregon he had a new song to sing. His family would be impatient to hear.

I have plunged through a thousand interesting and exciting adventures since we have seen each other. Indeed scenes of the most impressive sublimity are [illegible] in infinite variety through the immense district of mountains that occupies three fourths of the country between Independence and the Pacific Ocean. For the last *thousand miles* approaching the Pacific in front, behind and around you rise towering piles of basalt hard and stern, the faces of the precipises [sic] for the most part, of packed pentagons.

No two fragments of the earth's surface present a more complete antithesis than the valley of the Mississippi and Oregon—yet both are equally grand and complete, extensive and comprehensive—both equally fit to receive and give development to the last and grandest nation of the human family—both essential to one another to complete the territorial symmetry of that nation.

I have neither seen or heard of any place any where in the world which surpasses in grandeur and richness of scenery the mouth of the

---

[35] Uncle Tom was gone six weeks, returning via Galena, Chicago, Mackinac, Detroit, Buffalo, and Albany. True to family tradition he told Henry and Eliza that *they* should go west, too (Thomas Gilpin to George Sibley, September 16, 1844, Sibley Collection, Missouri Historical Society).

Columbia, and the magnificent mountains in its rear whose peaks bathe themselves *two miles* deep in the 'eternal snows, thrice winnowed in the northern blast.'[36]

Until the legislative session ended he would remain in Jefferson City—"My occupation and labor are incessant"—concerned with the thousand details thrust upon a chief clerk. In the midst of these labors William gradually realized that his long trip to Oregon had turned him away from the moderate stand on expansion held by Benton and his closest partisans in the West. Missouri Democrats were dividing on various national issues—slavery, Texas, and Oregon—and it was over the last of these that William split from his chief.[37]

Benton believed that the forty-ninth parallel was the proper settlement line and frequently suggested that the administration should accept that compromise. Benton must have known that his stand was unpopular, just as his Texas position was losing him strength. He, nevertheless, maintained his ground, hoping that most Democrats, at least, would come around.

William Gilpin was one of those who did not. While his loyalty to Benton was great, he felt that Old Bullion was wrong, and William made plans to go to Washington to do something about this mistake. "Even Benton went back on us," he reported years later. "We wanted the line of 54°40', and got it into the Democratic platform in 1844. The salt-water politicians were afraid of war, and abandoned us for the line of 49."[38]

William's attitude was that of most Democrats in the presidential election of 1844, and Polk, their spokesman, defeated Henry Clay, who tried to explain away his own obvious reluctance to risk war over either Texas or Oregon. In his inaugural address Polk talked of America's "clear and unquestionable" title to Oregon, but he still felt that there was room for negotiation with Great Britain, and for several months matters were in the hands of the diplomats while Congress recessed.

The Missouri legislature also adjourned—March 28, 1845—and William could finally make his visit to the Brandywine. How long

36 William to Richard, December 1, 1844, Gilpin Folder, HSD.
37 McClure, *Opposition to Benton*, pp. 100–103.
38 *New York Daily Tribune*, March 22, 1879.

he remained with his family is not clear. He told his mother and his sisters of the many sights in the Great Valley and in Oregon, of the Indians, the buffalo, and the mountain men he could call by name. He went to Philadelphia and enjoyed Henry's parties with Eliza, Richard, and the local Democrats who were in better standing with Van Buren than with Polk. Henry had to hear again about the endless Congressional lands and how his capital and William's knowledge wisely put together would make them all rich.

William's fund of western information was no longer locked in family correspondence. In widely separated locations people were reading what William had to say and quoting him. William had no way of knowing it, but on the Kansas prairie, along the banks of Big Soldier Creek, an Oregon-bound party paused to reorganize and choose permanent officers. Recorded one pioneer:

> . . . *now* when we had reached the spot and the period for attending to the matter in earnest had arrived, the excitement was intense. The most important officers to be elected were the pilot and the captain of the company. There were two candidates for the office of pilot, one a Mr. Adams from Independence,—the other a Mr. Meek, from the same place. Mr. Adams had once been as far west as Fort Laramie, and had in his possession Gilpin's Notes, had engaged a Spaniard, who had traveled over the whole route, to accompany him, and moreover had been conspicuously instrumental in producing "Oregon Fever."

William had published these notes on Oregon in a local newspaper when he returned to Independence in the winter of 1844–1845. Clearly Mr. Adams considered ownership of the "Notes" worth much, for he asked $500 in advance to pilot the train to Fort Vancouver. The election was not settled until the next day, when Adams lost to Stephen Meek, who had once been to Fort Vancouver, was a brother of old Joe and wanted only $250 for the job.[39] The peculiar syntax of the diary nothwithstanding, William must already have earned a reputation as a western exhorter, precisely the claim he would have made for himself.

On the other side of the continent William was doing battle for Oregon in person. He made several visits from Kentmere to Wash-

[39] During this typical western expression of the democratic process the Indians drove off 2,000 head of cattle (Joel Palmer, *Joel Palmer's Journal*, pp. 39–40).

ington to see members of the Polk Administration who were friends of his family; Robert Walker, George Bancroft, William Marcy, and James Buchanan were all in the cabinet. Of these, William thought that Secretary of State Buchanan would probably best remember him from Philadelphia days.

So William made an appointment, met Buchanan and told him of his Oregon adventures and of the needs of the Oregon pioneers. According to William, Buchanan insisted on taking him to see President Polk. The Secretary told William, "You must come with me instantly to see the President and give him word for word, as near as you can, all you have told me."[40]

William talked with Polk about Oregon at some length; additionally, before the opening of Congress, William hunted up his two Missouri senators, Benton and David Atchison, and let them know of his willingness to appear before Congressional committees on the Oregon question. Then he returned briefly to Delaware to await the convening of Congress to present his memorial.

By great fortune Charles Jared Ingersoll represented a Philadelphia district in the Twenty-Ninth Congress; he was another close friend of Henry—they lived only a few blocks apart—and he was chairman of the House Committee on Foreign Affairs. Not only the Oregon question, but that of Texas as well, was within the jurisdiction of Ingersoll's committee. William discussed the petition of the Oregon settlers with Ingersoll, and Ingersoll agreed to introduce the memorial to the House of Representatives for its consideration and disposition.

On December 2, 1845, Ingersoll rose from his seat in the House and asked leave to present a memorial from the citizens of Oregon. He was shouted at and accused of being out of order. He replied that the petition was an urgent matter and that he would soon be leaving Washington and sought permission to move his business ahead on the calendar. In spite of some sharp objections the House voted the necessary two-thirds to suspend the rules and granted consent that the memorial be read.

The clerk then began to read: "Memorialists, citizens of the United States and residents of Oregon assembled in mass lay before your honorable body . . . statement of members, wants, and condi-

---

[40] *Kansas City Star*, April 30, 1905.

tions for legislative action." The paper, which ran some 2,500 words, went on to ask for a territorial government and to describe the Oregon settlement and the problems of its residents. Much of the paper included flowery, Gilpinlike descriptions of the American west; these began to pall on the listeners, and a motion was made and passed that, since few Congressmen were listening, the reading be discontinued. The matter was then tabled with instructions that the memorial be printed and distributed. Temporarily discussion on the Oregon question ended at that point.[41]

William had planned to have his memorial presented to the Senate during this same session of the Twenty-Ninth Congress, but other circumstances made this unnecessary. Since his departure from Oregon the settlers had prepared another statement. This request for territorial status was signed by sixteen men— entirely different from Gilpin's 1844 group. The second memorial was dated June 28, 1845, at Oregon City and signed by Osborn Russell, Peter Stewart, and J. W. Nesmith as the officers. Jesse Applegate and Doc Newell were among the better-known signers.

This document is more easily traced than the one William drafted. Dr. Elijah White and three others were instructed by the settlers to bear the paper to Washington; they left on July 30, reached Fort Hall on September 19 and Laramie on October 15, meeting meanwhile large numbers of west-bound immigrants. For two weeks they were held captive by the Pawnees but were finally freed. In December White reached Washington, located Senator Benton and got him to introduce the memorial to the Senate on December 8.

White's paper, more acceptable to Benton than was Gilpin's, carried much the same theme, and some phrases were identical, sparking the belief that a copy of William's draft had been retained by the settlers. In 1845, as in the year before, the Oregonians were concerned with land under the Linn Bill, Indian threats, postal service, forts, more shipping, and the like. The greatest difference in the two lists of demands was a significantly milder attitude toward Great Britain in the second. While William had written of the dangers from a "haughty government on a foreign conti-

[41] *Congressional Globe*, 29th Cong., 1st Sess., Dec. 2, 1845, p. 12; U.S. House of Representatives, *Executive Document No. 3*, 29th Cong., 1st Sess., 1845, pp. 1–5; *Niles' National Register* (Baltimore), Dec. 13, 1845.

nent," the second paper declared that relations with Great Britain were fine and hoped they they would remain so. Something of William's enthusiasm for geographical description was lost from the 1845 memorial also.[42]

The dual requests from the Oregon settlers now revived one of the great debates in American history. Prior to the presidential election of 1844 the Oregon question had centered around various efforts to pass the Linn Bill. This measure, as will be recalled, passed the Senate by a narrow margin that indicated some of the forthcoming bitterness. It failed of passage in the House; Linn's death in October meant the elimination from the scene of one of Oregon's chief spokesmen.

The Democratic convention at Baltimore in 1844 had nominated Polk on an expansionist program designed to please everyone, and Oregon to 54°40′, became a popular adjunct to the demand for Texas. With the annexation of that republic some shifting of position took place. Eminent Democrats such as Calhoun and even Benton talked of diplomatic negotiation with, not ultimatums to, Great Britain. On Benton's suggestion, Secretary of State Buchanan proposed to the British ministry the acceptance of the 49th parallel as a boundary. The revelation of this compromise greatly excited a number of Democrats who concluded that the Administration was deserting them; Buchanan was forced to withdraw the offer. Then on December 2, 1845, just before Ingersoll introduced William's memorial, President Polk threw open the whole Oregon matter in his first annual message to Congress. He told of the repeated failure at compromise on the basis of the 49th parallel as the boundary and asked for a law giving the required one year's notice to Great Britain ending the joint occupation convention of 1827.

Polk went on to make a number of recommendations that Congress might carry out for the benefit of the American settlers in Oregon. The conclusion is nearly inescapable that Polk's suggestions came from the Gilpin memorial. Both papers mention the need for extending the laws of the United States over the Oregon settlers, the need for protection from the Indians, the need for Indian agencies, the need for forts along the Oregon trail, the need for

[42] *Missouri Democrat* (Fayette), December 2, 1845; *Niles' National Register* (Baltimore), December 6 and 13, 1845; *Congressional Globe*, 29th Cong., 1st Sess., December 8, 1845, p. 24.

overland public mail, the need for carrying out some measure to grant land to the settlers.[43]

Necessarily Polk's language is more moderate than William's, and he left out William's effusive descriptions as well as reference to touchy subjects such as navy yards and the threat to "create a new nation rather than linger in doubt." The general theme and numerous specifics are too similar to be coincidence—Polk was repeating the settlers' requests to Congress and forcing the British to a decision.

For the next four months the two Houses discussed Oregon almost daily. The particular question was whether or not to give Great Britain the year's notice, but various other resolutions concerning an Oregon settlement were debated during the same period. William listened to all of the debates and was often called upon by speakers to supply information about the Far West. Calhoun charged that William expected to be the first Congressman.

Some of the details of these events cannot be confirmed by official records, but Gilpin's memory for the roles of certain individuals appears to be absolutely accurate. He lists, for example, Simon Cameron of Pennsylvania, Lewis Cass of Michigan, Sidney Breese and James Semple of Illinois, William Allen of Ohio, and Edward Hannegan of Indiana as the few men who held out for 54°40′. The opposition was led by Webster, Clay, Calhoun, George McDuffie of South Carolina, and most disappointing to William, Tom Benton. This division, recalled by William in 1879, exactly conforms with the debates recorded in the *Congressional Globe*.

Many of this latter group—the compromisers or "salt-water despots" to William—talked of the danger of a war with England. Others, including some southerners who had been most anxious to acquire Texas, now felt that the United States was large enough,

[43] James D. Richardson (ed.), *A Compilation of the Messages and Papers of the Presidents, 1789–1797*, IV, 382–398. White reached Washington too late to see Polk before the annual message—the Pawnee captivity preventing the meeting if White had such plans. I see no reason to doubt that Gilpin had serious talks with Polk and Buchanan about Oregon. Buchanan, of course, talked frequently with Polk about Oregon, but the President favored a much firmer stand against Great Britain than did Buchanan. Polk seems to have given careful consideration to the recommendations of Benton, however (James K. Polk, *The Diary of James K. Polk*, I, 68–72).

that Oregon was nearly worthless and separated from the states by a Great American Desert.

These arguments made William bristle as much when he was an old man as they did in 1846. He was particularly incensed against Webster for an alleged attack on Oregon which he called a

region of savages and wild beasts, of deserts, of shifting sands and whirlwinds of dust, of cactus and prairie dogs. . . . What can we ever hope to do with the Western coast, a coast of 3,000 miles, rock-bound, cheerless, uninviting and not a harbor on it? What use have we for such a country? Mr. President, I will never vote one cent from the public treasury to place the Pacific coast one inch nearer Boston than it is now.[44]

In January, 1846, through the efforts of Charles Ingersoll (supported by his brother Joseph, a Whig Representative from Pennsylvania) a bill to give the one year's notice was introduced as a joint resolution; it passed the House in the same week and the Senate on March 31. Polk signed the bill on April 27.[45] Now the British government would have to determine what the measure meant, for Congress was in no hurry to make Oregon into a territory.

During this winter of such importance to the American West, William kept in close touch with the scene in Washington. Elijah White called upon him to intercede with the War Department (which from 1832 had included the Bureau of Indian Affairs) to help settle his financial accounting for the four years that he had served as sub-Indian agent in Oregon. The new Commissioner of Indian Affairs, a family friend from the Brandywine country, was William Medill, later Governor of Ohio. William wrote to Medill that he wanted

to say a word in behalf of my friend, Dr. Elijah White, Indian agent in Oregon. . . . Dr. White with whom I passed the winter of 1844 upon the Wallamet, has had unnumbered difficulties surrounding him, and has performed his duties with great delicacy and happy success. . . .

[44] *Kansas City Star*, April 30, 1905. This often-repeated quotation reads a great deal like a speech of Senator McDuffie, made in 1843. I have found no contemporary evidence that Webster made this speech.

[45] William M. Meigs, *The Life of Charles Jared Ingersoll*, pp. 270–272; Marion M. Miller (ed.), *Great Debates in American History*, II, 308–332.

All whom I heard comment upon the administration of his office have accorded to him great praise for ardor and industry . . .[46]

White completed his audit satisfactorily and passed out of William's life by moving back to New York to write his recollections.

For the next two months William spent his leisure writing about the West in the event that someone in authority should ask for such information. One of the officials who did just that was Missouri's Senator David Atchison. Pursuing one of the points of Polk's December message, Atchison sought William out to get fuller information about a mail route to the Pacific. William submitted a reply to Atchison who used it as an enclosure to the report of the Senate Committee of Post Office and Roads. So impressed was the committee with Gilpin's work that it printed the letter as part of a Senate Report and ordered 3,000 other copies run off for Congress' use. William's claims for Oregon now became widely known and the reprinting by Congress can explain the similarly exaggerated discussions of the region found in so much of the press of 1846 and 1847.

William wrote a half-dozen pages of statistics and glowing descriptions (his letter to Atchison is dated January 23, 1846). He said that Oregon had nearly 10,000 population now, 20,000 cattle, 100,000 bushels of surplus wheat from the 1844–1845 crop, all of this developing in less than a decade. But William did not emphasize Oregon as farm country; the farmers of the Middle West already knew of the fertility of the Willamette Valley, just as they were critical of the near-deserts between. Without doubt William considered himself a spokesman for his "pioneer army," but his letter to the committee indicates his far greater interest in Oregon as something besides a new Eden. "Oregon is the maritime wing of the Mississippi Valley upon the Pacific as New England is on the Atlantic." Oregon had a superlative position—it was to Japan like New England was to the Old World. Already was there a continual traffic with the Sandwich Islands. The 675 whaling vessels in the Pacific had to visit these islands and Japan "*because the United States has no domestic port in the Pacific*" (William's italics).

The American people, he wrote, had acted in defiance of the

46 Gray, *History of Oregon*, pp. 417–418.

frowns of their government when they settled Oregon, and he wondered if they would be forever "banished" while their officials were "debating whether American wisdom had not better suffer British hyenas to gorge country, people, commerce and all and stop our republic short at the Rocky Mountains?"[47]

When he got around to the question of the postal road, William could speak with authority but had trouble terminating the mail at the mouth of the Columbia. He recommended that the road begin at Independence because it could also service New Mexico (still Mexican territory). Beyond the Rockies Indians might be used, but he knew three former mail contractors now in Oregon who would cover the route for ten dollars a mile. Then back to his grander theme went William—provision should be made in the same law to extend the route to the Sandwich Islands and China. He cited instances of the American fleet's "embarrassment" in the Pacific because of slow communications from Washington.

He calculated that 651,014,100 Pacific peoples were about to be attacked by the mighty agriculture and commerce of the United States. His letter continued:

The opening of the Chinese empire; the independence and civilization of the Sandwich islands; the occupation of the north Pacific by the American whaling fleet; the completion of a wagon road across the continent and the establishment of the advanced guard of the American nation in permanent position upon the Columbia, are detached events which have all transpired simultaneously, though apparently without any connection the one with the other, but which when linked together by this simple connecting line of intelligence, will be found to be in *fact* and *full operation*, this new field of commercial enterprise which orators sportively ridicule as Utopian. . . . deep designs of destiny work steadily.

William concluded the letter with remarks about the Pacific trade. More specifically, he suggested that the United States could easily destroy the British monopoly on commerce with China, since the distance between China and the United States was so much

[47] William's occasional outbursts of Anglophobia were never personal. His ancestry and business ties prevented this. He might have acquired some of the feeling from Benton—it was good for votes in St. Louis, but I believe that he felt that only Great Britain prevented the United States from achieving its true destiny.

shorter, and the area through which trade would pass was entirely within the temperate zone.[48]

This letter by William was printed on March 4, 1846; the following day the Senate adopted a resolution that the Committee on Post Offices and Roads should investigate measures for the transportation of mail through Panama and along the Pacific coast to Oregon.

The Chairman of the Committee was James Semple of Illinois, one of the holdouts for 54°40′ and a friend of William Gilpin. On the 16th Semple sent William a note asking him to provide the committee with more information about Oregon, "knowing that you have traveled a great deal through that country. . . ."

William replied the next day that he had "thrown together" some notes as Semple requested for he held the "conviction that no human efforts can restrict our Union as at present to one ocean . . . all on one side of the continent," like the handle of a cup. Then followed nearly 20,000 words on Oregon, the geography of the United States and Europe, world commerce, and Great Britain's attempts to monopolize the Asiatic trade. Control of Oregon, William wrote, was the key to unlocking the oriental riches which the United States had yet to share.

Recurring frequently throughout the "notes" is a text very dear to William: his belief that the government was failing in its responsibility to support the Oregon movement. The impetus instead came from the American people. A "vast army of pioneers . . . numbering 500,000, at least, has the movement and obeys the discipline of a perfectly organized military force." Each man is a platoon. "He makes a farm upon the outer edge of the settlements, which he occupies for a year, and then sells to the leading files of the mass pressing up to him from behind. He again advances twenty-five miles, renews his farm, is again overtaken and again sells."

This pioneer army had mobilized itself at Plymouth and James-

[48] U.S. Senate Report No. 178, 29th Cong., 1st Sess., 1846. This letter includes the first writing by William which suggests his later obsession with climatic zones. Norman Graebner, in *Empire on the Pacific*, p. 218, concludes, "Any interpretation of westward extension beyond Texas is meaningless unless defined in terms of commerce and harbors." While westward expansion had many motives, Graebner's thesis is clearly strengthened by Gilpin's writings.

town. The progeny of Plymouth gave the United States its mercantile fleet, its whalemen, its factories, and Michigan. The progeny
of Jamestown, said William, created a dozen agricultural states,
then added Texas, Louisiana, Arkansas, Missouri, and Iowa. Thirty
more states were yet to be formed, he added.

Now by land and by sea the two pincers of the army were about
to reunite in Oregon. What impelled these soldiers? Oriental markets, he frequently mentioned, free land, patriotism in the form of
Anglophobia, but yet another factor—a mystique, thought Bernard
De Voto a century later. Said William, "since 1842, forced by the
mysterious and uncontrollable impulse which drives our nation to
its goal, a body of the hardiest" had moved on to Oregon. Sometimes few people could see this urge, but it was apparent to William. Already the "irresistible tide of population, fulfilling that
inscrutable destiny which drives it on to absorb the continent,"
was "rushing from all sides" on Nebraska.

Whatever a pioneer's motives, William could voice them.
Whether he invented the language or formulated it one cannot say,
but thousands of copies of his reports to the Senate were circulated,
and many must have found their way into the hands of editors.
Later in 1846, and in 1847, editors frequently spoke of the Valley
of the Mississippi and the road to Oregon as offering greater riches
than those of the Ganges, the Nile, or some other ancient civilization, in the same vein that William so often employed.[49]

Few writers, however, were as harsh on the government as was
William. Democrats and Whigs alike received his scorn although
his attack was not particularly personal. As Henry Nash Smith
wrote, "Gilpin is too much a bardic seer to argue with anyone.[50]
Gilpin's letter to Semple went on:

Whilst the great pioneer army is thus noiselessly establishing new
nations, grasping a continent and throwing open a new ocean, an
American Congress and American statesmen, . . . are laboring to convince the world . . . that the prairies are impassable to their troops,
and the ocean and rivers to their ships; asserting sovereignty, yet re-

---

[49] U.S. Senate Report No. 306, 29th Cong., 1st Sess., 1846, contains William's
long letter to Semple. Graebner's *Empire on the Pacific* quotes many of these
editorials.

[50] Henry Nash Smith, *Virgin Land: The American West as Symbol and
Myth*, p. 40.

fusing protection. Proving that what women and children have performed by their unassisted means is impossible to be attempted by the select braves, the enormous revenues and resources of the great American people. . . . If, whilst this sublime scene is enacting at Washington, ten thousand isolated Americans perish by the tomahawk, and Oregon is lost thereby, what imperishable glory will surround our statesmen!

In one important regard William's report was not endorsed by Semple's committee. That body wanted the President to decide whether a mail route might as well go through Panama as across the plains. William favored no Panama mail system until the Isthmus was in United States hands.

In his peroration he turned from the present to the future.

The *untransacted* destiny of the American people is to subdue the continent—to rush over this vast field to the Pacific ocean—to animate the many hundred millions of its people . . . to set the principle of self-government at work—to agitate these herculean masses— . . . to set free the enslaved—to regenerate superannuated nations— . . . to confirm the destiny of the human race— . . . to unite the world in one social family— . . . to absolve the curse that weighs down humanity, and shed blessings around the world. Divine task! immortal mission.[51]

Except for a sentence or two used in letters or editorials, this report to Semple seems to be William's first broad attempt to outline his beliefs about the West and its destiny. Almost everything is here that later appears in his speeches, articles, and books. The only difference is their greater detail and selective emphasis not found in this first work.

Precisely when William compiled and organized his information can only be a matter of conjecture. Much of the work came from his own observations as a traveler. We can probably believe William's story of what he had learned by helping De Tocqueville collect data in Washington back in 1831–1832; William had the winter of 1845–1846 to do the same for himself.

As for the writing of this essay, it is only reasonable to believe that William did it at this same time in anticipation of both the Atchison and the Semple requests. If we take the evidence at its face value—that is, Semple's request on the 16th of March and William's reply on the 17th—we have William preparing the

---

[51] U.S. Senate Report No. 306, 29th Cong., 1st Sess., 1846.

equivalent of a short master's thesis literally overnight. More acceptable is his own language, "I have thrown together . . ."

When he performed his work is of less importance than the wide acceptance of it. William was becoming the spokesman of the West and its destiny, and he was anxious to go back to Missouri and devote himself to writing about the Oregon fever. But events from another quarter suddenly intervened and William the soldier took the stage again.

Meanwhile debate over the Oregonians' memorial was lost in the broader context of the boundary question. Both England and the United States found reason for compromise. Decline of the Columbia Valley fur business and fear of the pugnacious American settlers had provoked the transfer of the Hudson's Bay Company from Fort Vancouver to Vancouver Island, leaving the British government little economic concern south of the 49th parallel. The United States at the same moment was engaged in critical discussions with Mexico, the breakdown of which brought war in the spring of 1846. England offered a settlement based on an extension of the existing boundary along the 49th parallel to the Pacific, and Polk, on the advice of the Senate, accepted. The treaty was signed in June, 1846.

The question of the prohibition of slavery in Oregon now arose and prevented passage of a bill to create a territory until the massacre of the Whitman mission late in 1847. Oregon Territory was created in 1848.

Besides the Whitman family, Joe Meek, Peter Ogden, Doc Newell, and other friends of William Gilpin played key roles in the tense days of 1847, but William knew little of this. His active Oregon career had ended with the first news of gunfire along the Mexican border.

CHAPTER SIX

# Xenophon's March

*Volunteer in the Mexican War, 1846–1847*

War began between Mexico and the United States because many citizens of both nations wanted it. Long before the clash of arms in 1846 there had been pretexts enough: a critical boundary dispute, unsatisfied American claims against transitory Mexican governments, the sharp clash of cultures that began with colonization schemes like those of Moses Austin, raids by Indians who fled from one government or the other by crossing the border, the successful revolt of Texas culminating in its annexation to the United States, and the complete breakdown of diplomacy as exemplified by the failure of the Slidell mission. The American believed that the Mexican could not govern himself and, therefore, stood in the way of progress. The Mexican believed that the American intended to swallow him whole. And so they fought.

In the spring of 1846 the troops of General Zachary Taylor and

General Mariano Arista engaged in some weeks of angry dispatches, dirt-pawing, and distant sniping until April 25, when a small detachment of Americans was attacked by Mexicans in disputed territory. Some sixty Americans were killed, wounded, or captured.

President Polk agreed with Taylor and Arista that war "existed," and he called upon Congress for support. The declaration of war came on May 13 as Congress authorized the President to order the services of volunteers not to exceed fifty thousand in number, to serve for twelve months, or for the duration of the war.

Taylor was to lead the main attack on Mexico, with Scott's assault from Veracruz to the capital something of a Polk afterthought intended to dim Taylor's luster. Naval units, and Frémont and his mountain men were already in California. But to insure that conquest and at the same time to provide Taylor with a distant right wing, the War Department created the Army of the West to be commanded by Stephen Watts Kearny, then at Fort Leavenworth with his First Dragoons. This was the army to which William Gilpin sought and received assignment. William apparently asked for a reinstatement of his regular army commission but left Washington without knowing his status. He had written meanwhile to friends in Independence asking them to hold a place for him in their volunteer company.

War Department orders were to use the First Dragoons as the cadre of the Army of the West, while President Polk asked Missouri's Governor John Edwards to organize companies of infantry, light artillery, and mounted volunteers. Edwards acted promptly; recruiting began in St. Louis and several counties strung more or less across the state following the Missouri River. As each county reached its quota of 105 men, its contingent was sent to Fort Leavenworth to join Kearny. Letter designation was accomplished at the Fort on a first-come, first-served basis, and as a result, the company from Jackson County, where Independence was located, had the distinction of becoming "A" Company.

William arrived in Independence just after the detachment had left, so he hastened to Fort Leavenworth, hoping that his place had been saved. Volunteers abounded, however, and at Leavenworth William found that he had no billet. Providentially, one of the recruits turned out to be only sixteen (the law required that soldiers "appear to be at least eighteen") and was needed at home. William paid the boy $85 for his niche, and was back in the army.[1]

William did not remain long in "A" Company. The War Department had given Kearny considerable latitude in organizing his forces. Within the Army of the West he assigned about one half of his forces to the First Regiment of Missouri Mounted Volunteers, composed of eight companies representing as many counties. On June 18 the volunteers carried out Kearny's orders to elect their field-grade officers. Candidates for the various ranks made speeches on the parade ground to the assembled troops. With limited military experience to point to, the aspiring officers emphasized camaraderie and soldiers' benefits.

Only two men ran for the position of regimental commander and Alexander W. Doniphan, a private from Clay County, won handily. The choice was wise as well as popular. Doniphan had a bit of experience fighting the Mormons back in 1838. Moreover, Doniphan was a large, imposing man (an old photograph makes him look like an untormented John Brown) with a gift for oratory. He used his talents judiciously as a legislator and attorney and built an unusual frontier reputation as the defender of accused criminals, including Joseph Smith, whom he had just captured.[2] Doniphan had what the volunteers sought: common sense, leadership, and freedom from the taint of West Point.

For lieutenant colonel the volunteers had two more candidates, Charles F. Ruff of Clay County and William Gilpin of Jackson County. In what was described as a "very exciting" election Ruff defeated William by two votes. Ruff, a friend of William from Philadelphia and West Point, had five years of service in the dra-

---

[1] Outside New England most states oversubscribed their quotas of volunteers. In Tennessee, for example, 30,000 men met the call for 3000, and the places were filled by lot. Yet the war was very unpopular with many Americans, even in states like Ohio and Illinois with surpluses of volunteers (Justin H. Smith, *The War with Mexico*, I, 195). See Smith, I, 138–203, for the outbreak of the war and details of the higher command structure. See also Hubert Howe Bancroft, *History of the Life of William Gilpin*, pp. 30–31. I doubt that Polk seriously considered William for Kearny's post as Bancroft implies.

[2] William E. Connelley, *Doniphan's Expedition*, pp. 21–31. Doniphan gambled his future by refusing to obey a direct military order to put Smith and several other Mormon leaders to death. In spite of the bitterness of the era (1838) in Missouri, Doniphan seems to have gained popularity by his courage.

goons to match William's West Point, Florida War, and frontier experience. William believed that he had Doniphan's support but that Kearny preferred Ruff.

At this point in the elections William became a strong candidate for the remaining staff post of major. He had just delivered a twenty-minute speech when Kearny called him to his office to notify him that the War Department had offered William a commission as lieutenant colonel with the regular army, which Kearny urged William to accept.

William preferred to take his chances with his present regiment (probably because he knew the theater of action) and went back to the political arena. With little difficulty he defeated several other privates and became Doniphan's third in command.[3]

Company officers were also elected in similar fashion. The men of "A" chose William's old friend and creditor, David Waldo, to be captain. Waldo, a doctor of medicine from Transylvania, a naturalized Mexican citizen, and a Santa Fe trader, was frequently called upon as a translator for the regiment.

Doniphan and the Missouri Mounted Volunteers were, of course, under Kearny's command, but the vast distances of this army's campaign and the necessity of dividing forces to conserve grass and water, meant that Doniphan was often to be supreme in his theater.

The remaining half of the Army of the West was now a composite force under Kearnys' personal authority or marching as separate units. The dragoons (regulars) were augmented by recruits from other western posts to a final total of six companies. Two volunteer companies of light artillery (mostly from St. Louis) were placed under Major Meriwether Lewis Clark, son of the explorer. Two volunteer infantry companies, a company of mounted volunteers from St. Louis called the Laclede Rangers, a detachment of engineers, and some fifty Delawares and Shawnees filled out the Army of the West, a total of 1,650 to 1,800 men, varying literally from day to day in strength.

The supplying and training of this army was scarcely underway when Kearny found it necessary to begin his march upon

---

[3] Marcellus Edwards, *Journal of Marcellus Ball Edwards*, p. 115; Bancroft, *William Gilpin*, p. 31. As in wagon train elections, the men lined up behind their choice for each rank. Doniphan's town of Liberty, Missouri, helped his campaign by offering free breakfasts at the inns, only a few miles from the Fort.

Santa Fe. An important and perhaps determining factor in this haste was the peculiar situation of the merchants of the Trail. Most of these men had bought their merchandise and organized their trains before war began, and some of the caravans had actually left Independence. Kearny's orders from Washington were that, so far as possible, he was to protect the merchants and their goods and to help them sell to the New Mexicans without the usual tariff charges.

Kearny now learned from Captain Waldo, who knew most of the merchants, that a caravan owned by a Prussian, Albert Speyer, was carrying munitions as well as goods. Kearney was led to believe that Speyer intended to deliver the arms to Mexican officials in Santa Fe. On June 6 Captain B. D. Moore, guided by Tom Fitzpatrick, took two companies of the dragoons out of Fort Leavenworth in pursuit of Speyer. Six days later a third company set out to reinforce Moore. In a technical sense this was the beginning of the invasion of Mexico from the west.

Almost immediately Kearny dispatched an enormous supply train of one hundred or more wagons. Once the troops reached the plains they were expected to live off the land, and this caravan was moving ahead to prepare wild meat for them.[4]

Although several dozen Missouri volunteers were with the supply train, the first to leave Leavenworth in their own units were mounted Companies "A" and "D." Lieutenant Colonel Ruff and four more companies followed in a day or so, and a day later, William Gilpin, commanding "E" and "H," the last two mounted companies, plus two companies of volunteer infantry, set out for Santa Fe; Doniphan accompanied Gilpin's element. Major Clark's artillery and the last of the dragoons under Kearny himself departed on June 30, the date his new rank of brigadier general became effective, a fact he did not learn for six weeks.

Each morning as the next echelon of troops swaggered out of the parade ground they cheered themselves, their units, and their flag. Often there were pretty faces, smiling and crying, as the deputations from neighboring towns came to wave their white handkerchiefs in farewell while some spokeswoman delivered an address

[4] The hunters, who were experienced buffalo men, estimated that from Pawnee Rock they could see a mass of 500,000 to 800,000 buffalo (Connelley, *Doniphan*, pp. 139 n.–140 n.).

to accompany the inevitable homemade banner. Only an occasional old army noncom could be seen standing about and shaking his head at the unbelievable rawness of this undisciplined mass.

Never had an American trail been so cluttered. Four hundred wagons of merchandise, a stray band of California-bound emigrants, 1,700 soldiers scattered for four or five hundred miles, buffalo hunters, Indians—all led by a foreign merchant rushing to Santa Fe before war should close all the stalls in that sleepy village. Kearny sent word ahead, "Tell the Mexicans that we do not intend to deprive them of their property but to stop its progress for the present."

From Fort Leavenworth to Santa Fe was about 950 miles, bypassing Independence and entering New Mexico by way of Bent's Fort and Ratón Pass. Some men like Gilpin, Waldo, Fitzpatrick, and Kearney's engineers knew the Trail well. Others had never seen it before, and the fervor of the volunteers was soon dulled by the boredom and discomforts of the endless southwestern prairies.

The Santa Fe Trail was marked as plainly as any highway, but so was the Oregon Trail, and perhaps not too surprisingly Company "D" got lost and briefly headed for Oregon until Captain Waldo of "A" sent a messenger to straighten out Captain Reid.

Hurrying to catch Fitzpatrick, Captain Moore, and the dragoons (who were hurrying to catch Speyer), "A" and "D" played leapfrog daily for campsites, with "A" usually winning the game because of Waldo's experience and trail knowledge. Meanwhile they began to overtake and order the merchant wagons to halt at the nearest of three rendezvous points and await the arrival of Kearny. These sites were Pawnee Fork, some three hundred miles from Independence, Arkansas Crossing, and Bent's Fort.

Some of the merchants were never overtaken within United States territory. Speyer, with teams of very fast mules, was weeks ahead of the army and in his haste passed other caravans, who first learned from him of the outbreak of war and in turn, whipped up their oxen to outdistance this unusual cavalry charge. As a consequence, Speyer reached Santa Fe by the 1st of July and blanketed under his Prussian or British passport the goods of Americans like James J. Webb, who arrived at about the same time. They paid several thousand dollars in duties and made plans for a more leisurely haul to Chihuahua and the goods-hungry southern markets, safe from the Army of the West. A few weeks passed before they realized that a more complex set of problems was to face them, and that the relations of the traders and the army were to become ever more involved.[5]

The daily lives of the soldiers that summer are recounted in the journals of men of sufficiently varied ranks and organizations to provide a good composite. Although William Gilpin kept no journal, we can calculate accurately how he lived and from time to time pinpoint exactly where he was.

The army was moving into July at the same time that it moved out on the treeless plains, and the men soon concluded that the elements of nature were conspiring against them. Wrote one soldier a few days out of Leavenworth,

The heat was often excessive; the grass was tall and rank; and the earth in many places so soft that the heavily loaded wagons would sink almost up to the axle upon the level prairie. The men were frequently compelled to dismount and drag them from the mire with their hands. . . . Numbers of wagons broke down.[6]

Camps were infested with gnats, flies, mosquitoes, and snakes. More pesky than dangerous to humans, these nuisances were hard on livestock, and large numbers died. One man was bitten by a snake but found relief for his foot when his company provided him with a quart of whiskey. Other soldiers suffered from measles, chills, dysentery, and sore and swollen feet, and many thus traveled long distances in the wagons.

Sore feet or no, the infantry soldier gradually realized his advantage over his mounted associates who had reveille at three in the morning to take care of the horses and who could not eat in the evening until the horses were watered and fed. The foot soldiers acquired pride in their ability to travel farther each day than the cavalry, although Captain W. Z. Angney made himself unpopular with his men by trying to set records.

---

[5] Max L. Moorhead, *New Mexico's Royal Road*, devotes one chapter to "Profit and Loss in Wartime," straightening out many of the scattered references found in the journals cited below. See also William J. Parish, "The German Jew and the Commercial Revolution in Territorial New Mexico, 1850–1900," *New Mexico Historical Review*, XXXV (January, 1960), 1–29.

[6] Connelley, *Doniphan*, p. 141.

Some of the infantry also took the Oregon road, and an Indian messenger was sent to bring them back. Said their lieutenant, "As we had enlisted for the wars we retraced our steps, and encamped at the same place we started from in the morning."[7]

For the Fourth of July Kearny permitted his men to purchase whiskey from various suttlers who still accompanied them. Somehow the infantry was left out, and, in fact, even wanted for water most of the day. The dragoons had a reasonable share, but Captain Waldo of "A" Company, Mounted Volunteers, had enough to give a surplus keg to "D." Of such considerations are trail reputations constructed.

At Council Grove most of the Army of the West paused for two days. Wagons were repaired from the abundant timber; men and horses rested in the shade and drank from the cool Neosho River.

Lessons of great importance were learned almost daily. The command found that oxen could haul wagons as far in one day as horses could be ridden, but they needed more rest during the hot hours. Thus the food and tents for the men arrived much too late each evening for the men's comfort, and drastic rescheduling was needed. Kearny reorganized his long supply train into companies of twenty or thirty wagons each. This move necessitated arming the wagoners, but, after some trial and serious error, made possible a closer coordination of marching men and their food supply.

In spite of delays of this kind the army made good progress across the plains: twenty to twenty-five miles a day was probably the average and both foot and mounted occasionally traveled more than thirty. The volunteers had yet to see an enemy, and only a few Shawnee and Delaware farmers, but they were developing a degree of esprit de corps and trail discipline. The soggy ground disappeared as they moved west, and some of the mornings were beautiful, so the men confided to their diaries. They saw their first mirages, the prairie dog towns, the distant antelope. For the first time they cooked with buffalo chips, and some of the troops would not eat that night, but were hungrier the next day.

Now they followed the north bank of the Arkansas. They camped one night at Cow Creek where Chávez, the Mexican trad-

[7] George R. Gibson, *Journal of a Soldier under Kearny and Doniphan*, p. 132 n.

er, had been killed in 1843. By coincidence Doniphan's and Gilpin's battalion overhauled Ruff's that night, and doubtless William told the other officers of his part in tracking down the McDaniel gang.

Kearney now received word from Captain Moore, fruitlessly after Speyer. In spite of traveling forty miles a day Moore had not caught the Prussian, and in fact, concluded from camp sites that he was not even gaining on him. Speyer had taken the Cimarron Cut-off; since Kearny planned a rendezvous at Bent's Fort, Moore returned to the Arkansas and reported that he would await the general at the Fort.

A disappointment to Kearney—nevertheless, the Speyer affair did not concern him and his men so much as another report, one from an agent who had returned from Santa Fe and believed that the Mexicans were getting ready to fight the Army of the West.

Military discipline in that organization was being tested daily by late July. Kearny was ordering very long marches that were breaking down men and animals. Scores of the men rode in the wagons and argued with their officers about their ailments. Several company commanders began dealing out punishment, often in the form of overtime marching and drill. Apparently nettled by the infantry's ability to outwalk his Mounted Volunteers, Ruff put his battalion to a severe march in 100° weather that placed them in the fore, then ordered close-order drill until Kearny and the main body arrived. That the drill occurred while winds "swept across the parched and heated plain . . . as withering as the breath of the Sahara" exaggerated Ruff's growing unpopularity with the men, who blamed him rather than Kearny for the driving pace.[8]

Kearny himself became sick one day and the whole army paused. Many of the men took the occasion to have a refreshing swim in the shallow Arkansas, or "rearranged the dirt" on their clothing, as one soldier put it.[9]

Toward the end of July the entire force moved upon Bent's Fort. Anticipation of something different improved morale; the first sight of the Rockies was greeted with echoing cheers through the ranks, and the realization that they were virtually in Mexican as well as Comanche territory added a thrill that made the troops

---

[8] Connelley, *Doniphan*, p. 175.

[9] Abraham Robinson Johnston, *Journal of Abraham Robinson Johnston*, p. 87.

appear a bit more military. (Doniphan and Gilpin, for some reason, crossed the Arkansas and traveled for a day on Mexican soil.)

In approximately a month the Army of the West had, blisters and all, walked over five hundred miles from Leavenworth to the most famous way-station on the Santa Fe Trail. They would have a day or two to rest, eat and drink and perhaps find an Indian maiden, while Kearny talked with Fitzpatrick, his own spies, and even some Mexican spies who were given a free view of the army before being sent back to Santa Fe to broadcast and perhaps exaggerate Kearny's strength.[10]

First named Fort William, Bent's Fort—or later, Bent's "Old" Fort—as it was popularly called, was completed about 1832 by William and Charles Bent and Ceran St. Vrain, very successful fur traders and merchants. A 137 by 178 foot rectangle with four-foot adobe walls, it was the second largest American trading post. The location was carefully designed to tap the Indian, Mexican, and natural resources at a point convenient to the settlements in Missouri. Built for the siege that never came, the fort had eighteen-foot towers containing small artillery and hand guns, sabers, and lances. A second wall inside kept Indians from entering the center of the fort, yet cashiers' cages permitted easy trade in safety. The fort abounded in small rooms or apartments on two different levels for transients and for the permanent party of about 150. This castle in the desert was complete with kitchen, dining halls, warehouses, offices, shops, an ice house, and a billiard room.[11]

But even the Bents were not prepared for this much company. In addition to the 1,700 soldiers, the army had by now accumulated half again as many civilians, merchants, extra teamsters, and drovers. Their tents reached to every horizon, and there was not enough grass on the whole upper Arkansas to feed the livestock.

Indians came from miles around to see the white man's show.

[10] Details of this portion of the expedition come primarily from the firsthand accounts of Doniphan, Johnston, and Gibson, cited above, and the *Journal of Marcellus Edwards*.

[11] David Lavender, *Bent's Fort*, pp. 136–139, provides the most reliable information on this enterprise. In 1849, after refusing to sell it to the government, William Bent deliberately burned the fort and built a new one a few miles down the Arkansas. A mixture of business and sentiment, Lavender concludes (pp. 313–319).

He provided some unscheduled excitement when something frightened the volunteers' horses, loosely picketed on the prairie. Over
a thousand stampeded in every direction, maddened by the flail-
ing *reatas* and the iron picket stakes which they jerked from the
ground. They ran themselves out in time, but not until many were
fifty miles from the fort or permanently lost to the army.[12]

Men were lost, too—a drunken dragoon fought and swam until
he killed himself with a stroke. Several volunteers were discharged
for various "weaknesses"—delirium tremens was a repeated cause.
Doniphan left a score of men at the fort as unfit for further duty.

The Colonel kept William busy for the three days they were at
Bent's, handling discharges, supervising his own battalion, and
arguing with the Bents about supplies and prices. William's brief
friendship with the brothers, stemming from their hospitality of
two years before, was strained by the behavior of the volunteers
who thought they deserved rewards and not $24 whiskey and $4
tobacco. They had been on short rations often during the month
on the march from Fort Leavenworth and had mistakenly assumed
that all would be corrected at Bent's.

One of the visitors to the fort who did not complain was a civilian, and a female at that. Probably the first American white
woman to pass down the Santa Fe Trail, Susan Shelby Magoffin
was accompanying the merchant caravan of her new husband,
Samuel, and his brother and senior partner, James. With other
Missourians, they were en route to Chihuahua by way of Santa Fe
to sell goods, but James Magoffin had just been to Washington in
mid-June at Benton's request, had talked with Polk, and had sped
along the Trail to catch Kearny (as well as Samuel and Susan)
before they met the Mexican forces. For James Magoffin had a
secret mission and his success would be of critical importance to
southwestern history. He was to move out ahead of the troops
with twelve men under Captain Philip St. George Cooke and proceed to Santa Fe, carrying secret proclamations from Kearny to
the Mexican commander, General Manuel Armijo. Kearny was
warning Armijo not to resist the peaceable occupation; Magoffin
was to negotiate with (and possibly bribe) him; while William Bent

---

[12] Connelley, *Doniphan*, p. 178. Johnston's *Journal* said four hundred animals,
p. 90.

and a half dozen scouts were to spy out the pass at Ratón to make sure there was no trap.

How much Susan knew of this plot is a matter of conjecture. She was as popular with the men on the Trail as she is with the modern historians of the West, and her press has been justifiably good. She kept a diary which helps date and place a number of events and people in the year of 1846. Susan had been ill for some time, possibly from a wreck of her carriage, and now she was pregnant, yet seriously thin. Samuel gave her every comfort possible and the Bents made room for her inside the fort.

Susan celebrated her nineteenth birthday (July 30) at the fort and found it a friendly place, if different from any she had ever seen. William Gilpin and other officers called upon her—Captain Moore claiming a distant relationship. She watched the scolding and the fighting of the Mexicans, the visit of some Indians, and the bustle created by the arrival of Kearny and the last of the troops.

That night Susan went into premature labor and, with much agony, suffered a miscarriage in spite of the efforts of a doctor with one of the caravans.[13] From her bed, during the next three days, Susan heard the Army of the West move out for Ratón Pass and Santa Fe, and learned that her brother-in-law had gone ahead with a small contingent.

One of the men with William Bent at Ratón Pass was Frank Blair, Jr., long-time friend of William Gilpin, now staying at Bent's Fort for his health following overwork in Benton's St. Louis law office. Frank and the Bents were probably related, and he was to become guardian of George Bent's children. Frank was soon to prove very useful to the army, but his future was to be on a more national scale.[14] He and William had a chance to reminisce briefly; then each made his own way south.

William, Doniphan, and the Missouri volunteers now followed closely behind the dragoons along Timpas Creek. They left the Arkansas with regret and for two or three long days' marches had nothing to drink except filthy mud. Then the clear waters of the Purgatoire refreshed them before the army tackled the Ratón Mountains. They crossed Ratón Pass with great difficulty and were

[13] Susan Shelby Magoffin, *Down the Santa Fé Trail and into Mexico: The Diary of Susan Shelby Magoffin*, pp. 59–69.
[14] William E. Smith, *The Francis Preston Blair Family in Politics*, I, 206–207.

given the next day to rest.[15] But the Kearny notion of rest was unusual. The men were lacking breakfast as well as dinner the night before, yet were required to drill several hours on their day off. Then they were informed that their rations had to be reduced to one-third. Never again during their year's service were the men of the Army of the West to receive a full ration in enemy country.

The suffering, illness, and hunger were resulting in an average of one death and many incapacitated each day, but the army's spirits improved with the first sight of tiny Mexican villages. Using their own specie funds, volunteers bought flour and an occasional chicken while listening to stories of the vast army that Armijo was deploying just east of Santa Fe.

William Bent returned to tell Kearny and Doniphan of 2,000 Mexicans at a pass just beyond Las Vegas. The Americans occupied Las Vegas without a shot; Kearny climbed a rickety ladder to a housetop and told the Mexican civilians assembled that he would respect their rights, protect them from the Indians, and keep the present officials in office under oaths of allegiance to the United States.

From time to time Kearny's men captured small groups of Mexicans that he assumed were spies. Five such, mounted on tiny burros, looked so pathetic alongside big Missourians and bigger Missouri horses that the sight convulsed old Tom Fitzpatrick, a man rarely amused by anything.[16] Doubtless such vignettes got back to the Mexicans, for their forces beyond Las Vegas simply disappeared and the army moved on again, Kearny repeating his speech and oath ceremony in each village.

Captain Cooke and Magoffin found it hard to outride the infantry but finally left them behind and entered Santa Fe on August 12 with their flag of truce. At the palace they held secret conversations with Governor Armijo and his executive officer, Colonel Diego Archuleta. Possibly Armijo was bribed by Magoffin to desert Santa Fe and remove the troops; Magoffin also might have undermined him by convincing Archuleta that the United States sought only to extend Texas to the Río Grande and that the land to the west could be Archuleta's if he, too, would not fight. This, at least, is Benton's

[15] One day Magoffin's wagons went only eight hundred yards.

[16] Lieutenant Colonel William H. Emory, *Notes of a Military Reconnaissance*, p. 21.

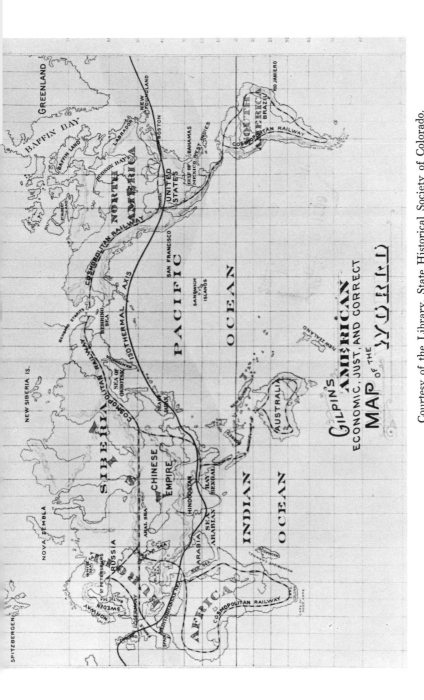

Courtesy of the Library, State Historical Society of Colorado.

1. "Gilpin's American Economic, Just, and Correct Map of the World." Copied from the frontispiece of *The Cosmopolitan Railway, Compacting and Fusing Together all the World's Continents* (1890), by William Gilpin.

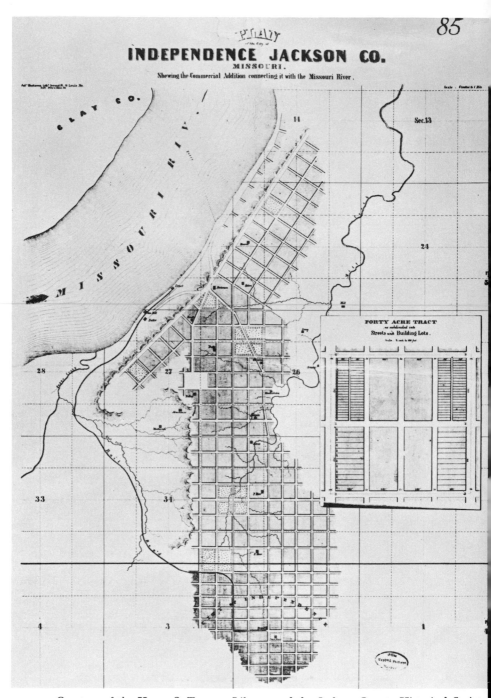

Courtesy of the Harry S. Truman Library and the Jackson County Historical Society

2. An undated map believed to be of Gilpintown, near Independence, Missouri

Courtesy of the Library, State Historical Society of Colorado.

3. William Gilpin in his late 40's.

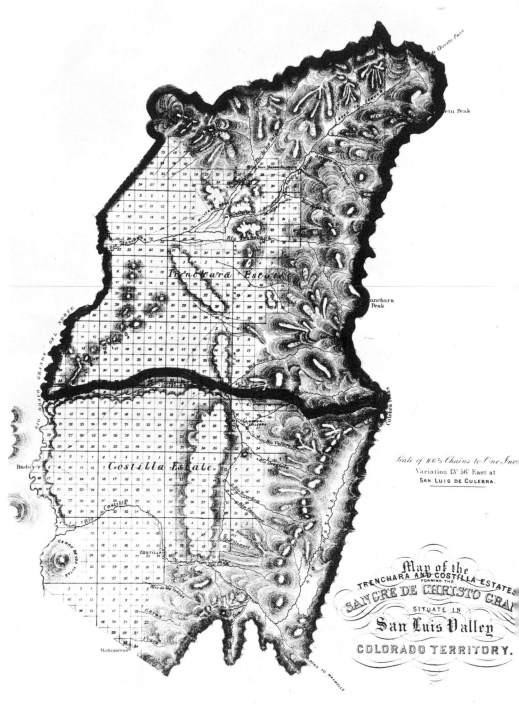

Courtesy of the State Historical Society of Colorado.

4. Gilpin's land grants in the San Luis Valley of southern Colorado and northern New Mexico territories.

5. William Gilpin, copied from *Colorado: Its Resources, Parks and Prospects as a New Field for Emigration, with an Account of the Trenchara and Costilla Estates in the San Luis Park* (1869), by William Blackmore.

Courtesy of the Library, State Historical Society of Colorado.

6. A draft made out by William Gilpin to pay a Denver merchant during the Civil War.

RESIDENCE OF HON. WM. GILPIN.

Courtesy of the Library, State Historical Society of Colorado.

William Gilpin's Denver residence. Copied from *History of the City of Denver, apahoe County, and Colorado* (1880).

Courtesy of the Library, State Historical Society of Colorado.

8. William Gilpin, in his 70's.

version in justification of a large "reimbursement" to Magoffin. Several explanations have been suggested that need not concern us here, but the fact is that the United States Congress a few years later appropriated $30,000 for Magoffin "for services rendered."

After only a day with the Mexicans, Cooke turned his horse out of the palace yard and rode back toward Kearny. The news he bore disappointed the volunteers—they had little chance for a fight. Yet, while Cooke was riding to report, the Mexicans improved the natural fortifications of Apache Canyon and increased the number of their troops to well over 3,000. With any will the Mexicans could have prevented the occupation of Santa Fe at this point, but the civilian soldiers had no interest in a fight. Armijo argued that fighting was useless, his officers disbanded the militia, and Armijo with a company of dragoons fled southward.

Kearny got word of Armijo's departure and on August 18 the Army of the West marched twenty-nine miles to enter Santa Fe unopposed.[17] The dragoons rode in front, then the infantry, and Doniphan's mounted regiment; the artillery remained on a hill overlooking the town. The Mexican citizens studied the entering army with fear and uncertainty; the soldiers viewed the town with disgust. Said one in his journal:

The appearance of the town was shabby . . . no gardens that deserved the name, the fields all unenclosed, the people poor and beggarly, and nothing to pay us for our long march. . . . To add to our disappointment, our teams are all behind, and we have a fair prospect of going without supper and of having no blankets.[18]

---

[17] Connelley, *Doniphan*, pp. 195–200. The same story is told by the other journals.

[18] Gibson, *Journal*, pp. 205–206. "The Army of the West marched . . . with rations calculated to last . . . until . . . Sant Fé. Is this war? . . . A colonel's command called, an army, marches eight hundred miles beyond its base, its communication liable to be cut off by the slightest effort of the enemy . . . the whole distance almost totally destitute of resources, to conquer a territory of 250,000 square miles; . . . the people of this territory are declared citizens of the United States, and the invaders are thus debarred the rights of war to seize needful supplies; they arrive without food before the capital—a city two hundred and forty years old, habitually garrisoned by regular troops! . . . This is the art of war as practised in America" (Philip St. George Cooke, *The Conquest of New Mexico and California*, p. 21).

In such fashion the Army of the West began its occupation of the romantic outpost of Spain's once-glorious empire. Kearny got an interpreter, called several delegations together and announced the conquest of New Mexico and the deposing of Armijo. Kearny gave his usual paternal talk—that he would protect them but that they must be good American citizens. Enough representatives took the oath of allegiance to satisfy the general, and he ordered the raising of the American flag.

The strength of the Army of the West now had to be divided. The primary mission was the conquest of California, and General Kearny began immediate preparations for that campaign, using his dragoons only slightly augmented by volunteers. The occupation of New Mexico was to be put in the hands of the Second Missouri Volunteers, just now leaving Fort Leavenworth under the command of Colonel Sterling Price, a congressman commissioned by Polk but confirmed into the colonelcy by frontier democracy at Leavenworth. Price had about 1,200 men and, it was mistakenly assumed, could easily control the Mexicans. Doniphan's regiment would then be free to continue the invasion southward along the Río Grande, and Kearny wrote to Brigadier General John E. Wool, commanding the "Army of the Centre," that he would shortly send Doniphan's regiment to help Wool capture Chihuahua. Wool was at San Antonio and was to do a good deal of marching before the war ended, but he never saw Chihuahua.

Kearny's final obligation was to create a government for New Mexico. He gave Doniphan the responsibility of framing a constitution for the territory, but except for some advice from Frank Blair, the labor was performed by Willard P. Hall, a private, but an unusual private. Like Doniphan, a frontier lawyer, Hall had been nominated by the Democrats for a seat in the United States House of Representatives and during his absence with the army was elected without campaigning. Doniphan, in fact, brought Hall word of the results one day while they worked on the constitution.[19] The translation of the code into Spanish was accomplished by David Waldo. Just before leaving for California in late September, Kearny appointed Charles Bent as governor, Frank Blair as district

---

[19] Hall nevertheless went on to fight in California before taking his seat in Washington. During the Civil War he was provisional governor of Missouri (Connelley, *Doniphan*, pp. 238–243).

attorney, and a mixture of Mexicans and Americans to other positions in the territory. Charles (or Carlos) Beaubien, a superior court justice, and Stephen Lee, an acting sheriff, were about to became participants in one of the largest land deals in American history. In their new jobs they probably met William Gilpin, for it was a portion of their estate that was someday to make William a rich man.

In the fall of 1846, however, William could only dream of an empire. His primary duty in life was to command the Second Battalion and to serve as chief assistant to Doniphan with the regiment. Colonel Ruff remained only briefly in Santa Fe and was sent with the "grazing detachment" a day's march into the hills from the capital to feed and revive the animals.

Ruff's men did not get enough to eat, and he had to court-martial a lieutenant who insisted upon going to Santa Fe to provision his unit. The lieutenant was dismissed from the service, although his "crime" was condoned by all the enlisted men. Nor were they happier with Doniphan's new orders: three roll calls and two and a half hours of drill each day. He kept a tight control on the town and unpleasant incidents with the civilians were rare.[20]

Fraternization seems to have been encouraged by the officers as well as the town fathers. Several fandangos were sponsored by Kearny or by businessmen; officers and enlisted men alike could attend and dance with the local girls although "the most decent and respectable were not there."

Briefly William replaced Ruff with the grazing battalion and missed some of the social life, but he could observe with others the unusual Spanish-Indian dancing described as waltz, country dance, and Indian swing mixed together. The dances were held on dirt floors (including that in the Governor's Palace). The girls were made less attractive by heavy coats of whitewash and red blossom streaks painted on their unscrubbed faces. The Americans were disturbed by the constant smoking of these women as much as they were by the appearance of drunken priests at every party. A saving feature of the fandango was—to some soldiers, at least—the

---

[20] Edwards, *Journal*, pp. 160–162. Captain Reid talked Kearny out of requiring the men to wear their coats when he reminded the general that the men had not been paid and were trading clothing for food.

music, played by two violinists and a guitarist. The same men played the music at mass the next day, changing only the tempo.[21]

Gradually Santa Fe got back to normal that August and September. The weather was beautiful, some local food was obtainable —grapes, melons, and mutton (often goat, sold by slick Mexicans) —and the construction of Fort Marcy near the plaza added comfort as well as military security. Rumors abounded that the war for New Mexico had never begun, and William, Kearny himself, and other officers made short tours of duty to learn if an uprising were planned. They found scant evidence of conspiracy but concluded that it was time to keep Kearny's promise that he would prevent the Indian tribes from molesting the Mexicans.[22]

Two unconnected events now thrust William Gilpin into more responsibility. Colonel Price sent word that his Second Regiment was well up the Arkansas and could soon relieve Doniphan; and Ruff was notified of his appointment as captain in the regular army. He could have declined and retained his higher rank with the volunteer regiment, but he had been having a difficult time with the troops. Ruff had won his rank from William at Leavenworth because of pressure from Kearny and other regulars, and he never learned the knack of catering to the civilian soldier. Doniphan appears to have shrugged off all discipline upon Ruff whose West Point experience was so often resented.[23]

Ruff resigned and returned East for reassignment. Kearny held an election for a replacement at dawn of September 18 amidst a great deal of excitement. Major Gilpin, Captain John W. Reid, and Captain Congreve Jackson were the candidates in spite of a verbal agreement among the troops to vote for no one but a private. William had a plurality as the men lined up behind their favorites, but Reid withdrew, and his supporters all moved over to Jackson's

[21] Gibson, *Journal,* pp. 215–234. The same men, same instruments, slower tempo for funerals.

[22] William wrote several letters to his brother, Henry, from Santa Fe. Henry passed on to the ex-President William's belief that the population was friendly and disposed to come under the government of the United States (Henry D. Gilpin to Martin Van Buren, January 29 and April 6, 1847, Martin Van Buren, Papers, Manuscript Division, Library of Congress).

[23] Ruff's men discussed throwing him into a dirty pond and voting him out of office; they filled his tent with sheep entrails during one absence (Connelley, *Doniphan,* p. 235).

line. Once again, the volunteers' prejudice had won; they had preferred William to a man with four years at West Point, but they favored a man with no military experience to one who had attended the Academy however briefly.

Jackson in combat was a brave man. In camp he was nearly useless: his "hobby"—emulating the local citizens by dozing in the warm autumn sunshine—did not add to his efficiency. In short, the departure of Ruff gave William Gilpin no more rank, but he now had the prestige and the onus of being the only staff officer in the regiment with West Point *or* true combat experience.

The period of recuperation was over. Kearny was ready to move west, Doniphan to move south, and some of Price's men were now entering Santa Fe. Kearny feared that the whole plan might collapse, however, if he failed to impress the surrounding Indian tribes with the might of their new great white father.

The Utes, Navajos, and Apaches roaming thousands of square miles of the Southwest, were in the habit of running off Mexican livestock with complete impunity. They would ride through the dusty streets of the isolated villages, taunting the Mexicans to pursue; they frequently boasted that they would kill off all the Mexicans but for this usefulness in raising animals for them. Occasionally the Indians did more than steal animals. About one hundred Mexicans were carried off by Navajos while Armijo was pretending to defend Santa Fe against Kearny.[24] To obtain the release of the Indians' prisoners and to get some assurance of good behavior, Kearny ordered William Gilpin to take Mounted Companies "A" and "E" into the Ute country for peace talks. Jackson and three companies departed for Navajo country, and Captain Fisher led about fifty artillerymen southward to Apache land for similar purposes. Jackson had a bit farther to travel than the other two men, but Fisher and Gilpin seem to have made rapid contact with a number of leading Indians and sent them promptly to Santa Fe to talk with Kearny. The general gave the chiefs presents, fed them, and warned them that he was the protector of all the people in New Mexico and would tolerate no more abuses. He insisted upon the return of prisoners, and this was carried out rather quickly, probably an indication of the Indians' initial respect for

[24] Susan Magoffin, *Diary*, p. 110; Edwards, *Journal*, p. 176.

the army. Kearny concluded his talks by declaring that he had to leave for California but that the Indians must obey Governor Bent. Kearny was putting the kiss of death on the merchant.

Having talked with enough Indians and having left his three subordinates in the field to conduct more talks if needed, Kearny finally left Santa Fe for California. He departed on September 25 with about three hundred dragoons to be supplemented by the Mormon Battalion under Captain Cooke as soon as they arrived in New Mexico.[25]

Three days after Kearny moved out Colonel Price arrived, extremely ill. Each day thereafter for at least two weeks detachments of his Second Regiment drifted in from the Trail. It should now have been possible for Colonel Doniphan to leave for Mexico and join General Wool for the attack on Chihuahua. An additional reason for haste was that Kearny had just released the merchants and their wagons and they were already strung along the road to El Paso for one hundred miles. Lacking military escort they feared both Indian and Mexican attack and called upon Doniphan for help.

The merchants included the Magoffin party—except James, who once again had gone ahead of everyone hoping to prepare for another bloodless conquest. For the time being, no one in Santa Fe knew what James was accomplishing or even where he was. Brother Samuel and his bride, Susan, had put behind them some of the grief accompanying their early tragedy. Susan had kept busy in Santa Fe riding, going to church or to the fandango with the ever-gallant Kearny, and even frostily driving from her rooms drunken teamsters and officers who may not have known the name "Magoffin," but knew a girl when they saw one.

What was delaying Doniphan was the fact that his forces were scattered all over the mountains and deserts of New Mexico. Jackson was at Cebolleta looking for Navajos; Gilpin was at Abiquiu

---

[25] Cooke, of course, was already in Santa Fe and did not know of his difficult new command until Kearny got word of the death of the Mormons' commander somewhere along the trail from Fort Leavenworth. The battalion was encumbered with twenty-seven women (some of whom were wives) and a number of children. Price ultimately sent them back north from Santa Fe in the general direction of the great Mormon migration.

awaiting new orders, and small groups were en route from Santa
Fe to relieve them so that they could move farther into the desert.

On the 11th of October Tom Fitzpatrick galloped into Doniphan's headquarters in Santa Fe with a new express from Kearny.
Plans had to be changed again. About 150 miles out of Santa Fe
Kearny had run into Lieutenant Kit Carson reporting from Cali-
fornia to President Polk. The news was exciting, yet once again
the troops felt let down; California had fallen to Frémont and the
United States Navy. The Stars and Stripes flew over Monterey. No
trouble. At the same moment, Kearny, hearing new complaints of
Navajo pillaging in western New Mexico, changed his organization
again. He sent some of the dragoons back to Price and ordered
Gilpin to move against the Navajos when he had finished with the
Utes. Jackson and Doniphan were to expand this show of force.
Kearny then resumed his march to California and ambushment,
drafting poor Kit Carson (who had been promised a leave in Santa
Fe) to be his guide to California. Fitzpatrick swapped duties with
Carson and would go on to Washington with the mistaken an-
nouncement that California was secure. The war was moving too
fast for the Army of the West to catch up.

William Gilpin had carried out his first assignment quickly. He
had reached the Chama River late in September and had left about
one hundred men there. For speed he took only eighty-five soldiers
some hundred miles above Taos, where he met his Utah Indians.
He talked solemnly with several tribes, got a good response, and
hustled fifty or sixty of their leaders down to Santa Fe to see Doniphan. That very day (October 13) they signed peace treaties with
the Colonel and gave their promise to let the Mexicans alone.[26]

That done, William rode back to his troops with the new mission.
Anticipating a winter campaign in badly broken country, William
spent the next few days getting extra supplies and mules and
horses. His wagons he sent back to Santa Fe as useless in the
mountains that he would penetrate. The men were not properly
outfitted, however, through failure of the army itself.

Most of the men, volunteer and regular army alike, had not been

[26] Gibson, *Journal*, pp. 252–253. Doniphan's official account stated that William rode two hundred miles "to the Rocky mountains . . ." (U.S. Senate, Executive Document No. 1, 30th Cong., 1st Sess., 1848, pp. 495–496).

paid since they left Fort Leavenworth five months before. The paymaster brought to New Mexico almost nothing but checks, normally good enough in the Santa Fe trade, but not acceptable now. The
Mexicans would take no paper at all and the "American" merchants discounted it up to 25 per cent. For the protection of his men
Doniphan ordered the paying held up until specie could be sent.
(Through extraordinary effort some gold was brought to Santa Fe
in January, 1847, but none was passed on to Doniphan's men, by
then in old Mexico.)

This scarcity of money worked a greater hardship on the troops
than the mere annoyance of not being able to distribute it in
friendly fashion to Santa Fe taverns. Part of the unreceived money
was clothing allowance and so the men were inadequately outfitted. Few had even one complete uniform. Worse, the one-half and
often one-third food ration put the men on their own to supplement
the mess, for even the army itself had no credit.[27] The Mexicans
suffered a surprisingly small amount of theft: on the contrary they
(and the Indians too) profited well by trading food for the scarce
articles of clothing. Many a Santa Fean's jacket was ornamented
with buttons bearing the insignia, "U.S."

Underfed and improperly clothed, William's battalion prepared
for a winter in the Navajo country. Some of Price's men moved
into Abiquiu to help that portion of William's command that remained behind. Since no man who accompanied William on the
Navajo campaign kept a journal, most of what is known comes
from remarks of these new men interpolated into official records of
Doniphan and Gilpin.

William began his search for the Navajos in early November,
1846, by riding north through the Chama River valley in the face
of a strong wind that turned chilly rain into a blizzard early on the

[27] One soldier paid a settler one dollar for a cotton handkerchief and traded
two needles to some Mexican girls for six ears of corn and some onions (William H. Richardson, *Journal of William H. Richardson*, pp. 29, 39; Gibson,
*Journal*, p. 245–250). One of Price's officers borrowed $1,000 to feed his men by
taking the female owner of a gambling establishment to an army ball. A war
correspondent tried to report the incident, but the officer promised to shoot him
if he did, so "he gave up the scoop instead of the ghost" (William Clark Kennerly, *Persimmon Hill*, pp. 191–192).

morning of his departure. For the next three weeks he and his men traveled in almost constant snowfall.

As William could not bring wagons with him he had substituted a pack-mule train driven by a number of Mexicans. He also had twenty Pueblos to make his force look stronger, two guides, and two interpreters, augmenting Companies "A" and "E."

For six days they plodded through the drifts toward the source of the Chama in the San Juan Mountains, so beloved by William. They crossed the Continental Divide, bringing them into what is now Colorado, probably by way of Cumbres Pass, just under 10,000 feet in altitude. They were in a region where snowfall averages three hundred inches a year, and in the same mountains where two years later Frémont suffered tragedy for failure to use the route William followed. Sleep was nearly impossible, for the men had no tents and had to move about to keep warm. Drinking water was unaccountably bad, and many of the soldiers took sick. Two died and were buried in the San Juan snows, far above ground.[28]

About the 8th of November William became more optimistic for his mission. Off in the distance he could see an occasional Indian or two—Navajos, he was told by his guides. On the same day he noticed that more and more of the unfrozen, swifter streams were flowing westward and inevitably would join the San Juan along which the tribe had lived protected from the outsider for three hundred years.[29] William sent scouts out to persuade the Indians to talk with him, but none would come until they grouped in such numbers as to lose their fear of Gilpin's weather-beaten battalion.

As the Indians indicated that they would treat with the army, William sent word to Doniphan that he would soon meet with him but would first try to reach the main group of Navajos. Doniphan was meanwhile moving by a more southerly route, by way of Albuquerque, to an encampment at Bear Springs where Fort Wingate was later built, and just south of the present town of Gallup.

William's detachment followed the San Juan River for about forty miles. At this point the river was some fifty yards wide, very clear, its banks brimming with Navajo horses, sheep, and goats.

---

[28] Connelley, *Doniphan*, pp. 298–300, 593–594.
[29] Edward H. Spicer, *Cycles of Conquest*, p. 213–214.

Somewhat reluctantly William then moved away from the river in a more southwesterly course toward the Chuska Mountains, known to the Navajos as the Goods of Value range, and the eastern border of the Navajo lands.

This part of the march was over barren sandy plains and immense fields of gypsum, covered with pebbles worn smooth by attrition, which rendered the travel extremely laborious, the whole way being entirely destitute of either wood or grass, and only supplied with water which is both bitter to the taste and nauseating to the stomach.[30]

The men had to lead their horses and wade through the snow when they ascended the passes of the Chuska range. Many animals were crippled and had to be left; others slipped and were killed on the granite slabs below. About half of the battalion no longer had animals to ride even when the trail permitted.[31] The pass downward posed almost the same problems, and horses frequently had to be dragged out of deep crevasses.

The Missourians finally camped in a high plateau region where the Navajos grew their wheat. In other times the land would have appeared attractive to William but the unceasing snow had so slowed travel as to threaten the existence of his whole detachment. Briefly William visited the Canyon de Chelly which he assumed was the military and religious headquarters of the Navajos. It was in this deep, twenty-mile long canyon, settled from the fourth century, that Kit Carson in 1864 ruthlessly destroyed animals and crops and brought the Navajos to final terms.[32]

[30] Connelley, *Doniphan*, pp. 300–301.

[31] Ruth Underhill says that the Chuskas are "jumbles of cliffs and boulders with only a few passes between them, which white Americans later found almost insurmountable" (*The Navajos*, p. 63). The same region was visited in 1849 by army engineers under Lieutenant James H. Simpson, accompanying Colonel John Washington and his force of about five hundred. Another treaty was forced from the Navajos, and it meant as little as Gilpin's. Simpson, aided by the Kern brothers, made a survey of the Navajo country. He disagreed with much of the detail found in Connelley but described the Chuska pass as the most formidable Washington had ever seen. James H. Simpson, *Navajo Expedition: Journal of Lt. James H. Simpson*, p. 75.

[32] The Navajo's "retreats and caverns are at a distance to the west, in high and inaccessible mountains, where troops of the United States will find great difficulty in overtaking and subduing them, but where the Mexicans have never thought of penetrating. The Navajos may be termed the lords of New Mexico."

William felt that his job was about done. A great many Indians visited his camp and gave assurances that they wanted peace with the white man. The Navajos gave him presents, restored many stolen horses, and agreed that nine chiefs would leave immediately for a meeting with Doniphan. (The horses, William learned, had been stolen from Jackson's battalion some days before.) Believing that his nine delegates could speak for the nation, William left the canyon country on November 19 with about thirty of the better mounted troops for the rendezvous at Bear Springs with Doniphan. William—proudly bearing pieces of petrified wood—was on time, Doniphan and Jackson trooping in the next afternoon.

Talks commenced at that time, but were postponed during an uneasy evening as white and Navajo considered the prospect of treachery. William and Doniphan felt more secure when on the following day Captain Waldo arrived with the remaining 150 men of Gilpin's battalion to help balance the surprising, and steadily increasing, mass of Navajos.

On the 22nd of November, 1846, the United States government concluded its first treaty with the Navajo nation. Doniphan, Jackson, and William signed this Treaty of Ojo del Oso with nine Navajo chiefs. Whether these were the same nine men that William found at Canyon de Chelly is impossible to say. Hundreds of Navajos arrived at the Springs in the course of two or three days. The treaty called for peace, commerce, the return of all prisoners and recently "acquired" property, and protection of the Mexican and Pueblo people. Doniphan exchanged his presents for colorful blankets (which he brought home), and the talks ended. Good work, well done—but knowledgeable men like the Bents knew better. No nine men could bind a few thousand Indians as though they were a state; moreover, too many scores were unsettled in the Southwest to permit peace, even had the Navajos wanted it.[33]

---

Observations of Lieutenant Emory just before William began his campaign (Emory, *Notes*, p. 47). William's men were the first American troops ever to enter the Navajos' country.

[33] Lieutenant Emory believed that Governor Armijo had kept himself in office in New Mexico by a deal with the Navajos whom he never let his troops attack. Mexicans, Pueblos, and many other people were spoiling for a chance at the lords of New Mexico. Some of Doniphan's men felt that the Navajos got off too easily. "But the Nabajoes . . . will continue to steal sheep and commit other

Among the tribes who suffered greatly from these Navajos were the Zuñis, whose country was due south of the Bear Springs area. Doniphan resolved to settle some of their disputes before returning to his command, now scattered up and down the Río Grande from Santa Fe to Socorro. He, Jackson, and three Navajos, protected by Gilpin's battalion, made a two-day, sixty-mile march to Zuñi pueblo.

Zuñi was a series of villages, presumably comprising one of the Seven Cities of Cíbola which had been reported by Fray Marcos to Coronado in 1540. William told the folks back in Missouri, "This people, many of them albinos, one of the lost specks of the antique Aztec race, inhabit a solitary city in the center of the immense plain traversed by a northern branch of the Gila River."[34]

This location was vulnerable to Navajo attack, and many Zuñi women and children were carried off to Chelly and captivity. At Zuñi Gilpin's men camped in the open just outside the main pueblos, but Colonel Doniphan and a few others took the Navajos and occupied an adobe building inside the town.[35] Doniphan, carefully guarding the three Indians with William's men, found himself faced by some two hundred Zuñis whose leaders began to rant at the Navajos about their many crimes. If we can believe the recorded rejoinder, the Navajos sneered at the Zuñis that their war was a matter of long standing, that the Navajos were winning it, and that the Zuñis were cowards who killed women and children. Zuñis now threatened Navajos, and Doniphan warned both groups that his was a mission of friendship which he would enforce.

The next day, November 26, the three parties moved to William's headquarters and drew up a treaty between the two tribes.

---

outrages, until they are well whipped a few times; but unfortunately, like the Seminoles or Comanches, they are not easily caught." Edwards, *Journal*, p. 212 n. Oddly enough, in his brief military career William campaigned against all three of these tribes.

[34] Connelley, *Doniphan*, p. 594. Lieutenant Edward F. Beale passed through Zuñi in 1857 on a road survey and confirmed William's report of many albinos, "very fair skins, white hair, and blue eyes" in Edwards, *Journal*, p. 203 n.

[35] Doniphan described the Zuñi town as four solid blocks with two right angle streets. All of the buildings were two stories high and made of sun-dried brick. The solid walls facing the streets were all joined. The Zuñis entered their homes by ladders to the second story.

Doniphan felt that he could do little more; he saw to the safety of his three Navajos, and set out for Laguna and Valverde to reassemble his command in the Río Grande Valley. The war could wait no longer.

What had William Gilpin accomplished? Probably nothing permanent and little that was temporary. Navajos not represented at Bear Springs were in these very days continuing their thievery in other parts of New Mexico, and it was to be eighteen years before their complete subjugation could be brought about, and then by the most ruthless methods.

This is not to belittle the campaign. William's march was extraordinary. Counting his missions to the Utes, the Navajos, and the Zuñi, he must have traveled over seven hundred miles in less than a month, not deducting time for parleys. The weather was miserable. In one day thirty-six inches of snow fell in the mountains that he was crossing. Bernard De Voto maintains that the march would have been prodigious even for well-equipped troops—which his were far from being—and that only the Missourians' audacity kept their scalps from hanging permanently in the Canyon de Chelly. David Lavender calls the march "tremendous." Byers' early study of Colorado compares the movement to Frémont's disaster for hardship and suffering. Contemporaries of the marchers were also impressed. One of Kearny's topographical officers, J. W. Abert (in Emory's *Notes*), sympathized with their "ragged appearance" from "constant exposure" when he saw the battalion along the Río Grande two weeks later. Another diarist, Marcellus Edwards, noted that most of the men had to be remounted three times before getting back to Doniphan.[36]

William's own account exaggerated when he declared that his command reduced the Utes and Navajos to peace, but at the time he could quite honestly believe that his mission had been a success. For about a year the Navajos were tolerably peaceful, and in the Taos uprising of the winter of 1846–1847 they took no part.

Immediately after the Zuñi treaty was signed, William led his battalion back across the mountains to Laguna, then down the

[36] Connelley, *Doniphan*, pp. 303, 594; Bernard De Voto, *The Year of Decision: 1846*, p. 390; Lavender, *Bent's Fort*, p. 274; William N. Byers, *Encyclopedia of Biography of Colorado*, I, 29; Emory, *Notes*, p. 506; Edwards, *Journal*, p. 212.

valley of the Río Puerco and the Río Grande to Socorro. On the latter's banks the men held reunions with the other Missouri Volunteers who had been slowly moving along the river. Rumors had been frequent that the Navajos had destroyed the Second Battalion, and doubtless all of the regiment felt more secure now that they were finally reunited for the first time in months.

Socorro was a "small, wretched place," looking like a prairie-dog town, full of begging women, decorated with alternate layers of facial paint and dirt, and of loafing, pilfering, dirty men. So said Lieutenant George Augustus Frederick Ruxton, twenty-five years old, traveler, adventurer, writer, possibly British spy. Ruxton, in this year of the southwest movement, was going from Veracruz and Mexico City north to Chihuahua and the Rockies.

Ruxton was a literate observer and had seen much of interest to the Army of the West; he had passed the trader Speyer well beyond Chihuahua, hoping to sell his goods in Durango. This had been in mid-October. With Speyer, but guiding seven wagons of goods of his own, was ex-Governor Armijo, asking about the price of cotton in Durango, and wondering what the people of Mexico thought of his defense of Santa Fe. Ruxton told this "mountain of fat" that the general and the New Mexicans were all considered "a pack of arrant cowards" by most Mexicans.

Ruxton estimated that he passed five hundred volunteers strung out over one hundred miles with their supplies and ammunition incredibly unguarded. At Valverde camp, a few miles below Socorro, he watched the reassembling and reorganizing of Doniphan's command. Most of the Missouri merchants had stopped at Valverde awaiting Doniphan's return from the Navajo country. Gilpin's men arrived and a rest for them would have been ordered, but the merchants had been at Valverde for several weeks and the grass was gone. Some cattle had even died of starvation. Provisions were disappearing and wild game was almost impossible to find except at great distances.

Doniphan's regiment appalled Ruxton. He found no discipline, no regulations, no cleanliness. Camp and men alike were filthy; unshaven, undressed, men lounged about, playing cards and swearing at their officers. The men voted not to mount guard duty and promptly lost eight hundred sheep to Navajos. Said Ruxton, "These very men, however, were as full of fight as game cocks, and shortly after defeated four times their number of Mexicans at Sacramento, near Chihuahua."[37]

Doniphan wanted more artillery and sent to Price in Santa Fe for it, but could not await its arrival. Several weeks elapsed before the company was available to him. He appointed a new adjutant to replace the one who had died in Navajo country, said good-by to Congressman-Private Willard Hall, who was en route to Missouri at last, and ordered the march on to Mexico, at dawn of December 12, 1846.

William Gilpin had enjoyed perhaps two days of rest since he had left Santa Fe in mid-September. Nevertheless, his battalion departed two days before Jackson's and five days before Doniphan with the rear guard and the merchants. William and four captains (including Waldo) had about three hundred men under their command as they set out for El Paso. Within a few miles of Valverde William entered the Jornada del Muerto, an extremely arid region which the army had to cross because steep mountains forced the Chihuahua trail away from the Río Grande. The Jornada was eighty to ninety miles in length, lacking wood and grass, and with seasonal water available only at a distance from the trail made risky by lurking Apaches.

The soldiers felt that Lieutenant Colonel Jackson properly should have commanded the forward echelon into the campaign, "but Doniphan, as everybody else would do, makes a distinction between the two men." Nowhere is there evidence that William felt that he was bearing the brunt of the southwestern struggle, but the comments of his subordinates became increasingly appreciative as time wore on. As for Jackson, one soldier recorded, "as long as he can get a rock to sit on in the sunshine and another little one to peck with, he will sit all day and forget his dinner. . . . He has been lying in camp here, where the dust nearly suffocates, not knowing or caring what to do."[38]

The battalion passed through the Jornada without serious consequences. The nights were bitter, and lacking fuel William decided to push his men as rapidly as possible. By resting only a few hours each night and resuming the march at two each morning the men

---

[37] George A. F. Ruxton, *Ruxton of the Rockies*, pp. 132–133, 168, 174–175. Drunkenness, insubordination, fights, even duels were commonplace.

[38] Edwards, *Journal*, pp. 186, 215–216.

were able to traverse the desert in three days. Men and animals were parched and exhausted and nerves were on edge from the long marches and occasional sneak visits by Mexicans and Apaches, but no men were lost. Long before the Río Grande could be seen again the horses smelled the water and dashed, riders and all, miles to its refreshing course.

At Doña Ana William's command nervously awaited the rest of the regiment. The men learned some disquieting news. In this very region James Magoffin had been attacked by Apaches, had lost his animals, wagons, and goods, and had been taken as a Mexican prisoner to Chihuahua where he might be shot for treason since he held Mexican citizenship papers. Gone were the dreams of another easy conquest if the negotiator was a prisoner.

Then the rumor (an accurate one) was spread that General Wool was not on his way to Chihuahua but might go somewhere else and leave the entire western Mexican campaign to Doniphan's thousand volunteers. And merchants and natives reported the massing of 2,500 Mexicans near El Paso, readying at last for a stand.

Doniphan, about four days behind Gilpin, sent a message to learn what William needed. His reply was, "Two hundred men," and so Doniphan hustled Jackson and that number on through the Jornada. Jackson's speed was so great that the popular explanation was that he was hungry.

For a change the Gilpin battalion could loaf until Doniphan arrived. The weather turned delightful; there was plenty of water, fruit, and corn meal. Sheep were confiscated from Mexican peasants but with valid promises to pay; for the first time in weeks Gilpin's horses had sufficient grain. William's men happily acknowledged his ability as a provider.

During the next three or four days several false alarms briefly aroused the men, but they saw no Mexican troops. Jackson arrived and then Doniphan with the struggling, swearing teamsters. William told the Colonel that they might have trouble taking El Paso; William's reputation for optimism was so strong that his comment worried the troops. Nevertheless, rejoicing and relaxation were the order of the day; one of Doniphan's men reaching Doña Ana on the twenty-third found his friends "all noisy and drinking." The next day they left Doña Ana in the direction of El Paso. On Christmas Day they had traveled about eighteen miles to a spot called El Brazito on the river where Doniphan decided to spend the noon hour.

As usual, William's battalion was in front and dangerously scattered while Jackson with about one half of the regiment was several hours to the rear. William's men were searching for wood, stripping and picketing horses, and preparing for dinner. Some woodgatherers, more than a mile from camp, sounded an alarm that the Mexican army was rushing on them. The shouts and dust clouds brought the Missourians back, throwing away logs, or resaddling horses as they ran. Only an estimated 150 men were in camp in any position to fight when the Mexicans appeared.

Doniphan and some officers were playing loo for a handsome Mexican horse that had been captured. The colonel was winning at the moment and was annoyed by the excitement. Before throwing down his hand he decreed that the game would be renewed after the emergency. He, William, and Lieutenant Colonel D. D. Mitchell (detached temporarily from Price's command) belatedly organized a defense. Hardly a score of horses was available so the regiment in its first battle fought as infantrymen. William and three companies held the right or southern wing, nearest El Paso; Mitchell and two companies took the left or northern wing, and Doniphan commanded the center. That portion of the baggage that was on hand was protected behind the center below a slight hill. Here Doniphan stationed himself.

The Mexican force, set at 1,200 by papers found after the battle, drew up in a single line with their cavalry facing Mitchell. Gallantly, optimistically, or incredibly, the Mexicans threw away their advantage and stopped for discussions. A lieutenant rode to about sixty yards from the Americans, lowered in salute a black flag enlivened with two skulls and cross bones and the slogan, "Libertad o muerte," and demanded that the Colonel appear before the Mexican general to arrange for the American surrender. In the American tradition an interpreter anticipated Doniphan's reply and called out a "Go to hell!" The lieutenant wheeled back to his lines and the battle of El Brazito began.

A small affair, it was nevertheless revealing. Some regulars with Doniphan feared that his volunteers would run from what appeared to be smartly equipped and well-disciplined Mexican troops. But the Mexicans were also a mixture of regulars and militia, and the latter were more conscript than volunteer. Furthermore the Americans soon made the happy discovery that Mexican arms were ineffective at almost any range. About twenty-five minutes were needed to demonstrate that the El Paso area had little better resistance than that of Santa Fe.

Several soldiers' accounts agree on the outline of the battle. As the Americans placed their backs to the river in a north-south line the Mexican dragoons concentrated their rifle fire on Mitchell's men holding the American left. Doniphan issued the order, "Prepare to squat," as clear as it was unprecedented, and he ordered the regiment to withhold its fire until the Mexicans were within sixty yards. The attackers fired three separate rounds rather harmlessly. Much of the wild shooting struck the hill behind the Americans; said Doniphan later (as reported by Herr and Wallace), "Their shot were falling thick all around me. I put spurs to my horse, charged to the front, hallowed 'Come on boys.' The boys thought I was brave as hell but they did not know what drove me there."

The Mexican left advanced against Gilpin's battalion, fired their three rounds, and turned and fled when William's men jumped up and took one shot at very close range. The same sequence occurred in the center except that Doniphan's company captured the lone Mexican howitzer, "drawn by one mule and as near of no account as anything could be." (It had fired a "bushel of copper junk" ten feet over the Americans' heads.)

The Mexican cavalry in their scarlet coats and plumed helmets, with dazzling sabers, lances, and pennants, made one gay dash at Mitchell's companies. They were easily turned to the extreme left of the American line and suddenly realized the possibility of sweeping in behind Mitchell toward the baggage. The wagoners, who included men with more combat experience than most of the regiment, now had their turn at the cavalry. The Mexican formation broke completely and fled. Captain Reid of William's battalion had organized 15 or 20 Missourians (usually with the wrong horse and saber) into a cavalry unit that was able to enter the battle at this moment and throw the Mexicans into complete confusion.

Casualties for the Mexicans were believed to be about 40 killed, 150 wounded (including some who died in El Paso), and a few prisoners. The American loss was 7 wounded, none seriously—an astonishing, and fortunate, result, considering the odds and the American lack of preparation. Colonel Jackson and the rest of the regiment arrived breathless and pouting as the Mexicans scampered back toward El Paso. Jackson had spent most of the battle trying to find his mule.

There was plunder enough, if not glory, for everyone. The officers went back to their cards, but found to Doniphan's disgust that the horse had disappeared. Some of the soldiers acquired decent blankets and jackets and every one of the "veterans" celebrated, for the Mexicans left behind bread, fruit, wine, and *aguardiente.* "Every one is *omega* today," reported one soldier to his journal.[39]

The army rested two days before approaching El Paso, which William assumed would be heavily defended. Several nighttime alarms were heard, bringing orders to spill the steaming kettles to put out the cook-fires. Rekindling the wet fires was fatiguing and discouraging work and after one more alarm, a loud, melancholy voice called into the darkness, "Save the soup!"[40]

On the 27th Doniphan marched on old El Paso (on the right bank of the Río Grande) and was met by a flag of truce and offers to surrender the city. Terms were settled upon and the occupation of the place began.

Reasonably secure in El Paso, Doniphan now faced his most important decision. He had had almost no official communications, but repeated rumors led him to conclude that higher headquarters were changing plans without informing him. His original instructions had been to march to Chihuahua and there to join General John Wool's army from Texas to capture that city if Wool had not already done so. But the War Department had decided that

[39] Details about this skirmish come from Connelley, *Doniphan*, pp. 370–379; Jacob S. Robinson, *A Journal of the Santa Fé Expedition under Colonel Doniphan*, pp. 64–68; John K. Herr and Edward S. Wallace, *The Story of the United States Cavalry*, p. 52; Edwards, *Journal*, pp. 217–237; Gibson, *Journal*, pp. 298–310; Susan Magoffin, *Diary*, pp. 180–182; Frank S. Edwards, A Campaign in *New Mexico with Colonel Doniphan*, pp. 80–84. Curiously, Bancroft does not mention the Navajo or Brazito campaigns at all. Logistical detective work seeking the still-unknown site of the battle is employed by Andrew Armstrong in "The Brazito Battlefield," *New Mexico Historical Review*, XXXV (January, 1960), 63–74.

[40] Edwards, *Journal*, pp. 237–238.

Taylor was in trouble near Saltillo, and had already diverted Wool's army to assist Taylor while Doniphan rested in El Paso.

Regardless of where Wool might be, Doniphan would not leave for Chihuahua without his artillery—still with Price in Santa Fe. Price feared to release this battalion because from mid-December on he heard whispers of an uprising by some of the less docile Mexicans and Indians. Just as Doniphan finished routing the Mexicans at El Brazito, Price thwarted a rebellion in Santa Fe. Price thought correctly that he might have more trouble, so he retained the artillery throughout January of 1847.[41]

While waiting, Doniphan strengthened his own position. As soon as he dared he brought his troops out of the wind and dust and let them camp in El Paso among the natives, many of whom wore bandages donned after Brazito. He put William Gilpin in charge of mounted scouts. William found some arms and ammunition and scattered a few hundred Mexican troops who appeared to be fleeing from Wool in the east rather than coming to redeem The Pass.

Within the town business was brisk. Some of the itinerant merchants set up shop, sold to Mexicans, then lent to Doniphan so that he could buy supplies from the Mexicans. A few of the daring businessmen sneaked their wagons out of town at night, headed for Chihuahua—270 miles to the south—a dangerous gamble for better prices. In his practical fashion Doniphan organized the remaining wagoners into a battalion under Major Samuel Owens, one of their own (and a leading creditor of Doniphan), and ordered them into the Missouri Volunteers.

The Missourians felt some uneasiness in El Paso; the four thousand or more Mexicans in the municipality could have done great damage to the regiment of less than a thousand, but they did nothing. Their poverty, ignorance, and isolation had developed no sense of Mexican nationalism that could help them overcome a vigorous, well-armed invader. The greatest fear, in fact, of most of the Mexicans north of the city of Chihuahua was of the frequent Indian raids—raids that made existence terrifying to farmers who settled too far from forts.

Wisely, Doniphan and Gilpin utilized this fact and made—and

[41] Price and Governor Bent were informed of the uprising by a Santa Fe prostitute (Connelley, *Doniphan*, p. 93).

kept—promises to protect the Mexicans from Indian marauders. In the El Paso area the Apaches played the same role as the Navajos played farther north, and when Apache attacks were reported, the Missouri Volunteers pursued them with enthusiasm and success, for the Apaches neglected to distinguish between Mexican and American livestock. Doniphan went further and hired professional Indian hunters to take the offensive. Some of these men were later to help him against Mexican troops in Sacramento.

William, as the leading disciplinarian of the regiment, found that during their weeks in El Paso, he and Doniphan encountered more problems with the Missourians than with the Mexicans. The numerous fandangos institutionalized a fraternization that in some instances was permanent, and not all of the Missouri boys went home to Missouri after the war. Three soldiers were court-martialled for attacking a Mexican girl. Gambling and horse racing so occupied victor and vanquished alike that Doniphan prohibited these activities to prevent disorder in the town. Drunkenness, however, persisted beyond the officers' control. Wine was as available as the friendly native girls and very inexpensive. With few military duties the soldiers thus brightened the soft winter days in their new-found Eden. One evening William gave an eggnog party for the officers; a fight ensued, and one Lieutenant Richard Wells had a bowie knife thrust through the neck just below the ear. Reportedly he bled both whiskey and blood, yet lived to practice medicine with the surgeon who patched him.

In this manner the time passed. William's men were rested if not reclothed, and more important, the animals were brought back to health and gotten in shape for the next long march. On February 2, 1847, Major Meriwether Lewis Clark rode into El Paso at the head of 117 men and six cannon, explaining that Price had held him up because of the uprising of the natives at Christmas time.

Clark's men fired the six pieces as a salutation, to the delight of the Mexicans standing on top of their adobe houses. In reply the captured Mexican howitzer was readied with powder for a blank round. Lacking better wadding, someone supplied a pair of socks and crammed them on top of the powder. The gun was fired with little regard for direction, and a Missourian was struck in the face by the socks. His cry was far greater than his injury, and he wanted the gunners punished. His reasoning was that he would have been better off struck by a solid ball than by a pair of socks that had been worn unchanged from Leavenworth to El Paso.[42]

With the arrival of the artillery Doniphan delayed no longer. Some of the merchants started to move, and Doniphan sent Mitchell with them. Four or five days elapsed before all of the regiment was ready, and during that interval the men heard of the second New Mexican rebellion. This one nearly succeeded: Governor Charles Bent was visiting his family in Taos on January 19, when a mob of drunken Pueblos stormed the jail for the release of two Indians charged with theft. When the sheriff, Steve Lee refused, he was murdered along with the prefect. The Indians then set out after Bent, who defended a number of women and children (including his own family and the wife of Kit Carson) in his home but was shot and killed. His scalp was taken and paraded around the streets as the Indians terrorized the town.

What had appeared to be a drunken riot now gave signs of being an organized revolt against the Americans. Lieutenant Governor Archuleta had not obtained his vice-royalty across the Río Grande; using the priests, he had fanned a spark of patriotism into Mexicans, and reinforced them with loot-happy Pueblos. In various parts of northern New Mexico about twenty Americans were murdered, and cries for help rang out to Bent's Fort and Santa Fe.

Suppression was Price's task, and he reacted energetically. Within three weeks Price won some skirmishes and a bloody pitched battle, and he captured Taos Pueblo. Several leading conspirators were killed and others captured. The latter were prosecuted by busy little Frank Blair before a judge and jury highly prejudiced against the insurrectionists. Those found guilty were put to death almost immediately.[43]

Fragmentary accounts of these events reached Doniphan, but he dared not send help to Price or remain longer in El Paso. A Mexi-

[42] *Ibid.*, pp. 395–397.

[43] Apparently about fifteen were hanged. The bad behavior of some of Price's command and the constant rumors of Mexican victories encouraged boldness on the part of the natives. Susan Magoffin heard numerous stories that William Gilpin's command had been captured or wiped out because they so often were beyond touch with the rest of the regiment. Most detail for the Taos revolt is from Lewis H. Garrard, *Wah-To-Yah and the Taos Trail.*

can counterattack could easily cut him off from all communication, just as the desert had already cut him off from most supplies. Living off the land of the conquered, the First Missouri Volunteers had to keep moving to be safe.

By the 8th of February the entire regiment, now over 1,100 in number, was on the trail again, taking along as hostages a few individuals who seemed most likely to fan rebellion in Doniphan's rear.

The march on Chihuahua moved William and the Volunteers three weeks deeper into Mexican territory. The road included several *jornadas* (a word now thoroughly dreaded by the Missourians), including one of sixty miles. The precious water was often patiently dripped into scabbards to provide men with a drink in the worst stretches of the desert. Drifting sand dunes required triple teams on the commissary wagons, and often the mules were assisted by cursing, sweating infantrymen. The merchants' huge Conestogas, eighteen- or twenty-feet high at the ends and creaking with two tons of goods, often sank to the hubs in soft sand, and six yoke of oxen were not enough to keep the wagons going. But the army could recover dangerously lost time on some places where the road was packed hard.

The diarists have much to say about the weather, however, good road or bad. Some days were hot, some balmy; once or twice it snowed, and the privates blamed Doniphan or William for the "northers" as well as the consistently chilly nights. The wind blew continuously, and the dust filled canteens and eyes and got into food and under saddles with equal disregard for the comfort of men and animals. On February 21 the regiment reached Ojo Caliente and enjoyed a bath of warm, clear water before another day without grass, wood, or water.

Only a few incidents seem to stand out in the men's minds during those weeks. They frequently saw Mexican soldiers who quickly dispersed and Apaches who stole livestock. Fair success was achieved by Reid or Waldo or other mounted units pursuing these lurkers. The greatest threat to the Missourians came from an unexpected source.

One noon in late February some of Gilpin's men were baking bread from the "wretched native flour, now our only fare." A fire spilled over into the tall grass where, driven by a strong wind, it soon got out of control. For several hours the fire raged more or less harmlessly because the wind was blowing it away from the camp. The next day, however, the fire enlarged itself and leaped across the desert and mountain in ten- and twenty-foot waves. William's battalion failed to control it in spite of clearing the brush with their sabers and driving their horses and wagons back and forth across a single fire break.

Almost the entire regiment was finally employed in setting backfires and cutting breaks that ultimately separated the fire from unburned grass. Many square miles of land lay black beyond the Army of the West, and smoke billowed to the Sacramento River.

William saw other signs of disaster along the Chihuahua trail. Villages, homes, and even magnificent haciendas had been abandoned during the past two decades because of the Mexicans' inability to cope with Apaches—an accurate indication that the Mexicans could do little with Americans as well.

The Mexicans in the northwestern provinces, such as Chihuahua, were receiving little help from the central government. Santa Anna concentrated as many men as he could under his own command opposite Taylor, and sent a mere 250 men from Durango to help the governor of Chihuahua. Nevertheless, a new governor and a new general in that state momentarily stirred a spirit of resistance to the Americans, a spirit they hoped would manifest itself against the Missouri regiment.

The Mexican forces moved fifteen miles north of Chihuahua where the road from El Paso passed some low, steep hills bordering the Sacramento River. Between three and four thousand troops were scattered in the hills above the road and a front echelon was placed on a low plateau between the Arroyo Seco (a completely dry river bed) and the river. The location was sound enough, giving the Mexicans depth as well as ideal artillery locations covering the road. Ready with ropes and hand-cuffs for their expected prisoners, the Mexicans awaited the Missourians.

On Sunday, February 28, 1847, Doniphan marched on Chihuahua. His organization was a pragmatic answer to his problem of the four hundred wagons and their million dollars worth of goods. They had to be protected, yet they might help protect the army. He placed three companies of cavalry in front, then shortened his line by putting the wagons into four columns or files about thirty feet apart. In the three moving alleys thus created, Gilpin's Second Battalion took the left, the First Battalion marched in the right, and the artillery was in the very center.

Given the situation, the Americans made a fortuitous change of direction. Out of range, they took an abrupt right turn from the road along the Arroyo Seco and crossed the bed at a point which served to flank the Mexicans. While the latter shifted the direction of their defense, the Americans raced into the soft sand; drivers yelled at their teams, while infantry shoveled, pushed wheels, or jerked at ropes. Once through the Arroyo, men, animals, and wagons together scrambled up the forty or fifty feet to the plateau.

Before the regiment could re-form, the Mexican cavalry moved across the plateau. At a range of one-half mile Major Clark's artillery began to fire, and the cavalry, perhaps one thousand in number, simply disintegrated, as horsemen fled to the hills across the river. For one very important hour an artillery battle was fought while Americans made their new positions secure.

The long-range artillery fight could have but one result, for the Mexican powder was so ineffective that balls hit the ground and bounded clumsily through the American lines. Jeering at Mexican marksmanship, the soldiers—and one extraordinary horse—hopped and skipped away from the lumbering projectiles. The only danger lay in the cannon balls that struck forty or fifty yards short and rebounded into the massed troops and wagons. In this fashion a few men were wounded and some animals were killed.

American artillery meanwhile was winning the battle and holding off the Mexicans until Doniphan was ready to attack. Doniphan always disclaimed any tactical skill, and on this day he let command get away from him. As he sat whittling, one knee hooked around his saddle horn (with about one thousand Mexican spectators watching from the hills nearby) he ordered a cavalry charge. Somehow Doniphan's adjutant ordered the unit commanders to attack, then halted some of them in exposed positions, an act that threatened the safety of the few that continued as well as those that had stopped.

William's battalion was in the latter group, and a soldier beside him heard Gilpin say, "Are these men to be sacrificed? I will not stand it!" as he ordered his men to resume the attack. His battalion was on the Mexicans' extreme right at a point where some of the

cavalry tried to re-form. William turned his attention to that group
and prevented a renewed cavalry charge while his remaining
companies drove through the Mexican redoubts.

By this time the First Battalion under Mitchell had also topped
the plateau, and the American artillery could move into position
to shell the Mexicans on the hills behind the river. Without their
horses, Gilpin's battalion climbed the rough hills in a flanking
movement, which combined with the artillery fire, caused the last
Mexican units to turn and run.

An incredible victory it was by any standards. The defeated
general said that he had only 1,200 men, but Doniphan's report to
the War Department declared that confiscated records set the force
at 4,200 against his 1,100. The casualties were literally almost unbelievable: a reported 300 Mexicans killed, a similar number
wounded, and 40 captured. The Americans lost Major Owens, the
wagon commander, who rashly left his wagons in the rear and
was probably the first man up the plateau. A half-dozen were
wounded, and one of these died a few days later.

No Mexican unit showed any will to resist, and only one Mexican officer was killed, yet the army was typically top-heavy. The
difference in artillery, resulting from defective Mexican powder,
was important. Years of being pushed around by poorly armed
Apaches must have influenced morale. Finally, several Americans
noted that the Mexicans fired almost blindly into the air and then
ran during the attack. Fear? Perhaps. But it might have been
something else. The American army was accompanied by an alleged million dollars worth of goods, the owners of which were
citizens of Chihuahua or temporarily incarcerated in Chihuahua
by the governor. (The one exception seems to have been James
Magoffin; too dangerous, he had been sent under guard to Durango,
from which he finally got free by dissolving "all charges, prosecu-
tions and enmities in three thousand three hundred and ninety-two
bottles of champagne wine.")[44] Perhaps a tendency on the part of

---

[44] Cooke, *Conquest of New Mexico*, p. 162. Cooke adds that Magoffin was reimbursed by the government, ". . . the secretary said to him, mildly, 'Mr. M.
ten thousand dollars is a very large item for wine.' 'Yes,' responded the Don
with gravity, 'but Mr. Secretary, champagne at $37.50 a basket counts up very
fast.'" Some of this account is doubtless Cooke's own creation.

the Mexicans to protect the wagonloads of merchandise played no part in the battle, but a reasonable doubt does exist.

The achievement of the Missouri regiment should not, however, be questioned. They could not know in advance the ineffectiveness of Mexican fire-power—whatever its cause—or the low level of Mexican morale. Doniphan cited several men for their courage. Major Owens rushed blindly on the Mexican redoubts, seeking death, some said, because of a family quarrel. Colonel Jackson refused to give Doniphan a post-battle report saying that all his men "fought like hell"; his slogan, "Every man for his turkey" was the Missourians' chief war cry that afternoon. Major Clark's report singled out William Gilpin for driving the Mexicans out of their fixed positions. William's report (so long that Doniphan apologized to the War Department) credited everyone, including wagon drivers, with great courage.[45]

The day after the battle the Americans systematically searched the field for plunder. Much of the glory of victory was dimmed for them by the sights and sounds of the Mexican wounded and dying; to its credit the army ministered as well as possible to these unfortunates.

Nevertheless the plunder was not ignored. Most prized were the animals, promptly put to work to spell those exhausted by the trail from Fort Leavenworth. Powder, cartridges, and souvenirs of all kinds were acquired—and, if possible, concealed from the officers. A large amount of silver and gold coin quickly disappeared among the Missourians; understandably, no official report was made of this loot, but some soldiers estimated its value at $50,000.

Then it was time to move on to Chihuahua proper. At noon March 2, 1847, the Army of the West took possession of this old city without incident. The men were much impressed by its elaborate twin-spired cathedral, the palace, and the public grounds

[45] William was unscathed. A horse beside him reared back from an ankle injury and smashed his rider's nose with his neck. Seeing the spurting blood, William asked the soldier how much he was hurt. The reply was, "I'll tell you tomorrow" (Connelley, *Doniphan*, p. 417).

Accounts of the march from El Paso to Chihuahua and various versions of the battle of Sacramento River are in Smith, *War with Mexico*, I, 303–313; Connelley, *Doniphan*, pp. 395–443; Richardson, *Journal*, pp. 53–64; Edwards, *Journal*, pp. 247–269; Moorhead, *New Mexico's Royal Road*, pp. 169–175; Kennerly, *Persimmon Hill*, pp. 196–199.

with their monuments to Hidalgo and Iturbide, as well as the upper-class homes. The governor had fled south, so Doniphan encountered no opposition in taking over the palace as his headquarters.

Of immediate concern was the fate of the alien merchants captured by the Mexicans since the past September. James Magoffin, alone, was presumably still a prisoner in Durango. The others, including the notorious Speyer, had finally been overtaken after a thirteen-hundred-mile chase. Some of the army wanted to hang Speyer as a traitor, but the members of the court-martial accepted the recommendations of the other merchants, and after two weeks of being entertained by Speyer, they acquitted him.

The army now settled down for the occupation of Chihuahua not knowing how long they would be there or even what their mission might be. Army and conquered combined to give Major Owens a formidable—and expensive—Catholic, Masonic, American-Mexican burial in a cemetery near the Bull Pen. William was in charge of the escort for this remarkable event. According to one soldier, prayer, genuflection, tricks, and $600 dollars carried Owens through purgatory instantly.

Colonel Jackson's First Battalion camped in the Bull Pen out in the suburbs and on one occasion held a bull fight with several thousand Mexicans in attendance. The five bulls and four matadors were equally inexperienced, and the American soldiers were disappointed.

William and the Second Battalion officers moved into the palace on the plaza where William commenced agitation to renew the campaign. Most of the enlisted men (often quartered with local families) quickly found divertisement.

Undoubtedly the most surprising occupation was created by Major Clark, who found that the books in the palace library were not classified properly and put a detail to work making corrections. A little theater group, not too freshly from Santa Fe, put on performances of such plays as "She Stoops to Conquer" and "Pizarro," with heavy-footed Missouri volunteers as Inca maidens. The troops also produced a minstrel show, to the delight of their Mexican audiences.

Less cultural activities were also available in Chihuahua. The wine was not so bitter as the beverages of New Mexico (although the soldiers discovered that in the coffee houses, local girls preferred coffee cooled with *aguardiente* rather than cream). Gambling was a full-time occupation for Mexicans, and they found many of the conquerors ready to share the excitement of cards and cock-fighting. The Mexicans staged a ball, annoying some Missourians because it was held on Sunday and annoying others because the tickets were two dollars. Public swimming pools were popular with the soldiers and señoritas alike; some of the more fortunate Americans were invited to upper-class homes, and received the impression that the American government was welcome to stay in Chihuahua.[46]

All of the men were impressed by the ease of life, a mixture of poverty and great wealth; by the flooded silver mine that had produced over $300,000,000; by the ruins of Jesuit property, abandoned eighty years before; by the cocks tied to chairs and crowing challenge during mass; by the abundance and variety of food. The question was in all the men's minds—should not the Army of the West remain in Chihuahua?

Doniphan called a council of his officers to discuss the next move. His orders simply directed him to help General Wool take Chihuahua. Since the Missourians had completed their mission—and without help—Doniphan felt that he should link with Wool, believed to be under Taylor's command at Saltillo, five hundred miles to the east. But in this unusual army the commander's wishes were not necessarily law. Several points of view were expressed in the council: many officers wanted to remain in Chihuahua until the one year's enlistment was ended—about June 1, 1847, for most of the regiment. Presumably they would return by way of Santa Fe and thus avoid any more of the conflict.

Doniphan felt scorn for this group. While they "might possibly have found *fair* reasons for staying . . . I'm for going home to Sarah and the children." Doniphan's motto was popular with some, who were willing to help Taylor until their enlistments ended and then go back home to their Sarahs via Monterrey and Texas.

Another group did not want Doniphan to go anywhere. These were the merchants, who now wailed that under the present conditions they could not sell their goods in five years. Some few began

---

[46] Susan Magoffin arrived with her husband and party April 4. She professed herself shocked at what the troops were doing to the town, although she and Samuel moved unceremoniously into an upper-class home in the wake of the fleeing owners (Susan Magoffin, *Diary*, pp. 228–229).

to pull out in disgust for Santa Fe, but the majority pleaded with Doniphan for protection against the Mexicans and bandits who would presumably move into the vacuum left by the departing army.

None of these factions was a match for William Gilpin, however. William's scheme was simple: the war was not over; there was fighting yet to be done. Why not push on to Mexico City![47] William argued cogently, and got the backing of many other young officers. Reluctantly, Doniphan agreed to the most quixotic of his choices. To protect Chihuahua and the merchants, Jackson's battalion remained behind; William's battalion and the artillery readied themselves to move south.

Some unfinished business had to be cleared away. Doniphan sent a personal messenger, one James Collins, with a small escort, to ask Taylor for new orders. In another one of the singular achievements of the Missouri regiment Collins traveled more than fifty miles a day through enemy territory, including a forty-eight hour period without water. Collins found Wool at Saltillo, but had to wait there a week for orders from Taylor before carrying them back to Doniphan.

Doniphan meanwhile had started on the road to Durango, "protesting at every step, and offering to resign his command to Gilpin and return home." The departure from Chihuahua had two brief delays: the men insisted on waiting one more day to see a bull fight, and William insisted upon breaking into the Chihuahua mint for its reported $800,000 as spoils of war. At cannon-point the mint was finally opened to reveal nothing but private property. So the Army of the West was still unpaid ten months after enlistment.

The expedition to Durango and Mexico City proved an instant fiasco. Two and one half days and seventy-two miles south of Chihuahua William waited at dawn for marching orders. To his amazement Doniphan and several friends mounted their horses and announced that they were returning to Chihuahua. A message from Americans to the south had warned the colonel that the Mexicans had massed a new army of 6,000 to retake the city. A

[47] The Missourians had demonstrated their ability to march and survive the desert country; how much military strength they might have encountered can only be a guess. That General Scott had just taken Veracruz the Missourians could not have known.

grumbling, complaining Major Gilpin was overruled, and the battalion sent back to Chihuahua, to the catcalls of friends and Mexicans. Momentarily William agreed not to push for his southern campaign if Doniphan would postpone his trip to Sarah. So once again the regiment went into garrison duty—a task for which the Missourians were completely unfitted, as even William and Doniphan agreed.[48]

Fortunately, only two weeks passed before messenger Collins arrived, returning from Taylor's headquarters with a triple escort and tales of sustained hardship. The orders he brought Doniphan were precise: bring his regiment to Taylor. For the first time the Missourians learned of Scott's campaign in the south. The war was nearly ended in the north.

To conclude his obligations to the businessmen Doniphan urged them to sell their goods quickly and return to the United States. Most did this and sustained some loss. A small number, of longer Chihuahuan residence, stayed behind, hoping for fair treatment from the Mexican officials waiting in the wings.[49] Doniphan gave the Mexicans a vague threat and ordered his army to move. After one more big party the Army of the West started for the east, Jackson's battalion and the artillery preceding William and the Second Battalion by three days. The 28th of April provided a sight both colorful and bewildering to the serape-clad Mexicans lurking in their doorways. Baggage and food wagons rolled out of one side of town for the long drive to Monterrey and General Taylor. From the north gates of Chihuahua passed many of the Santa Fe merchants, carrying little in goods but unknown and important quantities of bullion, a season's receipts a year late.

In the plaza William's battalion formed, impatient now to go, their major overruled by competent authority. As William and Doniphan made their final inspections, a number of Mexican girls raced their horses through the Missourians' ranks. "They accom-

[48] The Durango army report proved to be a hoax, probably created by merchants in Chihuahua.

[49] In June one merchant who remained was killed and his store robbed of $5,000 in money and merchandise. The criminals were punished. All other merchants seem to have been protected (Moorhead, *New Mexico's Royal Road*, pp. 180–182). Not yet planned was a second invasion of Chihuahua. Price's army reached that city from Santa Fe in March of 1848, after the war had ended.

panied their lovers on the march to Saltillo, and bivouacked with them on the deserts," reported one eyewitness. Doniphan made an honest effort to run the señoritas off, but their horsemanship and male attire complicated the task.

The march across northern Mexico provided the Missourians with little else in the way of new experiences. The days were long —reveille sounded typically at three in the morning. The weather was consistently hot. Once in awhile a pleasant stream or small spring could be found, but too often the water the men pursued for hours turned into a mirage. Thirty miles in a day seems to have been average; a few men were overcome by heat and fatigue and died in the wagons. They were buried in the sands of Durango far from Missouri.

At the request of a rancher, twenty troopers of Gilpin's battalion attacked fifty or sixty Indians (Comanches or Apaches, the men thought). Several Indians were killed as the rest fled, leaving behind Mexican prisoners, plunder, and horses. The dead chief was such an impressive figure that Frederick Adolph Wislizenus, a German doctor who had traveled with Speyer from Missouri, decided to save his skull. He chopped off the head, and carried it on a wagon pole, boiling it each evening to remove the flesh. "Whistling Jesus," as the Missourians called the doctor, became a much less popular traveling companion from that date.[50]

The regiment reached Parras in mid-May, a beautiful town where Wool once camped. Natives and Americans were a little tired of each other here, and Doniphan could not discipline his men. A teamster was officially drummed out of the service for punching Mexicans. He was marched to city limits, officially discharged, and kicked in the jeans by a committee of three.

Doniphan cut short the proposed rest period at Parras and moved in two more days to the Buena Vista battlefield near Saltillo. That battle had been fought in February and though the Mexican army had long since left, Taylor and Wool had not moved. The Missourians toured the field not yet cleared of Mexican dead, and listened to Wool describe the chief features of the struggle. Wool's narrative ended with a picture of the army of Santa Anna sneaking off at night unpursued by Americans. ". . . a brawny young Missou-

[50] Kennerly, *Persimmon Hill*, pp. 202–204.

rian, almost naked, dirty, bearded like a pirate, hair unkempt and falling over his shoulders . . . slapped me on the thigh and said . . . 'General! when they retreated you ought to have pressed them . . . like we did at Sacramento! . . . there is where you made a damned bad mistake!' " The General's critic was a private, but he spoke with the conviction of the entire Missouri regiment.

Not yet completely aware of how matters stood with the Missouri regiment, Wool ordered them into formation for a review. It was a failure; the dirty, ragged veterans could not keep a straight line had they wished to; and most preferred craning and shuffling to get a good look at the splendor of Wool and his staff. Wool cut the review short.

Wool tried to persuade Doniphan's men to re-enlist, since the year was almost ended. Only a few saw reason to remain in service, so steps were taken to begin demobilization of the regiment. The artillery was given to another unit, and the men were marched to Taylor's headquarters near Monterrey for a final inspection.

Taylor impressed the Missourians. He kept his hat off when he reviewed them and his uniform was nearly as rough as theirs, if not so ragged. One soldier mistook him for a camp-follower and asked the "fat, old rascal" to help him locate whiskey to buy. Formalities over, the Missourians were sent to the States by way of the lower Río Grande.[51]

At Cerralvo they happened upon six Texas Rangers about to execute a Mexican prisoner. The procedure so upset the Missourians that it took all of Doniphan's influence to keep them from releasing the prisoner.

Some of Taylor's men were also seeking ships home, so William was put in charge of a small detachment that rode ahead from Camargo to Reynosa on the Río Grande for the purpose of securing boats that could deliver the regiment to the river's mouth. By riding all one night he was successful, but lost a sergeant to a Mexican sniper on the way.

When the entire command reached Reynosa, Doniphan took the first ship, accompanied by his sick, and steamed to Matamoros. Many of the Missourians were indignant that they and their officers—Gilpin, Colonel Jackson, and Major Clark—were left be-

---

[51] Connelley, *Doniphan*, pp. 484–485.

hind, but Doniphan intended to procure transport across the Gulf. The regiment spent two miserable days at Reynosa without tents and in ceaseless rain, sleeping in mud on maggoty blankets, their mess fouled by "Millions of blue flies."

Enough ships were finally obtained for the river journey. War Department orders were to drive all of the animals by land to Missouri, but none of the soldiers would carry out the command. Thirty-five men agreed to take on the task for a fee, charging five dollars per animal C.O.D. to its owner's Missouri county. By mid-August deliveries had been made of about one half of the seven hundred animals that left the Río Grande.

Saddles and other equipment could not be taken on board the river boats, so a day was devoted to burning and destroying such items to keep them from Mexican hands. Three days were needed to get the entire regiment to the river's mouth. An insulting nine-mile walk through soft sand took them to their Gulf ships and out of Mexican territory for the first time in twelve months.

Once again Gilpin led the advance party for the regiment. With twelve men he embarked on the steamer *Telegraph* for New Orleans to arrange for the reception and payment of the Missourians. Two slower, overloaded ships carried the remaining eight hundred men across the Gulf of Mexico. Even now their ordeal was not at an end. A quart of water and a few crackers and molasses was the daily ration allowance. Two more men died during the six-day crossing. On the seventh day the men first saw the sunken meadows of the lower delta and entered one of the passes of the Mississippi. A steamer towed them across the bar, up the river, past Balize, Fort Jackson's ruins, and the site of Old Hickory's victory over the British at Chalmette. Three days after William Gilpin's arrival, the Missouri volunteers alighted on the New Orleans wharf, June 17, 1847.[52]

The people of New Orleans had been prepared by Gilpin to expect an army. But no one was prepared for the unkempt, bedrag-

[52] The events from the occupation of Chihuahua until the regiment's discharge in New Orleans can be found in: Connelley, *Doniphan*, pp. 444–495; Bancroft, *William Gilpin*, pp. 33–34; Robinson, *Journal*, pp. 80–91; Kennerly, *Persimmon Hill*, pp. 202–206; Edwards, *Campaign in New Mexico*, pp. 119–165; Richardson, *Journal*, pp. 64–89; James J. Webb, *Adventures in the Santa Fe Trade*, I, 272–278; Edwards, *Journal*, pp. 270–280; Gibson, *Journal*, pp. 353–363.

gled group who disembarked. Thirteen months before, they each had received a $42 clothing allowance. Since that time they had collected no pay, no allowance, no issue—from Fort Leavenworth to Chihuahua to Matamoros and, finally to New Orleans. Their original uniforms had long since disintegrated: bits of Mexican uniforms, Indian garments, and animal skins gave everyone only partial covering. William Richardson, suffering from fever and scurvy, landed in the city clad in torn underwear and an overcoat. Few men had shaved or had their hair cut in a year. "The unshorn beards and goat and deerskin clothes . . . reminded us of . . . the inhabitants of some of the countries of the Russian empire," noted a newspaper reporter.[53]

Clothes, food, and haircuts were available as New Orleans honored the heroes. William had done his staff work well; some of the men were paid off and discharged within twenty-four hours. He remained in the city for about a week, by which time nearly all the men had gotten their back pay. ($16 a month for privates) and a warrant for 160 acres of government land. Many of the warrants quickly changed owners in the Crescent City, at the minimum price of $1.25 an acre.

Discharged as they were in New Orleans, the men found their own way home. Every day more Missouri veterans boarded steamers for St. Louis. William caught the *Old Hickory*, and, with Doniphan and a number of other officers and enlisted men, reached St. Louis on June 30.

The city fathers were determined to celebrate the regiment's return before the men scattered throughout the state. On July 2, two more ships arrived, and their pasengers joined with those veterans already in town for a parade from the Planters' House to Camp Lucas where an enormous crowd awaited them. Committee members made brief talks of greeting, and Captain Reid acknowledged them on behalf of the soldiers.

The featured speaker was William's old friend, Senator Benton, fortuitously available for the occasion. "Old Bullion," in his classic and orotund fashion, described for the public the nature of the regiment's achievement. Doniphan thanked him, and a captain in-

[53] *The American Flag* (published by the United States Army at Matamoros, Mexico), June 7, 1847.

sisted that it was collation time. They adjourned to St. Louis Park and won their battles all over again.[54]

A few days later Gilpin, Doniphan, and other westerners took steamers up the Missouri for Independence and home, Doniphan to Sarah and the children, William to a lonely shack and a nearly fatal bout with malaria.

[54] William Cullen Bryant in the *New York Evening Post* compared Doniphan's expedition with Xenophon's retreat through Asia Minor (Kennerly, *Persimmon Hill*, pp. 206–208); Connelley, *Doniphan*, pp. 438–440, 495–509. Benton's speech was recorded; Doniphan's was not, but a newspaper account summarizes the latter as a sober warning of growing disunity in America (*American Flag*, July 17, 1847). Chairman of the reception was Thornton Grimsley, William's "bully" of six years before.

CHAPTER SEVEN

# High Jinks on the Santa Fe Trail[1]

*Indian Fighter, 1847–1850*

William Gilpin's Mexican War career ended with his discharge in New Orleans June 24, 1847, after one year and sixteen days of service. Then he accepted his back pay, his bounty land warrant, and the applause of the civilians in New Orleans, St. Louis, and Independence, who greeted him and the other veteran "Ring-Tailed Roarers," along the river highways leading home.

William did not receive the publicity of Doniphan, of course, but he was frequently cited for leading the charge on the Mexican center at Sacramento and toasted as "the essence of chivalry, the disciplinarian of the regiment." These descriptions fit the spirit of the journals of soldiers who knew William, and in no instance does his behavior dispute the claims.

Independence was home to William now, and he would consider it his residence until the Civil War moved him to Colorado. He

[1] Several portions of this chapter were previously published in my article "Gilpin's Volunteers on the Santa Fe Trail," in *Kansas Historical Quarterly*, XXX (Spring, 1964), 1–14. Permission of the *Quarterly* to use this material is hereby gratefully acknowledged.

did not at once file for his bounty land, but appears to have resided in a small cottage on the northern outskirts of town during the fews weeks that he was out of uniform.

William had plans for his future; he was thirty-two and ready to settle down. He had a small law practice and a little garden; he hoped to make money in land speculation and to commence writing his epic of the Great West. Furthermore, William was now famous, at least west of St. Louis, and he and friends gave thought to re-establishing his political career.

Late in July the citizens of Jackson County gave an "abundant" dinner for about four thousand people, and William was called upon as a featured speaker. But as usual Doniphan was the special guest, and his acceptance of a laurel wreath from the ladies dimmed some of William's glory.[2]

The next month he had a larger stage, with no Doniphan to keep him in the wings. The people of Jefferson City decided to pay tribute to their heroes, the Cole County Infantry, Company "F," which had served under William against the Navajos and the Mexicans. Because of this William was invited, although not a resident of the county.

With the firing of a cannon the people of Jefferson City went to the hall of the House of Representatives and awaited the veterans of Company "F" as they capered through the streets to the capitol. Two men of the outfit made talks about the gallantry of the soldiers and then there arose a popular outcry for William to speak.

Never unprepared for such an emergency William responded eloquently in what one newspaper called a "few" remarks. If the accounts are at all accurate William declaimed for more than thirty minutes about the Mexican War and the particular bravery of the Missouri Regiment under intolerable conditions. Long before this period of his life William had developed a great fondness for words. His amplification of the florid language of the public orations of his time by the addition of certain pet, key phrases and the frequent use of the passive voice resulted in a singularly identifiable style.[3] William's language was impersonal and grand, and

[2] *Weekly Tribune* (Liberty, Mo.), July 31, 1847.
[3] Henry Nash Smith, *Virgin Land: The American West as Symbol and Myth*, p. 40.

the folks of Jefferson City must have detected a vague feeling of greatness in the speaker, the listeners, and the events.

Two years earlier William had told the United States Senate of the "pioneer army" in which each man was a platoon, moving on the Great West to conquer and hold the land from nature, the Indians, or the British, with no help from an Atlantic-oriented nation. Now, in the heart of the Mississippi Valley he addressed some of this very army and shifted his vision a few degrees.

During the Revolution, little armies . . . passed over Kentucky, the Northwest Territory, and Tennessee. . . . recruited by a year or two of peace, these soldiers returned to occupy the choice spots which had been their bivouac and camping grounds. From the campaigns of war grew the settlements of peace, and populous States displaced the wilderness. Another war came with another generation—armies penetrated Michigan, upper Illinois, and into Mississippi. . . . and now, again, have come another generation and another war. Your little armies have scaled the eternal barriers of the "Mother Mountain" of the New World, and, . . . have *debouched* at many points upon the briny beach of the Pacific. . . . your soldiers resting for a time at home, will sally forth again, and, wielding the weapons of husbandry, give to you roads that will nurture commerce and a sisterhood of *maritime States on the new-found ocean.*[4]

The meeting adjourned for toasts and a barbecue.

For the first time William's neighbors began to look upon him as more than just a frontier wanderer and soldier. After all, he had held public office, he was educated, he was a leader. Some of his friends had a plan.

Almost immediately after the barbecue William's name was proposed for the office of governor of Missouri. He was lauded as a Democrat of the Jeffersonian school, an able expounder of democratic principles, who "bold and fearless," could lead the party to a victory as glorious and triumphant as Brazito and Sacramento.[5] The canvass was just beginning in the state so that few clues can be found to assess William's prospects. Almost instantly, however, his gubernatorial ambitions came to a halt, for the people of his

[4] William Gilpin, *Mission of the North American People*, p. 133 (first published in 1860 under the title *The Central Gold Region*). See also *Weekly Tribune* (Liberty, Mo.), August 28, 1847.

[5] *Jefferson Inquirer* (Jefferson City, Mo.), August 28, 1847.

state entered a prior claim upon his services. Scarcely three weeks after the Cole County barbecue William was back in uniform.

Once again the reason was trouble on the Santa Fe Trail; this time the enemy was not the Mexican, but the Indian of the Great Plains. Comanches, Kiowas, Pawnees along the Trail, Navajos, Apaches, and the Utes in New Mexico and Colorado were taking advantage of the Mexican War to raid and pillage and kill. Military units destined for Mexico in 1846 and 1847 passed down the Trail quickly with no time to pursue the Indians and punish them for their attacks. Equally advantageous to the tribes was the absence of the chief merchants who with their tough, experienced teamsters were the equal of the army in protecting themselves.

In the summer of 1847 the Indians concluded that they could strike with impunity almost anywhere along the road from the settlements on the Missouri to Santa Fe. Nearly every company of merchants and travelers was attacked; and since small groups were in Santa Fe or scattered along the Arkansas trying to get home safely, Missourians estimated that hundreds of whites would be killed if the government did not act quickly.[6]

The only available military force was the army occupying Santa Fe, which gave such help as it could, but was badly weakened by having to send companies into the Navajo country to punish the very groups who had signed a treaty with William the winter before. Also planned was a second invasion of Chihuahua, and Colonel Price could spare few men from this enterprise to patrol the road in his rear. Most frightening to the frontiersmen was the apparent confederation of tribes—Comanches, Pawnees, Apaches, and Arapahoes in unprecedented combinations against the whites.[7]

President Polk and his advisors concluded that controlling the Plains Indians required the use of a military force distinct from those engaged in fighting the Mexicans—a unit with one purpose,

[6] Even military units were not safe that summer. In June the Indians attacked a detachment of dragoons escorting the paymaster to New Mexico and killed five of the troops (Philip Ferguson, *The Diary of Philip Ferguson*, p. 295). A force of more than two hundred American soldiers was engaged by Comanches in May, but the casualties were slight.

[7] In July an alliance of three tribes turned one thousand warriors against thirty wagons of teamsters and a dozen guards near Walnut Creek. Every white was massacred (*The American Flag* [Matamoros, Mex.], July 10, 1847).

organized outside the normal channels of command. On July 24, 1847, the federal government asked the state of Missouri to raise the Separate Battalion of Missouri Volunteers, composed of two companies of cavalry, two of infantry, and one of artillery.

William Gilpin's personal recollection was that one day late in August he was sick in bed, attended by a physician, when Governor John Edwards came to his home and urged him to accept command of the new battalion. Allegedly William stipulated that he would assume the task if his health improved, if he could determine his own tactics, if he could have a priority for supplies, and if he could do his own recruiting in Missouri. Whether these conditions were met is not clear, but within less than a month he had his five companies. He was sworn back into service on September 18 and given the rank of lieutenant colonel by Governor Edwards. Then in the peculiar democracy of the frontier army, the volunteers voted to see if they would accept William as their commander. The vote of the first three companies was unanimously for William, and so he received his endorsement even before everyone had voted. Said the editor reporting the vote, "Gilpin is a soldier in the fullest sense of the term. Brave, energetic and intelligent he will retain the confidence of his men, and will lead them on to victory."[8]

William had these qualifications, but he would have needed several more to have brought victory over the Indians that year. Tom Fitzpatrick was quoted as saying that subjugation of the Indians of the Southwest would be more difficult than the conquest of the whole of Mexico; with the organization available to William, Fitzpatrick was dead right. William had hoped to enlist his "Ring-Tailed Roarers" of the Mexican campaign, but only a few could be induced to try the army again. Instead of Doniphan's toughened veterans, William had to lead a motley group of raw foreigners and city lads, completely lacking in military experience, volunteering as the cheapest way to get 160 acres of land.

William understood this problem and thought that his disciplinary skill could whip the men into the same level of sloppy effective-

[8] *Jefferson Inquirer* (Jefferson City, Mo.), September 25, 1847. See also Hubert Howe Bancroft, *History of the Life of William Gilpin*, pp. 36–37. Doniphan probably could have had the command but expressed no interest in leaving "Sarah and the children." He warmly recommended William in spite of their differences in Chihuahua (*Weekly Tribune* [Liberty, Mo.], October 15, 1847).

ness that characterized his old regiment. He could not foresee a serious difference; his new command would fight Indians who could not be bribed and who had no vulnerable towns to occupy in comfort.

William was tormented from the day he took over his battalion. A clue to his organizational problems is the fact that there was not even agreement for the name of his unit. Records in Washington as well as Missouri refer to it variously as the "Santa Fé Trace Battalion," "Gilpin's Battalion Missouri Mounted Volunteers," "Indian Battalion Missouri Volunteers," "Separate Battalion Missouri Volunteers for the Plains," and curiously, "Oregon Battalion." Irrespective of its name the battalion was "separate"; the War Department failed to establish any chain of command for Gilpin to use, and he had no superior officer to direct him. The battalion was mustered in and equipped at Fort Leavenworth, but was never placed under any department or other headquarters. William thus got into the time-consuming habit of dealing directly with the Adjutant General, the Secretary of War, and even the President when he sought help.

Within his command William's problems were as great. For tactical reasons the companies were usually to be scattered widely from the Missouri to Santa Fe, putting considerable responsibility upon captains and lieutenants. All of these were volunteers, almost completely lacking military experience, with their authority weakened even more by the fact that their election from enlisted ranks required substantial fraternizations and concession-making.

Two of the five companies came from St. Louis, and nearly all of these men were German. So few of them, and their officers as well, spoke English that William labored unnecessarily to get his commands understood. Worse, a hostile nativism immediately developed in the other three companies, and the immigrants concluded that the "Americans" would as soon attack them as they would Indians.

By reasonable standards William's battalion should never have left Fort Leavenworth. It was in sorry shape. Some units had three weeks of training, others had a few days. Haste was a factor, of course, but William blamed his predicament on "the ignorance, the laziness and the vicious character of officers in the frontier depots." The chief target of his attack was Lieutenant Colonel

Clifton Wharton, commanding officer of Fort Leavenworth, a man with long experience in Indian warfare and probably able enough. By coincidence this was the same Wharton who had visited Henry Gilpin's home thirteen years before and whose tales of the dragoons had influenced William to seek an army career.

The two officers quarreled immediately upon William's assuming command of the battalion at Leavenworth. Wharton had orders to supply him, and according to William, Wharton flatly refused. At this point William allegedly challenged Wharton to a duel. The duel was somehow avoided and supplies were forthcoming, if inadequate. William's report (the only side of the argument available) was that Wharton sent the command "naked" into the wilderness. Wharton issued no cavalry sabers, no sheet music for the band, no officers' side-arms, no copies of regulations, no forage, and insufficient provisions, ammunition, and medical supplies.

In fairness to Wharton it must be recalled that he was also the supply and fiscal agent for all of the United States military units in the Southwest, from the Missouri River to Chihuahua. Doubtless they had priority over William's battalion, and as has been seen in the case of Doniphan's regiment, they, too, suffered from shortages of all kinds.

William adds another charge which may have truth in it. He claimed that Wharton thought that the whole mission of the Separate Battalion was a mistake, pursuing the Indians into their own country at the beginning of winter, under the command of a young boy.[9] Jealousy, too, could have been a factor. Wharton was a veteran of nearly thirty years' service, yet he held only the same rank as William whom he might well consider a raw youth. Many a military grudge has grown from milder circumstances.

Unfortunately both men were ill: William seriously so, with recurring malaria contracted in Mexico; Wharton, wasted from an unknown fever, was to die while William was in the field. Unquestionably their mutual irritations were aggravated by poor health.

The bickering produced consequences within two months. Late

[9] Gilpin to Secretary of War William L. Marcy, January 8, 1848, Gilpin File, Letters Received, G62, A.G.O., National Archives; Elvid Hunt, *History of Fort Leavenworth*, p. 67.

in September, 1847, William led his two companies of cavalry, "A" and "B," out on the trail. The other companies followed shortly, the last one leaving Leavenworth on October 6, and the whole battalion was united on the 1st of November at Walnut Creek and the Arkansas River in central Kansas. They then moved as a unit up the Arkansas to Fort Mann, three miles west of the present Dodge City.

This small post had been hastily thrown up early the same year as an additional safeguard against the Indians. About half-way from Fort Leavenworth to Santa Fe, it was needed for repairing wagons and resting animals with reasonable safety for the troops.[10]

At Fort Mann, William determined to investigate the rumored alliance of the Plains tribes. The continued labor of the Bent brothers to trade among the Cheyennes had so far paid off. The Bents were influential with Cheyennes and their allies, the Arapahoes (William Bent successively married two Cheyenne sisters) and had so far helped keep them peaceful with the whites.[11]

As a show of force Gilpin left Fort Mann in mid-November with the two mounted companies to seek out these two tribes located near Bent's Fort. His other three companies he left at Fort Mann with two hundred supply wagons. Since they could not move as easily as the cavalry, they were left behind to enlarge and repair the post.[12] This rear echelon William placed in command of Cap-

[10] Fort Mann was permanently abandoned by the army in 1850. Fort Atkinson was located near the same site in the mid-1850's. "Kansas History as Published in the Press," *Kansas Historical Quarterly*, XV (August, 1947), 329–330. I am indebted to the *Quarterly's* managing editor, Nyle H. Miller, for helping me locate material about Fort Mann. Comanches had little fear of the post and attacked it at least once. Whites were killed within sight of its occupants before William's battalion arrived. The fort was made up of four small log houses, connected by timbers with loop-holes cut through. The walls were twenty feet high (Lewis Garrard, *Wah-To-Yah and the Taos Trail*, pp. 330–360). While working on the fort, Garrard met Frank Blair, who was on his way from Santa Fe to Independence.

[11] David Lavender, *Bent's Fort*, dramatically and as faithfully as is possible analyzes this relationship. George Bird Grinnell, *The Fighting Cheyennes*, adds a few details.

[12] Fort Mann had been left untended for a few weeks that summer, and the Comanches made "a perfect wreck" of it. William evidently drove a number

tain William Pelzer, commanding officer of Company "C," the artillery battery.

Pelzer was one of the German immigrants in the Separate Battalion and completely unequipped to manage Indians or troops. A day or so after the cavalry's departure, about sixty-five Pawnees wandered up to Fort Mann, looking for some cheap meals. Reported Pelzer to William, "Sir! . . . they shekt Hands with us and i envoited them to come with me to the Fort." Pelzer planned to hold them prisoners until he could get instructions from William, but the Pawnees became wary and tried to escape. The captain ordered his men to fire; two Indians lay dead, two were wounded, and about twenty-five other wounded managed to scramble away. The captain of company "D" and one private were slightly injured. Pelzer was holding the two prisoners—chiefs, he called them, and planned to have them shot. He wrote William that he was disturbed about the incident; for one thing Captain Napoleon Koscialowski of "E" had "forbitten his men to load after i hat given the Command, he could not see any necessity of it . . . I wish you was here with Mr. Fallon [Gilpin's guide] to get information how to get these other savages. P.S. i dont like to feet them [feed the prisoners] any longer."[13]

Captain Koscialowski was not the only one who could not see any necessity of it. William blustered over Pelzer's report but could do nothing while the units were separated. Frontier farmers shuddered at the report that Pelzer had deliberately planned a massacre. Thieving Pawnees were not popular, but the local citizens did not want the Pawnees to have any legitimate excuses for their tactics. Most whites considered the event an outrage, and the War Department took slow steps toward an investigation. Defense for Pelzer came from an unusual source. The Bents' partner, Ceran St. Vrain, told officers at Jefferson Barracks that bad motives had not caused

---

of Pawnees away when he occupied the fort (*Weekly Tribune* [Liberty, Mo.], November 19, 1847).

[13] Capt. William Pelzer to Gilpin, November 19, 1847, U.S. War Department, Record Group 94, G 368, Adjutant General's Office, National Archives (hereafter cited as Record Group 94, G—, A.G.O., National Archives). Very possibly Pelzer refers to the same Fallon who had been the unsavory leader of one of the parties relieving the Donners in California the previous spring.

the incident, but the ignorance and mutual suspicions of Germans and Indians had brought about an accident. The army gave due consideration to this suggestion by an old authority and decided to withhold judgment on Pelzer.[14] But William's mission had started badly.

Along the trail from Santa Fe William met a merchant headed toward Independence who later told the press his impression of the state of the Separate Battalion. The merchant (B. F. Coons of Santa Fe) reported that the unit was already in very bad shape. The animals suffered from lack of feed alarmingly early in the campaign. The land was "a vast black crisp, the grass and all kinds of vegetation having been entirely burnt up by the Indians." William had told Coons that he would resign his command if Wharton did not hasten to furnish the winter subsistence.[15]

As William and the cavalry forged ahead toward Bent's Fort (about two hundred miles up the Arkansas), a more unusual problem was about to brighten the gray Kansas winter for the troops at Fort Mann. Unbelievably, back in September at Leavenworth, First Lieutenant Amandus Schnabel had recruited into Company "D" a young woman named Caroline Newcome. Caroline used no such old stratagem as calling herself a laundress; she was enrolled as a genuine soldier—Private Bill Newcome. How many men were in on the game is a company secret, but she traveled with the troops to Fort Mann. Schnabel disguised Caroline in soldiers' clothing and helped her escape detection by sending her "off from duty in the Company under different pretexts . . . [Schnabel meanwhile] tenting, sleeping and cohabiting with the said female . . ."

The fraud was revealed when Private Bill Newcome became pregnant and went absent without leave. Schnabel had already been reprimanded in October for spreading a rumor that Company "E" was planning an attack on the two German companies ("C" and "D"). William, disgusted, initiated court-martial proceedings against the artful lieutenant. William's charges would indicate that he was neither shocked by the immorality nor amused by the cleverness of the trick. For he alleged "gross fraud upon the United States" in his specifications. Schnabel, he said, was guilty of "de-

14 Col. John Garland to General Robert Jones (The Adjutant General), May 24, 1848, Gilpin File, Letters Received, G 210, A.G.O., National Archives.
15 *Weekly Tribune* (Liberty, Mo.), November 19, 1847.

frauding the United States of the service of a good and competent soldier . . ."[16]

A serious-minded William Gilpin saw nothing humorous in his own language; he probably also failed to draw the conclusion that Caroline Newcome's presence on the roster deprived the army of the services of more than one "good and competent soldier." Months were to pass before a general court could be assembled; Pelzer and Schnabel retained their positions throughout the winter and helped create more mischief.

Fate was unkind to an otherwise respectable enough officer, Second Lieutenant William O'Hara. O'Hara was a young Irish-American in "D," a company almost exclusively German. He had no respect for Pelzer and the other officers of his unit, but worse, his men had no respect for him. He commanded a small detail ordered to bring supplies from Fort Mann to Gilpin. Privates Fahlbush and Goldbeck, angered because O'Hara promoted an Irishman to corporal, talked about him in German in his presence. Then, when he ordered night travel, they became most insolent. They cursed him, threatened him, and refused to camp at the site ordered. Then they stole a baggage wagon and deserted their unit with O'Hara unable to act.

A few days later, they rejoined the already cowed O'Hara on his return to Mann. En route Goldbeck threatened, pursued, and shot at O'Hara, driving him from camp. Once again court-martial machinery moved ponderously. Before Colonel Gilpin could get the charges and arrange for the officers required by the Articles of War, Fahlbush quarreled with another private and shot and killed him.

Pelzer had meanwhile not settled down. Throughout much of the winter (1847–1848) he was habitually drunk, made frequent speeches against the absent William, interfered to prevent supplies from reaching the cavalry, and engaged in a sword fight with another German, Captain Paul Holzscheiter, commander of Company "D."[17]

---

[16] Court-martial record, January 4, 1848, Record Group 94, G 368, A.G.O., National Archives.

[17] *Ibid.*; Court-martial record, undated, Record Group 94, G 368, A.G.O., National Archives; Charges and specifications against William Pelzer, undated, Record Group 94, G 368, A.G.O., National Archives. The excessive use of for-

Clearly William had lost control of his battalion, or at least that portion of it still at Fort Mann. He had entrusted the command to an officer who was completely incompetent, and he could do nothing to correct the situation so long as he remained in the field.

Camped near Bent's Fort William and the cavalry had problems of their own. His animals were broken by the country—no grass, and no feed from Wharton—and so the cavalry became infantry and, therefore, was unable to police six hundred miles of trail. His men were inadequately housed (in tents) for a freezing winter, and for food they relied upon trade with Indians and New Mexicans.

Bitterly, William learned that near Bent's Fort were a thousand cattle, property of Bent and St. Vrain, and not for sale to him; William Bent was willing to sell but Ceran St. Vrain was not, St. Vrain arguing that he had experienced too much trouble getting repayment for requisitions made by field commanders in the past. The partnership was shaken, but William got no beef.[18]

A westerner might encounter a number of his counterparts in a winter at Bent's Fort, and William was not surprised to meet his friend, Tom Fitzpatrick, who, back in 1846, had become Indian agent for the plains tribes on the suggestion of Benton to President Polk. Meanwhile Fitzpatrick had guided General Kearny part of the way to California until they met Kit Carson returning with news from Frémont. Carson and Tom then swapped roles, with the latter becoming the messenger to Washington. By the summer and fall of 1847 he was performing his Indian duties, moving in and out of Santa Fe and Bent's Fort.

Fitzpatrick, too, found much to complain of that winter. He did not like the Mexicans; he was sick of the licentiousness in Santa

eign recruits was frequently deplored by the army's Inspector General, Colonel George Croghan. At Fort Leavenworth in 1840 he urged the army to forbid enlistment of "Dutch or Germans . . . [and] Irish . . . the very bane of our garrisons" (Francis P. Prucha [ed.], *Army Life on the Western Frontier*, p. 148).

18 Frank Hall, *History of the State of Colorado*, IV, 73. Hall says that the refusal not only made William Gilpin very angry, but it caused a split in the partnership of the fort, and William Bent "at once bought out the interest of his brother." Since the other brothers were dead, this statement could refer to Charles' or George's families, or to St. Vrain's share. Lavender believes the last to be the case (*Bent's Fort*, pp. 305, 312, 412).

Fe; he thought that many of the trail massacres were simply the result of stupidity, and there was little that he could say for the army or the way it dealt with Indians.[19]

With William Bent, Fitzpatrick talked sternly to the Cheyennes and Arapahoes to persuade them to turn farmers and to stay out of the war. He feasted them on bread and coffee but had nothing to give them. The Cheyennes considered themselves "good" Indians yet got no presents while the "bad" Indians were receiving gifts from other agents. This they could not understand.

The role of these two tribes now caused an argument between Fitzpatrick and Gilpin. William agreed with the Cheyennes that the government should locate them along the Arkansas as a buffer (probably with the Arapahoes, as well) and subsidize their introduction to agriculture. William thought that at the very least this would keep the Indians from attacking travelers on the Santa Fe Trail. Chief Yellow Wolf agreed with William and additionally offered to fight the "bad" Comanches.

Old Broken Hand was not impressed. He contended that the Cheyennes wanted to settle, but he told William that they could not be trusted. Furthermore, some of their Arapaho allies were already aiding the Comanches' raids. Fitzpatrick was worried; Arapahoes were not so brave as Cheyennes, but more insolent and sneaky—and numerous.

Fitzpatrick made his case; then, since neither had authority for any policy except harassment, he directed a proposal to the Superintendent of Indian Affairs in St. Louis. Fitzpatrick wanted more forts; the desert was too vast to expect settlers to push the Indians here as they had elsewhere. But mostly he wanted a new policy from the army. He said that they needed a special, different force of about 250 well-mounted men with short rifles, a company of Mexican mounted lancers with pistols, a company of regular dragoons, and a few highly mobile howitzers, all under one experienced commander. This tough unit should then wage a vigorous campaign of chastisement, just what Fitzpatrick said William was not doing.

[19] The Bureau of Indian Affairs was created within the War Department in 1824. In 1849 Indian affairs were transferred to the new Department of the Interior (William T. Hagan, *American Indians*, pp. 67, 109; Le Roy R. Hafen and W. J. Ghent, *Broken Hand*, pp. 182–186).

In truth the men disagreed more on the tactics of the campaign than anything else, and neither man had much use for eastern editors who sobbed their sympathy for the misunderstood savages. Both were reasonable, informed men, but they had a further falling out when William refused Tom a ten-soldier escort to the Platte in pursuit of a renegade, bootlegging whiskey to the Indians around Fort Laramie. (Fitzpatrick, also, complained of suffering from a severe illness that winter.) The argument was not very fundamental, however, and William was in these same days drafting a message to the Secretary of War urging the government to listen to Fitzpatrick as the ablest advisor available on Indian matters.

On at least two important items Fitzpatrick and Gilpin agreed completely: for one, they could not talk with Comanches and Kiowas. These tribes understood force and force only, and treaties meant nothing. Secondly, while volunteers often made good soldiers, their discipline was ruined by the practice of allowing them to elect their own officers. Both men felt that William's battalion could be saved only by a reorganization, a series of courts-martial, and the discharge of the German companies.[20]

William could bring none of this about through his own authority and had to make his plans for a winter campaign with almost no help from Washington or Leavenworth. The details are not clear, but he appears to have detached Company "E" and some of the artillery from Pelzer at Fort Mann and added them to his two mounted companies at Bent's Fort. Pelzer and a number of his Company "C" men remained behind with all of Company "D." In essence William was leaving all of his trouble-makers at Fort Mann.[21]

By February of 1848 William's situation was public knowledge. Missouri papers related the latest rumors of indiscretions in the

[20] Indian Agent Tom Fitzpatrick to Superintendent of Indian Affairs Thomas H. Harvey, September 18, 1847, U.S. House of Representatives, *Executive Document No. 8*, 30th Cong., 1st Sess., 1848, pp. 238–249; Hafen and Ghent, *Broken Hand*, pp. 192–211; Gilpin to Marcy, January 8, 1848, Letters Received, G 62, A.G.O., National Archives. William here told the Secretary that he wrote to him because he did not know who was his commanding general.

[21] When Fort Mann was replaced on or near the same site about 1850, its successor, Fort Atkinson, was significantly called by its soldiers "Fort Sodom." It is not unlikely the name was used for Fort Mann, earlier (Grinnell, *Fighting Cheyennes*, p. 121 n.).

battalion, and Pelzer became infamous. The editorials upset the War Department more than William's own reports, and slowly the bureaucratic wheels moved. The troops acted faster. Over one hundred men, all with German-appearing names, drafted a petition to Gilpin asking that he relieve Pelzer of his command by reason of his misconduct and his inability to sustain military order. About the same time, three officers under Pelzer made approximately the same request, additionally detailing that Pelzer had failed to punish O'Hara's men, that officers were drunk during Indian scares, and men were shooting at one another on hunting trips. Government property was being misused, and, in general, "things was being made disagreeable."[22]

William paused long enough to fire off another salvo at the War Department, and then left Bent's Fort, heading over Ratón Pass for the south and the Comanches, unable to waste more time with insubordination. He had meanwhile solved his requisition problem (how is not known), for St. Vrain and William Bent had taken a party to Santa Fe and planned to meet William's troops along the trail with the supplies he would need for his campaign.

His winter and spring campaign was successful in two objectives, if only for the short run. First, the Kiowas temporarily broke off their aggressive alliance and joined the Cheyennes for peace talks at Bent's. Second, Gilpin's battalion, augmented by twenty invaluable mountain men, began a systematic hunt through scores of miles on each side of the Santa Fe Trail for Comanches and Apaches. Remounted on fresh mules and enriched by one or more six-pound guns, William waged the kind of "war" that Fitzpatrick had prescribed.

The program had a serious flaw: William found no Indians. Warned of the cavalry, the Indians burned the grass and drove off all the game they had time for, and then fled. The Apaches rode all of the way to Chihuahua, the Comanches back into Texas. For the moment, William could boast that the road from Santa Fe to the "states" was open and safe. He knew better than most how

[22] Petitions to Gilpin, February 20, 22, 1848, Gilpin File, Letters Received, G 62, A.G.O., National Archives. Doubtless the men did not enjoy *this* much liberty and democracy and wanted new officers. However, they knew that Gilpin's threat of a discharge *en masse* would deprive them of their 160 acre bounty-land grants.

temporary was his victory: he had not fought a battle nor killed an Indian. In fact, so far, his whole battalion's toll for nine months was two more-or-less innocent Pawnees. Nevertheless William felt that he had overawed the Indians with his striking force and had prevented their "annual migration" to the north.

Beset with recurring fever, in mid-May he gave up the pursuit and turned his horse northward to the Arkansas once more. At Fort Mann he found chiefs from Kiowa, Cheyenne, and Arapaho tribes awaiting him to discuss annuities and other treaty terms. William disappointed them when he informed them—correctly—that he had no authority to negotiate treaties, but most of these Indians obeyed his request to move to the upper Platte and await instructions from the government.[23]

As William reunited his command at Fort Mann late in the spring of 1848, General Robert Jones, the adjutant general, finally took steps to curb the Separate Battalion's insubordination. Jones told Secretary of War Marcy that the two companies of Germans should be discharged, but he could see no way to hold a court-martial for Pelzer (and any other officer), because regulations required that such a court be made up of volunteer officers equal to or higher than Pelzer in rank. No such group existed on the western frontier within Gilpin's call. Therefore, Jones directed Colonel John Garland, commanding officer of the Third Military District at Jefferson Barracks, to visit Fort Mann, investigate all of the facts, and take such measures as were necessary.

Garland left St. Louis on May 31 for Fort Leavenworth, where he was to pick up Wharton to accompany him the rest of the way to Fort Mann. Wharton, as Jones had predicted, was very ill. He traveled a few days with Garland then had to return to Leavenworth where he died on July 12. Meanwhile Garland took a small escort and proceeded down the trail across Kansas, reaching Fort Mann on July 2.

Garland found that Gilpin was at the fort and in control of his battalion. He had arrested Pelzer and instituted court-martial proceedings against all enlisted men charged with breaking any of

[23] *St. Louis Reveille*, May 29, 1848; Gilpin to Adjutant General, August 1, 1848, Record Group 94, G 449, A.G.O., National Archives; Gilpin's Battalion, Record of Events, 1847–1848, Adjutant General's Office, National Archives.

the Articles of War. Slow in getting around to his problem, William was acting decisively now.

Garland began his investigation armed with the knowledge that the Mexican War Treaty had just been accepted by both nations and that the War Department would discharge all volunteer units as fast as possible. His justice, therefore, could be swift.

The revelations of the inquiry brought little credit to anyone at any level of authority. The War Department, with no chain of command for the Separate Battalion, literally had lost William; that he had been at Bent's Fort during the previous winter came as a surprise to Jones, who thought that the battalion had wintered at Fort Scott, five hundred miles to the east. Gilpin had no executive officer to whom he could delegate part of his command, and his orders were ignored during his frequent maneuvers. Both Wharton and "green lieutenants" had engaged in "injurious scribbling" to St. Louis papers about the battalion. In William's absence several officers had been drunk on duty; one broke his leg wrestling with an Indian; several made near-mutinous speeches, and the jealousies and suspicions between "Germans and Americans were discreditable to both." Garland concluded with William and Tom Fitzpatrick that allowing volunteers to choose their own officers was "the most fruitful cause of that insubordination."

Garland treated with Captain Pelzer first. Oddly, at that remote post, Pelzer was able to obtain quality legal counsel. A lawyer, Orville C. Pratt, bound for Oregon and a judgeship in the Second Oregon Judicial District, had traveled from Leavenworth to Mann with Garland. Pratt convinced Pelzer that he should not fight the charges but should resign immediately and leave the Indian country.

One of the Pawnees, shot by Pelzer's orders, was still a prisoner at Fort Mann. Garland released him now and told him to tell his chief that the guilty white man had been disgraced and punished.

Four other officers, including O'Hara and Schnabel, were also induced to resign as "absolute drawbacks to the battalion." The impropriety of Pratt's "placing [the charges] in form" against the officers and then passing on to them Gilpin's wish that they resign was probably not called to their attention. Justice, doubtless, was done.

The enlisted men were also handled quickly. Fahlbush and Gold-beck had already been punished (probably by a special court), but Garland brought more serious charges. Fahlbush was turned over to the United States district attorney at St. Louis to be tried for murder, and Goldbeck was given a dishonorable discharge. Several men accused of stealing horses and mules were released for lack of evidence. William and Colonel Garland agreed that further actions were not needed.

Garland, his work done effectively and fairly, hastened back to Jefferson Barracks, completed his report for Jones and with a new star on his shoulder moved out of William's life and on to another assignment.[24]

During those same summer weeks of the investigation, plains warfare broke out again. Save one, all of the tribes that William had dealt with were behaving themselves. The Comanches had merely run and hidden in the West Texas arroyos and by June were ready for their old system of "triangular trade." The neighborly Osages were plentifully supplied by the government with tobacco, lead, powder, firearms, and other necessities of life which they swapped for Comanche products. According to the Osages' own agent, the Comanches delivered them some fifteen hundred mules in 1847, worth $50 to $75 each. By some grapevine William Gilpin had already surmised what was happening and knew that his only recourse was to eliminate the trade by protecting the rightful owners of the mules. The Osages and Comanches completed their business, the Osages going home, and their partners distributing themselves along the Santa Fe Trail from Walnut Creek (insolently near the

[24] Post Returns, Fort Leavenworth, 1847–1848; Gilpin to Marcy, March 10 and June 10, 1848, William Pelzer to Marcy, May 30, 1848, Garland to Jones, May 24 and June 9, 1848, in Gilpin File, Letters Received, G 62, G 270, G 210, and G 217; Gilpin to Marcy, undated, Jones to Garland, May 9, 1848, Garland to Jones, July 14, August 3 and 16, 1848, in Record Group 94, G 368; all in A.G.O., National Archives. See also *St. Louis Reveille*, July 3, 1848; unpublished diary of Orville C. Pratt, July 1, 5, 7, 1848, Coe Collection, Yale University Library; *Weekly Tribune* (Liberty, Mo.), April 7, 1848. This paper wished Gilpin every success as a good officer and a gentleman, but for his sake hoped that the Germans would be ordered home promptly. I can find no reason why the War Department thought William was at Fort Scott.

Kansas settlements) to the adobe villages of northeastern New Mexico.[25]

As well as the chronology can be reconstructed from the local press and the official reports of William and his lieutenants, he now divided his battalion into several small units; some daily "screened the train" to protect the merchants, while others resumed the offensive to drive the Comanches back into hiding. William himself led an attack on the warriors near Mora, New Mexico, and killed "many" Comanches with the loss of one or two soldiers killed and a few wounded.[26] The Comanche horses outrunning William's mules, he appears to have returned then to Fort Mann, unable to continue pursuit.

Probably during these same days in early June, William ordered First Lieutenant W. B. Royall to escort the paymaster from Leavenworth to Mann. A few days later artillery Company "C" under First Lieutenant Phillip Stremmel (replacing Pelzer) left Fort Mann to meet Royall for the last stage of the relay in which the paymaster was the baton. Both detachments were scouted constantly by distant Indians. On June 7 at Pawnee Fork the Indians quietly surrounded Stremmel and his sixty-five men at supper. Two Indians had reached the corral before any alarm was given. The Indians, who were a combination of Pawnees and Comanches, fired a few times at the troops with no damage. While the soldiers beat back the Indians, Stremmel finally touched off a six pound gun aimed rather fruitlessly at the fast-circling horsemen. The noises frightened his own animals so much that they stampeded.

The Comanches suddenly "let loose a white horse who running among them [the cavalry mules and horses] succeeded in drawing them off toward the main body of Indians." Perhaps five Comanches were killed, but under very dangerous circumstances their comrades removed all of the bodies as well as the wounded. At this cost two hundred Comanches had in ten minutes acquired twenty-two riding animals for next year's fair.

---

25 Rupert N. Richardson, *The Comanche Barrier to South Plains Settlement*, p. 186.

26 William makes no mention of this battle in any letter, but two papers published the same story as reported by residents of Santa Fe (*Weekly Tribune* [Liberty, Mo.], June 9, 1848; *St. Louis Reveille*, June 5, 1848).

Stremmel reported later that the Indians kept his men in sight constantly as he sent back to Colonel Gilpin for more animals, then hurried on to Walnut Creek where he joined Royall with the paymaster. At dawn of June 18, just as the united groups began the return march to Fort Mann, they were attacked again. With spears and shields the Indians charged in from all sides on the animals, perhaps one hundred paces from most of the troops. Again about twenty animals were stolen, including two being held by troopers. As before, the use of artillery had to be delayed because of the close quarters, but finally a few rounds were fired at the escaping Indians.

Royall and two-score men went in pursuit and suddenly found themselves ambushed by five to seven hundred warriors. The soldiers were happy to escape with only four men wounded (in lance charges) as the Indians drifted away. Royall and his men were all puzzled by the nearby presence throughout the fight of "a female who seemed to be their queen mounted on a horse, decorated with silver ornaments on a scarlet dress, who rode about giving direction about the wounded." Her efforts were so successful that the troops had trouble assessing the Indian casualties and got no prisoners. This time probably twenty Indians were killed, again no soldiers killed, but four wounded.

The experience was shaking to whites all along the trail. The boldness of an attack upon troops, the unprecedented specter of a queen, and the presence of a combination of an estimated one thousand Comanches, Pawnees, and Osages greatly unsettled Gilpin's battalion, already torn by the Garland findings.[27] Amid rumors that the battalion was to be disbanded William concluded that he must once more take the offensive as the only way to protect the travelers on the trail. Crippled by the uselessness of Company "D" (confined to Fort Mann) he gave up his shuttling and sent the cavalry to search out the Comanches and destroy their will to pillage, for that summer at least. Already the trail was crowded, and William estimated later that 12,000 persons, 50,000 head of stock

---

[27] First Lt. W. B. Royall to the Adjutant General, June 21, 1848 and First Lt. Phillip Stremmel to William Gilpin, June 23, 1848, Record Group 94, G 449, A.G.O., National Archives. In March Stremmel had charged Pelzer with cowardice and thievery.

and 3,000 wagons had gone past Fort Mann that summer.[28] They needed his protection.

William ordered Captain John Griffin of Company "A" out to the Cimarron and along its north bank to hunt a reported Comanche village. At a point where the river bisects the Kansas-Oklahoma line Griffin found a grove that had recently been the camp of "thousands" of Indians. A few miles off he encountered six hundred warriors moving in broad formation to protect their traveling village.

The cavalry attacked the tribe at noon on July 9. In spite of the efforts of the warriors the entire village was put in flight. Two soldiers were wounded and about thirty braves killed in the three hour affair. No red queen, no white stallion were seen, for the Indians were the surprised party this time; the same superb task of saving wounded and dead was noticeable, however, as the Indians even tied their dead onto horses to escape the soldiers.

Satisfied that the Comanches were on the run, William sent Captain Thomas Jones and Company "B" (Griffin and Jones each commanded only one hundred men in these "companies") to complete the task. Near the same grove that Griffin had found, a small unit of Jones' company was ambushed by Pawnees and had to fight hand-to-hand until the Indians were frightened off by the balance of the detachment. From the litter and the abandoned food, salt, and animals Jones concluded that both Pawnees and Comanches were in full flight from the Arkansas and Cimarron to the wilds beyond the lower Canadian. Leaving twenty dead Pawnees, Jones brought his company, with only five wounded, back to Fort Mann.

As far as the Separate Battalion was concerned the Indian war was over. With verbal orders only, William began moving his scattered detachments to Fort Leavenworth. Griffin's and Jones' paused only briefly at Mann; two squads rode to Bent's to recover some government equipment, and William with the balance trooped east. He stopped at Independence long enough to describe the military picture in letters to the War Department, then sent the battalion to Fort Leavenworth to accomplish its mustering-out. His

[28] *Weekly Tribune* (Liberty, Mo.), July 14, 1848; R. L. Duffus, *The Santa Fé Trail*, p. 222.

military duties finished, William remained in Independence, dragged his feverish, weary frame into the Noland House and collapsed in bed, his health almost destroyed.[29]

In a year of service on the trail what had William's battalion accomplished? The skirmishes could mean but little in the ultimate solution of the Indian question. He had proved again the accepted belief that a tight military organization could defeat far more numerous bands of Indians burdened with their women and children. He also proved that he could drive the tribes away from the Santa Fe Trail but could guarantee to the merchants no permanent protection once his back was turned. Toward the end of his tour of duty he had become more bitterly aware of the futility of pushing nomads one way or another.

Since the battalion's discharge coincided with the end of the merchant's year on the Trail the Indians had no reason to return to their old business until the next spring. For a few months, therefore, the Trail would remain quiet. But William knew that his job was not half done; in his opinion the permanent settlement of the frontier required a string of forts, as opposed to General Kearny's proposal of a constantly moving cavalry. William recommended constructing four new adobe posts, purchasing Bent's Fort for the army, and keeping the cavalry active. These steps would solve the problem of security for that trail and would set the example for the Oregon and other trails to follow. Before the winter ended treaties must be signed with the Cheyennes, Arapahoes, and Kiowas, and a cavalry of a thousand men must "invade" the lands of the Comanches and Apaches, chastise them and release their hundreds of Mexican prisoners, otherwise, he told the War Department, ". . . all the atrocities of a very severe Indian war may be momentarily looked for and are certain to burst forth with the early spring."

These recommendations William put into his final report to the War Department, added some of his usual descriptions of the Great Plains, and concluded with one more swipe at the lazy and ignorant officers who had brought such suffering to his battalion.

[29] Captain John C. Griffin to Gilpin, July 12, 1848, Record Group 94, G 368, A.G.O., National Archives; Captain Thomas Jones to Gilpin, July 23, 1848, Record Group 94, G 449, A.G.O., National Archives; *Weekly Tribune* (Liberty, Mo.), August 25, 1848.

This summation of his year's work on the Santa Fe Trail was reliable. In fighting nine battles and killing 253 Indians the battalion had merely prevented a terrible war. That was all. The Indians, momentarily on the defensive, could be contained if the government acted at once. But it did not.

Tom Fitzpatrick, in his winter arguments with William Bent and William Gilpin, had a plan for a vast assembly of all the plains tribes with agents of the United States government. Several tribes were willing, and Gilpin had punished others enough so that a comprehensive plan of peace, food, and gifts made sense. Gilpin's campaign ended too late to make the meetings possible in 1849. Congressional inactivity held up Fitzpatrick the next year, and it was not until the summer of 1851 that the great gathering took place at Fort Laramie. Fitzpatrick, aided and frequently handicapped by Jim Bridger, was in charge of negotiations, made very touchy by the tribes' fears of one another. The treaties were signed but failed to solve the problem because the Indians claimed that the annuities were too small.

So perhaps it did not matter that the Comanches were conspicuously absent from Fort Laramie. Their battles with William Gilpin were now three years old and only small events in the tribe's chronicles. William's recommendations were not carried through, either. No new punitive action in the south was tried; the string of forts was not built, and even Fort Mann was once again deserted; William Bent refused to see his fort in any other hands and burned it. Another generation would have to face the threats of Comanches and Apaches in the American southwest.[30]

In spite of these failures William was not lacking commendation for his campaign. The Secretary of War praised the battalion's work in a report to Polk, and the Missouri State Senate unanimously presented the thanks of the people of Missouri to William, his

---

[30] Gilpin to the Adjutant General, August 1, 1848, Record Group 94, G 449, A.G.O., National Archives; Gilpin to Colonel Garland, August 18, 1848, Gilpin File, Letters Received, G 398, A.G.O., National Archives; Bancroft, *William Gilpin*, p. 41; Lavender, *Bent's Fort*, pp. 312–323. A terrible epidemic of cholera among Bent's Indian friends may have been a factor in his setting fire to his buildings and property (Hafen and Ghent, *Broken Hand*, pp. 165, 228, and 244). Most of the Indians that Gilpin fought had no rifles yet, an advantage that the government lost by its delays.

officers, and his men "for their brave and energetic conduct" against "wild and restless" Pawnees and Comanches.[31]

During the next few months William was too ill to follow these developments. He scarcely left home that fall and winter and in the spring of 1849 he decided to go to St. Louis to find the competent medical care that Independence lacked. He reached St. Louis in May, the day after 361 people died of cholera. Concluding that his move would help little, he traveled on to Lexington, Kentucky, seeking treatment there from Dr. Benjamin Dudley, founder of Transylvania University's medical school.[32]

Apparently William came close to dying in Lexington. Always spare of flesh, his six-foot frame was reduced to one hundred pounds, and Dudley said that William was the sickest man he had seen in forty-five years of practice. Living at the old Phoenix Hotel William lay on the porch listening to planters talk of cotton and secession, his chats violently broken three times a week by the doctor who treated him with raw calomel, ipecac, and rhubarb. After three months, still sixty pounds underweight, but on a slow road to recovery, he returned to St. Louis for the winter of 1849–

[31] Marcy to President, December 1, 1848, U.S. House of Representatives, *Executive Document No. 1*, 30th Cong., 2nd Sess., 1848, p. 77; *Weekly Tribune* (Liberty, Mo.), February 23, 1849. In 1875 the government was still facing a suit over William's arrest of a merchant and the destruction of sixty barrels of the man's beer at Fort Mann in June, 1848. The Secretary of War did not know why William had done it, but we can make a reasonable guess. Bureau of Legal and Departmental Information to Secretary of War, July 3, 1875, and endorsement July 20, 1875, Gilpin File, Letters Received, G 62, A.G.O., National Archives.

[32] In 1849 St. Louis suffered its worst epidemic in history. German immigrants were believed to have brought cholera to New Orleans and St. Louis in December, 1848. Deaths from the plague reached a peak betwen mid-May and mid-July, 1849, the precise period of William's stay in the city; 4,285 persons died of cholera in St. Louis in 1849 (John Thomas Scharf, *History of St. Louis City and County*, II, 1574–1575). I have to assume that William had malaria before his Indian campaign and contracted cholera during it. Obviously this is only a guess. Dr. Dudley was a graduate of the University of Pennsylvania Medical School and a specialist at Transylvania in cholera. He introduced many techniques to medicine at the university and retired in 1850 when the school closed down (Bancroft, *William Gilpin*, p. 42). William's doctor in Philadelphia was Samuel Jackson, also widely known as one of America's early specialists in cholera treatment (J. S. Chambers, *The Conquest of Cholera*, pp. 34, 72–74, 173–174, 233–238).

1850 and then, feeling only a little better, paid a visit to his family in Philadelphia. He lived with his mother and two sisters for the summer, escaping the middle western heat, while remembering old times and telling the women of his adventures among Mexicans and Indians.

He was not greatly tempted to stay in the East—either to take up some of his father's many enterprises or to work in law with brother Henry. He merely rested and saved himself from renewed exposure to the waning epidemic which had now crossed all Missouri. The West still called him and in the autumn of 1850 he returned to his shack in Independence.

CHAPTER EIGHT

# The Great West Is "Some"

*Geopolitician, 1850's*

During his months of illness William Gilpin had time in abundance
to consider his future once again. Aged thirty-four (in 1849), he
had been soldier, politician, writer, and amateur real estate speculator. Only his military career was ended, and then just in a technical sense, for he was to be commander-in-chief of Colorado's
militia when he became governor in 1861. But he had fought his
last Indian and led his last cavalry charge against Mexican forces.
Although he was a good disciplinarian and a brave soldier, he did
not seem to enjoy the life. Too many other officers were lazy and
inefficient, and William was frustrated by men who he thought
were just putting in time. In the absence of war, he realized, conditions would be worse. Even after the recovery of his health William made no attempt to re-enter the army.

His military service had now made him modestly famous in the
West and especially in Missouri. Frontier voters, looking for men
of action with legal background, found in William a near-perfect

candidate for numerous state offices. He was intelligent, very widely read, a gifted (if long-winded) orator, and as extravagant about
the future of the region as any man alive. His political prospects'
seemed limitless.

He faced one problem in his political life, however, that he could
not resolve prior to 1860. A Jackson, Locofoco,[1] Benton Democrat,
who very late developed an antislavery feeling, he, by the early
1850's was in the minority wing of his own party in Missouri.
Benton, defeated for the Senate in 1851, served one term in the
House, retired, and died in 1858; his influence in the party was
gone early in the decade. William still supported Benton on many
issues, but found that most Missouri Democrats were becoming
more ardently proslavery and following the leadership of Senator
David R. Atchison.

William's opportunities were further limited by the fact that he
was a more aggressive westerner than any of his party. Uncon-
cerned with the crucial question of the extension of slavery, he
favored all territorial expansion in any direction. Additionally, he
quarreled with Benton over the selection of a railroad route through
the Rockies. No longer a member of a strong machine, William was
often campaigning alone. So, in spite of frequent popular suggestion,
as well as official nominations, William was unsuccessful in his
immediate political aims. Toward the end of the decade he bet on
a new horse, however, and his winnings were substantial.

Throughout most of the 1850's, then, his energies were princi-
pally applied to combining his other two vocations of publicist and
town planner—the jobs he loved the best. Independence (his home
until 1860 in spite of numerous visits to St. Louis and the East)
provided him with the ideal headquarters for his work.

According to Gilpin, about 1824 the two westernmost counties
of Missouri, separated by the river, had sought incorporation by
the legislature at the same time. Most of the residents north of the
Missouri had come from Kentucky and called their county Clay,
with Liberty the seat. "On the South," he said, "as if in rivalry,
emigrants from Virginia, Carolina and Tennessee, selected the

---

[1] The Locofocos were a wing of the Democrats, opposing monopolies and seeking tight restrictions upon private bank operations.

name of Jackson for their county, and Independence for their City."[2] Liberty grew very slowly, but Independence, because of its better location for the Santa Fe trade, expanded rapidly.

When he had first moved to Independence in 1841 William had bought some of the land between the center of the town and the river. He probably used funds from the sale of some of his father's lands in Kentucky or Pennsylvania; how much he spent, and how many acres he bought is unknown.

Adding some of his own theories to those of Homboldt, William concluded that a great continental city would grow near the site of Independence. His enthusiasm and warmth swept through the town and he created a development which his contemporaries called "Gilpintown." The heart of Independence was then about four miles from the Missouri, and William built his bachelor farmhouse about half-way between the county court house and the river. The people of Independence, lacking dock facilities generally used those at Wayne City, and William persuaded the county to macadamize a road between the two towns, and incidentally past his farm (apparently this is the present Liberty Street and Courtney Road).

How much help William had in planning and developing Gilpintown is unclear. He had a few partners, including his good friend David Waldo, and some of his frequent trips to the East were in part to seek funds for his suburb. He did not get far beyond the mapping stage. He laid out—on paper—an enormously expanded Independence, with wide, straight, paved streets and roads, with locations for schools, colleges, parks, churches, and industry as well as homes. Nevertheless, property sales lagged.[3]

Independence, according to its town historian, was "the pioneer of all western booms . . . the work chiefly of one man, Maj. William Gilpin, a resident here, who distinguished himself as an author, a

[2] Carrie W. Whitney, *Kansas City, Missouri: Its History and Its People 1808–1908*, I, 35.

[3] W. Howard Adams, President of the Jackson County Historical Society, and Philip C. Brooks, director of the Harry S. Truman Library, helped obtain for me a copy of a map which probably is of Gilpintown; only thirteen homes are shown, and two of these are designated as Gilpin's. The plat has no date. Some sections of Gilpintown are not yet developed, but the Truman Library is located on land that was once part of William's scheme. See the *Kansas City Star*, February 18, 1900.

soldier, an explorer. . . . He created the wildest enthusiasm." But when William returned from Washington and New York without the capital for his town, the project lost its energy.[4]

Not so with William; he merely broadened his aims. He could hold onto Gilpintown to see what the future could mean, but at the same time he would publicize the whole western Missouri area and even give his blessings to the Great Plains and the Rockies beyond. William never ran out of dreams.

How he lived in these years is not clear. He performed various legal chores, but in his own letters William never mentions prosecuting a case in court. He had a bounty land warrant of 160 acres for his Mexican War service, and he used it to locate a quarter-section six miles southeast of Grandview in lower Jackson County. He did not live there, and may have sold or leased it. He perhaps received funds from his father's estate. Old settlers remembered, however, that he lived simply and frugally, probably growing enough to feed himself while financing a few luxuries, such as a fine horse, with law fees. Recalled one neighbor,

The people around him looked on him as an eccentric scholar. . . . His attainments were far greater than those of any other man in the county. . . . He was six feet tall, with an athletic figure, and dark, curly hair. He paid no attention to dress. He went about town in old, baggy clothes part of the time with a frayed rope around his waist for a belt. . . . He spent most of his time making maps, reading and making speeches about the West. His enthusiasm over the future of the West was almost without limitation.[5]

[4] William L. Webb, *The Centennial History of Independence, Missouri*, pp. 19–20; *Independence Examiner*, July 2, 1942.

[5] *Kansas City Star*, May 26, 1901. This version of William's personal carelessness does not at all coincide with several descriptions drawn at both earlier and later stages of his life. Probably his illness and concentration on his writing brought about the change temporarily. William collected some bills for the Waldos in St. Louis, saving them from a "suit which wd have cost at least a good share of it to a lawyer." David also wrote to his brother in Oregon that when Gilpin came back from St. Louis he (David) "would burn up the papers as you request." I can shed no light on these curious comments. David Waldo, it should be recalled, lent money to William for his Oregon trip; Daniel was a homesteader in the Willamette Valley. David to Daniel Waldo, November 6, 1851, and March 1, 1852, David Waldo Manuscript Collection, 1851–1852, Missouri Historical Society. William's bounty land is described as "NW 1/4 of Section 35, township 47 North, Range 32 West" recorded at the Clinton, Missouri

In the minds of most residents of the Mississippi Valley was the belief that their future progress was closely tied to railroad construction, and William was an early leader in expressing this conviction. Beyond the bend of the Missouri, water transportation was sharply limited; if Independence (and Gilpintown) were to grow further, they needed rail highways across the plains and the Rockies. But more than logic urged itself upon William, for transportation development was in his blood. His grandfather, father, uncles, and brother had all played key roles in this activity, and William had grown up in a household that believed that good market roads stood only a little behind godliness. One of William's earliest and fondest memories was that of waiting for a British train to pass through a tunnel—the first train William had ever seen.

The first national railroad promoter in the United States was Asa Whitney, whose ideas must have had some influence on William. Whitney was a New York merchant who made a fortune in China and returned with it just prior to the period when the Chinese-United States commerce was first regularized by treaty. Convinced that great commercial, political, and social gains would accrue to the whole world when the Orient was linked to the United States, Whitney memorialized Congress in 1845 for permission to build a railroad from the Great Lakes to the mouth of the Columbia by way of South Pass. All that Whitney asked was the right to purchase a sixty-mile-wide strip of land from Lake Michigan to the Pacific coast at ten cents an acre. Then he would build the railroad.[6]

Whitney acquired two powerful opponents in Benton and Stephen A. Douglas, who had little in common with one another about railroad building but could agree that Whitney's plan was nonsense; Congress did nothing about it. By 1850 Whitney had given up his scheme and retired from public life.

Congressmen generally felt that a transcontinental railroad was indeed now needed but would give no individual the power that

Land Office (letter to author, June 19, 1961, from National Archives and Records Service).

[6] Asa Whitney, *A Project for a Railroad to the Pacific*; U.S. House of Representatives, *Executive Document No. 72*, 28th Cong., 2nd Sess., 1845.

Whitney sought. Furthermore, the government could probably afford to assist in the construction of only one route. By the end of the Mexican War a regional struggle had developed as various cities and sections of the Mississippi Valley sought to prove that they should be the departure point for a Pacific road. Two such rivals were Memphis and St. Louis with the naval scientist Lieutenant Matthew Maury and Senator Benton, respectively, the chief proponents. Memphis planned a railroad convention to drum up interest, and St. Louis immediately copied the idea.

After delays resulting from the close of the Mexican War, gold discoveries, Benton's congressional campaign, and the cholera epidemic, the St. Louis conference assembled October 15, 1849. The citizens of St. Louis and smaller Missouri towns had worked hard to raise funds and advertise their convention, and they were disappointed in the attendance. More than one-half of the approximately nine hundred delegates were from Missouri and few of the outsiders had national reputations. Van Buren, Clay, Calhoun, and Cass all sent greetings but did not come. Young Stephen Douglas was the best-known non-Missouri statesman at the sessions; representing the scientific world was Lieutenant Maury.

William Gilpin, seriously ill with cholera, returned from Transylvania in time for the railroad convention. What part he played must be conjecture, but the evidence is ample that he kept careful account of the proceedings and reported them to his friends in Independence.

The list of Missouri's delegates included most of her notables of the mid-nineteenth century. Benton attended only as guest speaker, but Montgomery Blair, Sterling Price and Trusten Polk (both future governors), Henry Geyer, many of William's war comrades, and most of the leading citizens of St. Louis were representatives. W. P. Darnes, who killed Gilpin's publisher nine years before, was a delegate, and Thornton Grimsley, the "bully" William had chastised, was the marshal.

In spite of the fact that Stephen A. Douglas had come to the convention to speak for Chicago and not St. Louis, he was elected permanent chairman. Other regions had their spokesmen—Maury favored Memphis as the terminal, and some of Whitney's agents spoke out for Prairie du Chien on the upper Mississippi. St. Louis was loudly protected by Benton; as usual there was no unanimity among Missouri points of view. Opinion differed also upon the proper route as well as the point of departure: Douglas advocated the Platte River and South Pass, while Benton, doubtless spurred into something of an absurdity by his son-in-law, held out for the Arkansas River and the San Juan Mountains of Colorado in spite of their terrible snows. Memphis proponents usually preferred a Texas route to the now widely reported gold fields of California. William Gilpin, motivated by a combination of self-interest and experience, supported St. Louis with Benton but maintained that after leaving Independence the tracks must follow the old Oregon Trail and cross the mountains at South Pass. William, who had as much experience in the Colorado Rockies as had Frémont, remained ever critical of Benton for his blindness.

The St. Louis press was, of course, also playing in the game. So bitter were the editorials against Douglas' partiality that he resigned the chairmanship in favor of Henry Geyer—new evidence of Benton's decline, for Geyer, a Whig, was soon to defeat him for the Senate seat that no one but Benton had ever held.

Seeking a compromise, the delegates petitioned the Congress for prompt government action on a *central* route with branches to Chicago, Memphis, and St. Louis. They then voted to adjourn until the following April for a new session to be held in Philadelphia.[7] Almost immediately after the convention's close William took passage back to Independence. Here he was instrumental in calling a public meeting on November 5 to ratify the actions just taken in St. Louis. After the selection of officers (William's friend, James Chiles, was chairman) Gilpin was called upon to speak about the railroad question and the St. Louis convention.

William tipped his hat in general reference to St. Louis, added a

[7] R. S. Cotterill, "National Railroad Convention in St. Louis, 1849," *Missouri Historical Review*, XII (July, 1918), 203–215. Cotterill points out that no one at the convention raised the question that organization of the territories was a prerequisite to transcontinental railroad construction. I have found no evidence of a Philadelphia convention, but curiously William was in that city during the period scheduled for the sessions. (Herbert Howe Bancroft, *History of the Life of William Gilpin*, p. 42). Geyer had defended the slayer of William's publisher when William edited the *Argus* back in 1840; in 1851 William Walker's journal reported that cholera was "still raging" in Independence (William E. Connelley [ed.], *The Provisional Government of Nebraska Territory and the Journals of William Walker*, p. 327; *St. Louis Reveille*, October 22, 1849).

few lines about Missouri's war heroes and then took off for a ninety-minute ramble on the pioneer army, the seven great basins and the four great valleys of North America, the route to the Pacific (South Pass), and what the products of the Mississippi Valley would do to the Orient and the world balance of power. He concluded that scientific methods and geographical scrutiny would solve the problems if people would cease arguing about details.

His words begin to sound familiar. Much of what he said he had previously written at the request of Congress when he returned from Oregon. He admitted, in fact, making the same talk earlier "at the camp of five thousand California emigrants, at Wakerusa [now the city of Lawrence], Kansas."[8] But not yet were his neighbors tired of his vision. How could they object if Gilpintown or Independence became a railroad center and brought them riches from Cathay in exchange for their hemp and tobacco?

William finished his portrait of a continent and moved that a committee be appointed to draw up resolutions of response to the St. Louis convention. Chiles chose twelve men—William first. The committee drafted twelve resolutions that were approved by the whole body; the only amendments were intended to give greater publicity to William's address. The resolutions, in spirit and language unquestionably William's work, endorsed the St. Louis convention and urged the people of Missouri to hold similar assemblies to direct their Congressmen to work for a "central, domestic" railroad.[9]

[8] William Gilpin, *Mission of the North American People*, App. II. How much earlier he does not say. He probably referred not to the present village of Wakerusa but to the junction of that stream and the Kansas River east of Lawrence. If five thousand emigrants were located at that spot it must have been in the spring; William could have added a few references to the convention when he spoke to the Independence meeting. Louise Barry and Secretary Nyle H. Miller of the Kansas State Historical Society doubt the 5,000 emigrants figure and so must I. I cannot explain the reference, however. (Letter from Mr. Miller, April 6, 1965.)

[9] William Gilpin, *Mission of the North American People*, App. II and III. William's writings are detectable primarily through the style and wide range of subject matter. Minor clues are numerous. For example, the Rockies are the "Sierra Madre" or "Mother mountain of the World"; the Cascades are the "Andes"; Mississippi Valley soil is "calcareous"; South America is always lumped with Japan and China in the Pacific market, and so on. Such conjecturing is needed in William's life because he did much anonymous publishing.

The coincidence of growing public interest in a subject so dear to William's heart contributed to his expanding reputation. In the heavy westward movement of 1849 and 1850 were many argonauts who read William's article, heard his speeches, or stopped off for a visit. Some even camped near the Gilpin home as the last stop before leaving civilization.[10]

Soldiers, politicians, pioneers were among his listeners. A close friend was William's neighbor, the Catholic priest, one Bernard Donnelly. William persuaded Benton to come to Independence on one occasion and the two men visited Father Donnelly and talked of the West and of the future. Donnelly remembered William as a cultural oasis in the West—"well read in the Latin and Greek classics. He spoke French fluently and had traveled abroad extensively." Donnelly said that William lived in the West because he loved it and wanted others to feel the same way. His predictions of gold in Colorado, pastoral wealth on the Plains, and commercial prosperity for Kansas City were things he believed. "His well stocked library was at my disposal and from its shelves I conned much useful lore and renewed my acquaintance with many loved authors."[11]

In spite of his illness William's growing fame now pushed him gently back into politics. He had spent the summer of 1850 in Philadelphia with his mother and sisters then returned to Independence that autumn. His name was placed in nomination for the House of Representatives from Missouri's Fifth District. William ran as an "Independent Democrat" in a field that included a Whig, a Benton Democrat, and an anti-Benton Democrat. William claimed to be running on the invitation of members of both parties, but the obvious split among the Democrats gave the victory to Sam Woodson, the Whig incumbent.

Unsuccessful and undaunted, William and his supporters raised their sights; in 1852 the Jefferson County Democrats nominated him for the post of governor. This time he ran as a Bentonite against several candidates, the strongest being Colonel Sterling Price, an anti-Benton man, who had been the commanding officer

10 Ralph P. Bieber (ed.), *Southern Trails to California in 1849*, p. 354.
11 William J. Dalton, *The Life of Father Bernard Donnelly*, p. 169.

of the United States troops in Santa Fe during the Mexican-Indian uprising.[12]

William's office-seeking was never very energetic nor even very well directed. A letter (doubtless biased) tells of a campaign speech that William made at the Rotunda in St. Louis. The occasion was the celebration of the battle of New Orleans, a big event for western Democrats. In attendance was "a slim collection of anxious looking individuals" who waited an extra half-hour before starting the session. After organizing some committees the chairman introduced William Gilpin, candidate for governor.

William's address explains his weakness as a political campaigner. Said a reporter who was present:

His speech was one *sui generis*, not belonging to any particular class or rank. He didn't make an 8th of January—Andrew Jackson, Battle of New Orleans speech, nor did he make a Benton speech (for he didn't deign to mention the ex-Senator), nor did he deliver what would ordinarily be termed a good Locofoco speech. He took a broad spat at the face of all creation, and wound up with a set of resolutions which he intends to stand upon (I suppose) as a gubernatorial platform.

He evidently thinks the great West is "some," and intends to array it against the East. Poor Indians are very much in his way—he wants them pushed to the Pacific giving their lands to the patriotic Democratic Dutch now flocking to this country.

Sometime during the evening partisan spirits were raised by the arrival of a band and many noisy Irish and Germans. After William finished, the practicing politicians endorsed the Democratic Baltimore platform of 1848, Benton for Congress in 1852, and Irish patriotism; they noisily condemned Senator Atchison, nullifiers, and national banks.[13]

Such following as Gilpin had was probably composed of Locofocos, hyphenates, land speculators, and farmers in varying proportions, with a few professional Bentonites still clinging to a capsizing ship. Doubtless he had a personal claque who believed in his grand design of Manifest Destiny. But William was running for office in the days of the stump speaker like Benton from whose

[12] *Weekly Tribune* (Liberty, Mo.), July 19, 1850, and January 9, 1852.

[13] *Ibid.*, January 23, 1852. See also William E. Parrish, *David Rice Atchison of Missouri.*

throat specks of blood would issue when he accused a man of having no heart; "he only has a gizzard and he has lied upon Benton from the bottom of his gizzard to the tip of his tongue"; who could describe "Claib" Jackson, "as demure as a prostitute at a christening."[14] William could not solicit votes that way. As he grew more mature his opponents became faceless and distant. They were vague: Atlantic shippers, blind capitalists, or salt-water politicians—useful comments, perhaps, but too mild and impersonal for Missouri in the 1850's. His real interest, in his own words, was "working to get this started as the territory of Colorado, forwarding the gold fever and seeing physicians."[15]

In short, Price was an easy victor in the gubernatorial race, and William went back to his writing. During his journeys in the Rockies William had seen geologic formations that convinced him that gold and silver could be found in many places. The California discoveries were mere endorsements to him, and from 1850 on he added great mineral wealth to his predictions for the future of the West. The danger lay in literal beliefs in William's words, for gold was not quite everywhere, and it required ten years to get from Sutter's Fort to Pike's Peak. Said one traveler:

The first statement which appeared worthy of serious attention was made by Colonel William Gilpin of the United States Army. This gentleman, a zealous student of the natural sciences, crossed the continent with a party of Oregon explorers, and again with his command during the Mexican War. . . . as the result of all his observations, he asserted the abundant existence of gold, silver, and precious stones throughout the Rocky Mountains. But his hearers voted him an enthusiast; and for ten years longer the only white inhabitants of the remote mountains continued to be trappers and traders.[16]

And Gilpin admitted that:

I tried to get parties to come across the plains and strike the mountains, but they would come a little way and then go back and some threatened to hang me for deceiving them. . . . The first party was some of my neighbors, and they thought all they had to do was bring

[14] William M. Meigs, *The Life of Thomas Hart Benton*, pp. 64, 456.
[15] William Gilpin, "A Pioneer of 1842," October 18, 1884, P–L28, Bancroft Library.
[16] Albert D. Richardson, *Beyond the Mississippi*, p. 136.

on their wagons and load them up with gold in a week or two. They came as far as Fort Riley. . . . They came from Jackson Co. Mo. my home.[17]

William's months with his own battalion on the upper Arkansas had given him some prominence as an authority on the mineral deposits of the region, and his prestige was raised by stories of "color" found by California-bound Cherokees who later decided to return to the Pike's Peak country and dig seriously. One historian wrote that Gilpin's addresses

obtained considerable circulation through the newspapers along the border. Colonel Gilpin was, of course, well grounded in the natural sciences . . . [and] convinced . . . of the presence of gold and silver in the Rocky Mtns. . . . the clearness with which he presented the results of his personal observations may be said to have first given substantial footing to reports of gold existing in the Pike's Peak country.[18]

William's personal success as an exhorter can not be calculated, of course, particularly since the gold rush to the Rockies achieved such enormous proportions before the end of the decade and perhaps encouragement was not needed. As early as 1850 an estimated 90,000 persons started across the plains from the mouth of the Kaw River, and by 1859 the prairie roads bulged with thousands of wagons going to—and coming from—the western Kansas Territory gold fields.

Guide books became very popular and those that have since been found indicate that William was frequently cited as an important authority for the fact that gold did exist in the Rockies. About one-half of one book is devoted to a Gilpin address on "Pike's Peak and the Sierra San Juan." It followed then, that many who found no gold—the "busted"—had a convenient scapegoat in William; their diaries and letters reveal some very angry men bound for home in the 1850's. One man in Leavenworth wrote to the *Republican*,

Since my arrival here, however, my faith has been considerably shaken in the Kansas gold mines. I have met some people who would say that the whole thing is a grand humbug, gotten up by persons interested

[17] Gilpin, "Pioneer of 1842."

[18] Jerome C. Smiley, *History of Denver*, p. 179. See also, Floyd B. Streeter, *The Kaw*, p. 5, and Le Roy R. Hafen (ed.), *Pike's Peak Gold Rush Guidebooks of 1859*, pp. 219, 241, 244–245, 249, 288.

in embryo towns on Mr. Gilpin's "plateau," and by merchants along the Missouri River who have goods to sell. Be this as it may, the Pike's Peak crowd has got up steam for the trip, and nothing can stop it.[19]

William's belief in the future of the whole West was too sincere to cause him to try town-building by such chicanery. He thought he was correct, and continued his publicity campaign in spite of talk by the "humbuggers" or the threats of their ropes. So he continued to work, undoubtedly writing many more articles and making many more talks than are now substantiated, for the press of his time often deemed it unnecessary to identify him.

A Jefferson City paper, for example, headed an article as merely "Gilpin's Maps," and went on to describe how he had presented the two houses of the Missouri General Assembly with several copies of his hydrographic maps of North America, "compiled from astronomical data of all existing authority, which contain very valuable information. Mr. Gilpin has spent several years, and much labor to publish these maps." The editor urged the legislature to purchase a few hundred from Gilpin and distribute them throughout the counties.[20]

Some weeks later William addressed "an immense concourse [in Liberty, Mo.] for two hours on the subject of a Pacific railroad at their request." He demonstrated by "Hydrographic and other maps prepared by himself at great labor and expense" that the only practicable route was the Platte River, South Pass, and the Snake River, and he took issue with Benton and others who preferred a more southerly passage. He included in his discussion an attack upon the "Atlantic Seaboard Merchants" whose ruinous monopoly of shipping was preventing a national railroad.[21]

Two significant observations must be made about this speech. First, neither the Liberty *Weekly Tribune* reporting the talk nor the St. Louis paper quoting it thought it necessary to use Gilpin's name and merely called him "the Colonel," especially strong evidence of his renown because Missouri was bursting with famous colonels. Second, this article clears William of being primarily a speculator. If his first interest were the booming of Independence

[19] Le Roy R. Hafen (ed.), *Colorado Gold Rush*, p. 283.
[20] *Jefferson Inquirer* (Jefferson City, Mo.), February 19, 1853.
[21] *St. Louis Evening News*, May 5, 1853.

he would have cooperated with the Benton faction for the St. Louis-Independence-Arkansas River route. But William's insistence on the Platte and South Pass could mean—and so it turned out— that the Chicago and Great Lakes sponsors would push Independence out of the picture. In short, William was arguing for the "right" road even though it strained his long friendship with Benton and weakened Gilpintown.

Not just gold and homestead seekers asked William to talk. In 1854 he was invited to appear before the dignified Mercantile Library Association of St. Louis. Copying some eastern cities, the chief merchants of Missouri combined business and culture to promote the growth of St. Louis. Organized in 1846, the Association soon had about one thousand members who read its publications and heard its distinguished speakers. Some of William's predecessors were the world traveler, Bayard Taylor, Senator Benton in 1850, Ralph Waldo Emerson in 1852, and Louis Agassiz in 1853. It was lively, intellectual company for William, but he was eloquent and at ease. Doubtless the "Table Lands of North America" impressed the merchants as much as did Transcendentalism or the Arabs.[22]

Even though he occasionally moved in these cultured circles William did not forget that he had an investment in his adopted hometown. Signing himself Wm. Gilpin, Esq., he wrote "The Cities of Missouri" for the October, 1853, issue of *The Western Journal and Civilian* then in its eleventh volume (pp. 31–40). Tucked in with articles on manufacturing, iron mountains, and self intellectual culture, was a ten-page discussion on Independence, second in Missouri only to "Metropolitan St. Louis." About one-half of the pages were devoted to tables illustrating the agricultural production of eight counties including William's own Jackson (it led all of the others in "Asses and Mules").

The theme, however, was that Independence would by nature have to be the emporium for the Territory of Nebraska now being discussed by the Congress. William predicted that a state would be carved out of this area within four years. His boundaries coincided

[22] Brad Luckingham, "A Note on the Significance of the Merchant in the Development of St. Louis Society as Expressed in the Philosophy of the Mercantile Library Association," *Missouri Historical Review*, LVII (January, 1963), 184–198.

well with present-day Kansas, pushed about one hundred miles north to follow the river basins. His name for this state was Washington, whose goods must pass to the east through Independence.

But his home town had other virtues which the businessman and homeseeker must note. It was due north of Galveston, and seven hundred miles of railroad across the "most delicious of all countries, at the divide between timber and prairie lands," would "blend . . . in the natural social ties . . . the great fraternal States of Texas, Arkansas, Missouri and Iowa." His road was "tabooed," however, for "Federal power, made the meretricious engine of maritime monopoly and spleen, declares it an Indian waste, and interdicts it to the white millions."

William concluded that Independence's central position in the Mississippi Valley and the United States assured by natural law the great future of the town.

In a different issue of the same journal the editor, attacking the Great American Desert theory, quoted William on the "slopes and valleys of the Rocky Mountains" and concluded that Gilpin was a "highly intelligent gentleman" who might exaggerate but who was "a man of much learning . . . well acquainted with the region."[23]

William's steady publicizing of the West began to bring him attention from some of the many travelers who passed through the Great Valley and described America as they saw it. One of these was Ferencz or Francis Pulszky, who, condemned to death for his political liberalism, fled Hungary with his wife and Louis Kossuth. Exiled in America, the visitors examined the institutions of the United States and reported on them with both fairness and charm in *White, Red, Black*. In sections on the western movement of the pioneer and the "Physical Configuration of North America" they relied primarily upon William Gilpin as their authority, quoting from a speech he made at St. Louis in 1851. The occasion of the talk and how they obtained a copy they do not say, but passages that they repeated can be found in several of William's speeches or writings.

Once again William is not introduced but simply referred to as "Colonel Gilpin, a man whose comprehensive mind and indomi-

[23] "Slopes and Valleys of the Rocky Mountains," *The Western Journal and Civilian*, X (April, 1853), 1–11.

table energy, may yet give him an important place in his country."
As usual he described the mountain ranges, the basins, the valleys,
and the great advantages of North America over other continents.
That the Pulszkys (who were not just heroes of Hungarian liberalism, but noted in art and science as well) gave so much of their
attention to William is singular and enlightening.[24]

Another famous traveler who spent some time with William in
Independence, was the German mineralogist, journalist, and liberal
politician, Julius Froebel, one more of the many who had to escape
from Europe in 1848. For several years Froebel lived in New York,
writing and editing and making extensive tours of the United States
and Central America. Froebel wanted to accompany a merchant
caravan from the Missouri border to Chihuahua and in this connection waited in Independence from July 5 to August 17, 1852,
during which time he made the acquaintance of Gilpin.

As recorded by Froebel the conversations were indeed strange,
for William apparently expressed himself in terms that he never
used in print or public address. Froebel loosely linked Gilpin with
various noisy eccentrics in the United States of that time—spiritu-
alists, vegetarians, and religious fanatics. According to Froebel,
William held a highly respected position in Missouri in spite of
some of his extravagant ideas.

He regards the "American" as the "most ancient and primitive civilization of mankind," and laments that this is not acknowledged by the
world at large. This culture, he admits, has become degenerate in
America itself; but in China it is still found in a pure state. Hence
salvation must come to America from China, and this consists in the
introduction of the "Chinese constitution," viz the "patriarchal democracy of the Celestial Empire." The political life of the United States
is, "through European influences," in a state of complete demoraliza-
tion, and the Chinese constitution alone contains the elements of re-
generation. For this reason a railroad to the Pacific is of such vast
importance, since by its means the Chinese trade will be conducted
straight across the North-American continent. This trade must bring
in its train Chinese civilization. All that is usually alleged against
China is mere calumny, spread purposely, just like those calumnies
which are circulated in Europe about the United States.

[24] Francis and Theresa Pulszky, *White, Red, Black*, I, 96–112.

Froebel went on to classify William as one of the "better element of Know-Nothings," an American malcontent proud of America's future, but unsure of her past.

"We want the prestige of antiquity," said Mr. ———— to me; "but we have it! See the Indian mounds in our West!" . . . It is an endeavor, mentally and historically, as has been done politically, to emancipate themselves from Europe; and they imagine they can attain this object by denying their physical and mental origin.

While William had often spoken of the benefits of oriental trade to the United States and the advantages of increased intercourse with the Pacific nations at the expense of the Atlantic, he had never made such sweeping assertions for the benefits of Chinese democracy. What prompted Gilpin's odd exaggerations? Likely, as Kenneth Porter says, if he believed in the superiority of Chinese institutions he dared not say so to any but a passing stranger. Possibly, like many another frontiersman, he enjoyed pulling the leg of a learned traveler; possibly he was misquoted. Suffice it that William Gilpin made an impression on Julius Froebel.[25]

Thus the months passed for William, his living as simple as his writing was grandiose. But the swift events of a moving frontier had a way of sweeping William along, and this happened again with the Nebraska problem.

The end of the Mexican War, the discovery of gold in California, and the substantial European immigration all combined to quicken the already rapid westward movement. By the 1850's pioneers in number were for the first time poised beyond the Mississippi River, contemplating homes on the edge of the Great American Desert. Mass production of the reaper, rising grain prices, and the beginnings of better transportation from the Middle West to the eastern cities made such settlement seem reasonable. In 1850 California obtained statehood; heavy travel to that region as well as the continued flow to Oregon increased the demand for better protection

[25] Julius Froebel, *Seven Years' Travel in Central America*, 222–223; Kenneth W. Porter, "William Gilpin: Sinophile and Eccentric," *The Colorado Magazine*, XXXVII (October, 1960), 245–253. Professor Porter, whose article led me to Froebel's book, declares that even though Froebel did not use Gilpin's name, there can be no doubt of the identity of "Mr. ————." I agree. Froebel was one of the youngsters in Friedrich Froebel's famed experimental school. Like William Gilpin, the younger Froebel was a devotee of Alexander von Humboldt.

and accommodations for travelers. A first step necessarily was the organization into a formal territory of the regions between the Missouri and the Rockies.

This harmless issue was now fused by the transcontinental railroad question and turned into a terrible explosive. In 1853 Congress authorized the survey of four possible routes to the Pacific and concluded that although requiring the purchase of Mexican territory, the one posing the fewest problems would pass from New Orleans by way of Texas and the Gila River to southern California.

Led by Stephen A. Douglas, a number of Congressmen with important political and economic goals quickly jumped to stymie the Pierce Administration (and especially Secretary of War Jefferson Davis) with a bill to organize the vast "Platte Country" and make possible a central railroad. Entirely unacceptable to southern congressmen, the bill was debated and amended to get their vote by dividing the area into Nebraska and Kansas Territories and throwing the whole question of slavery open again through popular sovereignty. Thus the people of the new territories would decide through their legislatures whether or not they would have slavery. A prerequisite was the repeal of portions of the venerable Missouri Compromise, and the United States began running down the road to disunion.

Innocent by-standers to these proceedings were a few thousand "civilized" Indians, residing just west of the Missouri in present-day Kansas. Moved from Ohio and Illinois a dozen years before, Shawnees, Delawares, and especially Wyandots had prospered as farmers in the Kaw Valley. Some of the Wyandots were white men, captives of an earlier day who had grown up with the tribe, or Missouri traders who had married into the tribe—for love of maiden or land we can only guess.

The Wyandots held a superb, central location (approximately that of present Kansas City, Kansas) which they might lose to white claim-jumpers or "sooners." They reasoned that while creation of a territory might force the sale of some of their unoccupied lands, ownership of their developed properties would be permanently protected by the federal government.

Another group with a stake in Nebraska was the usual assortment of land-hungry pioneers, speculators, and legitimate farmers who had not yet crossed the Missouri because the federal government made it impossible for them to get title in the Indian lands. Some of these men wanted the Indians removed, but most were satisfied that the tribes owned surplus land that could be sold once the government gave its approval.

Thus it appears that for a variety of motives most of the people directly concerned favored creation of the new territory before the question of slavery was ever raised.

In the western tradition the Wyandots in 1852 chose one of their whites, Abelard Guthrie, as delegate to Congress. Guthrie was to request a territorial government and remain as Nebraska's representative after the bill was passed. His chief function then, apparently, would be to negotiate a treaty guaranteeing Wyandot land titles.

Traveling to Washington with Missouri senators Geyer and Atchison, Guthrie discovered the southern requirement for repeal of the Missouri Compromise as a prerequisite for a new territory. Assuming the impossibility of repeal, Guthrie and his associates were depressed but continued with their plans. They threw their support behind Congressman Willard Hall's bill calling for a "Platte Territory," appropriating $100,000 to purchase Indian lands, and leaving the slavery question untouched.[26]

Soon other bills for the territory were introduced, and the Wyandot's role was obscured more and more as Nebraska became a national issue. Guthrie received no seat in Washington and returned home to help with a different approach. On July 26, 1853, a small group of men met in the Wyandot council house in Wyandot City and organized a provisional government of Nebraska Territory, chose various officers including William Walker as provisional governor, and drew up a number of resolutions, proclaiming the government and calling for elections to Congress.

The purpose and importance of this convention has been the subject of a great deal of speculation. Both Hall and Benton supported the meeting; Atchison claimed that Benton intended to move to the mouth of the Kansas so that he could become Nebraska's Senator. The Methodist Church, the Wyandots, the Indian traders, all had their motives. But of more concern to this biography

[26] Hall was the man who helped draft the constitution of New Mexico for Kearny during the Mexican War and was elected to Congress at that time. See Chapter 6.

is the question of what William Gilpin was doing in a Wyandot meeting.

For the testimony of one delegate is that William was there and that he addressed the session. William was evidently then editing the *Independence Agrarian* and was invited as a writer and authority on the West.[27] One author claims that the final copy of the resolutions was in William's handwriting, and some of the language could well be his. William might have enjoyed the excitement of planning a territory (as he had in Oregon) and being an old resident, doubtless knew many of the Wyandot leaders. But his overpowering interest in these years was the Pacific railroad, and that undoubtedly was the subject he proposed at Wyandot.

The preamble and most of the resolutions (including the *first* three) are concerned almost entirely with the railroad and not with Nebraska Territory. Several newspapers referred to the convention primarily in terms of railroad routes, and at least one writer called it a "Railroad Convention." The tenor of the resolutions, in fact, closely followed those drawn up by Gilpin at the Independence rally of November, 1849. Rather than a preliminary to the Kansas-Nebraska struggle, the Wyandot meeting more logically is another expression of frontier railroad fever in a town that coincidentally was not yet in an organized territory.[28]

William was usually far ahead of his time on most issues. His friend, C. C. Chiles, said that they used to call him "Prophet Bill."[29] But William was slow to grasp what was at stake in the Nebraska question—slower than Benton or Atchison or many another politician. Probably he reflected majority frontier opinion that trans-

[27] I have not been able to find a copy of the *Agrarian*. Other press references to it indicate that William edited it during 1853–1854.

[28] Connelley (ed.), *Provisional Government of Nebraska*, pp. 30–42, 76–79, 388. Connelley was convinced that Gilpin wrote the resolutions and that they served as the first territorial constitution. William E. Connelley, *Doniphan's Expedition*, p. 151 n. *National Intelligencer* (Washington, D.C.), August 16, 1853. The *Intelligencer*, citing several Missouri papers, declared that the Wyandot meeting showed the impatience of Missourians for a new territory. Frank H. Hodder, "Genesis of the Kansas-Nebraska Act," *Proceedings of the State Historical Society of Wisconsin, 1912* (Madison, 1913), 69–86; Webb, *History of Independence, Mo.*, p. 251; James C. Malin, *The Nebraska Question, 1852–1854*, pp. 80–85, 179–203.

[29] Webb, *History of Independence*, p. 234.

portation, land, Indians, and protection were paramount; slavery was unimportant. Publishing a summary of his views on Nebraska in November, 1853, in Jefferson City, he called upon the Democrats of St. Louis to have a "prodigious meeting" on settling Nebraska, proclaiming it completely open to the people now and forever. The motto must be "Nebraska, homesteads and no federal land tax." For Gilpin the enemy was unchanged. "Maratime [sic] tyrants have always defined it to be a desert, and not worth selling." They had already settled the Indian question in their favor. For the Indians were "under the control of Eastern tyrants, who will use them for a restraining barrier to the white pioneer population, so long as ten of them are still alive."

As he saw it the national government, dominated by seaboard interest, had deliberately prevented further westward expansion by placing the Indian lands "like blocks of stone in the wall of a jail" athwart the moving frontier line. Strangely, William (and many other Missourians) felt no malice toward the Indians and did not want them removed again. The Redman should be on an equal footing with the white; the government should break up and sell the reservation lands, give each Indian and each white a homestead and equal protection of the law. They would then live peacefully alongside one another like the "twelve to fifteen millions of Indians in the Spanish republics of Mexico and South America." The Indian would thus be made a useful citizen—civilized. New states would be formed, and the continental railroad could move grandly ahead connecting the central country with the western sea. He concluded that there was no hostility on the frontier except that created by the "bloody Indian policy . . . of the federal government."[30]

That body meanwhile began discussing the report of Senator Douglas' Committee on Territories, and between January and May, 1854, the sectional pot was brought to boil. While slavery in the new territory (or territories as the bill now provided) made no economic sense, fired-up sensitivities in Washington paid little attention to facts. Repeal of the Missouri Compromise bitterly aggravated abolitionists while the possibility of free soil just west of Missouri seriously threatened the investment of slaveowners.

[30] *Jefferson Inquirer* (Jefferson City, Mo.), November 12, 1853.

Sooners, speculators, and railroad schemers added to the confusion and antagonisms. And most unfortunately for the nation the Benton-Atchison feud had permanently divided the Missouri Democrats, the one powerful agency that might have prevented war in Kansas. Douglas' labors and Pierce's use of his office narrowly negotiated passage; in May the President signed the bill into law creating a Kansas and a Nebraska Territory divided by the fortieth parallel and leaving the slavery question to the citizens of each.

Already eastern emigrant societies were forming and though no pioneers had yet arrived, frontier slaveowners were greatly concerned for the impact of hundreds of migrant poor as much as for the safety of their slaves. Most likely affected were the towns of William Gilpin's home county, Jackson. Holding mass meetings in June, slaveowners in Westport and Independence resolved to do all possible to move to Kansas as permanent settlers, bringing their property, including slaves, with them. They urged their neighbors in adjacent counties to do the same. More—they planned to meet in Kansas to arrange protection against the coming zealots.

Speaking through the *Agrarian* Gilpin promptly denied that these meetings reflected true Jackson County spirit. He charged that a few men had sprung the resolutions on unsuspecting audiences and that the measures were carried because most present took no part. While it was true, he said, that the majority of his neighbors were deeply concerned that Kansas not be abolitionist, they would do nothing to destroy law and good government.

That William had support for his moderation is indicated by renewed efforts to nominate him for the United States Congress. He was praised as a steady Democrat, a brave soldier, an unflinching friend of the organization of Kansas and Nebraska Territory, a true Jeffersonian, an untiring advocate of the Pacific Railroad, one of the most enlightened companions of western interests, and the best informed man on the frontier—but he was not elected. Moderation could carry no election in Missouri, 1854, and William's thinking and feelings could not yet drive him out of a splitting party.[31]

Legitimate settlers were moving into the two new territories, but

[31] Malin, *Nebraska Question*, pp. 366–372; *Jefferson Inquirer* (Jefferson City, Mo.), February 24, 1853, and January 14, 1854.

history was being made by the border ruffians, proslavery and anti-slavery, who went to Kansas in 1854 and 1855. (The *Nebraska* migration was relatively peaceful.) Southern Baptist Bibles and rifles tried to stem the tide of Congregational Bibles and rifles as fanatic met fanatic. Small civil war broke out and perhaps two hundred people were killed in the next two years of rival govern-ments and constitutions. Only the power of federal troops could end the strife.

The war in Kansas was the turning point in the party allegiance for many Democrats (as well as Whigs) in the West. Probably for most the shift from old principles was a gradual and difficult process, reluctantly recognized and accepted. William Gilpin left little record of how he felt about making this adjustment but some of the steps can be reconstructed through the career of his good friend, Francis P. Blair, Jr. Frank, as he was called, was still a fervid Benton man in the early 1850's, and with B. Gratz Brown kept St. Louis in the Benton fold, if somewhat restlessly. Close to Van Buren, these men had some sympathy for the Free Soil move-ment of the late 1840's and early 1850's and promoted it in St. Louis. In that city the heavy foreign population was opposed to slavery. Without being an abolitionist Blair could get the immi-grant vote by favoring voluntary emancipation and opposing the Know-Nothings, a weak platform "out-state." Hence Blair was elected to the Missouri legislature in 1852 and 1854 although he could do little for Benton in the latter's statewide campaigns. For Benton could not aggravate the slave-holders.

Out of the Kansas-Nebraska struggle the Republican Party was born in 1854, and its leaders appealed to Northern Whigs, Know-Nothings, and anti-Douglas Democrats, abolitionists, and Free Soilers—like Frank Blair. The party planned a canvass for the presidency in 1856. In a preliminary meeting at Pittsburgh Frank's father was chairman and one of the party organizers. Frank was Missouri's delegate on this occasion and became a member of the national committee, yet still calling himself a Benton Democrat. Apparently reconsidering his position, Frank did not attend the Philadelphia convention that nominated John C. Frémont for the presidency—nor was there any other Missourian in attendance. Of immediate concern was his own candidacy and in the same year Frank Blair was elected to the House of Representatives from his

St. Louis district. Probably a Republican, he did not dare admit it yet and refused to say whether he would support Frémont or Buchanan.

William Gilpin's part in these affairs is frankly a puzzle. Blair, Benton, Brown, Buchanan, and Frémont were all personal friends of William's of many years standing. Buchanan might get the Gilpin support for old family reasons, and William's loyalty to Benton was traditional. Benton, himself, opposed his son-in-law's candidacy in 1856. A safe assumption is that William was still a Buchanan Democrat.

His principles or what were purported to be his principles were widely publicized: the Democratic State Convention met in January at Jefferson City, supported Benton for governor and named a committee to declare the Benton platform. The members, listed in this order, were: Gilpin, A. A. King, C. F. Holly, F. P. Blair, Jr., and J. D. Stevenson. In June the committee made its report in language unquestionably Gilpin's.

The party favored, first, the suppression of slavery excitation and, second, the immediate construction of the national railroad and internal improvements—harmless enough. But the third point must have terrified party workers. Wrote William, by the Kansas-Nebraska law,

The arbitrary obstruction to central growth has been repealed, but this great triumph of the true genius of America is signalized by a malignant renewal of the slavery agitation in the seacoast states of the North and South—The convention is in all particulars, and in the sternest sense devoted to the maintenance of slavery in the states, and to its extension into any and every territory where it may peacefully be carried.

The next day Blair flatly repudiated the portion about extending slavery, declaring that he had not understood what Gilpin meant. Brown, editing the *Missouri Democrat*, categorically blamed Gilpin for using his own ideas in the address without the right to call them the sentiments of the party.[32]

---

[32] John H. Ulbricht, "Frank P. Blair, Jr. and Missouri Politics, 1856–1860," (unpublished M.A. thesis, University of Missouri, 1936), *passim*. Blair, the Free-Soiler, owned slaves until 1859; William, defender of the Kansas-Nebraska Act, never owned a slave.

Was William exceeding authority or were some of the Democrats using him? The language seems too clear for Blair's alibi to hold up, and he might better have taken Brown's stand. The extremely quick repudiations nullify the likelihood that the platform was a trial balloon—certainly Blair and Brown would have let a few days pass in order to feel the nature of Missouri's response before issuing their denials.

The appeal, however brief, to slaveowners appears to be a trick useful to collect "out-state" Democratic votes, easily refuted in St. Louis where Blair had to be a Free-Soiler. What part did William Gilpin play in this deception? Not himself a serious candidate, he might have joined with the other committeemen in framing the document with the understanding that to save Blair in St. Louis Gilpin would accept the entire responsibility. A frequent visitor to the larger city, William, nevertheless, called Independence home, and there he was secure from Free-Soilers.

The final possibility is that Brown was right. William enjoyed drafting resolutions and did it well. The committee could have given him the task and conceivably paid little attention to what he wrote until it came out in the press. If this assumption has any merit, it must be judged by whether the platform fits into Gilpin philosophy. About the first two planks there can be no question. William greatly opposed discussion of abolition as his editorials in the *Argus* proved, and, of course, he was second to no one in his demands upon the federal government for a Pacific railroad. The third, and controversial point, is curiously, the decisive one in favor of William's responsibility. For William thought of the Missouri Compromise and the Kansas-Nebraska Act solely in terms of western growth ("central" is his unique phraseology for this) and not as major episodes in the history of slavery. Then the platform casts the blame for renewed slavery arguments upon the *seacoast* states, North and South, William's favorite and personal devils. And what about slavery and its extension? William owned no slaves at any time, and in later years he spoke harshly of the "slavocracy," and as governor of Colorado he fought it with all of his vigor. Yet in these pre-war days William was so obsessed with westward expansion that he supported anyone or any agency that would encourage it. If abolitionists or slaveowning border ruffians threatened the development of the Great West, then they must be kept out of the territories. But "peaceful" people, in accordance with "law and good government," must be allowed to go where they wished and to bring their property along. Stirring, proslavery language had a different meaning when it came from William Gilpin.

The reader will seek in vain for William's rebuttal or explanation. He was on his way to Philadelphia and a vacation, conveniently or coincidentally away from the fire that he had lit.

During that summer of 1856 William spent much time traveling and could easily have attended some of the many presidential conventions, but evidence of such attendance is lacking. The Democrats met at Cincinnati in June, and the two rival Missouri delegations fought at the door for the right to be seated. The Bentonites lost the decision but voted for Buchanan, the nominee. Republicans, Know-Nothings, and their anti-Nebraska offshoot, the North Americans, all convened in Philadelphia that same month, and again William might have been an observer. On July 17 brother Henry wrote to Martin Van Buren that Henry and his wife were now leaving for their "usual ramble" which had been postponed until the arrival of William. Henry wondered if there would be room at Lindenwald for William, as well; they were all most anxious to see the ex-President.[33]

With his vacation over William returned to Independence. Circumstances helped to put politics aside for a while. Buchanan had been elected in the name of unionism without too much danger from various splinter parties, and moderate Democrats got their rewards: for instance, Lewis Cass became Secretary of State. Benton was defeated for governor of Missouri, and so Gilpin got no reward. Benton, already suffering from cancer, had run his last race and died in April, 1858.

William now directed his exertions into old channels and resumed his interest in Gilpintown. The Kansas troubles had brought

[33] Henry noted that Mr. Blair (Francis P., Sr.) had come to see the Gilpins during the Republican convention and looked so young that Henry considered going back into politics (Henry D. Gilpin to Martin Van Buren, July 17, 1856, Martin Van Buren, Papers, Manuscript Division, Library of Congress). Blair conducted Frémont's campaign while Frank, Junior, supported Buchanan. Ruhl J. Bartlett, *John C. Frémont and the Republican Party*, pp. 8–24; Edwin C. McReynolds, *Missouri: A History of the Crossroads State*, pp. 196–200.

extra migrants and excitement to Independence in the mid-1850's, but these were not always of the stuff that built cities. By 1858 antislave settlers were in a great majority and the civil war temporarily was suspended in Kansas. Tensions were eased in the western Missouri towns, and a visitor to Westport observed that for the first time in two or three years free speech was tolerated.[34]

The thousands of new, permanent settlers in Jackson County revived William Gilpin's speculative hopes. Gilpintown lacked adequate financing and never grew, even though it lay on the road passing from Independence to the river. (In 1852 Julius Froebel had noted what a terrible road it was and how the four-mile stretch was little better than an ox-killer.) When time permitted a restudy, Gilpin concluded that he had miscalculated in laying out his town lots; the true center of the United States was ten miles to the west at the point where the Kaw flowed into the Missouri from the west and the Missouri made its great bend on the journey from the northern Rockies. A metropolis must arise there.

William was not the first to discover this fact, but he thought he saw a growth that no one else anticipated. Independence had for many years monopolized the Santa Fe trade in competition with its little rival, Westport, a dozen miles west and south. The latter town, also away from the river, utilized the services of a dock called Westport Landing, and some Missourians assumed that in time Westport would absorb the Landing. But trade routes and river pilots determined a different future for the villages. Most persons crossing the state used the river as the best means of commerce and travel and found that the most convenient method was to pass Gilpintown-Independence and disembark at the Landing, the end of the river line, so to speak.[35]

The superiority of Westport Landing seemed to lie in the angle of the river which caused the formation of a solid levee that the

[34] William P. Tomlinson, *Kansas in 1858*, p. 23.

[35] William H. Miller, *The History of Kansas City*, pp. 244–246. A recent history of Kansas City suggests that the town grew faster than Leavenworth, St. Joseph, and Independence during the Kansas "war" because Kansas City's businessmen minimized stories of conflict and so stressed to the eastern press the opportunities for peaceful progress in their city (A. Theodore Brown, *Frontier Community: Kansas City to 1870*, pp. 97–114). This "westernism" is identical with that of William Gilpin.

river man preferred. Furthermore, the teamsters at this point had one less day of travel than if they had come from Independence. So the Landing grew rapidly and by the late 1850's, under its more popular name of Kansas, it was beginning to absorb Westport.

Probably in part to salvage something from his Gilpintown scheme and in part because he loved encouraging town development even when it did not benefit him, William now conceived of a giant city. Its name would be "Centropolis" and it would be composed of "the condensed cities of Independence, Kansas, and Westport, Jackson County, Mo." He drafted a number of maps of this city and apparently served as attorney for Sublette, Campbell, and others when they began laying out Kansas City. He recalled:

My idea about the townsite was to take in the territory now comprising Independence, Westport and Kansas City and call it Centropolis. . . . [a] great influence with me was my association with De Tocqueville, the French writer, who visited this country, whom I assisted in collecting data in the libraries at Washington. He taught me the importance and value of statistics and how to look into the future with a good deal of reliability from the data the present affords. . . . I thought that a great city would spring up where Kansas City now stands.[36]

Why would it arise at that site? William explains in Humboldt's terms:

The distance from the European to the Asian shores (from Paris to Pekin) traveling straight by the continuous line, in this country, of the Potomac, Ohio, Missouri, Platte and Snake rivers and across two oceans is only 10,000 miles. This straight river line is the axis of that temperate zone in the northern hemisphere of the globe, 33 degrees in

[36] *Rocky Mountain Herald* (Denver), January 14, 1913. Some old settlers believed that William had drawn an earlier map of Centropolis when first trying to market Gilpintown. Reputedly he had the national capital and the national observatory in the center of Gilpintown. This map has never been found. The existing Gilpintown map locates streets and lots, but no national buildings. Charles N. Glaab, who is active in urban history, shows some of Gilpin's theories and their influence on other promoters and writers in "Visions of Metropolis: William Gilpin and Theories of City Growth in the American West," *Wisconsin Magazine of History*, XLV (Autumn, 1961), 21–31. One newspaper sets 1851 as the year that William "and others laid off Kansas City," but the Centropolis maps that I have seen are dated between 1858 and 1861. See also, *Kansas City Star*, April 30, 1905; Richard S. Elliott, *Notes Taken in Sixty Years*, p. 162.

width which contains four-fifths of the land and nine-tenths of the people of the white races and the commercial activity and industry of the civilized world. Here in this favored region we are in the very center of that zone, so far as our northern continent is concerned.

William did more than add his scientific blessing to the Holy Writ of the Landing's growth; he was responsible for the construction of the first pike, a rock road, from Independence to the Landing at the foot of Main Street, evidence enough that William had lost a skirmish while winning a war. For Centropolis was his:

As the site for the great central city of the basin of the Mississippi to arise prospectively upon the development now maturing, this city has the start of the geographical position and the existing elements with which any rival will contend in vain. There must be a great city here, such as antiquity built at the head of the Mediterranean and named Jerusalem, Tyre, Alexandria, Constantinople, such as our own people name New York, New Orleans, St. Louis or San Francisco.[37]

In a political sense the villages, towns, and cities never united into one metropolis, but in the commercial sense the Centropolis' limits are even larger than the predictions of William's charts.

The *Kansas City Star* in 1913 discussed the relationship of Gilpin and Benton and their joint importance to Kansas City and the West. Concluded the article, "If Kansas City should ever build a monument to Benton there should be placed on the same pedestal a monument to Gilpin of equal height and workmanship. And if Kansas City should make but one monument, that should be to Gilpin."[38]

A reassessment by the same paper a generation later declared, "If any man deserves a statue in the greater Kansas City of today upon some high elevation and preferably in near proximity to that Indian Scout who is peering towards the west—that man is William Gilpin, now almost a forgotten man."[39]

William continued his writing, his map-drawing, and his publicizing as the decade drew to a close. He wrote for the *Western Journal and Civilian*, sometimes anonymously. He contributed to

[37] *Kansas City Star*, December 17, 1937.

[38] *Ibid.*, September 14, 1913.

[39] *Ibid.*, December 17, 1937. The same paper has similar accounts on May 26, 1901, and January 10, 1915.

the *National Intelligencer*, the *New York Times*, and *De Bow's Review*, and his articles and speeches were often cited by other writers. He discovered the "Hemp Growing Region of the United States," twenty counties bisected by the Missouri River and especially favored by nature for the growing of this important product. But he lingered only briefly with the hemp. This river was to be far greater than the Nile, for Egypt's growth was restricted by her deserts, "But on every side . . . of the ravine of the Missouri, expands with a radius of one thousand miles, that variegated calcareous plain which we define as the 'Basin of the Mississippi,' destined to be the most thronged and wonderful in the world."[40]

A few weeks later he played the same tune but with a verse that he had not recently used, reminding his public how fortunate the United States was to have its Mississippi bowl—"the most remarkable feature of America is the Basin of the Mississippi." Europe, Asia (and probably Africa and South America) he pointed out, have their mountains in the center, dividing peoples and spilling them off in centrifugal fashion. The American people, however, were held "in unity" by the Great Basin. Excited by his own ideas William's vision now went far beyond the outspread Kansas horizon: "Viewed as the dominating part of the great calcareous plain formed by the coterminous basin of the Mississippi, St. Lawrence, Hudson's Bay and Mackenzie, the amphi-theatre of the world, here is supremely, indeed the most magnificent dwelling-place marked out by God for man's abode."[41] A citizen army with axe and plough was marching on to plant a hundred states, he concluded.

Surely no one in western Missouri or Kansas could be anything but bullish about such tidings. William's speaking services were in great demand. Said a Liberty paper:

This gentleman, distinguished alike as an orator and soldier, having been invited by a large number of our fellow citizens to deliver an address in this city, has kindly consented to do so. The subject of the address: "The Mississippi Valley and Mountain Ranges of North America, and the newly discovered Gold Regions." . . . We can safely promise the ladies and gentlemen of the county, the Students of our

[40] "The Hemp Growing Region of the United States," *De Bow's Review*, XXIV (January, 1858), 56–58.

[41] "The Great Basin of the Mississippi," *De Bow's Review*, XXIV (February, 1858), 159–165.

Colleges and Schools, an address abounding with the results of great research, scientific attainment and elegance of diction.[42]

Next door, Kansas Territory was, of course, a part of the expansion. One contemporary noted that for a few years Kansas had been fettered by politics, but by 1858 "progress and money-making ideas" were growing. The day would soon come,

that Kansas Territory will occupy her true position in the interior, or rather in the "pastoral regions of the world," so ably and graphically described by the master scholar of Interior Geography, Col. Gilpin, from whose writings we make the following extracts, in order that we may exhibit fully the true character, both in extent and resources, of the "Great Plains of America," of which the Territory of Kansas is the major part.

Then followed four pages of a Gilpin attack upon the notion that the Great Plains were really the Great American Desert.[43]

Later in the same year William began emphasizing the recent gold discoveries along the front range of the Rocky Mountains in western Kansas Territory. For a decade he had preached the riches of the region; now he was a prophet with considerable honor. He wrote articles for various newspapers (that were often copied verbatim by others) discussing what he usually called the "Pike's Peak region and the Sierra San Juan." William linked the gold discoveries along Cherry Creek with the San Juan Mountains of present southwestern Colorado and in his elaborate prose described the topography, beauty, and resources of this extensive area.

William never forgot his romantic and solitary journey back from Oregon in 1844 when he had first passed through much of the land that he pictured for his readers. In particular his heart had gone out to the San Luis Valley, sheltered on the north and west by these San Juan Mountains. Evidently from this first acquaintanceship he had determined to own a portion of it. Not yet was he an investor in Colorado lands but by 1858 his writings singled out this valley as adjacent to the gold regions and an ideal homesite as well. Calling it San Luis Park, he described it as the most

---

[42] Alexander Doniphan was a member of the committee issuing this invitation. *Randolph Citizen* (Randolph, Mo.), October 22, 1858, quoting the Liberty *Weekly Tribune*.

[43] Charles C. Spalding, *Annals of the City of Kansas*, pp. 9–14.

beautiful of all the parks of the mountains, and he urged the governments of Missouri and the United States as well as the merchants of New York to invest in its development.[44]

William probably received no compensation for either his talks or his journal publications, yet his steady production of western propaganda must have cut critically into his livelihood. For example, he published a series of articles in early November, 1858. He composed four long columns on the "Physical Geography of North America" printed November 13. The same paper announced Gilpin's acceptance of a Chamber of Commerce request to lecture on the "Gold Region," adding that, "It is useless for us to urge full attendance. A lecture from Col. Gilpin, before the New York audience on this subject, would crowd the largest building with the science and intellect of that metropolis." The only hall in town large enough was the Methodist Church.

The meeting was held two days later and William's words were given most of the front page of the *Western Journal of Commerce*. This one time, at least, he explained his manner of presentation, declaring, "I have been criticised—often censured, for appealing to abstract truths of science when speaking to the assemblies of the people." But he felt that he could rely on the people's intelligence to comprehend his studies. He considered himself a scientist, and his audience should not expect him to reveal the exact spot for thrusting a miner's spade.

In this Chamber of Commerce speech (which was afterward printed in various forms) he explained how *specific gravity* would predict the location of precious metals. When the earth was a liquid mass, gold with its high specific gravity settled toward the center first and was "congealed in the *Mountain Formation* of the "primeval crust of the globe." The calcareous plain was secondarily formed and so contained the lighter, base metals. The maritime slope is the "external mountain base partly revealed, and partly covered by the washings of the sea."

[44] William usually minimized western distances, but in one article he doubled the mileage between Bent's Fort and the San Luis Valley for no apparent reason. I have no evidence that William had any investment in Colorado yet; probably his enthusiasm bubbled forth before he was in any position to profit by speculation (*Western Journal of Commerce* [Kansas City, Mo.], November 6, 1858).

In the mountain formation, occupying two-sevenths of North America, men would find their gold. So far they had looked only along the waters and, therefore, had discovered only grains and small lumps.

It is *beneath* that we must search for the sedimentary mass; the possibility to do which now first presents itself as we advance within the labyrinth of the volcanic masses and canyons of the Plateau. . . . The facts . . . collected by me are so numerous and so positive, that I entertain an absolute conviction . . . that *gold in mass and in position* and infinite in quantity will, within the coming three years, reveal itself to the energy of our pioneers.

So that no one could be mistaken by these words one paper distributed nine thousand maps of the gold region to its readers.[45]

William did more than spread gold fever. He continued active in Pacific railroad promotion and was instrumental in organizing a railroad convention for Kansas City, which feared the Hannibal-St. Joseph line nearly complete across Missouri. The delegates met at the Court House on November 26 for an organizational session. William was one of several elected to the position of vice president. The groups reassembled after supper that night and heard the "Continental Railway by Col. Gilpin of Independence. The address was a masterly production and was listened to with intense interest throughout its delivery."

This talk was not copied by a reporter but appears to have been an involved and broadly based argument for the Platte River and South Pass as the route to China. The convention drafted several resolutions on railroad costs and methods of construction, and ignoring their keynote speaker, called upon Congress to build the line straight west of Kansas City along the 39th parallel, approximately the highest road in the United States.[46]

Gilpin was doubtless a very popular orator. A modern reader can wonder if people listened to him or got lost in some of his parks, bowls, and calcareous plains. Nevertheless, one history of Kansas

[45] *Western Journal of Commerce* (Kansas City, Mo.), November 6 and 13, 1858, and December 25, 1858. The map covered approximately Kansas Territory from Missouri to Pike's Peak. Several issues of the *Journal* refer to Gilpin's talk and quote parts of it.

[46] *Western Journal of Commerce* (Kansas City, Mo.), November 27, 1858. See Miller, *Kansas City*, pp. 92–95, on the railroad convention.

City said that Gilpin, a friend of Presidents, was a major reason that national railroad fever struck hard in Kansas City in the 1850's. "Gilpin's prestige was tremendous," as he predicted a brilliant future for the town.[47]

Little of the profitable future of Kansas City rubbed off on its chief spokesman, however. He sold a few lots in Gilpintown, but never acquiring the funds for real development, he was unable to retain local interest in the suburb. Values dropped, as they did in so many frontier "towns," and in March, 1858, William's creditors began foreclosure proceedings that dragged out for several years. One writer declared, "He was an honest man, but he had failed to interest Eastern capital in his rather gigantic and in many ways quixotic undertaking, and thus it was necessary to bring the project to a close.[48]

By agreement and judgment William's cases cost him several thousand dollars which he could not have had in cash. Many years passed before his Missouri land suits were cleared away; occasionally he was to lose more by default because his change of residence to Colorado prevented his appearance in Jackson County courts.[49]

The failure of Gilpintown was a factor in persuading William to seek another home after nearly twenty years. A stronger reason was the split in the Democratic Party reaching so bitterly across Missouri. While William's publicity from his writing and speaking spread his name throughout the frontier, it had brought him little income. Now his losses in land speculation made it necessary to find better employment. Perhaps he could return to politics, but no longer was there a place in Missouri for his brand of Democracy, save only in St. Louis dominated by Frank Blair and Gratz Brown.

In 1856 those men had repudiated Gilpin's platform for Benton and in the years since had gradually drifted away from what was

[47] Henry C. Haskell and Richard B. Fowler, *City of the Future*, p. 44. Of course, Kansas City had many other men who talked of her great future, usually in terms of railroad construction. Real estate promoter-businessman Johnston Lykins and editor Robert Van Horn were the best known, aside from Gilpin; their writings often use William's exact terms as well as his abstract philosophy of city growth (See Brown, *Frontier Community*).

[48] *Kansas City Post*, April 13, 1924.

[49] Webb, *History of Independence*, p. 165.

probably the majority wing of the Democrats. Although talking
of supporting Edward Bates for President of the United States on
a Whig–American–Free Democrat coalition ticket, Blair was lean-
ing more toward the Republican Party and holding conversations
with Abraham Lincoln in Springfield. In November, 1859, Blair
emancipated his own slaves, symbolizing the end of his long association with the Democratic Party.[50]

William Gilpin did not record the circumstances of his own
switch from his beloved Democracy, but it must have occurred
about the same time as Blair's and probably for the same reasons.
Almost life-long friends, they must have consulted one another
often about party politics. Neither man was an abolitionist, and
William, at least, liked Douglas' popular sovereignty because of its
assumption of frontier democracy. But, in truth, the Democrats of
Missouri were squeezing the men out. The Republican Party began
to look like their proper home.

Gilpin assisted Blair and Brown in organizing the Republicans
in Missouri. William's share of this joint task was doubtless the
most difficult and frustrating, for the other two men were secure
in St. Louis while Gilpin's neighbors in Independence were by a
wide majority proslavery men and often violently so; many had
been to Kansas to help drive out the New Englanders four years
before.[51]

While working for the Republicans, William continued to labor
for the transcontinental railroad. The ceaseless efforts of Kansas
City's leaders seemed finally to be repaid when in June of 1860 the
Pacific Railroad announced plans to begin work outside that city.
Ceremonies held the next month included cannon salutes, parades,
bands, symbolic dirt-moving, barbecues, and balls. The featured
speaker necessarily was William Gilpin. "We are ready at last,"
he observed, "to debouch out upon the great plains to the once far
West. . . . We start out under the shadow of names of great and
intrepid men, and should there be any trepidation on our part?"[52]

The debouching had to be delayed, however, as problems of fi-

50 Ulbricht, "Blair," pp. 178–203.

51 Vincent G. Tegeder, "Lincoln and the Territorial Patronage: The Ascendancy of the Radicals in the West," *Mississippi Valley Historical Review*, XXXV
(June, 1848), 81.

52 Charles N. Glaab, *Kansas City and the Railroads*, p. 91.

nancing and the Civil War interfered. That autumn the nation divided itself bitterly over the presidential election. In Missouri Abraham Lincoln ran a poor fourth behind Douglas, John Bell, and John C. Breckenridge. Out in Jackson County, Republicans were even less popular than in the state as a whole; practically all of them lived in Kansas City, and 185 strong, they protected themselves by marching to the polls together. In the town of Independence the circumstances were even more bizarre. More than twelve hundred votes were shared by Bell, Douglas, and Breckenridge; Abraham Lincoln received a total of one! The solitary, determined voter was William Gilpin. Unable even to obtain a Republican ballot, William had some problem voting, but he succeeded and thus took another step toward the governorship of Colorado Territory.[53]

Lincoln's election changed Gilpin's life dramatically. As the secession movement got underway William permanently broke his ties with Independence and traveled once more to St. Louis. Perhaps he felt that the Republicans owed him a job for his lonely efforts to build the party in the Far West. Perhaps he sought out Blair and Brown for advice—or work. By January or February, 1861, he was in the St. Louis area and waging his own peculiar war against secession.

He addressed a series of at least three letters to the St. Louis *Daily Missouri Democrat* arguing the wrongness of those Missourians who wanted to join the Deep South in the confederation then being created. William's thesis might well be unique. On February 8, signing himself "Union," he ran through his old hymn of the enormous riches of the Mississippi basin, whose "central wealth of lead, iron, coal, copper" lay in Missouri. "The balance of power of this continent must eventually culminate around that great flat-

---

[53] Brown, *Frontier Community*, p. 199 and n.; *Tri-Weekly Missouri Republican* (St. Louis), November 7 and 10, 1860. William was quoted as saying that he cast the only vote for Lincoln in all of *Jackson County* (Bancroft, *Gilpin*, p. 43): a statement that must be marked up as another near-truth. The one Lincoln vote in *Independence* was undoubtedly William's. Some of the physical dangers attendant to voting for Lincoln in Western Missouri are recalled in the relation of D. P. Hougland "Voting for Lincoln in Missouri in 1860," *Kansas State Historical Transactions, 1905–06*, pp. 509–520. Missouri's behavior between 1861 and 1865 is analyzed in William E. Parrish, *Turbulent Partnership: Missouri and the Union, 1861–1865*.

tened cone of palaeozoic and azoic rocks, that have the iron mountains of this State as a center."

Why should the poorer regions dictate to Missouri?

. . . with all these national resources our Governor would be content
to tie this great State, with all its advantages, to the little fire eating,
seceding State of South Carolina, to become a single spoke in the wheel
of the Palmetto car. Verily this must be the age of treason and imbe-
cility in high public functionaries. Not a word in the inaugural about
the wonderful wine-growing capacities of our State, and how we can
furnish homes to hundreds of thousands of the down trodden of
Europe. . . . No word about our being the half way house between
London and Canton . . . —our railroad system nothing! . . . The
physics of this continent oppose the idea of a dissolution of this confederacy. . . . The secession movement may spread until the whole
people will resolve themselves into a vigilance committee, and traitors
will then get their dues.

Apparently William was in Potosi when he composed that attack
and he may still have been there when he wrote his next two
signed "Syenite" (March 1) and "Missouri" (March 4). In these
editorials he repeated his assertions of the great mineral wealth of
Missouri, and professed in geologic terms his belief that southeastern Missouri had the same character as the Washoe and Pike's
Peak regions.

He announced that the "brethren" of the Pelican and Palmetto
states thought that cotton was king; "we say it is iron and Missouri
holds the keys of this kingdom," and with them the balance of
power of the Great Basin. Missourians did not want to secede from
the Union, nor did they want to join the "outside rim or slice of
Atlantic states known as the Southern confederacy." Palmettos, he
said, belonged to the palm family and were "mostly buried in
coal strata." William predicted that within a century the world
would need 100,000,000 tons of iron annually, about one-half from
the United States and one-fourth from the state of Missouri: "Nature has given us the balance of power in our mineral masses. . . .
Missouri is the hub of the republic."[54]

[54] *Daily Missouri Democrat* (St. Louis) February 8 and March 1 and 4, 1861.
Once again I must admit to guessing that William wrote these letters, but the
flavor is all Gilpin. His estimate of 1961 iron production is interesting; he badly

William still hoped that a Missouri state convention would declare its loyalty to the Union in spite of the strong southern sympathy of Governor Claiborne Jackson. On March 1 the convention almost unanimously voted against secession, and perhaps William had played a small part in mustering opinion, but he had already left the state, headed toward Washington, this time, and toward a new task.

William was in St. Louis about the 1st of February when, probably seeking a military assignment, he visited Colonel Edwin V. Sumner, commander of the Department of the West, and Major David Hunter, commanding officer at Fort Leavenworth. Gilpin had known Sumner from the days of Doniphan in New Mexico, and now it seemed Sumner had also known the President-elect from the Black Hawk War days. Sumner had a job for William.

Hunter in particular (but others felt the same) feared an attempt would be made upon Lincoln's life somewhere between Springfield and Washington. The War Department had assigned four officers to protect Lincoln until the inauguration. Sumner and Hunter were two of these officers and they handpicked a number of trusted men (including William) to give them support. William agreed to the job enthusiastically and hurried to Springfield to join the company.

A large, silent crowd of personal friends stood in the Springfield rain early in the morning of February 11, 1861, to bid good-by to Abraham Lincoln. He said a few sad words of farewell from the rear platform (there were only two cars), and the packed train slowly moved out of the station. Thirteen days, many stops, short talks, and visiting politicians later, the party arrived in Washington. The President-elect was safe; the danger of the threat is still difficult to assess today.[55]

---

exaggerated Missouri's future but underestimated world demand and United States supply by one-half or more.

[55] Bancroft, *Gilpin*, p. 43; *Daily Missouri Democrat* (St. Louis), February 11, 1861. Curiously the *Democrat* knew in advance the names of the leading bodyguards and published them the day of the departure from Springfield. For the exciting and convincing story of the plots and counterplots and especially the role of Allan Pinkerton in this journey see John Mason Potter, *Thirteen Desperate Days*. Potter says that a list of passengers with Lincoln could not be compiled because many politicians rode short distances only and then returned home (letter to author, May 4, 1965).

In Washington William was one of a company of one hundred men under Hunter to act as bodyguards until the inauguration. Some accounts (including Gilpin's) declare that the men stayed in the White House. Since President Buchanan's life was not in danger the men probably were quartered elsewhere, the most likely spot being the Willard Hotel where Lincoln insisted upon residing until the inauguration.[56]

In the weeks immediately before and after March 4, William had several opportunities to meet Lincoln, doubtless often in company with the many office-seekers who harassed the President-elect. The logical reward to William for his services as a new Republican would have been command of a regiment of troops raised in Gilpin's neighboring counties. Manifestly impossible of achievement in western Missouri, the gift was not forthcoming. Instead many people began to think of William as deserving some political post on the frontier—the most promising area being the lands just torn from western Kansas.

William qualified on many points. Few westerners were better known in 1860; his personal achievements and writings had made him nationally famous. In addition to his many articles and editorials he had just completed *The Central Gold Region*, published by Lippincott in 1860. How widely the book sold cannot be calculated, for a fire destroyed Lippincott's records in 1899, but statesman and pioneer both seem to have read Gilpin's writings, and many of the former corresponded with him.

For example, Edward Everett, former Secretary of State, senator, and America's best known orator, wrote to William in 1858 asking for maps and pamphlets about the West and its railroads. Thanking William later he wrote, "I am extremely indebted to you for these valuable papers. I have found them more suggestive and replete with instruction than anything which has yet fallen in my way relative to the mighty West."[57]

[56] Robert C. Schenck, "Major-General David Hunter," *Magazine of American History*, XVII (February, 1887), 138–152. The Hunter article in the *Dictionary of American Biography*, IX, 400, says the men were in the White House. Potter thinks this unlikely.

[57] Edward Everett to William Gilpin, Boston, March 31, 1858, cited in the *Commonwealth and Republic* (Denver), July 31, 1862.

In March William autographed a copy of his book and presented it to Schuyler Colfax, Indiana representative and later to be Vice President of the United States.

Salmon P. Chase, governor of Ohio, defeated by Lincoln only months before at the Republican convention, wrote to Gilpin of his difficulty in buying *The Central Gold Region*. He finally located a copy in St. Louis. He said, "I prize it highly. The views it puts forth are bold, striking and highly instructive. If statesmen would rise to its height how would the insane babble of disunion be hushed and silenced! I wish the book could be pondered and read by every intelligent American."[58]

Older friends did not have to purchase *The Central Gold Region*, for William had some copies to give to distinguished elders such as Charles Ingersoll, nearly eighty and doing his own writing.

I can hardly tell you how much edified and gratified I am by the volume which I take for granted is your gift, as its very striking contents are undoubtedly your performance. I am just going to press with a work on "American Historical Politics," of which the first chapter treats entirely, and all the rest more or less, of that Continental Union you so powerfully dwell upon and which I shall show was Washington's, Hamilton's, Monroe's, Rufus King's, and other fundamental statesmen's aspiration and anticipation.[59]

Scholars and statesmen might have read William for his theories on national growth, but pioneers from the 1840's on read his descriptions of wealth for personal reasons; just as the Oregon-bound read him for clues to reaching that frontier, so did the Pike's Peak miner read Gilpin in the guidebooks so popular around 1859 for descriptions of the new gold fields.

Two former newspapermen, in preparing their guide to Kansas and the Rocky Mountain region, quoted Gilpin at some length, and had, in fact, urged William to publish his letters and lectures into a single volume: "They are more thorough, clear and comprehensive than anything we have ever read on the same subject. We

---

[58] Governor Salmon P. Chase to Gilpin, Columbus, Ohio, December 15, 1860, in *ibid.*

[59] Charles J. Ingersoll to Gilpin, Philadelphia, July 2, 1860, in *ibid.*

think it would be beneficial both to the author and public if they could be issued in some collected form."[60]

Gilpin knew the West, and westerners knew him. Did these facts qualify him for important office? Many of the men around the tormented new President thought so; in the immensity of his task Abraham Lincoln had to stop for a few hours and worry about a distant frontier that only one of his immediate following had ever seen.

[60] James Redpath and Richard J. Hinton, *Handbook to Kansas Territory and the Rocky Mountain Gold Regions.* Their suggestion was made a year before *The Central Gold Region* was published.

CHAPTER NINE

# The Government to Which We Gave Existence

*Colorado Governor, 1861–1862*

During February and March of 1861 Abraham Lincoln was besieged with requests for the appointment of William Gilpin as governor of the new Colorado Territory. The petitioners included the lieutenant governor of Kansas, Pike's Peak miners, an Oregon pioneer who met Gilpin in 1843, and senators and congressmen in large numbers. Probably the more important—and convincing—names to correspond with the President-elect over the appointment were George Washington Julian of Indiana, Free-Soil candidate for Vice-President in 1852, Simon Cameron, a Gilpin family friend and new Secretary of War, Ben Wade of Ohio, soon to be one of the strongest men in American politics, and Frank Blair of Missouri, whose brother was to be Postmaster-General.

Most zealous in the Gilpin cause was Frank Blair. Besides holding conversations with Lincoln about Gilpin, Frank wrote a glowing recommendation that described William as a man of unimpeachable integrity, as a scholar and statesman, and as one more familiar with the Territory than any other man. He reported that Gilpin had spent fifteen years exploring the West and especially "Colorado, whose topography, mineral resources and climate have been illustrated by him." It seemed, in fact, that the nation was indebted to Gilpin "for the systematic names and classification of the Mountains of the West." Blair persuaded several men to sign this letter, and others to write their own endorsements, even when they did not know Gilpin.[1] Blair, of course, took a personal interest in forwarding his friend's career, but this was not unusual. He was so active in the first weeks of the Lincoln Administration that the New York *Herald* observed that he was saving the President and his cabinet a great deal of trouble by handling all of the Missouri appointments. Said the editor, "Verily, Frank has got to be a power in the land."[2]

Rumor had it that during one visit Frank told the President, "Billy Gilpin has done more for that section of the country than any man now living. Why, Mr. President, Billy Gilpin built Pike's Peak."

[1] William N. Byers, *Encyclopedia of Biography of Colorado*, p. 48, says that Gilpin's appointment as governor was not so much due to his valiant service in the Florida and Mexican wars as to his eminent qualifications as a scholar and the application of his learning to all of the western country. A popular local candidate for the post was General William Larimer (Jerome C. Smiley, *History of Denver*, p. 298). The *Leavenworth Conservative* saw a mixture of political reward and scholarship: "Mr. Gilpin was one of the Lincoln electors in Missouri. He is an able man, and has written the best book on the Plains of the West, yet published." Quoted in *Rocky Mountain News* (Denver), March 27, 1861. Although some Democrats wrote to Lincoln for William, most of the recommendations came from men who had just switched to Republican ranks and who were beginning long public careers by this circumstance. With two exceptions the men came from the West and Middle West. Probably to repay one of these debts, William recommended John G. Stephenson of Indiana for the post of librarian of Congress in a letter to Lincoln dated March 30, 1861. James W. Nesmith, senator for the new state of Oregon, wrote the President that he had gone to Oregon with Gilpin and would endorse him highly. A New York police commissioner, James W. Nye, supported Gilpin. In July Nye became Governor of Nevada Territory and permanently placed the family name in the history of that state. These letters, many with several authors and no dates can be found in the Gilpin File, Letters and Applications, Foreign Affairs, National Archives.

[2] Quoted in *Weekly Missouri Democrat* (St. Louis), April 2, 1861.

Lincoln replied that it was a strong statement, "If I knew that to be true I think I should appoint him. Can you furnish any proof of it?"

"Yes, sir," said Blair, "I saw him do it."[3]

Brushing aside the claims of other candidates, Lincoln made his choice. On March 22, 1861, he sent to the Senate for ratification the names of Gilpin for governor; Lewis L. Weld of Colorado, secretary; Copeland Townsend of Colorado, marshal; Francis Case of Ohio, surveyor general; William L. Stoughton of Illinois, attorney general; B. F. Hall of New York, S. Newton Pettis of Pennsylvania, and Charles L. Armour of Ohio, chief justice and associate justices, respectively, of the Colorado Supreme Court. All of the nominations were promptly confirmed.[4]

While these proceedings were being completed, William Gilpin remained in Washington—probably until late April. Anxious to take up his new post, William fretted over the time spent scurrying about Washington in search of Simon Cameron, Secretary of War, who was to give him the President's instructions concerning some of the problems of the territory. But Colorado could hold small concern for Lincoln in those desperate days. Facing the tragedy of Fort Sumter and the decision to ask for 75,000 volunteers, the President and his cabinet were left little time for Governor Gilpin. William evidently failed ever to meet with the Secretary of the Treasury and found Cameron only once, late at night outside the White House, talking with Lincoln and General Winfield Scott. In their hurry and preoccupation, the President and the Secretary gave William only verbal orders to leave immediately for Denver and protect the mountain region from secession. Said the President: "We have not a cent. I have just negotiated a loan of fifty millions of dollars from the banks of New York, and have called a special session of Congress to meet on the 4th of July, to know if they will hang me for treason for this unconstitutional act. If you are driven to extremities you must do as I have done, issue drafts on your own responsibility." As for troops, William was to call them

---

[3] "Why President Lincoln Made Gilpin Governor of Colorado," unidentified clipping in archives of State Historical Society of Colorado.

[4] *Daily Missouri Democrat* (St. Louis), March 23, 1861; Smiley, *History of Denver*, p. 492. The Senate recessed shortly after confirming Lincoln's appointments.

up in such numbers as were needed, command them himself, and
send the bills to Cameron for payment.[5]

Since Congress was not in session, Colorado Territory could get
no appropriation. Gilpin was given $1,500 from a contingent ex-
pense fund, which sum was supposed to maintain the territory
until July 1, 1861. He did not receive this credit until he reached
St. Louis, and he got no instructions in Washington about vouch-
ering or accounting procedures, but was told to get such information from the office of the Assistant Treasurer in St. Louis.[6]

William left Washington for the West by way of Philadelphia
and New York and reached St. Louis on May 6. That city, as well
as most of the state, was in a turmoil which William saw firsthand.
His friends Frank Blair and B. Gratz Brown were regimental
commanders training volunteers to oppose the pro-secession movement led by Governor Claiborne Jackson and Sterling Price (also
old friends). Most of Jackson's State Guards were stationed at
Camp Jackson, near St. Louis. Fearing this concentration of rebellion, Blair and Captain Nathaniel Lyon of the regular army forced
a surrender of the post on May 10. The action was bloodless until
the prisoners were marched into the city before crowds of southern
sympathizers. Name-calling, rock-throwing, and an accidental shot
precipitated a riot, with federal troops firing on the mob. Twenty-
eight persons, including a small child, lay dead in the streets in
the "Camp Jackson Massacre."[7]

Passing through the city in these very days, Gilpin for the first
time realized the scope of one of the problems he would face in

[5] Two generally similar versions—both recalled by Gilpin—are in existence.
Hubert Howe Bancroft, *History of the Life of William Gilpin*, pp. 43–44;
William Gilpin, "A Pioneer of 1842." This conversation was extremely perti-
nent to William's reputation as governor. Logic supports the memory even if
evidence is slim. William is here making a case for himself by showing the
parallel between his actions in Colorado and Lincoln's at the national level.
William claimed that he never received any written orders from Cameron in
spite of the Secretary's promises. I have found none.

[6] These should have been minor administrative matters, but when the Civil
War broke out in the territories William was unequipped to process funds cor-
rectly (W. Medill [comptroller] letters to Gilpin, April 11, 1861, Comptroller,
Fiscal Branch, National Archives).

[7] *Daily Missouri Democrat* (St. Louis), May 7, 1861. Governor Jackson offered Doniphan a brigadier generalship. Gilpin's old commander first accepted
and then declined it.

Colorado. When he reached western Missouri he found a picture that was no brighter; he was probably not surprised that his old town of Independence had become strongly secessionist, but now even Kansas City was so threatened by terror that the mayor was asking for federal assistance from St. Louis and Fort Leavenworth to protect Unionists and their property.

These events seem not to have endangered William personally, but he must have been increasingly impressed with the prospect of civil war as he crossed the plains in the cradled, swinging box that was the Concord coach. About two weeks out from the Missouri River William finally reached Denver. On May 27, 1861, he and his eight companions (including two ladies) disentangled themselves from the vehicle and climbed down into the dusty street. Guns sounded, bands played, and a gathering crowd pushed its way to the front to see the new governor.

Judge Hiram P. Bennet acted as spokesman for the territory, making proper comments of greeting. Governor Gilpin responded with his story of passing through Colorado years before and camping near the site where the crowd now stood. He recalled predicting greatness for the area even then because of its resources and its location along the world's commercial highway.

As usual William talked too long, but when he finally concluded with a call for cooperation, loyalty, and a reunion of hearts, his listeners gave him a loud cheer. They submitted to a few more speakers and adjourned to the Apollo Theatre for entertainment.[8]

Long before William Gilpin had brought legal government to Colorado the local residents had taken steps to organize themselves. The area of the gold rush of 1858–1859 was included in four existing territories—Kansas, Nebraska, New Mexico, and Utah. With only some two hundred people living in the so-called Pike's Peak region, they nevertheless held an election in November of 1858 and chose a delegate to the United States Congress and one to the Kansas Territorial legislature, the body with jurisdiction over the greatest portion of the "diggings."

The delegate in Washington had tried to bring about the establishment of a territorial form of government, but he got small attention from the Congress. Concluding meanwhile that the Kan-

---

[8] *Rocky Mountain News* (Denver), May 28 and 29, 1861.

sans were too far away to help with their problems and only interested in political appointments to the mineral region, the Pike's Peakers held several elections in 1859 to determine a course of action. They voted against statehood as being too expensive, declared the creation of Jefferson Territory (some 320 by 418 miles in area), drafted a constitution, and elected officers. With little legality (except for a vague foundation in Anglo-Saxon traditions) and no cooperation from the active miners who preferred the purer democracy of the mining camp, the government, nevertheless, stumbled along. The city of Denver was chartered and brought face to face with problems of crime, land titles, and public utilities. Delegates in Washington meanwhile bombarded Congress for territorial status. The slavery question caused Congress to stall, even after Lincoln's election in November, 1860, and the effect in Colorado was to weaken the various governments because of lack of recognition from Washington.

That winter, Congress, minus most southern legislators, finally acted upon the petitions, considering many names and an abundance of boundary arrangements before passage. On February 28, 1861, President James Buchanan signed the measure into law.[9] Most Coloradans seemed satisfied and none of the numerous provisional officers indicated any objection to the incoming administration. "Governor" R. W. Steele, in fact, relinquished whatever authority he and his officials held in a formal proclamation which directed them to

[9] Smiley, *History of Denver*, pp. 305, 313–322, 490, 633; U.S. Senate, *Journal*, 36th Cong., 1st Sess., 1859–1860, pp. 180, 335; U.S. State Department, *Territorial Papers, Colorado Series*, I, July 23, 1860. Many Congressmen were ignorant of Colorado affairs, often confusing it with New Mexico. Most of the settlers preferred the name Jefferson, but Colorado was a last-minute choice made in the Senate. Other proposals included Lula, Weappollao, and Tahosa as well as the more sedate Franklin and Colona. Gilpin claimed that he was responsible for the name Colorado, asking Senator Henry Wilson of Massachusetts to make such an amendment ("A Pioneer of 1842"). Wilson said in the Senate that he did so at the request of "the delegate," whom he did not name. Much of the delay was caused by Senator Stephen A. Douglas who complained that possible slave-holdings were endangered by proposed territorial taxes on property (Frank Hall, *History of the State of Colorado*, I, 245, 258; U.S. *Congressional Globe*, 36th Cong., 1860–1861, 2nd. Sess., pp. 639, 729, 1274).

yield unto Caesar the things that are Caesar's . . . and further I advise and recommend to all law and order loving citizens to submit to the laws of the United States and restrain themselves from deeds of violence which so long have made our Peculiar Position almost a bye word in the eyes of the civilized world.

Whether or not Colorado had become famous for its violence, this area was to provide William Gilpin with critical problems that he could not solve even though his well-known westernism prepared the public to accept him readily.[10]

Typical of new territories, Colorado suffered from a good bit of town rivalry. Colorado City had been very active in the demand for territorial status and often maintained a delegate in Washington to lobby for that purpose. Denver's growing advantage was its proximity to the newest mineral discoveries. But even Denver had only very recently united itself into a single community: prior to April, 1861, at least three separate Cherry Creek villages had vied for political supremacy in that region. Pressure was to be exerted on William to place the capital outside of Denver, but this seems not to have bothered him, and he did not identify himself with any of these factions.

His constituents had other needs that were beyond the Governor's power and which he could only refer to the general government at Washington. The Indian problem to Coloradans was chiefly one of getting the Plains tribes to sign treaties that would extinguish their land titles and make possible a general survey and sale of the public lands. Just before William reached Denver some Cheyennes and Arapahoes had signed agreements with Albert Gallatin Boone, but the majority of these bands refused to sign and the Kiowas would not even attend the council. Open warfare did not exist in Colorado in mid-1861, but the danger became greater as the Civil War in the East forced the withdrawal of regiments from frontier forts. To William Gilpin the threat was a constant one.[11]

[10] *Fowler Tribune* (Fowler, Colo.), September 29, 1939; Augustus Wildman to Frederick S. Wildman, April 29, 1861, Augustus and Thomas G. Wildman Papers, 1858–1865, Coe Collection, Yale University Library. According to William some of the men greeting the coach were old friends from years before.
[11] U.S. Senate, *Executive Document No. 15*, 36th Cong., 1st Sess., Feb. 20,

More commonplace questions for him were those of civil administration, most elements of which had broken down in the past few months while Congress dallied with the territory's status. Much of the legislature and several of his chief officers were men of little ability or, worse, early examples of carbetbaggers. William had nothing to do with the selection of any of them and probably did not even know them prior to his arrival in Colorado.

At every turn, however, Governor Gilpin primarily was faced with the question of secession. He struck at it with shrewdness and vigor, perhaps too much of the latter, soon turning many people against him because they felt that he foolishly or deliberately exaggerated the menace. When he proved right it was already too late, and he was out of office after a term of less than one year.

The date for the beginning of Gilpin's administration is not officially established. The Organic Act creating Colorado was passed in February, 1861; William's appointment as governor was dated in March. He reached Colorado in May, and finally took the oath of office on July 8. In his prime (age forty-five) as full of energy and enthusiasm as always, William went to work immediately upon his arrival in Denver. He rented the upper floor of a store on Larimer Street, taking the front room for himself, holding the middle for the territorial offices, and reserving the remaining room for the territorial secretary, Lewis Weld, who arrived a few days after Gilpin.

Weld was to be very useful to the new governor. Related to the explorer, John Ledyard, and the abolitionist, Theodore Dwight Weld, the twenty-eight-year-old attorney had moved from the East to Kansas in 1858 and joined the Colorado gold-seekers in 1860. He was one of several Denver attorneys who concluded that their practice was useless without organized government and, therefore, refused to accept any more business. He went to Washington seeking the secretaryship; successful, he returned to Colorado after a brief delay due to illness.[12]

1860, pp. 1–23; Irving Howbert, *Memories of a Lifetime in the Pike's Peak Region*, pp. 18–20, 68; George B. Grinnell, *The Fighting Cheyennes*, p. 126.

[12] *Rocky Mountain News* (Denver), June 12, 1861; Le Roy R. Hafen, "Lewis Ledyard Weld and Old Camp Weld," *Colorado Magazine*, XIX (November, 1942), 201–207.

Just before Weld's arrival Gilpin began a tour of the principal towns and camps of the territory. He was accompanied by his United States marshal, Copeland Townsend, and the publisher of *The Daily Rocky Mountain Herald and Colorado Republican,* Thomas Gibson. (Giving this advantage to one paper was Gilpin's first error in office; William N. Byers of the *Rocky Mountain News* soon became the mouthpiece of the Administration's opponents.) Weld joined the party after the men had visited Boulder, Golden, Central City, and other more northerly towns. The four men spent the last two weeks of June traveling to Fairplay, Breckenridge, Cañon City, Pueblo, and Colorado City.

Several missions were accomplished: Gilpin renewed acquaintances with people and land; be began to measure the size of the secession movement; he exposed his new government to the miners and welcomed their loyalty and their requests; he and his companions made speeches and listened to others; they enjoyed various entertainment, and they took the census.[13]

This tabulation showed some 25,000 people, including only about 4,000 white females and 89 Negroes of both sexes, the total being a significant drop from the presumed thousands of gold-seekers of a year or two before.

Now, in mid-July, the chief justice arrived and Governor Gilpin could set into operation a system of courts. He divided the territory into three districts with a separate headquarters for each of the justices. Rarely, if ever, were all three men in Colorado at the same time and much juggling of areas ensued. As late as October Justice Hall complained that Armour had not yet reached the territory and that Pettis was a mere boy who knew no law. Both associate justices objected to leaving Denver except for brief circuits, and Hall seems to have carried an abnormal load.[14] The

[13] Sheldon S. Zweig, "The Civil Administration of Governor William Gilpin," *Colorado Magazine,* XXXI (July, 1954), 179–193. In Cañon City where Confederate sympathizers were reputedly numerous and rough, a United States flag was raised—with great cheering—during the meeting of welcome (Hall, *History of Colorado,* III, 394).

[14] One writer says that Justice Armour was talented but tyrannical and that many citizens signed petitions for his removal. Failing of this the legislature set up Conejos and Costilla counties as his district, hoping that these isolated Mexican counties would discourage him to the point of resigning. Instead Armour filled out his term without leaving Denver (Wilbur Fisk Stone [ed.],

Supreme Court was organized on July 10 and Gilpin and Weld were two of several attorneys admitted to practice.

Fortunately for the people of Colorado, Justice Hall was able as well as diligent. The courts were facing unusual problems and lack of manpower was only one of them. Hall had been a law partner of William Seward in Auburn, New York, back in the 1830's. He became a member of the state legislature, then mayor of Auburn in 1852. A rising Whig, he had carried out a formidable task of compiling decisions of the United States Attorney General at the request of President Millard Fillmore. Appointed chief justice of Colorado at Seward's request, Hall brought with him as much legal experience as any territory could hope for.[15]

Nevertheless, even Hall, with the sympathetic understanding of Gilpin, encountered matters for which he was not prepared. As one judge put it, it was easy to carry the law from the Atlantic to the Mississippi Valley, but in the Rockies, "Irrigation, mining and non-agricultural public domain begot new rights. . . . demanding new legislation, which in turn exacted judicial interpretation, construction, application, consideration of possible results, and the application of the doctrine and rules of selection and adaptation."[16]

Miners, between 1858 and 1861, established scores of districts in Colorado for very effective administration of the laws that the miners themselves drafted. Gilpin's courts recognized districts and laws as well as the decisions of the miners' courts. Any other procedure would have produced chaos. Just as Colorado to some extent borrowed California precedent, so Oregon, Idaho, and Nevada borrowed from Colorado. Referring to a Nevada case in 1865 Chief Justice Salmon P. Chase declared:

A special kind of law, a sort of common law of the miners, the offspring of a nation's irrepressible march—lawless in some senses, yet clothed with dignity by a conception of the immense social results

---

*History of Colorado*, I, 734). The same writer says that Pettis came to Colorado, took one look and left (*ibid.*). This is not true unless the passage means that Pettis looked at his *district* and left for Denver. Another writer calls Armour an offensive, unworthy man, and Hall agreeable and mediocre (Smiley, *History of Denver*, p. 708).

15 "Benjamin F. Hall," *National Cyclopaedia of American Biography*, XIII, 24.

16 Stone, *History of Colorado*, I, 734.

mingled with the fortunes of these bold investigators,—has sprung up on the Pacific Coast, and presents in the value of a "mining right" a novel and peculiar question of jurisdiction for this court.[17]

Generally, Hall and Gilpin supported miners' and ranchers' claims clubs as well as other practices that protected the older settlers. Later in 1861, when the territorial legislature met, it confirmed the propriety of these actions and provided for the transfer of subsequent cases to the regular courts. The transition came about smoothly. In 1866 the United States Congress recognized the force of local mining laws and in this fashion endorsed Gilpin's legal administration.[18]

A different decision by Governor Gilpin gave the courts of Colorado some more business. In October, 1861, he vetoed an act of the territorial legislature which would have legalized the territory's first divorce. While this was still the practice of legislatures in many states and territories, William thought it wrong. To him, man and wife were parties to a civil contract and entitled to trial by jury if one party wished to terminate the contract. While the legislature had the right to establish tribunals and their procedures, the Governor said, "I recognize the sacred right reserved to the courts and to the Juries of the people, to hear and decide upon the evidence in such case, to determine the facts and to decree the disposition of Infants and property."[19] This precedent was closely followed in the history of both territory and state of Colorado.

At the same time that he organized the courts, Governor Gilpin called for a territorial election to be held on August 19. By decree he created three different forms of electoral districts: the territory as a whole would elect one man to the Congress in Washington; for the bicameral territorial legislature William established nine districts for councilmen and thirteen for representatives. The remain-

[17] The pioneer work on frontier government, written first in 1885, is Charles H. Shinn, *Mining Camps* (New York: Knopf, 1948).

[18] Thomas Maitland Marshall, "The Miners' Laws of Colorado," *American Historical Review*, XXV (April, 1920), 426–439, gives a detailed analysis of many of the codes.

[19] Quoted in U.S. State Department, *Territorial Papers, Colorado Series*, II, October 4, 1861. In "A Pioneer of 1842" William grandly claimed that he had despotic powers including absolute command of the Army and Navy. Perhaps He used his veto only a bit more than his naval command.

ing election procedures were completed with a haste that commends Gilpin and Weld for their efficiency. Almost immediately the campaigns opened on national party lines.

The Republicans met at Golden on July 1st and from eleven candidates nominated Hiram P. Bennet for delegate to the 37th Congress. Three weeks later the Union Party (largely Democrats) named Beverly D. Williams, one-time delegate for Jefferson Territory, to oppose Bennet. Although brief, the campaign was heated by the secession issue as Republicans hoped to gain votes through the association of disunion with the Democrats. The area had, until very recently, been predominantly Democratic, but many voters now switched (as Bennet himself did) to the Lincoln-Gilpin cause. The result was an easy victory for Bennet and most Republican candidates for legislative posts.[20]

At the call of Governor Gilpin the first Territorial Legislative Assembly of Colorado met in Denver on September 9, 1861, convened for a sixty-day term.[21] Before the members of the houses separated into two different buildings on Larimer Street they sat together to hear the Governor's welcoming address. Only seven printed pages long (if the entire talk was reported), it falls below William's quantitative standard. He told the men of his pleasure at greeting them and of the great work they must do together. His duty was to discuss conditions of the territory and recommend legislation—their duty, he said, was to create a stable government, "for this commonwealth of the primeval mountains, become, in the march of our great country one of the family of the American Union."

He revealed his plans for the legislators to divide the territory into counties, townships, districts, and precincts, for, he said, "it is in these complete little republics where the sovereign power of the

[20] Zweig, "The Civil Administration of Gilpin," pp. 186–189; U.S. State Department, *Territorial Papers, Colorado Series*, I, July 11, 1861; Le Roy R. Hafen, *Colorado: The Story of a Western Commonwealth*, pp. 157–158. Gilpin, hoping to keep moderate Democrats from allying with secessionists, made no campaign for the Republican candidates. Nearly 10,000 people voted.

[21] I see little evidence to confirm the advance opinion of one Denverite that in the Assembly "will be seen the greatest set of rascals that ever disgraced a legislative body," Augustus to Horatio Wildman, May 29, 1861, Wildman Papers.

people is always in exercise, where self government has a perpetual vitality and independent freedom is practiced and enjoyed."

Then the Governor asked for legislation to establish a system of "social" police, civil and criminal codes, taxation, roads, charitable agencies, and education. Schools and colleges were needed, he emphasized, because they were the basis of the "virtuous exercise of the elective franchise." Because he believed that no society was ever safe from revolution and conspiracy, he next asked for a territorial militia, adding that the program must include in its consideration the presence of 25,000 Indians in the area.

The new governor now distributed the results of the census to the legislators, his speech verbally expanding Colorado's population to 30,000. But he argued that even that figure was inadequate, for almost all of those people were adult males—family heads, whose families were elsewhere. Think how Colorado would grow when the wives and children arrived. He thought that this circumstance had no "precedent in any new society voluntarily planted and perpetuated in the wilderness."

No Gilpin talk could conclude without reference to his geopolitics. The precious and base metals, Colorado's universally fertile soil, her splendid and salubrious climate, "the facility of transit and penetration by roads over all varieties of surface . . . demonstrate that our country is supremely favored by nature with all the elements which promise unrivaled rapidity of progress prosperity and power." The great American dream of a "CONTINENTAL RAILWAY" was about to be fulfilled. Needless to say, it must pass through the center of Colorado. Added William, "Our territory will be besected [sic] East and West, by the grandest work of all time, constructed to fraternize the domestic relations of our people and . . . to draw the travel and commerce of all the nations, and all the continents of the world."

Governor Gilpin concluded his address to his legislature with an appeal to reliance upon the experience of the "Eagles"—Washington, Jefferson, and Jackson—and a prayer to the "Supreme Throne of Grace."

Copies of the speech were printed and circulated widely enough so that eastern newspapers occasionally quoted some of the more exciting portions. For his friends in the San Luis Valley William had his address put into Spanish and passed out as the blueprint

for Colorado of Governor Guillermo Guilpin.²² The legislature applauded; then the council left the small frame structure used by
the representatives and moved down Larimer Street to their "own"
borrowed building.²³

The volume of work completed by this first Colorado legislature
would indicate that the men held steadily to their tasks during the
two-month session. Under the Organic Act the governor shared the
law-making authority with the legislature, possessing an absolute
veto, yet there was no conflict between the two branches that au-
tumn.²⁴ Their list of accomplishments was substantial.²⁵ They
created seventeen counties, including six named for individuals—
Jefferson, Frémont, Douglas, Larimer, Weld, and Gilpin. Gilpin
and Secretary Weld sketched the territory's official seal, borrowed
from the Weld family coat of arms. The "Jefferson" laws were
endorsed or altered to meet the new status. Chief Justice Hall's
recommendations about court organization were enacted, while a
legal code (heavily borrowed from the state of Illinois) was
adopted. The city of Denver got a new charter, the territory speci-
fying the powers and marking out the city's organization and procedures. The previous acts of the town's "People's Government"
were legalized, meanwhile, and a territorial school system was au-
thorized.²⁶

²² U.S. State Department, *Territorial Papers, Colorado Series*, I, September
10, 1861; *The Denver Post*, November 2, 1919. The *Post* repeated sections of the
talk and added editorial comments about the session.

²³ Just at the close of this session the legislature passed a bill to move the
capital to Colorado City, a more central town. The primitive conditions there
(camping out and doing their own cooking) persuaded the men to move back
to Denver four days later. Gilpin's executive offices never left Denver (Hall,
*History of Colorado*, III, 85; Smiley, *History of Denver*, p. 493). See also Howbert, *Pike's Peak Region*, pp. 70–71. Howbert, whose father was chaplain in
the second territorial legislature, has some delightful reminiscences of those
days.

²⁴ William believed that this power was requested (before his arrival) by
proslavery men who had expected to control the governorship ("A Pioneer of
1842").

²⁵ Zweig, "The Civil Administration of Gilpin."

²⁶ Some argument arose over changing the name of Mountain County to
Gilpin; a few miners wanted it called Gregory after the man who made the
first important gold discovery in that district. The county is very small, but

The special interest of the Governor can be seen in measures to survey the territory with the aid of some old mountain men, whose work resulted in the first official map of the region. To assist agriculture the government passed an act to develop irrigation systems, and incorporated seven private water companies. The legislature sent a petition to the United States Congress asking for a branch mint and assay office to be located in Denver; Congress complied with the request in 1862 but for many years considerably restricted the amount of minting permitted.[27]

Preliminary plans were made for a future university at Boulder. Other measures discussed were aiding fisheries, higher per diem pay for the legislators, and increasing the representation in the next session. "Altogether the lawmakers under the guidance of Governor Gilpin enacted fifty-one general laws, forty acts relating to the practice of law, thirty-six private acts, eight joint memorials and three joint resolutions" a singular achievement for the first two months.[28]

While working closely with his legislature in civil administration, William Gilpin also had the responsibility for being superintendent of Indian affairs of Colorado Territory. This additional duty was typical for territorial governors of that era and in William's case provided him with nearly one-half of his annual $2,500 salary. In his capacity as superintendent William had no advice nor assistance from the territory but dealt solely with the Indian

rich in minerals (Hall, *History of Colorado*, III, 405). See also Hafen, "Lewis Ledyard Weld and Old Camp Weld," p. 205; Clyde L. King, *The History of the Government of Denver*, pp. 28–35.

[27] U.S. House of Representatives, *Executive Document No. 56*, 37th Cong., 2nd Sess., 1861; King, *History of Denver*, pp. 39, 47, 62. In July, thirty-two men met in Denver to form an agricultural society. Oddly, most of the men were business and professional leaders, and not farmers. The number included Governor Gilpin, William Larimer, Indian Agent Albert Gallatin Boone, and Alexander Majors, the genius of western freighting and transportation who had been a neighbor of Gilpin in Independence fifteen years before (Alvin T. Steinel, *History of Agriculture in Colorado, 1856–1926*, p. 54. Nothing seems to have come from the society.

[28] Zweig, "The Civil Administration of Gilpin," p. 192. The legislature created new posts for William to fill. These included a treasurer, an auditor, and a superintendent of public instruction, all of whom remained in office a year or more under William's successor (Stone, *History of Colorado*, I, 178).

Bureau, which had been transferred in 1849 from the War Department to the Department of Interior.

Gilpin had three agents under his jurisdiction: Harvey Vaile, whose district was the Western Slope of Colorado and included Utahs as well as some Shoshone and Snake Indians; Lafayette Head, who lived in the San Luis Valley and served Utes and some Navajos; and Albert Gallatin Boone, at Fort Wise among Arapahoes, Cheyennes, Comanches, and Kiowas. Offering the Bureau no reasons, Gilpin recommended that his superintendency should also include Kit Carson's Apaches and Utahs in New Mexico and a subagency among the Northern Cheyennes and Sioux. The expansion did not take place.

Among these men Vaile seems to have had the fewest Indian problems during Gilpin's term of office. In May of 1861 the Central Overland California and Pike's Peak Express Company, seeking a more direct route from Denver to Salt Lake City, had sent an expedition into the mountains. Aided by Jim Bridger, Captain E. L. Berthoud, the chief engineer, had found the high pass that bears his name. The same party left Denver again in July to mark out the road to Utah; Gilpin ordered Vaile to accompany the group, investigate Indian affairs along the way and report the condition of the Utahs to Gilpin.[29]

The survey of both road and Indians was completed without incident, but Vaile warned the governor that a new road would bring thousands of settlers into so lovely a region and the many Utes already there might resist when that invasion should come.

Down in Conejos, Lafayette Head had a touch of the same problem that was beginning to bother the Governor—he had no money to carry out his duties. Head came to Denver to ask for funds, but Gilpin had none to give and sent him to Santa Fe. The superintendent there gave him some provisions but not one-fourth of what he needed. Head, who impressed William as very able, distributed his goods in the early fall. Over five thousand Utes (out of eight thousand in southern Colorado) showed up, spoiling for trouble. They lived in the "gold region," said Head, and the miners coming

[29] Charles Mix to Gilpin, August 19, 1861; William P. Dole to Gilpin, April 15, 1861; Dole to Harvey Vaile, December 30, 1861; Mix to Gilpin, February 25, 1862; all in Gilpin File, Letter Book, Indian Bureau, National Archives. See also J. Cecil Alter, *Jim Bridger*, pp. 296–297.

in had already driven away their game. To restore their pride and
increase their supplies, the Utes frequently followed the Arkansas
through the mountains down to the plains, where they attacked
Cheyennes, Arapahoes, and whites indiscriminately and successfully. Worse, they were being pushed from the south by the ras-
cally Navajos. With the end of summer the raids were diminishing;
Head and Governor Gilpin hoped that the meager supplies would
keep the Utahs quiet until spring. Meanwhile, Head (and it should
be emphasized that it was *he*, not Gilpin) said that he needed a
minimum of five cavalry and two infantry companies at Fort Garland to guarantee peace. Many Mexicans and Americans in the
San Luis Park were now lending him supplies on credit, but this
charity would cease the moment that the new Confederate forces
in the West looked stronger than those of the Union.[30]

The Governor's third agent, Albert Gallatin Boone, posed the
most serious problem of all to the new superintendent. In the first
place, while the two men had been neighbors for years in Jackson
County, Missouri, William could not be sure how much trust to
place in this grandson of the old pioneer, for in the late 1850's
Boone had been an active member of the proslavery forces in Kansas. Upon the resignation of William Bent, Boone had been given
the Cheyenne-Arapahoe agency by President Buchanan. Then
Boone sold his Denver store and managed to get a few of the chiefs
to agree to the Treaty of Fort Wise just before Gilpin arrived in
Colorado.

This agreement decreased the Cheyennes' and Arapahoes' holdings to an arid reservation in southeastern Colorado in exchange
for an annuity to each of the two tribes of $15,000; this sum being
reduced by the costs of a number of improvements that the government promised to make. The treaty was amended but still not
signed by the majority of the tribes directly concerned when it
was ratified by the Senate and proclaimed in December by President Lincoln.

The treaty, signed or not, meant little. Most of the Indians

[30] A curious sidelight is Head's enthusiastic description of the climate and
resources of the San Luis country. His attempt to interest William in the area
could only reinforce a seventeen-year-old opinion (Lafayette Head to William
Gilpin, October 3, 1861, No. 36, in Interior Department, *Report of Secretary of
Interior*, November 30, 1861, I, 1.1, 1861.

hunted buffalo until September when they began massing on Fort Wise demanding their annuities. Shrewdly Gilpin had ordered Boone to issue nothing that summer knowing that the Indians would be much hungrier in the autumn. Enough food was now issued at the fort to keep the Indians temporarily satisfied.

Gilpin sent a private message to William Dole, Commissioner of Indian Affairs in Washington, describing the scene: Colorado needed treaties with the Kiowas, Comanches, and the remaining Cheyennes immediately; annuities must be paid in full; the funds for Colorado Indians' supplies must be authorized at once, for not one cent had yet reached the Governor—in fact, he had not even received a letter of instruction and was already in debt. Now, worst of all, Governor Gilpin had evidence that the Colorado Cherokee miners and other rebel sympathizers were trying to incite the Indians to attack the troops and white settlements. So serious was the plot that Gilpin could not trust the Overland to carry his mail —hence the secret messenger. Gilpin concluded by asking Dole to warn the President and the Secretary of War of the threat to the territory.[31]

William's superintendency of Indian matters can be assessed, therefore, as a period of marking time. No massacres took place nor even any action more than isolated raids. Perhaps William neither improved relations nor injured them. Completely lacking support from Washington, he could do little. He had a philosophy for treating with the Indians, and he had specific plans, but none of them was ever used. Events were very soon to prove him right in one important regard though—serious, bloody trouble was coming and no one knew how to stop it.[32]

To Governor Gilpin, during his few months of office, however, all of these issues were secondary to the defense of Colorado against

[31] Gilpin to Dole, June 19, 1861, No. 35, and October 8, 1861, No. 37, in Interior Department, *Report of Secretary of Interior*, November 30, 1861, I, 1.1, 1861; Stan Hoig, *The Sand Creek Massacre*, pp. 14–17. Hoig concluded that the federal government was driving the Indians into war. Boone did nothing to support the Confederacy. Without consulting Gilpin, who opposed the change, Lincoln replaced Boone with an agent whose reputation is badly tarnished.

[32] Relations between settlers and Indians became much worse after Gilpin left office. By 1864 the territory was in a state of siege, and Governor John Evans was powerless to protect the citizens. The Sand Creek massacre was one of the atrocities of this period.

secession. With all of his heart he was convinced that the Confederacy would try any measure to conquer the territory for its vast mineral deposits and its strategic location. If the Southern forces could take Colorado, the mines would build their army, and a handful of their troops could cut off the wealth of Utah, Nevada, Oregon, and California from the Union. Furthermore, in all of those areas feelings of westernism were already so strong that the possibility of a third American state was popularly being considered. The consummation of such a plan would, of course, be nearly as damaging to the Union as to have the region in Confederate hands.

These things William believed, and they explain his decisiveness, or perhaps overenthusiasm, in meeting the emergency of 1861.[33]

How real was the secession movement and the danger of invasion in Colorado? A frequently reported figure is that about one-third of the population came from the South and that many from northern states held no strong attachment to the Union because they had so often been ignored by that government when they had asked for assistance. One Denver newspaper was outspoken for secession, and an occasional Confederate flag was flown over the stores and saloons in the territory. While there was a tendency in the later 1860's for residents to play down the Confederate menace, the evidence is that during Gilpin's administration much of the Colorado public was frightened.

One young pioneer woman declared that Denver was about evenly divided on secession when Gilpin took office in 1861.[34] Another girl, wife of a miner, wrote in her journal that "Denver has a great many rebel sympathizers."[35] A visitor who published an emigrant's guide said that the crimes and outrages of the early terri-

[33] In Bancroft's biography as well as Gilpin's own accounts of his term as governor the signal achievements in administration are almost ignored for discussions on the military phases. George Willing, one-time delegate to Congress from "Jefferson Territory," advocated Colorado's entrance into a confederation of the Pacific in 1860 (William M. Wroten, Jr., "Colorado and the Advent of the Civil War," *Colorado Magazine*, XXXVI [July, 1959], 174–186). Wroten analyzes the press reaction to secession during 1860–1861.

[34] Susan R. Ashley, "Reminiscences of Colorado in the Early Sixties," *Colorado Magazine*, XIII (November, 1936), 226.

[35] Mollie D. Sanford, *Mollie: The Journal of Mollie Dorsey Sanford in Nebraska and Colorado Territories*, p. 162.

tory had just been crushed when "Rebel sympathizers [became] active and influential and for a short time it was a matter of serious doubt whether Colorado would remain true to the Government or drift away into the folds of the Confederacy."[36]

Justice Hall considered conditions so serious that he corresponded directly with Lincoln in September to describe the threat. He told the President that 6,000 adult males with strong "southern proclivities" lived in Colorado. These men had first gone to Kansas to make it a slave state; failing that, they had moved on to Colorado. Stirred by the rebellion they had got in touch with leaders in Missouri, Arkansas, and Texas. Secretly they had organized and begun the collection of arms, which Hall had seen for himself.

Colorado Confederates were bold enough to post notices that they would purchase arms from the settlers—and at good prices, Hall went on to say.[37] He agreed with Gilpin that many Indians (the chief justice specified Arapahoes) were in the pay of the Confederacy and that the Overland Express Company was untrustworthy. Hall believed that Bennet's victory over Williams was a triumph for unionism but that the rebels, led by one A. B. Miller, who claimed 1,200 followers in Denver alone, were now threatening to burn the city and overthrow the Administration. The danger ended only when Miller and his men left Denver for the southern army.[38]

Perhaps it is needless to add that Governor Gilpin agreed with all of these assessments. Presumably better informed than the public on the nature and degree of the threat, he, rather curiously it would seem, wrote to a Washington newspaper of his trials in office during the crisis:

My labors here are incessant, and the struggle with treason is a perpetual death-struggle. Emissaries swarm here as they have done in Baltimore, Washington, and St. Louis, in the worst time of insurrection. . . . The want of money, together with the total oblivion by the Government of the critical condition caused by the withdrawal of its military force, the agitated condition of the Indians, and the extreme

[36] Frederick B. Goddard, *Where to Emigrate and Why*, p. 161.

[37] L. A. McGee, "Colorado Pioneers in the Civil War," *Southwestern Social Science Quarterly*, XXV (June, 1944), 33.

[38] United States Government, *The War of the Rebellion: A Compilation of the Official Records of the Union and Confederate Armies* (hereafter cited as *Official Records*), Ser. III, Vol. I, 504–509.

cost and scarcity of food, (where it has all to be imported), complicate the tangled condition of affairs, and strain the ligaments of government to a perpetually bursting tension.[39]

In an interview some twenty years later Gilpin said that he, like Lincoln, had been surrounded by professional assassins. The extravagances of William's reports are clear, and probably are little more than his usual rhetoric; they were not more pronounced in later years, when he might be justifying his actions, however, than they were in 1861 in secret correspondence to Washington.[40]

Colorado's leading historian concludes that Gilpin made some honest mistakes, but

At the very time that the Governor's political enemies were asserting that the army of troops in Colorado was the height of folly, there was being organized a Confederate army in Texas to conquer New Mexico, Colorado and the great Southwest. . . . the Colorado troops recruited and equipped by the aggressive first Governor of Colorado were destined to strike the decisive blow in thwarting those well conceived plans of the South.[41]

The military phase of the Gilpin administration began in June of 1861. Two militia companies authorized by the "Territory of Jefferson" had just been disbanded (the commander of one of these was an ardent southerner). Gilpin felt that he should at least create a military staff to make some preliminary plans for normal protection of the territory as provided by law. He therefore named Richard Whitsett, adjutant general; Samuel Moer, quartermaster; John Fillmore, paymaster; and Morton Fisher, purchasing agent. Gilpin had no troops at his disposal; only a handful of federal forces were in the territory, split between Fort Garland in the San Luis Valley and Fort Wise, near Bent's New Fort on the Arkansas, each too far to be of any use in Denver or the mineral districts of the north.

A Texan, Captain Joel McKee, began purchasing arms for the Confederacy from among the Coloradans. Concerned, the Governor ordered Fisher to buy up all of the arms and ammunition that he could find, irrespective of condition or caliber and even paying

[39] *National Republican* (Washington, D.C.), November 29, 1861.
[40] Gilpin, "A Pioneer of 1842."
[41] Hafen, *Colorado*, pp. 159–160.

unreasonable sums if necessary to keep them from the hands of McKee's men. Then Gilpin arrested McKee and about forty others for treason, bringing an end to Confederate purchases in the territory.

When Judge Hall empaneled a grand jury to examine evidence against McKee, other southerners, led by A. B. Miller, demonstrated in front of the court house but failing to get public sympathy, soon left town untouched; Hall and Gilpin lacked the manpower to test Miller's strength.

While the immediate danger to the territorial government had passed, the Governor could not be sure that it was a permanent change; he therefore sent messengers to various military posts to ask for the delivery of arms to Denver. He knew that the forts in Colorado could not help, but he thought he could get assistance from Forts Laramie, Kearny, or some other farther east.

Gilpin learned that the War Department was moving the Second Dragoons from Utah to the Potomac. He sent messengers to intercept the troopers and beg for ammunition. Congressional Delegate Hiram Bennet saw the commander Colonel Philip St. George Cooke at Fort Leavenworth. According to Bennet, Cooke gave him nothing but oaths against the government; the report wound its way to Lincoln that Cooke (a Virginian) was a Confederate in sympathy at least and should be replaced. But Cooke was loyal, and one of his subordinates still back at Laramie dispatched eighteen wagonloads of ammunition and 1,800 new rifles to Governor Gilpin. This was probably the turning point in the defense of Colorado.

Now Governor Gilpin and Hall could move with more confidence. They set up a Union Defense Committee, built a prison for the Confederates, used military arrests, and suspended the privilege of habeas corpus for McKee and his followers. Hall suggested to the President that Gilpin be made a brigadier general to command a new brigade to protect the Rocky Mountain area.[42]

Gradually the War Department took some cognizance of the

---

[42] William C. Whitford, *Colorado Volunteers in the Civil War*, pp. 38–41; Stone (ed.), *History of Colorado*, I, 701; Bancroft, *William Gilpin*, p. 46; *Official Records*, Ser. III, Vol. I, 506–507; Otis E. Young, *The West of Philip St. George Cooke*, pp. 322–326. Cooke's son, John Rogers Cooke, and his son-in-law, J. E. B. Stuart, were two prominent members of his family who had already sided with Virginia.

trouble in Colorado. (That Hall regularly wrote private notes to Secretary Seward, and Gilpin used personal messengers such as Seward's son, Augustus, and various army officers, probably forced Colorado upon the Administration's attention.) In July Colorado Territory became a part of the new Western Department under command of Major General John C. Frémont.[43]

Some of his contemporaries accused Gilpin of being "trigger-happy" and overly fearful of military danger to Colorado that summer. The facts support the charge scarcely at all. While still in Washington in April, 1861, and again writing from Denver in July, William had asked the War Department for authority to raise a territorial militia. Getting no such power, he did no recruiting but merely set up his skeleton staff as we have seen. He took no further action until he was forced to by a cry for help from New Mexico.

On July 6, Colonel E. R. S. Canby, commanding officer of Union troops in New Mexico, wrote from Santa Fe to Gilpin requesting that he quickly enlist two companies of infantry volunteers to garrison Fort Garland. A very young post, Garland had been commanded in 1860 by Canby when he and three companies had moved there from Utah after the "Mormon War." Subsequently Canby and most of the troops had moved into New Mexico, leaving only a small detachment at Garland. Canby's request had War Department authority behind it, and Gilpin quickly complied.

He opened recruiting offices in villages and mining camps and commissioned John P. Slough and Samuel Tappan as the two company commanders. Both companies were full by August 13 and ready to move on New Mexico. Canby warned the Coloradans that he could not supply them, however, and hoped that somehow Governor Gilpin could feed and clothe them; arms would be sent from some eastern post, he hoped.

Both the Governor and the Colonel knew that the two companies were only sufficient to patrol southern Colorado, and they both correctly assumed that many more men were needed. Ironically,

---

[43] *Official Records*, Ser. I, Vol. III, 390, 567. William dealt directly with the field commanders in the remaining months of 1861. In November New Mexico became a separate department under Canby, while Colorado was placed under the new Kansas Department commanded by Major General David Hunter, another old friend of William Gilpin.

Canby had authority to raise a regiment in New Mexico and could not find the men; Gilpin lacked the authority but had an abundance of manpower.[44]

The exchange of this information must have been a factor in William's next step. Before receiving any *written* authority he decided to expand his two companies of volunteers into a regiment of ten companies. In a technical sense William was perhaps premature in this action. But he already had learned from Canby that the War Department planned to create several new companies in the Rocky Mountain area just as he also knew that they were unavailable in New Mexico. Furthermore, Canby had orders to transfer his 2,400 regulars to Fort Leavenworth. Whether Gilpin had informal word from Frémont in St. Louis is neither clear nor important.[45] For on August 29, Headquarters, Western Department, ordered Governor Gilpin "to increase your force to 1,000 men, so that you can send the companies to relieve the garrison at Fort Wise. That garrison, when relieved, is ordered to repair to Santa Fe and report to Colonel E. R. S. Canby."[46]

William had correctly assessed the situation and had put the machinery into motion that would save the Rocky Mountain area for the Union. The Confederate government of Jefferson Davis had no comprehensive plan for the conquest of the Far West. His administration recognized the mineral wealth of the region and perhaps had some vague notion of the link to California, but too many other matters were more urgent. In the Confederacy and the Union alike western military affairs were not directed—they happened.

Two Confederate officers were primarily responsible for the attack on New Mexico as the prelude to a general western campaign. One of these was Lieutenant Colonel John R. Baylor, who, with a few hundred Texans, opened the invasion in July of 1861 by taking Fort Fillmore in extreme southern New Mexico. Baylor, apparently

[44] *Official Records*, Ser. I, Vol. IV, 53–54, 68; Mollie Sanford's husband, a second lieutenant, told her that in the mountains, "They do not have to drum up the recruits, they come in from all quarters, from the mines, the shops and stores, all ready to fight for their country" (Sanford, *Mollie*, p. 158).

[45] One writer, Whitford, reported that Gilpin's authority for the regiment was "obscure" (Whitford, *Colorado Volunteers*, p. 45). See also *Official Records*, Ser. I, Vol. IV, 63; Ray C. Cotton, *The Civil War in the Western Territories*, pp. 11, 13.

[46] *Official Records*, Ser. I, Vol. III, 466.

satisfied with his progress, settled down in the nearby town of Mesilla, proclaimed himself governor and established Mesilla as the capital of the new Confederate Territory of Arizona, a rough, narrow rectangle of land extending from Texas to the Colorado River and from the Mexican border to 34° north latitude. Baylor's military efforts against federal troops were henceforth meager as he concerned himself primarily with Indian warfare and getting Jefferson Davis' support for his unexpected coup.[47]

The other Confederate with a plan for New Mexico was Major Henry Hunter Sibley, who as a regular had seen much western duty before 1861, had dreamed a grand design for that area, and had hastened to Richmond for the blessing of Jefferson Davis. In July Sibley, now a Brigadier General, returned to Texas with orders to commence recruiting two regiments, to organize his forces, to drive the federals out of New Mexico, and to set up a military government.

Sibley soon had three cavalry regiments under arms and in training at San Antonio for the invasion of New Mexico. In November this army started for El Paso, the last elements arriving there in mid-December. Sibley, from his headquarters at Fort Bliss, announced the Confederate plan for New Mexico—with 3,500 men he would defeat the federals, impress the Spanish, and cow the Indians. He urged the New Mexicans to be peaceful and industrious, and he welcomed the enlistment of disgruntled Union men. Although short on supplies Sibley was ready to move north by the beginning of 1862.[48]

The early information about Sibley's recruiting and training did not greatly disturb Colonel Canby, but he did fear what he called "combinations of the lawless" who might seize government posts and property. But as reports from spies, native civilians, and even Indians trickled in, Canby became increasingly concerned and turned more and more to Gilpin for help.

By the autumn of 1861 the Governor was in trouble. His recruiting had gone almost too well and he now faced an impossible task

[47] Briefly Baylor gave his troops to Gilpin's boyhood friend, Brigadier General Albert Sidney Johnston, en route from California to Richmond, but Johnston wanted a greater challenge than protecting a small western territory and lingered only a few days.

[48] Colton, *Civil War*, pp. 21–25; *Official Records*, Ser. I, Vol. IV, 93.

of provisioning his men. In spite of scurrying messengers with pleas to St. Louis and Washington, the arms problem was never solved. Food and clothing were generally obtainable, however, within Colorado. The question was the proper method of payment to the numerous suppliers.

On this matter William Gilpin tripped and fell, badly bruised. Neither the federal nor the territorial government had appropriated funds for the troops, and the War Department continued to give the Governor no information on how to proceed. Turning to his own experience as his sole guide, he recalled the days of 1846–1847 when Doniphan's Missouri Volunteers and Gilpin's Santa Fe Battalion were given similar treatment by Washington. With the intuition of one who has dealt with bureaucracy before, Governor Gilpin dared wait no longer; he assumed that ultimately accounts would be righted, and in payment for his military purchases he, in July, began issuing sight drafts to local (and a few out-of-territory) merchants bearing his own promise to pay.

At first the drafts were readily accepted, particularly because the mines were not producing well and specie was scarce. Most of the leading business firms took the paper at face value and soon began sending it to Washington for payment. A few drafts circulated as currency, and there was some speculating with them, but most began to show up at the United States Treasury. Approximately $375,000 in drafts were issued by Governor Gilpin that year in payment for military purchases.

Gilpin knew that he was adopting unusual measures and took advantage of a visit of Major Augustus Seward to get a confidential message quickly to the President. The note carried by the Secretary's son described the value of Colorado to the nation, the dangers threatening it, and the actions that the Governor had taken to prevent disaster. He hoped for the President's "sanction of what I have done and will continue to do."[49]

In September the merchants began getting concerned for their money. Hiram Bennet, the territorial delegate in Washington, wrote to the Governor that payment had been delayed by a misunderstanding, but would be made. In November the Treasury

[49] Gilpin had already told the Secretary of War of the drafts (Gilpin to Lincoln, September 13, 1861. Abraham Lincoln, Papers, Vol. 54, Manuscripts Division, Library of Congress).

declared that payment could not be paid. The drafts dropped 10 per cent in value; merchants became angry with Gilpin, and some made the long journey to Washington to seek reimbursement.

On November 2 an assistant quartermaster of the United States Army, Captain Charles H. Alley, reached Denver and soon announced his glum opinion that the drafts could not be redeemed. A significant part of public opinion now turned sharply against Governor Gilpin and many cries were made for his removal from office.

This autumn of 1861 was clearly the lowest point in William's life. Most of his businessmen friends, long accustomed to daily chats with him, were now his enemies, sniping at Lincoln with complaints. His only hope for more supplies for his troops was from the already stripped western forts. Drafts were accepted only at discount—some reaching a bottom of forty cents on the dollar. But most distressing to the Governor, and entirely beyond his control, was that his favorites—the troops—his "Pet Lambs" they were popularly called, had yet to receive a cent of pay. Several of those still in Denver began looting ("foraging") for Christmas parties, threw rocks at Gilpin's home, and chased away the police.[50] An ungrateful people whom he had saved from secession, invasion, and Indians—in William's thinking—had turned on their deliverer and sought his blood.[51]

Unfortunately for the Gilpin Administration the drafts question was not the only one attacking its popularity that fall. Several subordinates were proving to be untrustworthy or worse. William's confidence in Judge Hall and Secretary Weld seemed well placed, but other officials did him much harm. Both the Governor and Hall believed that the other judges were useless, and the Chief Justice went so far as to ask Seward (whom he called "Governor") to

[50] Hubert Howe Bancroft, *The Works*, XXV, 426, says that Gilpin threatened confiscatory measures to merchants reluctant to accept the drafts. No other authority says this. Paper money was issued by Clark, Gruber and Co. backed by their coin. The five dollar bill bore Gilpin's picture (*Rocky Mountain News*, August 7, 1861). David Moffatt was one who traveled to Washington; the government owed him $30,000 (Sheldon S. Zweig, "William Gilpin: First Territorial Governor of Colorado," unpublished M.A. thesis, University of Colorado, 1953, pp. 131–133, 138–142).

[51] The sorry financial condition of New Mexico Territory was very similar to Colorado's during the Civil War. Canby's regulars went unpaid for a year.

replace the justices with outsiders and "none of the *applicants from this territory*. They all belong to the William H. Russell [president of the Overland Express Company] School and are all infected with treason."[52]

Harvey Vaile, the Indian agent in western Colorado, "failed to account for property in his possession" and refused to maintain his office where Governor Gilpin ordered. William removed him from his post but was overruled by William Dole, commissioner of Indian affairs.[53] Then without consulting Gilpin, Vaile got sixty days leave from Dole who listened to Bennet's urging of "unusual circumstances," whereupon Vaile went to Washington to demand Gilpin's removal. William had accused Vaile only of failure to do his work, but Hall hinted at something worse in the agent's conduct. Vaile, he said, was the instrument of the rebels in Colorado and could not attend to his job because he spent so much time thwarting the Governor's legislative program.[54]

Some of the rebels remained in prison in Denver and this, too, created problems for the Administration. Hall evidently released a number of McKee's men but as late as November still refused to issue writs of habeas corpus for six rebels. The Governor and the Chief Justice thought it dangerous to free known Confederates, yet the territory lacked funds to feed them, and Hall preferred not to convict them in the face of much hostile public opinion. Hall asked Seward, Cameron, and Lincoln for advice on the matter, and got none.

The Indian danger never eased during Gilpin's administration. He somehow secured a copy of a treaty between Colorado Cherokees and Confederates and concluded that an "erruption [*sic*] of

[52] Hall could not live on his $1,800 salary (the surveyor received $3,000) and wanted a raise. He considered himself responsible for keeping Colorado in the Union, for Gilpin was all alone and listened to the Justice's advice—"kept him up to our Auburn standards" (Hall to Seward, October 9, 1861, Lincoln Papers, Vol. 58).

[53] Gilpin to Dole, January 24, 1862, Gilpin File, Letters Received, 1861–1862, Office of Indian Affairs, National Archives.

[54] Vaile to Gilpin, December 31, 1861, Gilpin File, Office of Indian Affairs, National Archives; Dole to Vaile, December 30, 1861, and Charles Mix to Gilpin, February 25, 1862, Gilpin File, Letter Book, Indian Bureau, National Archives.

Cherokees" was imminent. Both he and Hall were obsessed with the notion that Colorado was surrounded by anti-Union Indians and needed a large standing militia against that threat.

Another group of people bothered the two leaders. They estimated that in Colorado resided about five thousand "border-ruffians" and disappointed office-and-contract-seekers. Normally loyal, some even Republicans, they had no sympathy for any cause but their own. They were dangerous if the government appeared weak; "I presume that they are the worst people on the face of the earth to govern," reported Hall.[55]

Perhaps the most powerful enemy to the Administration came from an unexpected direction. From the date of his arrival in Denver Governor Gilpin had counted upon the support of the two large Republican papers, the *Daily Colorado Republican* and the *Rocky Mountain News*. But the former got the plums—editor Thomas Gibson had gone on Gilpin's tour, for example. William Byers' *News* gradually became more critical of the Administration and grew very bitter when Secretary Weld gave the entire territorial printing contract to Gibson.[56] To the end of his term Gilpin was harried by editor Byers, and the *News* became the rallying point of unsatisfied contractors and political enemies of Gilpin.

In a confidential letter to Lincoln, Justice Hall summed up William's role thus far in Colorado. He wrote that Governor Gilpin's wisdom and discretion in handling the complicated administrative and Indian problems alone vindicated the appointment. His excellent military education, knowledge of frontier people, and qualities of statesmanship gave him a superior advantage over common men. Hall wrote to Lincoln: "I know of no other Statesman or soldier in this Republic who could have served the country better, if as well, or who better deserves the confidence of the Federal Government.[57]

[55] *Official Records*, Ser. II, Vol. II, 119, and Ser. III, Vol. I, 636–637; Hall refused to grant McKee a writ on three different occasions. His reason was that McKee (a Texan) was not a citizen of the United States, nor an alien claiming protection (Hall to Seward, May 26, 1862, U.S. State Department, *Territorial Papers, Colorado Series*, I, National Archives).

[56] Zweig, "William Gilpin," pp. 135–137.

[57] Hall to Lincoln, October 9, 1861, Lincoln, Papers, Vol. 58.

Suddenly war in New Mexico was to prove that Hall had judged Gilpin correctly. Sibley was finally commencing his drive northward from El Paso, and Canby needed help.

Gilpin placed the First Regiment of Colorado Volunteers under the command of Colonel Slough and following the War Department orders sent three companies to Fort Wise to release regulars for Canby's use. The remaining seven companies under Major John M. Chivington, presiding elder of the Methodist Episcopal Church for the Rocky Mountain area, remained in training at Camp Weld.

This post had just been completed in the summer of 1861 on the Platte River about two miles from the center of Denver. Doubtless a camp was needed, but Weld was too imposing and expensive to suit many Denverites, and Governor Gilpin accumulated more criticism. The camp, which included the usual army buildings spread out over thirty acres of low bluff, cost $40,000 plus soldiers' labor, and seemed too comfortable to many of the nonmilitary visitors.[58]

Nevertheless, Chivington trained these men rigidly while holding them for Canby or the needs of Colorado. To reinforce Canby, Gilpin created the Second Regiment of Colorado Volunteers, only two companies of which were ever mustered for New Mexico. In December, 1861, he sent these two units south; Company A under Captain Theodore Dodd marched down the Río Grande and joined Canby at Fort Craig. Company B, Captain James H. Ford commanding, held up at Fort Union, northeast of Santa Fe on the supply line from Fort Leavenworth. These were the first Colorado companies to leave the territory.[59]

Colorado troops were the decisive factor in the Civil War in the Far West. General Sibley was progressing slowly but with little opposition as he rode northward through the Río Grande valley. Canby's resistance to him was minimal: New Mexican volunteers deserted as a matter of habit, and the absence of any pay caused

[58] The troops at Camp Weld spent their days drilling or out on patrol after Indians. Much social life revolved around the post; Gilpin gave a regimental ball and a theater party. A number of men brought their wives to live in barracks. See Sanford, *Mollie*, p. 159; Albert B. Sanford, "Camp Weld, Colorado," *Colorado Magazine*, XI (March, 1934), 46–48 (Sanford was Mollie's son, born in 1862 at Camp Weld); Ashley, "Reminiscences of Colorado," pp. 226–227; Whitford, *Colorado Volunteers*, pp. 45–50.

[59] *Official Records*, Ser. I, Vol. IV, 82; Ser. I, Vol. IX, 630–631.

other volunteers to mutiny and desert, Canby wasting manpower and time pursuing his own useless militia. At Fort Craig, Sibley tried to taunt Canby into a battle, but failing, by-passed the fort. This movement Canby opposed and on February 21, 1862, at Valverde, the first significant Civil War battle was fought in the Far West.

Sibley was victorious. Each side lost perhaps two hundred or more men in killed, wounded, and missing. Canby's one company of Colorado Volunteers had been of immense value, but he was not sure whether the desertion of more than one hundred men—New Mexicans—was a disadvantage to him or not. Canby, however, was able to scramble back to Fort Craig; and knowing its limitations, General Sibley decided to ignore the post and continue northward. His Texas army was beginning to suffer from shortages, but he concluded that he could subsist off supplies in Albuquerque and Santa Fe as well as by deals with the natives of shifting loyalty.

The southern army reached Albuquerque in early March, and a few days later a smaller detachment took Santa Fe, now deserted by federal forces. Without contact with Canby, who remained at Fort Craig athwart Sibley's supply line, various individuals concluded that the federal offensive in the Southwest would have to begin at Fort Union.[60]

The commander of that post, Colonel Gabriel Paul, had decided to collect the expected Colorado troops, join Canby and open a campaign to drive Sibley out of New Mexico. His intention was to leave on March 24, anticipating the arrival of the First Regiment of Colorado Volunteers before that date.[61]

Conditions in Colorado were such that a cry for the troops was probably a godsend. Gilpin's vouchers were creating so much ill will and financial chaos that the Governor found it necessary to go to Washington in December, 1861, to try to get payment. Weld

[60] Whitford, *Colorado Volunteers*, pp. 57–72; thorough secondary accounts from different perspectives include Martin H. Hall, *Sibley's New Mexico Campaign*; Robert L. Kerby, *The Confederate Invasion of New Mexico and Arizona*; and Colton, *Civil War*, previously cited.

[61] Paul, second in rank to Canby in New Mexico, of a St. Louis creole family, was at West Point about the same time as Gilpin, also fought the Seminoles, and, according to Bancroft, was first cousin to the lady whom William subsequently married.

remained as acting governor, and William was back in Denver by late February of 1862, but his absence frightened the business community which seems not to have been informed of the purpose of the trip.

The unpaid, unused troops had reached a state of near-mutiny at Camp Weld that winter and Colonel Slough acted promptly when the Department of Kansas ordered him to combine all the men available for the relief of Fort Union. The two groups from Wise and Weld moved rather leisurely at first until they encountered messengers who brought word of Canby's defeat at Valverde. Thereafter, often through several inches of snow, they hurried forward at an average of forty miles a day. At a ranch on the Purgatoire River the two elements were united. Somewhere near Ratón Pass they were charged by another messenger with the news that Sibley had taken Albuquerque and Santa Fe and was approaching Fort Union. The Coloradans agreed to continue to march all night and covered an additional thirty miles before exhaustion of men and animals called for a halt. In thirty-six hours the First Regiment had marched ninety-two miles. On March 10 they entered Fort Union, thirteen days and four hundred miles from Denver.

In the usual fashion of regulars versus volunteers, a conflict now arose over matters of seniority and mission. Claiming earlier date of rank, Slough assumed command of Paul's regulars and volunteers as well as his own regiment. Then the two colonels diverted their argument to interpretations of the most recent orders from Canby. Slough, supported by New Mexico's Governor Henry Connelly, wanted to start immediately to intercept Sibley even if his departure endangered Fort Union. Paul contended that they were to hold Fort Union at all costs, then wait until Canby was ready to pinch Sibley between the two Federal forces.

Notwithstanding Paul's protests to Washington, Slough won both paper wars, rested his men a few days, and on March 22 left the post in the direction of Las Vegas and Santa Fe. His army was composed of the First Colorado Volunteers, Captain Ford's company of unattached Coloradans, one company of New Mexican volunteers, and a few-score regular infantry, cavalry, and artillery, a total of 1,342 men.

At the same moment Colonel William Scurry and some 1,100

Texans left Santa Fe (Sibley's headquarters) with a plan to capture Fort Union. The two small forces approached each other through historic Glorieta Pass, the southern extreme of the Sangre de Cristo Mountains. Advance guards stumbled upon one another on March 26. In a first engagement Major Chivington drove the Confederates back to Apache Canyon at the western end of the pass. Suffering much more severe casualties than his opponents, Scurry committed his reinforcements into the Canyon just as Slough brought the rest of his brigade up to join Chivington. The key maneuver of the second day of the battle of Glorieta Pass was Slough's decision to send Chivington and seven companies into the mountains south of the Pass in the hope of getting behind the Confederates. The movement succeeded. The two main bodies fought at close range for several hours; casualties were heavy and both sides were exhausted when darkness began to fall. Slough was preparing to withdraw from the field when he received a request from Scurry for an armistice to care for the dead and wounded.

The reason for the unexpected armistice was Scurry's discovery that Chivington's men had got to his rear from above, let themselves down sheer cliffs with ropes, and fallen upon the guard and supply train with complete success. All of Scurry's supplies were burned, his animals killed or scattered, his prisoners released. While Scurry had been winning a battle, he had lost a campaign. The Texans could only flee to Santa Fe and join Sibley for a complete withdrawal from New Mexico.

When Canby refused permission to try to capture the Texans, Slough resigned his command, and his officers elected Chivington to replace him. Almost deliberately, Union forces under Canby, Paul, and Chivington drove Sibley down the Río Grande valley once again.[62] By May Sibley was in El Paso, his army scattered all over New Mexico and his dream ended.

[62] Whitford, *Colorado Volunteers*, pp. 75–127. The New Mexico campaign had more than its share of army rumor. Many soldiers believed that Canby was married to Sibley's sister, explaining to the troops' satisfaction the reluctance of Canby to wage a vigorous war. Hall finds no evidence of this (*Sibley's Campaign*, p. 79 n.). Slough was not popular with his men and one of his officers was said to be watching him closely for any "suspicious move" during the battle. Many soldiers considered Chivington the true leader of the Colorado troops, but even he had detractors who thought he took credit for the work of too many others. Fortunately for Union forces, almost identical problems existed among

Most of the First Regiment remained under Chivington in New Mexico for a few months and then returned to Colorado to serve against the Indians, some, unhappily, at Sand Creek. The Second Regiment was filled out, trained at Fort Lyon, and then sent to fight in Arkansas and Oklahoma. Several other companies of Colorado Volunteers fought in Missouri and Kansas. But the Civil War in the Rocky Mountains came to a close at Glorieta in March of 1862. Colorado troops had saved at least two territories for the Union and freed several regiments for duty in the major theaters of the war. The gold and silver of the mines was at the call of Washington, and the transcontinental highway was secured.[63]

The man responsible for these triumphs was soon to be removed from office by President Lincoln. Criticism of Governor Gilpin—in Denver and Washington—had been growing that winter. His brief visit to the Potomac had resulted in the payment of only a very few vouchers, and the Colorado contractors were angry and often in desperate financial condition. While William Gilpin deserved censure for his unorthodox financing, the trait was not his alone. His own pay as well as that of Secretary Weld, was many months in arrears because of clerical errors in Washington. The national government placed no military funds at his disposal, nor told him how to borrow. Yet he was under orders to recruit one or more regiments of men. One writer suggests that even Lincoln's cabinet could agree on no method of assisting William.[64]

The decision to remove Gilpin from office was forced slowly upon Lincoln. Oddly, the first official attack on William came from Justice Hall. Before the Denver merchants had become much concerned about their money, Hall reported the danger in another of his secret messages to Seward. Hall wrote that he still firmly en-

---

the Texas forces; Baylor accused Sibley of hiding in an ambulance during the battle of Valverde, for example (Colton, *Civil War*, p. 37). One writer concludes that Slough resigned because of the danger of assassination as well as argument with Canby over strategy (Arthur A. Wright, "Colonel John P. Slough and the New Mexico Campaign," *Colorado Magazine*, XXXIX [April, 1962], 89–105).

[63] Percy Fritz, *Colorado: The Centennial State*, p. 202.

[64] Hall, *History of Colorado*, I, 272. See also Gilpin File, Auditor's Certificates, August 15, September 20, December 20, 1861, and March 20, 1862, Fiscal Branch, National Archives; Weld to Seward, October 16, 1861, U.S. State Department, *Territorial Papers, Colorado Series*, I.

dorsed Gilpin's loyalty to the government but not his "financier-ring." Greatly exaggerating the amounts involved, Hall went on to say: "It is another Frémont affair on a smaller scale, convincing you no doubt that these old army officers are not just the men to make contracts for the government." Hall wanted his remarks passed confidentially on to the President.[65]

Hall's criticism was honest, and in all other matters he was completely loyal to Gilpin. More properly he should have counseled the Governor about the vouchers, but if he advised against their issuance, neither man makes mention of his advice in correspondence.

Hall, however, was William's friend and included no malice in his criticisms. The case was different with a handful of others whose animus was great and yet often puzzling.

The leader of this anti-Gilpin faction was Hiram Bennet, territorial delegate in Washington, and a close friend of William Byers, editor of the *News*. In October Bennet took up the cause of dividing the territorial printing so that Edward Bliss of the *News* could share some of the profits then monopolized by Thomas Gibson. Bennet went to the Secretary of the Interior, then to the Treasury Department, and eventually to Seward with his plaintiff's case. Bliss came to Washington to do his own pleading with the same negative results. For, in spite of luke-warm instructions from Seward, Weld refused to make any change in the printing contract because he felt that the *News* was venal, irresponsible, and touched with secessionism.[66]

Weld's counterattack was severe enough, and serious enough, to make the Washington Administration cautious about stepping into a quarrel among Republicans who questioned one another's loyalty.[67]

[65] Hall to Seward, October 23, 1861, Lincoln Papers, Vol. 59. The Frémont reference probably concerned the current accusations of fraudulent purchases in the Western Department under Frémont.

[66] Bennet to Caleb Smith, Secretary of Interior, October 29, 1861; Bennet to Seward, November 12, 1861; Bennet to Seward, February 18, 1862, Weld to Seward, March 12, 1862; Edward Bliss to Seward, February 18, 1862, U.S. State Department, *Territorial Papers, Colorado Series*, I; Smiley (*History of Denver*, p. 656) says that it was "generally understood" that Gibson was Gilpin's partner—at least in 1862.

[67] One Denverite wrote home that Bennet was "an unscrupulous politician,"

One consequence of the charges against Gilpin's government was that his military purchases came under the surveillance of a special committee of the House of Representatives on "The Purchase of Army Supplies." This diligent little group traveled from New England to St. Louis checking on contracts made by leaders such as Grant and Frémont. They called four persons to testify in Washington about Colorado affairs.

The first witness was Harvey Vaile, peripatetic Indian agent. Vaile's replies to the committee were a damning indictment of the Gilpin management. Frequently prefacing his comments with "It is said," or "I have heard," Vaile alleged that Morton C. Fisher had a contract from Gilpin to buy horses in Colorado for the cavalry; that Fisher paid between $40 and $100 for each, including small, useless, Indian ponies and sold them to the troops for $175, the price including a cheap saddle and blanket.

Vaile said that the Governor's means of disarming the secessionists was equally scandalous. One firm was authorized to buy weapons from anyone in the territory to prevent the enemy from building a supply. The evil, said Vaile, was that the individual could not sell directly to the government, and thus middlemen bought at $5 to $18 per gun and sold them for $20 to $60. Perhaps 1,800 were sold in that fashion.

The story of supply purchases was fully as noisome, according to Vaile. Shirts worth $1.00 in Denver stores brought $4.00; pants, even flour, enjoyed similar mark-ups. The committee, accustomed to such profiteering on much grander scale in war zones, wanted to know whether Gilpin's measures had any justification. Vaile thought not. The Indians posed no danger at all, and the soldiers had so little to occupy themselves that they had become a nuisance in Denver. The troops wanted to go east and fight; in Colorado they were just serving time, breaking into shows by paying valueless Gilpin drafts, brawling with city toughs, and occupying expensive quarters. He concluded that a few hundred men could accomplish the entire Colorado military mission.

One week later (January 18, 1862) Edward Bliss testified before

---

and that Gilpin "has a strong opposition to contend with both in and out of his party" (Augustus Wildman to father, February 14, 1862, Wildman Papers, Coe Collection, Yale University Library).

the same committee. Bliss, the would-be printer, had an obvious personal stake in the Gilpin war. He repeated some of Vaile's complaints and attached a few of his own. He declared that Fisher, a young man in his early twenties, who was "said to be" Gilpin's cousin, was making a great profit for someone on purchases of horses. Bliss thought that in all of Colorado there were only 250 secessionists willing to fight, and few of them were armed. The loyal citizens of Colorado had no fear of secessionists or invaders, he concluded.

The third witness was Richard E. Whitsett, for a few months in 1861 Gilpin's adjutant general, in which position he should have become far more informed than his testimony bore out. Whitsett was one of the founders of Denver, a speculator and businessman who was to hold office under a surprising variety of Republican factions. Why Whitsett had just left Gilpin's government is not clear, but he soon turned up as auditor in the next administration.

Whitsett added little to the story of purchases in Colorado. His estimates on prices paid for horses, guns, and supplies were much more modest than those of Vaile and Bliss; furthermore, he testified that Fisher bought directly for the government, was not a middleman, and did no selling. He agreed that Fisher could have been related to Gilpin but maintained that Fisher's business had been entirely with Samuel Moer, the quartermaster, and that Fisher owed nothing to Gilpin. Whitsett thought that many Coloradans made too much profit selling to Fisher, but the supply of horses and guns was clearly limited and everyone knew it. On one point Whitsett agreed with the other two witnesses—Gilpin had recruited too many men for duty in Denver. But, he added, the Governor could not have known that in advance. In spite of his job Whitsett contended that he knew nothing of the Governor's authority for mustering the troops and had not heard of any such directions from Frémont.

That same day (February 18) the last witness appeared. It was William Gilpin himself, getting ready to leave for Colorado after his unsuccessful attempt to secure payment for his vouchers.

The committee's questioning was not very adroit, and many unresolved issues were not tossed at the star witness. Instead the Governor merely made a statement, surprisingly temperate, matter-of-fact, and brief. He declared that Vaile and Bliss relied solely upon rumor and hearsay and should be ignored. He repeated his usual story of the value of Colorado to the Union, the many threats against the territory, and the need for a substantial and permanent militia. Gilpin was positive about one significant matter that the other three witnesses had challenged: he declared flatly that the War Department had authorized his recruitment of two regiments in addition to Canby's call for five companies.

The special committee concluded its work by publishing the hearings and condemning extravagance and fraud wherever found. The Colorado episode was minor in the total investigation, and Gilpin got only a rebuke for carelessness in fiscal matters.[68]

Gilpin's enemies were at the same time resorting to the direct approach to rid Colorado of its chief executive. Soliciting signatures and letters of complaint from Coloradans, Bennet and friends petitioned President Lincoln to step in and remove Gilpin from office. The petition was signed by Bennet, Bliss, Vaile, and three members of the territorial legislature, Jerome B. Chaffee, Jacob B. Stansell, and Napoleon Bond. Their theme was that without authority Gilpin had raised an unneeded regiment and four companies of troops at great cost. The expense adversely affected the region's business, and the soldiers' presence created a suspicion of disloyalty among the people, ". . . thereby prejudicing their just claims for appropriations for civil purposes in the minds of many members of the present Congress." The six prayed that Gilpin be removed and replaced by "a more prudent and practical man."[69]

Accompanying the petition was a letter to Bennet from a Colorado miner who had bought Gilpin drafts with gold and could not

[68] Fisher *could* have been a cousin; William's grandmother was Lydia Fisher (see chapter 1). William told Bancroft that he was a friend. The Cameron scandals in the War Department set off many investigations. See U.S. House of Representatives, *House Committee Report on Purchase of Army Supplies*, 37th Cong., 2nd Sess., 1862, pp. 373–385, 458–464, 670–680. Some work sheets of Lincoln make it appear that he had considered appointing Vaile attorney-general of Dakota Territory in March, 1861, on the recommendation of Gilpin. How often must William have regretted that he had not urged the appointment with more vigor. (Abraham Lincoln, *The Collected Works of Abraham Lincoln*, Roy P. Basler [ed.], IV, 294.)

[69] Bennet to Lincoln, January 25, 1862, Gilpin File, Letters and Applications, Foreign Affairs, National Archives.

get repayment for the paper. He wanted to know if the government contemplated a swindle. Bennet passed the message on to the President with a note that it was typical of complaints that he was receiving.

Possibly thinking that he was protecting himself, but more likely just because he liked to write about the West, William published several newspaper articles that winter. Sometimes signing them as letters, sometimes using the third person, the articles talked of Colorado's glorious resources but also of how a brave governor had destroyed the disease of secession. The writings did his cause no good, for too many Coloradans could see themselves described as rebels.[70]

Even while the House was condemning Gilpin finance, it maintained its solemn respect for his geopolitical skill. By resolution it asked Seward to give them Gilpin's annual report so that they might consider his charts, maps, and road surveys while the House contemplated a transcontinental railway.[71]

The grand highway through the snowy Cordilleras was a matter for the future, however. For the present Lincoln had enough of the strange behavior in Colorado. His final—and determining—cue came from the man who had sponsored Gilpin in the first place, twelve bewildering months ago. On March 10 Frank Blair wrote to the President: "I feel myself constrained to say that from conversations with Governor Gilpin himself and his own statements of his actions there, I am decidedly of opinion that he should be removed and some man of plain common sense put in his place."

Eight days later, on the suggestion of Senator Lyman Trumbull and others, Lincoln named John Evans of Illinois second governor of Colorado Territory.[72] Gilpin had already returned home, probably knowing that he would quickly be relieved. His friends and neighbors were unaware of the change, however.

[70] *National Republican* (Washington, D.C.), November 29, 1861; *New York Times*, January 27, 1862.

[71] U.S. House of Representatives, *Executive Document No. 56*, 37th Cong., 2nd Sess., 1861–1862.

[72] Trumbull's letter is dated February 19, 1862, suggesting that Gilpin's removal had been considered for several weeks before Blair swung his weight into the balance (Lincoln, *Collected Works*, V, 173–174).

On March 8, Mollie Sanford told her diary that,

The Governor took dinner at our house today [at Camp Weld]. He is a bachelor, grave, but very gentlemanly. Today while he was in the room I dropped a spool of thread that rolled under the bed. He crawled halfway underneath, got the spool, bowed, and handed it to me and kept on talking with the gentlemen without noticing my thanks.

William had reason to be grave: he had failed to get money for the "Pet Lambs" (his hostess's husband, a lieutenant, had not received any pay in six months of service), his political career must have seemed at an end, and the fate of Colorado hung yet on the efforts of her untried volunteers down in New Mexico.

Even light entertainment could be disappointing: the next week Denver's German Vocal Band formed under Gilpin's windows and

. . . made the air ring with most sweet melody, in honor of the return of our Executive. They sang several pieces in a masterly manner which did honor to the loyalty of our German citizens. The Governor had the windows thrown open and was about to address them in return for the honor they had done him, when it was perceived they had left.

What more cutting rebuke could be given William than a refusal to hear his usual talk![73]

William's career scraped the bottom when on March 28, Denver got official word of his dismissal. Crushed, he nevertheless cast no blame on Lincoln or Blair and recognized no mistakes of his own, but declared that two sets of men had accomplished their mutual goal. One group thought that Gilpin should not be trusted with anything; the other, he declared, feared him as an able soldier who would set up a new "Western Rocky Mountain Republic and would be harder to get rid of than Jeff Davis."

By coincidence that same week brought developments that buffed most of the tarnish off William's reputation. Captain Alley had been working since November at the wretched job of auditing the army accounts. Now he was nearly finished and had word from Washington that most classes of indebtedness would be paid immediately. A few less well-substantiated accounts would take a

[73] Sanford, *Mollie*, p. 171; *Colorado Republican* (Denver), March 13, 1862. The *Republican*, being pro-Gilpin, probably intended no malice in reporting the band's walk-out. Of more interest is the assumption that "loyalty" and support of William were the same thing.

bit longer, but they too would be paid. The *News* had been guessing an expenditure of over $500,000, but Alley's labors brought a calculation of about $375,000, doubtless a great enough benefaction to Colorado's economy when Major Fillmore returned in May, weighed down with greenbacks.

Of course the Treasury Department was not thus saying that Governor Gilpin's financial methods had been right. But it was admitting that the expenditures were legitimate and were the proper obligation of the government.

To William an even happier vindication of his methods was another piece of news, the decisive victory at Glorieta Pass and the rout of Sibley's army, clearly an accomplishment impossible without the Colorado Volunteers.

Vindicated or not these events occurred too late to save William's job. In his solemn, yet tense, fashion he went about completing some odds and ends. Evans was in Washington and wanted a delay; Lincoln asked Gilpin to act as governor pro-tem, a measure of questionable legality, but Gilpin complied. Weld resigned and went back to Connecticut to enlist. Since the Secretary's replacement, Samuel H. Elbert, did not reach Denver until May 26, Gilpin of necessity became a very active lame-duck.

The troops led by Chivington flooded back from New Mexico, and on May 1 Gilpin held a ceremony for them and extended the territory's "grateful admiration" for their triumphs.

Governor Evans assumed his post in Denver on May 16, and William Gilpin was unemployed once more.[74]

One must agree that "badgered" or not Lincoln acted correctly in removing William from office. A substantial element in Colorado had concluded that he was eccentric, impractical, visionary, or even chimerical, and had lost confidence in him. His conversation with

[74] Gilpin, "A Pioneer of 1842"; *Rocky Mountain News* (Denver), Supplement, March 22, 1862. Treasury Department audits reveal bureaucratic niggardliness and Gilpin's administrative carelessness alike. He was not reimbursed for traveling to Colorado, nor for conducting the census. Gilpin File, Letters of Auditor to Gilpin, October 1, 1861, March 27, June 4, October 20, 1862, Fiscal Branch, National Archives; Gilpin proclamation, May 1, 1862, Gilpin Collection, Chicago Historical Society (hereafter cited as Gilpin Collection, CHS); Hafen, "Lewis Ledyard Weld," p. 206 n.; Evans to Seward, April 8, 1862; Elbert to Seward, May 28, 1862; Evans to Seward, May 30, 1862, U.S. State Department, *Territorial Papers, Colorado Series*, I.

Frank Blair is convincing. No one knows what was said, but a fair guess is that Frank listened to too much exaggeration of the secessionist threat in Colorado and concluded that his old friend was beginning to see bogymen in the territory. So on grounds of politics and smoother administration William had to be dropped.

The propriety of William's measures as governor is a more complex question. The success of his Administration in matters clearly civil can not be doubted. In spite of its peculiarly unstable population (as of 1861–1862), Colorado under Gilpin acquired a framework for solid development, pushed on by a surprisingly progressive spirit of civic pride—a spirit which often disappeared in Colorado's later years. Histories by men more or less contemporary with Gilpin make these judgments:

Governor Gilpin was an honest, brilliant man, but his tastes, inclinations and life-training unfitted him to deal with political and other conditions found here; and the kind of executive ability he possessed was that of a military commander and not that of the successful head of a civil organization. His personal character was beyond reproach.[75]

In substantial agreement is this extract:

While not well equipped for the conduct of civil affairs, owing to the scholastic tendency of his thoughts, studies and habits, he was essentially patriotic and sincere, performing his duties with unselfish devotion. He was a great explorer, geographer, map-maker, a student of the abstruse sciences rather than a well balanced executive officer; a fine soldier as well. In battle he was brave and fearless, frequently very skillful. . . . This was the effect of his military training. Civil government, however, requires something of statesmanship, and this he did not possess.[76]

These men were being fair to Gilpin, but they appear to have missed the point. They ignored the fact that for twenty years William Gilpin had ridden in the slickest political machine of his time. He had watched the master, Tom Benton, hold together factions and interests of the most diverse sort until his followers fatally divided on a greater issue that caused them to shoot at one another. William prospered in that machine; he could not have been ignorant of politics. Had there been no war in 1861, Gilpin would

75 Smiley, *History of Denver*, p. 493.
76 Hall, *History of Colorado*, III, 13.

have been remembered as the very able, first chief executive of Colorado.

What went wrong, then? Hindsight provides an explanation. In purchasing supplies William assumed a military authority which in other states and territories belonged to the army commander. In Colorado no such officer existed. By War Department order Colorado was under the Western Department, commanded by Major General Frémont, with headquarters in St. Louis, from July 3 until November 9, 1861. The only regulars in Colorado were at forts Wise and Garland, both very new and possessing the smallest of cadres and no supplies. Canby, clearly responsible for Colorado in Frémont's eyes, could not help at all but rather hoped that they would reinforce *him* through Gilpin's efforts in Denver. In short, Gilpin faced an emergency which in his opinion threatened the entire West, an emergency that could not wait for the approval of a cumbersome, badly strained, bureaucracy. Supplies must be had.

A comparison with New Mexico's plight is revealing. Canby, too, lacked funds to make purchases for troops. He, too, begged Washington for help and got none. New Mexico had triple the population of Colorado, however, and more important, in Santa Fe were many wealthy merchants—a group yet lacking in young Denver. Canby resorted to borrowing from the merchants, pledging a gratifying 7.3 per cent interest on the loans. With these funds (which were really nothing but credit extensions, little cash circulating) Canby got his supplies and partially paid his men. In effect, New Mexico, by agreement of theater commander, governor, and merchants, became an enormous company store. No Santa Fe businessmen went to Washington seeking payment; the greater the delay, the greater the interest. William Gilpin would not, and could not, use the same procedure and so he lost his job.[77]

Gilpin was also accused of grossly exaggerating the threat of

---

[77] Gilpin would have been fortunate if in Colorado there had been a ranking regular officer with whom he could have shared responsibility. There was none. Gilpin told Bancroft that Colorado jobbers ran down the value of the drafts, then bought them cheaply for speculation. "The other band [Governor Evans' Administration, probably] went into the contract system, multiplied their greenbacks, and then funded them and started banks" (*New York Daily Tribune*, March 22, 1879). See *Rocky Mountain News* (Denver), May 7, 1862, for an offer by Cass and Brothers, Bankers, to purchase Gilpin drafts at seventy-five cents.

Indians and secessionists and calling up far more troops than needed. This charge must surely have appeared sound in those weeks of late 1861 when Denverites witnessed the waste and nonsense of hundreds of encamped soldiers lacking any apparent mission.

Oddly enough, however, Gilpin mustered into service fewer men than he was authorized. A compilation of requests to him from Canby and Frémont reveals that they asked for 2,500 men during 1861, a few hundred more than Gilpin could locate. Then in early 1862 when the Sibley threat mounted, Colorado was twice ordered to enlist "all of the men possible" for New Mexico. By comparison Gilpin's estimate of the needs of New Mexico and Colorado is minimal; just before learning of Sibley's defeat the War Department had readied five regiments and two batteries at Fort Riley to aid New Mexico. With news of victory the men went to Tennessee— a saving of $10,000,000, said the government.[78] If the number of Colorado men under arms was excessive, the responsibility was the Army's, not Gilpin's.

How many soldiers were needed in 1861 and 1862 to watch Colorado Indians can not be calculated, of course. The tribes did almost nothing of harm to the settlers in Gilpin's era. Should one conclude that there was no threat, and Governor Gilpin exaggerated again? The only evidence that can be utilized is what took place after William left office. Depredations commenced in earnest in 1863, Colorado became isolated by 1864, the terrible massacre at Sand Creek took place, and Governor Evans had to use three regiments solely for Indian duty.

William claimed that his withdrawal from office encouraged the Indians. "When I came out here I just wrote them orders and they obeyed them. I kept them out of the way of the people," was his boast.[79]

If it is correct to say that Gilpin's financial measures were necessary, though unusual, and if he did not muster an excessive number of volunteers, was his administration wholly proper? The answer must be a negative one. Gilpin's worst mistake in judgment and in tactics was his assumption and charge that his opponents were all

[78] Whitford, *Colorado Volunteers*, pp. 128–142.
[79] Gilpin, "A Pioneer of 1842."

rebels. In this he performed a serious disservice to men and territory. His action here had no justification, although it probably had a reason.

The explanation likely lies in William's experiences of the late 1850's when the Democratic Party tried to destroy itself, when long-time political associates, even friends, could no longer be trusted. William brought this emotion with him to Colorado; he found rebels, and he found political opponents. He did not know how to distinguish them from one another, and he considered the Democrats who voted against Bennet in 1861 to be Confederates. Although other northerners of that time might have shared his view toward Copperheads, he was wrong, and, significantly, most Coloradans were sure that he was wrong. He was vilified, but he had called the first name.

In February of 1863 William wrote to Slough, back in the army, but in Virginia now. William congratulated him on his recent promotion to brigadier general, thanked him for his great service to Colorado in the New Mexico campaign. Colorado, he told Slough, was now a success, safe and prosperous. Then, in a rare moment for William, he let his own feelings appear.

At times I am for a moment lonesome at being excluded from the activity of the struggle, in which all my life and experience fits me to take part—Calumny is not always eternal in its duration, nor virtue perpetually in a minority on earth! but its dismal frown thickens the atmosphere like dust, which we can neither combat nor escape.[80]

William was hurt. His pride had never taken such a blow. "The ordeal he has passed is not unlike yours," Hall had told Lincoln. "It is too severe for doubt."[81] The attacks from the press were at times cruel, perhaps libelous. Yet no one recovered more easily than William; while he licked these wounds he prepared to enter another fray. He might try for other public office; he would do more

---

[80] Gilpin to Slough, February 24, 1863, Gilpin Collection, CHS.

[81] Hall to Lincoln, October 9, 1861, Lincoln Papers, Vol. 58. Concluded one contemporary, Colorado and California would have been lost to the "myrmidons of secession, . . . if it had not been for the untiring zeal of Governor Gilpin, who . . . commenced the organization of the 1st Colorado Regiment. . . . For thus disregarding 'red tape' formalities, Governor Gilpin's decapitation followed in the wake of that of many others . . . like Gen. Wool, Fremont, and co. . . ." Charles Stearns, *The Black Man of the South and the Rebels*, p. 23.

writing; he thought that he knew a way to make a great deal of money. He made his own assessment of his year as governor: "The government to which we [he and Slough] gave existence and the Commonwealth founded here is a success, which harmonises with the instincts and fits the temper of the people, this new geographical area and the regenerative energies of the era. It will not and cannot be shaken upon its foundation."[82]

[82] Gilpin to Slough, February 24, 1863, Gilpin Collection, CHS.

CHAPTER TEN

# Let Us Go to the Audience of the People

*Western Speculator, 1862–1894*

William Gilpin governed Colorado for one year. In twelve crucial months be became the territory's most famous citizen, honored as the spokesman, prophet, and planner of the West. Yet a substantial number of Coloradans, although accepting these estimates, also considered him harebrained and impractical, entertaining, even useful to the community, but so lacking in common sense that he should not hold public office again.

Still ambitious for title and seeking some vindication for the mistakes of his gubernatorial career, William decided to campaign for the position of territorial delegate. His timing was poor, for the election was scheduled for October of 1862 and too recently had the accounts of many Colorado business houses been settled by the government.

His opposition included the incumbent, Hiram Bennet, running as the "Union Administration" candidate and supported by most Lincoln Republicans, "War Democrats," and the powerful *Rocky Mountain News*. The Democrats "of suspected Southern sympathy" nominated J. M. Francisco, to appeal to the Mexican vote. Gilpin called himself a Republican and sometimes the "People's Candidate"; his support seems to have come only from his personal following.

The campaign, unimportant though it must have been, foreshadowed on a small scale the struggle that was to tear at the Republican Party of the Lincoln-Johnson era. Bennet was classified as a "conservative" by his press; Gilpin was denounced by the same forces as a "radical," a very early use of the term indicating Gilpin's popularity with abolitionists. He found no fault with Lincoln, even for removing him from office, but the circumstances would now cause him to oppose the pro-administration men in Colorado. Probably, voters of radical bent saw an attitude in William that he did not have.

The *News* ignored Francisco and concentrated on Gilpin that summer. The paper opposed him on several grounds including some of an unusual nature. It declared that he had been an irresponsible governor, that he lacked common sense, and that many people considered him insane. William was accustomed to such criticism but not to Byers' new approach—an attack on Gilpin's book, *The Central Gold Region*. The paper denounced Gilpin for writing that South Pass was the proper highway through the Rockies, for his undoubted exaggerations about Colorado's climate, for his wild boasts about western trade with Asia. The *News* even declared that William was not really much of a scientist or scholar but simply a man who drew beautiful maps, had a large vocabulary, and by accident had once led an expedition of scientific explorers (curiously the *News'* last concession to William was not correct).

Because he was in office, Bennet had the determining advantage over William and Francisco that he could take credit for any piece of legislation that the United States enacted for Colorado. Largely through the efforts of Schuyler Colfax, several postal roads, a land office, a mint, and money for Indian treaties recently had been voted for Colorado. The combination was convincing: Bennet's wining vote was 3,655; Francisco's, 2,754; and Gilpin's weak third, 2,312.[1]

The election seemed to mean little to William. Throughout the 1860's and 1870's he remained a force in Colorado politics, especially during the twelve-year battle over statehood; but when he ran for office, as in 1862, it was always halfheartedly. Although his role in the political scene must, therefore, be recorded, the evidence is that he had already gone back to his abiding interest—the exploitation of western land. He had, in fact, taken his first steps toward acquiring a fortune while the election of 1862 was being conducted.

As he records the events, his interest in western lands was stirred on his return from Oregon in 1844. He had passed through the San Juan Mountains and the San Luis Valley, then in Mexican hands, and had fallen in love with the entire region. He was additionally excited by finding a few flakes of what he took to be gold. At Bent's Fort he learned of the system of enormous land grants then being issued by Mexico, as an economical way to protect the settlements from Indians, Texans, and Americans. Between 1846 and 1848 military service obliged William to visit Bent's Fort and Santa Fe again, and doubtless he spent as much time as possible making further inquiries. For William had determined to obtain a grant somewhere along the American-Mexican frontier.

From 1837 until the war of 1846, governors of New Mexico, under authority of Mexican laws of 1824 and 1828, issued scores of land grants in parcels of a few hundred to as much as one million acres. The method, available to Mexican citizens only, was to make application to the governor with a description of the land requested and a promise to bring in settlers. The governor, aided by local officials, investigated the title, theoretically visited the ground

---

[1] The election of 1862 provided William with a new and brilliant friend, Henry Moore Teller, who moved to the Gilpin County diggings from Illinois in 1861 and began a long political career in Colorado by campaigning for Gilpin. The miners enjoyed Teller's speeches—and voted for Bennet (Elmer Ellis, *Henry Moore Teller*, pp. 62–64; *Miner's Register* [Central City, Colo.], August 25, 1862). Frank Fossett, *Colorado*, pp. 130–131; *Rocky Mountain News* (Denver), May 10, September 25, and October 2, 1862; Frank Hall, *History of the State of Colorado*, I, 289; Hubert Howe Bancroft, *The Works*, XXV, 429.

in person to mark out the limits, and then, if everything was in order, issued a patent to the petitioner. Governor Manuel Armijo, the officer who admitted Kearny's army through the front door to Santa Fe in 1846, was especially active in authorizing grants; for not only did he assume that the land was worthless, but he feared the increasing pressure from the Yankee.

In 1843 Armijo approved the petition of Stephen Luis Lee, sheriff of Taos County, and Narciso Beaubien, the minor son of Charles (or Carlos) Beaubien, a French-Canadian trapper who had turned storekeeper in New Mexico and acquired Mexican citizenship many years before. Lee and young Narciso thus received a reported 1,038,000 acres centered in the San Luis Valley. In the uprising at Taos of January, 1847 (following Kearny's departure for California), both Sheriff Lee and Narciso Beaubien were killed. Subsequently Charles Beaubien successfully claimed inheritance of his son's land; the administrator of Lee's estate (Charles' son-in-law) sold the other half of the grant to the elder Beaubien for $100 in May, 1848, to satisfy some debts.

In this fashion the entire Sangre de Cristo grant, as it became known, entered the hands of Charles Beaubien, probably already land-poor and facing the responsibility of placing scores of families upon his acreage. The treaty ending the Mexican War recognized this and similar land patents, although the United States Congress later set a limit that significantly reduced the size of some tracts. The Sangre de Cristo grant was never diminished by the United States surveyor general of New Mexico Territory, who concluded that while Beaubien had never run a survey of his holdings, he had met all of the obligations of Mexican law, including the location of settlers on his lands. The surveyor general, therefore, recommended to Congress the confirmation of Beaubien's title. This was done in 1860.[2]

----

[2] Charles (Carlos) Beaubien was undoubtedly a silent partner in the grant to his thirteen-year-old son. Armijo could not very well give one man several million acres; and Carlos already held a share of the Miranda-Beaubien estate (better known as the Maxwell estate). Collusion was manifest in the land deals of the 1830's and 1840's. A dozen men who were the chief grantees were also the usual witnesses and even the officials advising the governor (Colorado Governor's Papers, Ralph Carr, 1939–1943, Mexican Land Grant Series, Colorado State Archives [hereafter cited as Carr Papers]). See also Harold H. Dunham, "New

Meanwhile, the United States Congress for the first time discussed the propriety of levying taxes on these lands. (A Mexican governor had been assassinated for such a proposal back in 1837.) Charles Beaubien, part-owner of at least 3,000,000 acres of the Southwest (the Beaubien-Miranda or Maxwell grant was even larger than the Sangre de Cristo), decided that it was time to start unloading some of his earthly possessions. In friendly fashion he transferred title to one-half the Sangre de Cristo estate to his daughter, Luz Beaubien Maxwell, and two associates, Joseph Pley and James H. Quinn. Pley held his one-sixth a few years and in 1858 conveyed it to Ceran St. Vrain.

William Gilpin, who had first dreamed of such an opportunity for himself nearly twenty years before, now moved into this family picture. Not yet aware of Beaubien's transactions, William had by February, 1862, acquired an option to purchase another large tract near Beaubien's holdings but in southern Colorado. Through his numerous acquaintances in that region he had arranged to purchase 100,000 acres from the heirs of one Luis María Baca at terms reported to be thirty cents an acre payable in five annual installments, the first of which would not be due until two years after the act of sale. William would meanwhile pay 5 per cent interest. Such a bargain can be explained only on the basis that there were no other purchasers—yet—for Colorado real estate, and that the title was a questionable one. Baca, an alleged descendant of Cabeza de Vaca, had petitioned Congress to confirm title to his land but had instead received scrip entitling him to 100,000 acres of floating grant, that is, an area located within larger outside boundaries. Baca had been permitted to transfer his claim to any unassigned land within the original boundaries of New Mexico. Optimistic and broke as usual, William staked out his claim less than one hundred miles north of the New Mexico line, his 156 square miles encompassing much of the northern portion of the San Luis Valley, along the western base of the Sangre de Cristo Mountains.[3]

Late in 1862, while visiting this estate, known to the General

---

Mexican Land Grants with Special Reference to the Title Papers of the Maxwell Grant," *New Mexico Historical Review*, XXX (January, 1955), 1–22.

[3] For the background of this grant, see U.S. House of Representatives, *Executive Document No. 14*, 36th Cong., 1st Sess., 1860, pp. 3–46. See also Hall, *History of Colorado*, IV, 307; *Colorado Chieftain* (Pueblo), June 18, 1868.

Land Office as Baca Float Number Four, William received an urgent message from Charles Beaubien to call upon him at Taos. In a long talk at Beaubien's home the one-time trapper explained to his friend that he wanted to return to Quebec for his final years. Remembering Gilpin's many inquiries about Mexican grants, Beaubien was offering to sell his half of the vast Sangre de Cristo estate, second only to Lucien Maxwell's holdings as the largest privately owned piece of property in the United States. Moreover, with some luck Gilpin might purchase more than one-half. Beaubien helped him get an option on St. Vrain's sixth and took steps (completed in 1864) to get the sixth held by Luz and her husband, Lucien Maxwell. William never dealt with Quinn but the latter's holdings were purchased in several increments by Gilpin's successors.

So far all of these transactions involved no funds, for William had none. Beaubien gave him until March of 1863 to arrange financing and William went back to Denver. From there he wrote a number of letters to friends who might care to share his great fortune. In the midst of his search for investors he was visited by Bela Hughes, attorney and president of the Overland Express. Hughes was headed for Salt Lake City to defend Joe Holladay, brother of Ben, against a charge of murder. Hughes asked William to accompany him to Utah, and assuming that his letters would bring no immediate replies, William consented.

The records indicate that William spent several weeks in Salt Lake—for no apparent reason. He visited various Mormons, and with Hughes called upon Brigham Young, possibly, but not probably, to talk about Colorado real estate.

Perhaps William was merely waiting for the trial's conclusion, for on March 29, 1863, he, Hughes, and Frederick Cook, assistant treasurer of the Overland Company, departed for California. None of the available records explains this leisurely conduct but William possibly concluded that a personal visit to the coast would help him locate some investors. In California William's search was completely unsuccessful when another's tragedy proved beneficial to him.

Gilpin and Cook were in Sacramento on their way back to Utah when their horses were suddenly frightened, shied, and ran away, dragging the carriage containing the two men. The vehicle overturned in the city's streets, Cook and Gilpin fell out, the former landing on his spine, causing injuries that resulted in his death. William was hurt enough to be hospitalized for more than a month, and it was during this period that he remembered San Francisco friends whom he had once assisted in Independence. The men not only entertained him, they lent him $1,000 to make possible travel to New York to seek out investors.[4]

By way of Panama William sailed to New York, arriving in early summer, 1863. His San Francisco friends gave him letters to smooth the way, and, with the aid of Morton Fisher, his recent procurement officer, now living in New York, he obtained a $30,000 loan from Duncan, Sherman and Company.

William was now in business. He hastened back to Denver, picked up a friend and rode south to Taos. Passing through his beloved San Luis Valley he encountered an acquaintance who informed him that Charles Beaubien had died just a few weeks before. Momentarily shaken, William wondered if there were any point in continuing the trip. But Beaubien had not forgotten Gilpin even though the option date had expired a year previously. For Beaubien had told his widow and children that if Gilpin raised the money, he should have first chance at the Sangre de Cristo estate.

Learning this from the friend, William Gilpin proceeded to Taos and concluded the transaction. He paid $15,000 to Beaubien's widow for her half, $20,000 to St. Vrain for his one-sixth, and $6,000 to Lucien and Luz Maxwell for their one-sixth. At a cost of $41,000 (a little less than four cents an acre), William Gilpin had acquired five-sixth's interest in a ranch of 1,000,000 acres, an area larger than Rhode Island.

Several questions remain unanswered about the windfall: how could he afford to pay more than he had borrowed in New York,

---

[4] Herbert O. Brayer, *William Blackmore: The Spanish-Mexican Land Grants of New Mexico and Colorado*, 62–66; Hubert Howe Bancroft, *History of the Life of William Gilpin*, pp. 48–49. Bancroft says the deceased was Frank Clark of Wells, Fargo, but since this is another piece of information provided by Gilpin late in life I will use contemporary evidence. *Deseret News* (Salt Lake City), April 28, 1863; J. V. Frederick, *Ben Holladay*, p. 169; Church of Jesus Christ of Latter Day Saints, Historian's Office, Journal History, February 17 and March 10, 1863, E K 2678, 2679. There are some internal contradictions in the dates reported by the *Deseret News*, but they affect the story very little. See also *Commonwealth and Republican* (Denver), July 30, 1863; Carr Papers, Colorado State Archives.

for one example. He had no savings. Perhaps he borrowed elsewhere; probably he paid only such down payment as was needed
immediately against the hope that he could pay off the balance
from the re-sales which he contemplated. Secondly, it should be observed that he could purchase the Baca Float with no down payment at all and with a purse so empty that he failed to meet the
first installment in 1864—yet held onto the title. The answer explains William's role as advertiser of the Colorado-New Mexico land
story. Prior to his participation in these events, the southwestern
desert holdings were often virtually given away; once William became a salesman and brought into play his hyperbole, his maps, his
prophecies, and his writings—fortunes could be made from dealing
in these selfsame sandy acres. He received his share.

William's next step was to learn the nature of his empire. His
frequent visits to the San Luis Valley convinced him that it was
ideal for agriculture and grazing, but he also believed in its mineral
resources and knew the necessity of evidence from the expert witness. He arranged for an expedition of scientists and prospectors to
study his grant with great care and to report its value to him.[5]

Gilpin called in three specialists to supervise the task. From
Brown University he secured the services of an able young chem-
istry professor, Nathaniel P. Hill, off-campus for the summer of
1864 but worrying that he might be late for the autumn term (he
was). A second specialist was James Aborn, a Colorado mining
engineer supervising ten prospectors. Redwood Fisher, with six
"teamers" who doubled as chainmen, directed the survey. Since

[5] Brayer, *Blackmore*, I, 66–68. Fisher was a representative western entrepre-
neur. Born in Pennsylvania, from college he went to Missouri and entered
freight business under St. Vrain. He opened his own trading house in Las Vegas.
He took six wagons of goods to Denver in 1859 to sell to gold rush prospectors.
He engaged in a great variety of businesses in Denver and aided Gilpin by his
purchases during the Civil War. Hill's letters home state that Gilpin had sold
one-half of his estate to Fisher and one Colonel William Reynolds of Providence
and that these men sent Fisher to Colorado at Gilpin's request. Brayer's research
in the New Mexican archives indicate that Gilpin sold $7/12$ of his grant to Fisher
and Reynolds in 1865, *after* Hill examined the estate. The dates could be of little
significance, for Fisher obviously did not pay Gilpin the $162,000 recorded in the
county records. I agree with Brayer that this was a bit of deceitful advertising
on the part of two good friends. Reynolds was a manufacturer who helped promote the telephone by demonstrating it to Queen Victoria.

Gilpin would go along and head the whole party, Hill concluded that the expedition had "four savants."

Hill spent many weeks with Gilpin that summer; his letters to family and friends provide the most personal information about Gilpin available for these years. One letter explains casually one way that Gilpin was able to function successfully without money; Hill told his wife that he would get a share of the estate if the report were favorable! He makes no mention of a salary from Gilpin in the unhappy event that the land proved worthless. Aborn and the other men might have been given this same option.

Hill had reached Denver in June and soon left for Central City with Gilpin to meet Aborn and plan the expedition. Doubts immediately pierced Hill's mind about the "Gov."[6] He ". . . knows almost everything but he is the most unpractical man I ever knew." He talked incessantly, to Hill, to the horses drawing the old buggy, and to himself. He planned careful travel schedules and did not meet them. He said that he never traveled after sundown, yet they drove through canyons in such darkness that nothing was visible except the stars. The buggy was pulled by Toby and Fanny, two horses so small that Gilpin could lift them out of the mud that they regularly found. "Gov." considered them splendid and exceptionally dependable. Hill found them "the ugliest, homeliest and meanest little rats I ever saw," quitting every hour to kick at buggy and Gilpin.

Gilpin loved to brag about the climate and in the occasional torrents continued to drive coatless, top down, happily oblivious to his sodden condition as Hill huddled inside his rubber coat. Gilpin was kind-hearted and highly respected and seemed to know every man in the territory, "but his mind is filled with great abstractions." He told Hill that when he died he wanted to be buried on the highest summit of the Snowy (Sangre de Cristo) Range, on his back, with one eye pointed toward each ocean.

Early in July the party was ready to move south from Denver. They were very well equipped for the projected one-hundred-day task. The twenty-two men were mostly mounted, except Hill and William in the old buggy behind Toby and Fanny. They traveled

---

[6] "Nathaniel P. Hill Inspects Colorado," *Colorado Magazine*, XXXIII (October, 1956), 241–276. See also Brayer, *Blackmore*, I, 67. Hill was United States Senator, 1879–1885.

two hundred miles by way of Colorado City, Pueblo, and La Veta Pass to Fort Garland, headquarters for the survey.

Hill was often impressed—by the sterility of much of the desert to the east and by the beauty of the mountains to the west. He wondered that he and his friends could eat seafood fresh daily in Central City, then have to live on ham, beans, biscuits, and "rot gut" every day that they were in the field.

The young chemist, who drank nothing but lemon juice, was awed by the endless consumption of whiskey. The "Gov." never protected himself with extra clothing against the changing temperatures, but continued his "usual remedy," and cured his morning headache with whiskey in far more than "homeopathic doses." (The same measures may have bred the fear of snakes that gave Aborn nightmares.)

Delayed a little by the necessity of stops while Gilpin transacted business along the way, the group reached Fort Garland on July 11. The country became more appealing as the men studied its potential. Rain was rare in the San Luis Valley and the "nights are always cool," a discovery that every neo-Coloradan lays claim to still. The Mexicans produced fine wheat by irrigation and while life was simple, some of the families (probably brought from Taos by Beaubien) lived in considerable comfort. These people loved Gilpin, too. Fandangos were held in his honor, and the wine flowed like whiskey.

Aborn and his prospectors left Fort Garland to spend two months examining minerals in the mountains; Hill appears to have divided his time between the valley and Central City, making personal investigations that did not directly concern the Gilpin lands.

By fall the work was complete and the reports made. Aborn published his letter to Gilpin declaring that he thought the southern Colorado mines were as rich as those of the wealthy Gregory District of 1859. Hill's report was never released, and rumors spread that he saw little of value on the Sangre de Cristo grant. Whatever the true story it seems clear that Hill had found wealth that would now consume *his* interest, if not Gilpin's.

Hill went back to Brown for the school year then returned to Colorado in 1865; from Black Hawk and Central City in Gilpin County he took tons of various ores by wagon to the Missouri, then by ship via New Orleans to Swansea in Wales for a thorough testing. Satisfied with the results, he built a smelter at Black Hawk and henceforth made Colorado his home.

While Hill was using his Colorado visits as a springboard to an illustrious career, his temporary employer, William Gilpin, concluded that he had enough evidence from outsiders to put his lands on the market. He journeyed to New York in 1865 and now (if not the year before) conveyed about one-half of his estate to Fisher, William Reynolds (for whom Fisher was evidently an agent), and Hiram Hitchcock, banker, hotelman, and promoter of such diverse activities as Madison Square Garden and a Nicaraguan hotel. Allegedly William had received $277,000 and still held a controlling interest in the grant.[7] Fisher next completed a transaction that brought a fifth member into the partnership. He was Dr. Isaac Hartshorn, rubber manufacturer and chief agent for General Ambrose Burnside's Rifle Company.

In spite of wide publicity and many personal contacts the partners failed to locate any New York firm that could raise enough funds for the development or sale of the grant. So the men concluded that Gilpin should return to Colorado and guard their interests, and Fisher should go to London and attempt to attract European investors.

In England Fisher incorporated the estate into the Colorado Freehold Land Association and expanded the partners' (or stockholders', now) publicity campaign. Although this was an era of vast foreign investment on the part of British citizens, and grazing lands were almost as popular with them as mineral holdings, the Sangre de Cristo promotion got nowhere. One authority contends that the English were reluctant to invest in foreign land unless they could share in the management and direction.

Through an official of the Union Pacific Railroad, Fisher was able to get the proposal to the attention of William Blackmore, one of the most spectacular financiers of the nineteenth century. Blackmore had been to the United States in 1863–1864 with an awesome proposal to finance the Union army by selling gold bonds secured by American public lands. Lincoln, Chase, Seward, and others seri-

---

[7] For the details of Gilpin's promotions and sales I rely heavily on Brayer's *Blackmore*, I, *passim*. Brayer performed prodigious service in following Blackmore's western land dealings, a trail the more obscure because so many parties preferred secrecy.

ously listened to Blackmore, but in the end refused to approve the plan because of the expected public reaction to foreign speculators. Blackmore used his time well though, and made close and useful acquaintance with public and railroad officials as well as many generals, including Sherman, Meade, Sheridan, and Grant.

Blackmore was interested in Gilpin's land and in 1868 made his second trip to the United States for a tour of the West. He, too, wanted a specialist's opinion of the Sangre de Cristo grant. He made friends with Ferdinand Hayden, one of America's leading scientists and chief of several governmental surveys. Blackmore asked Hayden to report to him on the estate. Hayden convinced Blackmore: (The grant contained) "by far the finest agricultural district I have seen west of the Missouri River . . . The time is not far distant when some of the choicest stock on this continent will be raised in this valley."

As for minerals Hayden went on to say that on the edge of Gilpin's land was

a lofty range of mountains, which seems to be charged with ores of gold, silver, copper, lead and iron. Mines of great value have already been opened and wrought, with rich returns of gold. . . .

Within the last fifteen years I have carefully explored Kansas, Nebraska, Dakota, Montana, Idaho, and Colorado, and I can affirm that I know of no region of the West more desirable for settlement than this just described, combining as it does all the elements of wealth and productiveness.[8]

While most of this report proved accurate, some of it can be dismissed as stretching the truth; in particular no "rich returns of gold" had yet been made. Whether Hayden was somehow fooled, or whether he deliberately misrepresented the land cannot be settled on the present evidence. Brayer points out, however, that significantly, Hayden never again would work for Blackmore in spite of very substantial inducements frequently offered. More to the point, in 1871 Hayden is listed by Blackmore among the insiders who were rewarded for their assistance in land promotion. His share—$10,000 worth of stock.[9]

[8] Brayer, *Blackmore*, I, 70–74.
[9] Hall, *History of Colorado*, I, 468; J. V. Howell and F. M. Fryxell are preparing a biography of Hayden. Their diligent research has turned up no evi-

William Gilpin could have been no more satisfied if he had written the report himself; had he played any part in the survey? The most convincing conclusion is that Gilpin's mountain of publicity, his undoubted chairm and air of innocence caused Hayden to let down his scientific guard for one short season and commit a serious error in judgment.

For three years before he met either Blackmore or Hayden, Gilpin had been telling the world of the wonders of his grant—and the better for its value, he now had others to tell the story for him:

In February, 1866, William had written to his friend, Father Pierre de Smet, in St. Louis, telling him of the spiritual needs of the 6,000 Spaniards living on his land (approximately the total population of Costilla County today), and asking de Smet's influence to have the church establish a mission and schools among the "primitive" and "worthy" settlers. It is probably unnecessary to say that Gilpin's plea was surrounded by "graphic and beautiful descriptions" of that part of Colorado. De Smet was interested and promised to pass the word on to the proper officials.[10]

At approximately the same time Allen Bradford, associate justice of the Colorado Supreme Court, enjoyed a visit to Gilpinland and wrote a letter (published by Gilpin) that the people living on the grant owned 50,000 head of livestock.[11]

In 1866 two English travelers toured the American West and sought out William Gilpin. One of the men was Hepworth Dixon, a prolific writer, whose accounts of America went through many editions. Dixon wrote that Gilpin was the most significant man on the plains and that his Denver office was headquarters for the gold region and its politicians. Dixon ascribed many virtues to Gilpin and concluded that he was establishing an empire.

Dixon's new-found friend (they first met in the United States) was Sir Charles Dilke, M.P., who, according to rumor and a modern drama, failed to become Prime Minister only because of a no-

---

dence of the stock in Hayden's hands. They believe that there was no fraud but that Blackmore had to lend Hayden money because the General Land Office so often failed to send him his funds (J. V. Howell, letter to author, December 16, 1965). See also Brayer, *Blackmore*, I, 36–46, 91–92.

[10] Hiram M. Chittenden and Albert T. Richardson (eds.), *Life, Letters and Travels of Father Pierre-Jean De Smet, S. J.*

[11] Wilbur Fisk Stone (ed.), *History of Colorado*, I, 528.

torious scandal about his personal life. Dilke also gave Gilpin credit for exploring the Colorado area and heading the "pioneer army" that civilized the territory. He liked Colorado and wished that he could stay; Gilpin offered to name a mountain for him. Dilke wanted the Constitution amended so that he could be President of the United States. Said William, "I'll see about it."[12]

Gilpin had clearly become famous—a tourist attraction—and his own frequent publications about the "auriferous regions," vague, grand writings often unsigned, or published as sections of others' books, had a powerful effect even upon the educated or skeptical, one of whom must have been Ferdinand Hayden.

It is necessary to add that when Hayden surveyed Gilpin's holdings at Blackmore's request, he was accompanied by the ubiquitous Morton Fisher, Richard Whitsett (holder of numerous territorial offices, but remembered here as Gilpin's adjutant general back in 1861–1862), and Gilpin himself.

If this were not pressure enough to place on a scientist, fate or Gilpin decreed that Secretary of State Seward and several generals should come west to see Gilpin that summer, and an unknown "Apache" was reported to have found gold on the Conejos River (just west of the Sangre de Cristo Grant) immediately before Hayden's arrival in southern Colorado. A Pueblo paper hoped the discovery would "vindicate Governor Gilpin's prophecy."[13]

In short, Gilpin had so prepared the public to expect great wealth in his holdings that, as of the 1860's, at least, neither Hayden nor any lesser person could decree otherwise. Unscientifically, Hayden told Blackmore what everyone wanted to hear.

Back in London Blackmore and his partners worked out various arrangements with Fisher to market the grant. The Gilpin group stipulated in January of 1869 that since Fisher could represent them in England, Blackmore's associates should concentrate on the continental market. Blackmore's suggestion that the grant be divided was also carried out.

By this split the Sangre de Cristo Grant became the Trinchera Estate in the northern, and the Costilla Estate in the southern half

---

[12] William Hepburn Dixon, *New America*, pp. 81–82; Charles W. Dilke, *Greater Britain*, pp. 92, 104; Stephen Gwynn and Gertrude Tuckwell, *The Life of the Rt. Hon. Sir Charles W. Dilke*, p. 63.

[13] *Colorado Chieftain* (Pueblo), September 17 and October 29, 1868.

of Gilpin's land. To market the Trinchera Estate, Fisher incorporated the Colorado Freehold Land and Emigration Company with a capitalization of £300,000, replacing the earlier corporation of similar name. Gilpin was managing director, Fisher one of five directors. From this point Blackmore was primarily interested in the Costilla Estate although he obtained several thousand acres of Trinchera land for his own use and settled some of his family on the land.

Probably the bond-buying and emigrating public took little note of these details, for the heavy advertising spoke in terms of "San Luis Park" or "Sangre de Cristo Grant," as Gilpin and Blackmore obviously combined their powerful literary forces. Gilpin had, of course, been advertising the region for years; now Blackmore topped off his pamphlets and brochures with a book on Colorado, dedicated to Gilpin and packed with quotations from official reports, press accounts, travelers' guides, and the like. The post surgeon at Fort Garland was quoted as reporting only one death from disease in eight years at the post. The *Mining Journal* considered Gilpin's denunciation of the "Great American Desert" equal to the discoveries of Watt and Fulton. And Blackmore could quote the Attorney General of the United States, William Evarts, that he found Gilpin's "title free of exception" (Evarts had offered this opinion as Gilpin's attorney three years before taking office, a fact not stressed in the book).

Much of the book is straight Gilpin, some of it is Gilpin as quoted by Dixon or Dilke, and sometimes the citation to Gilpin is lost but the flavor remains. William had now found a very practical use for his hobby.[14]

During the 1860's while selling real estate, he managed to maintain most of his other interests in public affairs. Wartime conditions in the territory had changed little after William left the governorship. Governor Evans was accused of spending too much money on defense and asking Washington for too many troops. Colonel

[14] Brayer, *Blackmore*, I, 75–78; William Blackmore, *Colorado: Its Resources, Parks and Prospects.* The maps were drawn under the "direction of Governor Gilpin"; the frontispiece is a picture of Gilpin. Gilpin said that he hired Evarts because he was "the greatest lawyer in the world." Evarts defended President Johnson and Henry Ward Beecher, prosecuted Jefferson Davis, and represented the United States at the Geneva Tribunal of 1872.

Leavenworth charged Denver merchants with exaggerating the threat of disorder to keep prices high. Justice Hall asserted that during Gilpin's administration danger from rebel and Indian was real; now, he said, under Evans (1862–1865) it was trumped up. Others asserted that conditions had never been so bad, as off-scourings from the border states poured into the territory. Indian disorder culminated in the Sand Creek massacre of 1864, an event which Gilpin harshly condemned but which he said was understandable if one knew the nature of the Colorado settlers of the era.[15]

In the same year, with but small demand from the territory, the United States Congress passed an act to enable Colorado's statehood. The chief purpose of the bill (probably to bring to Washington two more Republican senators) was frustrated when the people of the territory rejected the proposed constitution and statehood that October.

The movement was not dead though, and throughout the winter many individuals switched to the statehood cause. In the spring of 1865 all three political parties called for a new convention and reconsideration of the issue. As slates were drawn William Gilpin received the Republican nomination for governor. In September the voters by narrow margin chose to request statehood for Colorado, and in the November elections Gilpin was elected governor. The territorial legislature met a month later and selected Jerome B. Chaffee and Evans as United States senators. Evans meanwhile resigning his position as territorial governor in favor of Alexander Cummings, an appointment of President Andrew Johnson.

Charges of irregularities in voting, and reasons for the puzzlingly rapid change in public opinion became of no consequence when Johnson refused to recognize the "state" and asked the Congress to consider whether Colorado had authority to act under the enabling act of 1864.

While Colorado's representatives remained in Washington, and Gilpin and Cummings each pretended to be the legitimate governor, Congress considered various solutions. A new enabling act in 1866

[15] *Official Records*, Ser. I, Vol. XXII, Part 2, 172–173, and Ser. III, Vol. III, 494; A. K. McClure, *Three Thousand Miles through the Rocky Mountains*, p. 125; Hall to Edward Bates, May 20, 1863, Lincoln Papers, Vol. III.

was defeated, probably in part, at least, because of the absence of Negro suffrage in the Colorado constitution, as Colorado's status gradually became a matter of great importance in the Johnson-versus-Radicals fight.

Republican leaders wanted two more obedient senators and later in 1866 and again in 1867 passed other enabling acts which Johnson vetoed on the grounds that Colorado had an insufficient number of people. The measures failed to get by the veto; another bill guaranteeing Negro suffrage (to obtain Senator Charles Sumner's support for statehood) was also effectively vetoed.

Although the matter of statehood never completely disappeared from public sight until its success in 1876, the question was no longer a real issue after 1867, especially when public clamor forced the removal of Cummings. Gilpin, while considered by many to be the proper governor, seems to have given the matter little concern. His "state" legislature met very briefly in December, 1865, then adjourned in time to let the territorial legislature resume acting.[16]

That his Trinchera interests had become dominant in William's life is also demonstrated by his attitude toward his land speculation of a decade before in Missouri. As early as 1857 he had defaulted occasionally on some payments due for land in Jackson County. Several individuals began foreclosure proceedings and in 1865 and 1866 the petitions were successful, in each case the "defendant still failing to appear." Since William traveled almost constantly, and frequently through Missouri, on his way to Washington and New York, one must conclude that distance had little to do with his lack of interest. A few hundred acres of Missouri

[16] Jerome C. Smiley, *History of Denver*, p. 495. Some writers believed that Johnson feared that Evans and Chaffee would vote for his conviction in the impeachment proceedings (Ellis, *Henry Teller*, p. 65–73; Stone, *History of Colorado*, I, 420; Hall, *History of Colorado*, I, 382). Playing both ends against the middle Gilpin got some recommendations to be re-appointed *territorial* governor after Evans' resignation in 1865 (Gilpin File, Letters and Applications, Foreign Affairs, National Archives). Gilpin's oath of allegiance to the "state" of Colorado and mention of his address to the legislature are reported in the *Daily Mining Journal* (Black Hawk, Colorado), December 20, 1865. Gilpin, Evans, and A. C. Hunt, all governors, testified in Washington when the House investigated Cummings' expenditures (U.S. House of Representatives, *Miscellaneous Document No. 81*, 39th Cong., 2nd Sess., 1867).

lands, two or three thousand dollars in arrears, could not matter now to an empire builder.[17]

Inevitably William's speculations in real estate tied him closely to the equally furious railroad building schemes of the time. No man had talked and written more of the necessity for linking the Mississippi Valley with the Rocky Mountains and Pacific coast areas. In the 1860's the financiers and builders reached the Rockies and caught up with Gilpin's dream.

The Union Pacific on logical grounds by-passed the high Colorado summits and traversed Wyoming, uniting with the Central Pacific in 1869. The Kansas-Pacific was begun in Kansas City and by 1870 had reached Denver where it joined a spur of the Union Pacific from Cheyenne. The Atchison, Topeka and Santa Fe reached Pueblo in 1876, and the Denver and Rio Grande starting from Denver in 1871 entered Pueblo the following year.

The substantial construction (and the far greater amount of dreaming) was heady stuff to the Gilpin-Blackmore breed who could foresee the migration of thousands of farmers to their lands if railroads could solve the transportation problems. Not surprisingly, land speculator and railroad magnate worked closely together, or often enough, were the same man. William Gilpin did not become a railroad magnate but instead used his land and reputation to maintain his position as the industry's prime exhorter. He worked in an assortment of fashions.

Meeting Otto Mears, famed toll-road builder, high in the Rockies, Gilpin advised him to build his wagon roads with a gradual enough grade to accommodate the railroads that must follow.[18] He blamed Evans (probably improperly) for letting the Union Pacific avoid Colorado.[19] To encourage the Denver Pacific to unite the Union Pacific and the Colorado capital he ". . . delivered a heartening address to his fellow-citizens, that became the talk of the town for weeks afterward, and is still recalled with feelings of satisfaction by many of the old-timers who heard it."[20]

[17] Missouri Circuit Court Records, Volume O, 417, 445; Volume P, 270, Independence, Jackson County, Missouri.

[18] David Lavender, *The Big Divide*, pp. 94–95.

[19] Richard C. Overton, *Gulf to Rockies*, p. 43; Edgar McMechen, *Life of Governor Evans*, pp. 84, 92, 165.

[20] Smiley, *History of Denver*, pp. 438–440.

In May, 1868, when the graders moved the first Denver dirt inaugurating the Denver Pacific line to Cheyenne, a cheering crowd was entertained by free beer and a band, then listened to the ex-Governor, who "made one of his remarkable speeches."[21] That same summer, visitors to Denver included Generals Grant, Sherman, and Sheridan, and Vice-Presidential candidate Schuyler Colfax, always popular in Colorado. Colfax made a campaign speech but it was eclipsed by the bright western future described by the presiding officer, William Gilpin; William in his Prince Albert suit, flowing tie, and soft black English hat got almost as much attention as Nellie Wade who in the romantic setting of South Park announced her decision to become Mrs. Colfax.[22]

Colorado had no electoral votes to offer the Republicans, but it had opportunities which the party leaders apparently wanted to see for themselves. (Frank Blair, Democratic candidate for Vice-President, also journeyed to Pueblo and South Park, but after the election.)[23]

One paper declared, "Southern Colorado is just now in the focus where Governor Gilpin's 'two great columns' are converging," as the daily accessions of Americans from the south, east, and north were meeting the Mexicans in Las Animas, Costilla, and Conejos counties. The paper concluded that the region had room to spare for the many migrants that the railroads would bring.[24]

For months William spoke and wrote so regularly about the future of Colorado and the expansion of its railroads that brief quotes or references to him were often published in the western press in such fashion that the reader was clearly expected to know Gilpin and what he would say. But the bullish westerner wanted to hear and read more; if a portion of the Gilpin message were correct (and understood) the prospects were unlimited.

In February of 1869 he addressed the Denver Board of Trade on the subject of railroads. The site of Denver, he said, was "pre-

---

[21] William N. Byers, *Encyclopedia of Biography of Colorado*, p. 85; *Deseret Evening News* (Salt Lake City), May 27, 1868.

[22] Hall, *History of Colorado*, I, 453; E. E. Stanchfield, Ms. of an Interview, no date, State Historical Society of Colorado.

[23] *Colorado Chieftain* (Pueblo), May 27, 1869. After the Civil War Blair returned to the Democratic party.

[24] *Ibid.*, July 16, 1868.

eminently cosmopolitan," for along the eastern base of the cordillera the "vast arena of the Pacific fits itself to the basin of the Atlantic." Colorado was surrounded by the Mississippi Valley (of less importance since he moved from Missouri), the plateau of tablelands, and the family of parks. Through Colorado, rich with its soil, grass, and minerals, must pass the "condensed commerce of mankind." "Railroads . . . are essential domestic institutions, more powerful and permanent than law, or popular consent, or political constitutions . . . to bind the seaboards like ears to the head, to secure equality and prosperity and room." Then William described once more how railroads would link the pioneer armies of Colorado and California and break the "London Asiatic monopoly."[25]

The Board of Trade of Southern Colorado, "taking advantage of the presence of Gov. Gilpin in Pueblo," invited him to make an address at Thanksgiving time in 1869. The meeting was called to order at the court house; a distinguished committee walked to the Valley House to escort Gilpin while the Pueblo Cornet Band played. Gilpin told the "large and enthusiastic crowd" that Colorado awaited only the completion of a railroad to make it pre-eminent in the world in mineral production as well as to permit the territory to supply the East with its food. Colorado's dryness was an advantage, for irrigated farming was the most efficient form of agriculture; and Colorado's manufacturing would be shipped cheaply by rail because of the favorable descending grades! Gilpin "kept the audience enchained from the beginning to the close of his remarks" and received a rousing vote of thanks.[26]

William's forensic platform was as broad as the nation now. During October of 1869 he was Colorado's only delegate to the "St. Louis Convention" favoring the removal of the national capital to some more central place. He served on several committees, was elected vice-president of the convention, and made another speech. Said William, "Let us go to the audience of the people with our facts and our cause, told in our own style and language." And in his own style and language he talked of the Great Basin, the prairies and the rich Rockies leading to the Orient.[27]

25 Smiley, *History of Denver*, pp. 438–439.
26 *Colorado Chieftain* (Pueblo), November 18, 1869.
27 *Colorado Tribune* (Denver), October 28, 1869. For the quotation, see Logan

The convention asked the United States Congress for a commission to recommend a new site for the national government, published their considerations as a book, and dedicated it to William Gilpin, "A man of rare genius and advanced thought, a prophet and pioneer of civilization."[28]

William's advertising was not limited to the United States. To aid Fisher during some important phases of the overseas financing, Gilpin traveled to England in September of 1870. The Royal Geographic Society invited him to make an address at Liverpool to the British Association for the Advancement of Science. He was introduced by Hepworth Dixon who told of their meeting in the Rockies four years before. He described Gilpin's successes as explorer, soldier, and governor, and of his zeal for a Pacific railway.[29]

William's address, which was published as a fifty-two page pamphlet, was basically his old theme—the geographical descriptions of the West, but he varied it for this audience and described how Colorado would feed Great Britain, and commerce would grow between the two. The "numerous attendance" applauded his analysis which demonstrated that Europe's troubles spun from her convexity so that commerce and nations split apart. The United States was concave, hence all was "harmony and condensed."[30]

The late 1860's were full years for William Gilpin; the hurt of the war years was all gone. He gloried in the speaking engagements, the pomp and drama with which he filled them. He loved being in Denver, talking with friends and visitors in his small room at the Planter's House (the "spittoon generally for the upper ten thousand," said Hepworth Dixon), and he was starting to get rich.

How much money William made is impossible to determine.

V. Reavis, *A Pamphlet for the People Containing Facts and Arguments in Favor of the Removal of the National Capital to the Mississippi Valley.*

[28] Logan V. Reavis, *The National Capital Is Movable.*

[29] *Colorado Chieftain* (Pueblo), October 27, 1870.

[30] *Colorado Tribune* (Denver), October 19, 1870. A confusion of dates suggests the possibility that Gilpin spoke more than once in England, for a Liverpool paper of September 19 reports the talk generally said to have been made on the 26th. The pamphlet was called *Notes on Colorado*; one lady observed, "Governor Gilpin is, I believe, a very remarkable man, but his writing is simply absurd. The charm of the country [Colorado] cannot be too highly praised, I believe, but how could the British Association have stood such rediculious [sic] language?" (Brayer, *Blackmore*, I, 90).

Once he reported that he had no trouble making "a million or two," but he and his associates publicized only the transactions that they wanted publicized, and court house records give only a partial, and at times false, picture of sales made. Even accounts contemporary with William are often contradictory.

William evidently held sole possession of Baca Float Number Four, an area of about 100,000 acres. Probably because it was considerably smaller, the Baca Grant received much less publicity than William's purchases from Beaubien, but he seems to have made a handsome return on this $30,000. He had located this Float in the northeast portion of the San Luis Valley. In 1866 the town of Saguache was founded just to the west of William's land and at the same time the territorial legislature carved Saguache County out of Costilla, the new boundaries putting William's land in Saguache County.

In 1865 a group of Philadelphians came to Colorado to consider purchasing this plot and their visit gives one of the few firsthand accounts of a Gilpin promotion. The men were distinguished enough (a postal inspector, a publisher, and a mint official) that Ben Holladay provided a special carriage from St. Joseph, Missouri, and they had a free banquet at one of Denver's "swell restaurants," but they had to pay twenty-five cents each for eggs—kept in the safe.

Gilpin led them to the San Luis Valley in his buckboard (horses' names unknown). The group witnessed the awesome slide of a six-mule team and wagon fifty feet down the mountain-side, and the postal inspector was almost crushed by his own wagon at the same icy point. But the imperturbable Gilpin, who was at the moment running for governor of the "state," brought them safely to Culebra and the inevitable fandango. Gilpin in red sash and frock coat led the grand march; the Mexican girls in bright curtain calico, rolled and lighted cigarettes when the gentlemen bought them drinks. The press reported Gilpin and friends finally wrapping themselves in blankets and falling asleep on the dirt floor at daylight. The town required three days to return to normal.

Then William took his party northward to look at the land; he was disgusted when the buyers concluded that his estate "was too far out of the world."

William, nevertheless, disposed of the Baca Float fairly easily, although he made no profit at all on some acres. In this region he had to cope with a number of squatters, some of whom he was unable to force off the land. He also had some difficulties in verifying his deed because of questions about Baca's original title. But this was not unusual with the Mexican grants.

One account declares that Gilpin sold most of his Baca grant to a syndicate headed by Wilson Waddingham, a young English agent who also helped to market the Maxwell Grant. Waddingham then sold the property in England and for many years the absentee owners hired one George Adams, a Gilpin friend, to manage it. Under the name Crestone the estate developed rapidly and valuably, with thousands of head of livestock, sixty miles of irrigation ditches, and significant mineral production. However, newspaper accounts declared that Gilpin sold the land in 1886 to Adams and others, describing the transaction as the largest ever made in the *state* of Colorado, William's gross being $350,000. Records of the ranch itself indicate that the second version is the correct one.[31]

As noted earlier Gilpin's Beaubien lands had been split in 1869 into the Trinchera and Costilla estates, with Gilpin and Fisher managing the marketing of the former and Blackmore that of the latter. The distinction between the two properties was not always clear, however—Blackmore, for example, holding some Trinchera acreage as his own personal ranch. The men planned to transfer

---

[31] American Guide Series, *Colorado*, p. 397; T. F. Dawson, Scrapbooks, Vol. LXII, p. 19, State Historical Society of Colorado; one of the Philadelphians remained in Denver and Gilpin told him he would get rich if he would move to Leadville. "Go there, my boy, and stay." He would not go and did not get rich; some materials on Gilpin's financing the Baca Float are in Pamphlet Box 183, State Historical Society of Colorado; Hall, *History of Colorado*, IV, 307; doubtless Gilpin's own advertising contributed to his trouble with the many squatters who could honestly doubt that the titles to these large estates would ever be confirmed by the United States Congress. One such settler described his class as lean and hungry, with ventilated pants, observing the Sabbath with horse and cock, swearing by Lynch and diluted Illinois laws and arguing that he lived on the "axis of intensity" no matter where "the great Gilpin" placed it. Meanwhile he waited for the courts to decide who owned the land (*Colorado Chieftain* [Pueblo, Colo.], June 11, 1868, and May 12, 1870. The press made conditions sound like a near-land rush. The sale to Adams is reported in the *Denver Tribune Republican*, January 3, 1886. A very helpful source of local information has been H. W. Glenn of Crestone, Colorado, who grew up on the Baca Grant and still ranches in the same area (letter to author, December 14, 1965).

the Costilla Estate to a corporation, the United States Freehold
Land and Emigration Company. Blackmore arranged for this corporation to sell to a group of Dutch investors who, in turn, insisted
upon a federal charter, since the Costilla Estate spread over into
two territories. Gilpin went to Washington to head the lobby assail-
ing Congress.

The bill ran into a great deal of opposition because of the large
and indefinite powers, more, thought some Congressmen, than any
corporation had ever been granted. Some favorable consideration
was due to the fact that the Company asked for the right to build
a connecting railway across the public domain but did not ask for
assistance in the form of free land or other subsidy. A few senators
wryly commented that the directors were too modest.

Guided by such individuals as General Robert Schenck, a director of the corporation, member of the House of Representatives,
close friend of President Grant, and soon to be minister to Great
Britain, the measure passed after four acrid months of discussion.
The Costilla Estate was then deeded to the United States Freehold
Land and Emigration Company, with Fisher, Gilpin, and partners
receiving $500,000 for the act.

The Company was capitalized for $5,000,000, half in 7 per cent
bonds, half in stock which was not offered for sale but held in a
syndicate for "insiders" like Gilpin, Schenck, Fisher, Blackmore,
and Hayden. The Dutch banking firm of Wertheim and Gompertz
then bought $1,000,000 worth of bonds for $500,000—in a sense
one dollar an acre, because most of the remaining bonds were never
sold.

Gilpin, who joined in the transaction at Amsterdam, said that a
delay in payment ensued because of the Franco-Prussian War but
that on January 17, 1871, the Dutch firm deposited the funds in
the Bank of England. From this point onward William's interest in
the Costilla Estate was basically promotion, for as stockholder and
director his assets naturally would increase with the success of the
Dutch owners.

These men soon abandoned their original plan to settle the estate
with a single colony from Europe (twenty thousand Hollanders
was one report) and agreed to place the task in the hands of residents on the land who might find homeseekers in the United States
or Europe. Gilpin was chosen resident managing director for three

years at $2,500 annual salary. Two or three others were employed to assist emigrants in getting located. Missing no bets, the Company "arranged" that an employee be elected recorder of Costilla County to help Gilpin in selecting farm sites. William was given broad powers to encourage the growth of agriculture and industry; agents were meanwhile employed on a commission basis to find migrants and send them to William. Churches, libraries, schools, and newspapers all took shape on paper.

Progress was slow, the land being too remote for many settlers. Others preferred homesteads in better known areas already occupied by folk from their own native lands. Blackmore, hoping to make a return on his personal acreage, sent his brother and a cousin with their families to settle in the valley. Blackmore and Gilpin came to America in the spring of 1871 and held several conferences with John Evans, Dr. William Bell, General William Palmer, and others interested in railroad or land promotion. Blackmore made his first inspection of southern Colorado and at Culebra (present San Luis) witnessed the inescapable fandango.

Gilpin helped Blackmore select the sites for his relatives, and the two men sat up half the night making plans for a model town, still nonexistent today. They had agreed upon a dozen or so items of policy when a matter of much gravity came to their attention for the first time.

The Mexicans in the San Luis Valley were uniting to oppose everything that the Company planned. Most of them had moved there at the request of Charles Beaubien, upon his promise that they would receive clear deeds to their ranches. These they had never received, yet for twenty years the families had worked the lands as their own. These people—with a legitimate grievance— were supported by outright squatters, Mexican and Anglo, who made no pretense of having titles but joined in opposition to the "foreign" corporation. The settlers had a weak case: Congress had confirmed the estate's title for Beaubien in 1860, and few of the individuals could provide any proof of ownership other than the testimony of older residents.

Gilpin and Blackmore met with a committee of these settlers on October 4, 1871, at Costilla and reached agreement upon some of the issues. The terms were so favorable to the Company that the settlers renounced them a few weeks later when their chairman,

Ferdinand Meyer, returned to the valley. Meyer, a German immigrant, was one of the few settlers who could read English, and he advised his neighbors that they were likely to lose everything.

Development by the corporation of the Costilla Estate virtually stopped now. The Dutch could afford to spend little more, and a newspaper campaign against Gilpin and the Company launched by Meyer played a large part in discouraging settlement by newcomers.

Blackmore lost interest in the promotion and had several unsatisfactory discussions with Gilpin about getting title to the 5,000 acres operated by the Blackmores. Gilpin became very evasive and missed appointments with the Englishman in Washington, but finally completed the transfer in May of 1872, after months of unexplained stalling.

The Land Company made no progress during the depression following 1873, and in 1878 and 1879 was unable to pay the taxes for the estate. The Dutch bankers held on until 1902 but appear to have made little or no profit and sold very small amounts of land. Several individuals, Blackmore especially, doubtless did quite well. But if the records are at all accurate, the handsomest returns went to Morton Fisher and William Gilpin.[32]

The story of the Trinchera half of the original Sangre de Cristo Grant is similar, but simpler because Gilpin got involved with no large-scale international development. When the Trinchera was split from the Costilla in 1869, the British investors decided to concentrate on the latter and let Fisher do what he could alone in Great Britain with the Trinchera sales, although advertising and bond sales were to be closely coordinated.

The original five partners—Gilpin, Fisher, Reynolds, Hartshorn, and Hitchcock—had incorporated and sold some stock but

[32] Gilpin, at one time, had the contract to survey the Colorado-New Mexico boundary, his intention being to put all of his holdings on the Colorado side. He did not carry out his obligation and the line was run by others in 1867: the Costilla Estate was roughly divided in half by the territory line (Hall, *History of Colorado*, III, 331); Blackmore was a large stockholder in the Emma Mine, source of a scandal with which Schenck became linked in London. This material is almost entirely from Bancroft, *William Gilpin*, pp. 50–51; and Brayer, *Blackmore*, I, *passim*. The newspaper citations confirm Gilpin's travel to Europe. See *Daily Central City Register* (Central City, Colo.), March 8, 1871; *Colorado Chieftain* (Pueblo, Colo.), May 4, 1871.

with no vast sales such as that made to the Dutch bankers. Some small parcels of land were sold, new squatting reduced the size of the estate, and two shifts in partnership occurred in the early 1870's, but basically the Trinchera Grant was still managed by Gilpin and Fisher.[33]

As railroad tracks inched closer to the San Luis Valley William increased the speaking engagements that stressed what progress must come to Colorado when the lines were finished. Settlers' complaints against anonymous corporations or individuals were more and more directed against William, the only big owner who regularly could be seen in southern Colorado, and who additionally was a target because of the prominence of his writings and speeches.

In these early 1870's William emphasized the newest addition to his long list of themes: the flow of migration to the cordillera was really moving in two great waves—the traditional one from the Middle West plus another that William observed coming from old and New Mexico. They washed up against the Rocky Mountains and left "their spray where they met."[34]

Obviously William realized that both Spanish and Anglo-Saxon settlers were interested in his acres, but the language also reflects the railroad man's discovery of Mexico. The recent French intervention in that nation suggested many possibilities; Colorado newspapers talked of annexation, partial acquisition, or, at least, large-scale economic penetration. Several of the railroad schemes (including one that interested President Grant) planned routes as far as Chihuahua.

Gilpin participated in no railway plan with a Mexican destination, but in December, 1876, he and his partners signed an agreement with General William J. Palmer giving the latter right of way for the Denver and Rio Grande through the Trinchera Estate to Fort Garland.

Palmer's problems seemed limitless; his achievements in construction were almost unprecedented. Competing with the Santa Fe for the use of Ratón Pass into New Mexico, Palmer did little more than feint in that direction, then used his Trinchera agreement to move into the San Luis Valley. The money market was

[33] Brayer, *Blackmore*, I, 87, 103–104, 119–120.
[34] *Colorado Chieftain* (Pueblo), May 25, 1871.

sickly, and the geography was incredible, but by mid-1877 the Denver and Rio Grande had tracks laid and trains in service a few miles beyond La Veta Pass, the north-east portal to Gilpinland. The narrow gauge cars, hauled by two and three engines, pierced the Sangre de Cristos at 9,300 feet, the highest point on a railway in North America. Then Palmer needed more than a year to cross the flat San Luis Valley to the new town of Alamosa on the Río Grande, the western limit of Trinchera.[35]

The railroad benefitted Gilpin and his partners in land sales. But William found no clear sailing in the 1870's, for depression, squatters, lawsuits, and even grasshoppers all created problems. An unsigned letter to the editor of a southern Colorado paper exhibits some of the bitterness of the homesteaders:

We ask once more, has Gilpin a right to sell and receive pay for the whole territory of Colorado, and a few thousand square miles of New Mexico? If so, let us turn it over to him and go to war with the friendly Utes. This would be one of the best countries of the west, if it was improved, but the ambition of people is destroyed by the continual howl of Gilpin and his agents, "this is my grant, I have an interest in this grant, do you know that you are improving my land for me? . . . [I] will sell you this claim for fifteen dollars an acre," and all such detestable stuff.[36]

A few years later some "Farmer Crank" still could inquire of the same paper "as to whether or not Costilla county belongs to ex-Governor Gilpin, or if the lands are still in litigation." This settler insisted that he and his neighbors had squatter's rights that were being violated by Gilpin's agents who even claimed the public highways.[37]

Given the stakes as well as the peculiar nature of the grant as originally made, the cry of "fraud" was inevitable. Settlers complained to the press, petitioned Congress and the Secretary of Interior, threatened Gilpin with bodily harm, and went to the courts.

The most important case was not directed against Gilpin and his Trinchera Estate, but his title was jeopardized by the Tameling

35 Brayer, *Blackmore*, II, 201–202, 235; George L. Anderson, *General William J. Palmer*, pp. 73–81; Robert G. Athearn, *Rebel of the Rockies*, p. 50.

36 *Colorado Chieftain* (Pueblo), June 13, 1872.

37 *Ibid.*, August 2, 1877. See also *Ibid.*, June 14, 1877.

suit against the United States Freehold Land and Emigration Company. Tameling sued the corporation (of which Gilpin was a stockholder) to recover 160 acres in Costilla County, land once held by Gilpin but sold to the corporation in 1870–1871. The case reached the United States Supreme Court in 1877. The Court made a thorough examination of title changes from the original Armijo deed to Beaubien, and concluded that while the plaintiff might be correct that Mexican law had been violated as to the *size* of the grant, an "action of Congress confirming a private land claim in New Mexico, as recommended for confirmation by the surveyor general of that Territory, is not subject to judicial review."[38]

In thus upholding the validity of the title to a portion of Gilpin's former holdings, the Court eliminated a number of other probable suits. Nevertheless, there were still many suits, doubtless stimulated in part by the controversies over the neighboring Maxwell Estate, and in part by the fact that most of Gilpin's boundaries were not surveyed until the commissioner of the General Land Office ordered the task commenced in 1875. The job evidently took three or four years; hundreds of squatters were found to be illegally occupying Gilpin's land. Many left; many sued unsuccessfully. Some even published a booklet (selling price $1) claiming that the survey was fraudulent. It read in part:

Gov. Gilpin may exult in the success of his triumphs, and sale of his grant and the pocketing of his ill-gotten gains, but he should remember that there is power in the gov. left to set aside this fraud, . . . and while it is pleasant to contemplate his vast acres, wrongfully obtained from both the government and the poor men, it is yet humiliating, or should be, to him that he has not only been threatened with violence for his conduct, . . . but cannot in safety revisit his possessions, and . . . say "I am rightfully Monarch of all I survey."[39]

For the rest of his life William Gilpin was never completely free from litigation over his land, although once again many documents contain confusing references, and many of the suits were probably not brought against him but against subsequent owners of land that

[38] *Tameling v. United States Freehold Land and Emigration Company*, 93 U.S. 644 (1877). See also Carr Papers, Colorado State Archives.

[39] C. E. Broyles and John W. Hamm, *The Beaubien-Gilpin Grant; The Fraud of the Kellogg Survey Exposed*.

he once held. If he engaged in fraud, the evidence does not show it; the evidence available is that William was a fortunate man who became rich because he stumbled onto an enormous opportunity at a rare time in history. Some of the less fortunate in the valley became his enemies; just as obviously he made many friends or he could not so often have been a candidate for office and have been so highly regarded by his Mexican neighbors in the San Luis Valley.[40]

The region is not a populated center yet, but its pastoral, agricultural, and mineral production are very significant. Without Gilpin's developmental program and his inducements to the railway men, southern Colorado's growth must surely have lagged an additional generation.

Gilpin's interest in southern Colorado and in western resources in general caused him to lend his name to one final scheme that did his reputation no good. For more than two decades he had been predicting that certain spots in the mountains were geologically suited for the location of mineral riches "in mass and position"—his usual expression. The "precious metals" that he so often anticipated were gold, silver, and quicksilver, and at times he referred to the prospects for lead and iron. But briefly in 1872 he got caught up in an enthusiasm for a different sort of wealth.

From various vaguely identified locations in the Rocky Mountain area came reports of rich diamond discoveries. Two miners permitted a handful of promoters to join in their fortune; they incorporated at $10,000,000, hired Ben Butler as attorney and took some of the gems to New York to permit examination by Tiffany specialists. A distinguished group that included Horace Greeley and generals George B. McClellan and Grenville Dodge accepted the lapidary's opinion that the diamonds were genuine. No one

[40] George W. Julian, "Land Stealing in New Mexico," *North American Review*, CXLV (July, 1887), 17–31. Senator Julian was surveyor general in New Mexico briefly. He claimed to have seen a great amount of fraud but does not include Gilpin among the thieves; Lena Paulus, "Problem of the Private Land Grant of New Mexico" (unpublished M.A. thesis, University of Pittsburgh, 1933). Miss Paulus discusses some of the practices, ranging from tricky to dishonest, used by corporations to expand their holdings of some of the old Mexican grants. Again Gilpin is not accused. The W.P.A. study of Colorado declares that a portion of the Trinchera Estate was sold for $500,000 in 1937 (American Guide Series, *Colorado*, p. 334).

seems to have suspected that the stones had not even come from the United States.

Once again the public asked to be deceived. Stock companies were founded in several western cities, reflecting the hope that diamonds might be located in many different areas. Rumor said that "pints" of the stones had been discovered on southwestern deserts and that eminent geologists had actually visited the fields and confirmed the discoveries. By October the fever had reached southern Colorado.

Secretive groups of miners passed through Pueblo "revealing" that they had found a "half a peck" of diamonds, rubies, and sapphires perhaps in Arizona, perhaps in New Mexico. Companies of men, including that of J. J. Holbrook, were organized in Colorado prior to moving into the fields. However, notwithstanding the assurances of duped mining engineers such as Henry Janin, the Colorado public demanded the word from its oracle, William Gilpin. A petition in a Denver paper brought Gilpin's prompt response that he would speak on the "Diamond Regions of Colorado and New Mexico" at the Denver Theater, November 5, 1872.[41]

The title was suggested by a number of Denverites, but it did not justify Gilpin's use of it nor the implications of his talk. He did not actually say that the San Juan Mountains bordering his lands contained the precious gems, but his enthusiastic audience could conclude little else from his words: ". . . the richest treasures lie, where the incandescence of the country has moulded the carbon into the sparkling gem in the Sierra La Plata of the San Juan country in the Territory of Colorado."[42]

*If* diamonds and rubies really existed on this continent, he concluded, inevitably they would be found in greater quantities, larger dimensions, and finer luster in the San Juan country than anywhere else.

Commented the *Tribune* the next day, "Say what persons may, Gov. Wm. Gilpin is one of the wonderful and gifted men of the age, and to him are the citizens of the Republic, in general, and the West, in particular, immeasurably indebted."[43]

---

[41] *Colorado Chieftain* (Pueblo, Colo.), August 15, October 31, November 3, 14, 21, and 28, 1872; *Denver Daily Tribune*, November 4, 1872.

[42] Hall, *History of Colorado*, II, 136–139.

[43] *Denver Daily Tribune*, November 6, 1872.

Gilpin mentioned diamonds because his listeners were interested in diamonds; they preferred to ignore the fact that his speech was more concerned with the mission of the American "soldiers" marching forth against despotism, ignorance, and poverty—a different verse to the old tune.

During that same month careful, scientific scrutiny by geologist Clarence King revealed many more hoaxes than diamonds. Yet the public loved to be humbugged, if not robbed; less than a week after Coloradans read King's report that the diamond rushes were frauds, a group of the most prominent citizens of Denver incorporated a diamond company with a capital stock of $5,000,000.

Gilpin did not join any of the diamond ventures nor receive any reward for encouraging the rush. He was party to a hoax but a nearly innocent party, for he honestly believed what he said. The studies of his hero, Humboldt, led to the prediction of the discovery of diamonds in the Urals; Gilpin thought he was doing the same for the San Juans.

In Colorado the diamond era did little damage; most of the profits and losses occurred purely on paper. It is even doubtful that the rush hastened the settlement pattern at all. However, only a half-dozen years passed before gold and especially silver, were discovered in the San Juan country in quantities exciting enough to let the sanguinary westerner forget diamonds.[44] Diamonds have not yet been found in the San Juan Mountains.

The diamond rush was a brief episode in the career of William Gilpin and could not have taxed his energies greatly. But with the constant traveling, speaking, and negotiating that he engaged in during the 1870's it is, nevertheless, most astonishing that he had time for any other activities. Yet he had several more.

To a limited and unclear degree he was involved with the Patrons of Husbandry. In November of 1872 he addressed the "Farmers' Clubs" in Denver in a meeting designed to incorporate all of the county representatives into a territorial federation—one year later the Patrons (better known as Grangers) held their seventh annual national meeting at St. Louis, the high point of the movement.

[44] Asbury Harpending, *The Great Diamond Hoax*, pp. 142–183; Helmut De Terra, *Humboldt*, p. 298. Harry H. Crosby in "So Deep a Trail" (unpublished Ph.D. dissertation, Stanford University, 1953), gives a fascinating account of Clarence King, the geologist who broke the diamond bubble.

Gilpin, who spent the winter of 1873–1874 in St. Louis, visited the Grange headquarters and talked with members of the executive committee. Gilpin's position and the purpose of the talks unfortunately are concealed, for the Grangers' discussions were secret.[45]

No secrecy attended Gilpin's next two efforts. Late in 1873 Lippincott's brought out his *Mission of the North American People: Geographical, Social, and Political.* This volume is almost identical with his *The Central Gold Region* (1860) but for changes in organization and the addition of some new appendices. Presumably the second edition was prompted by a different demand, just as the new (and more accurate) title reflected the broader scope of William's interests.[46]

That same winter William fell in love, or, more precisely could renew his expression of love. The lady was Julia Pratte Dickerson, a St. Louis widow. Julia was the daughter of General Bernard Pratte, Jr., of an old Missouri mercantile family. Pratte had been in the Missouri General Assembly of 1838 and mayor of St. Louis from 1844–1846 during which time he and Gilpin became close friends. Julia was born in 1836 and grew up in a brilliant, social world that was generally patterned after French style. William, of course, knew Julia as a child (he was closer to her father's age than hers), but in 1856, on one of his trips through the city, he proposed marriage to her.

But Julia refused William, and a few years later she married Captain John H. Dickerson of the United States Army. That marriage was an unhappy one in spite of the arrival of four children, born between 1865 and 1871. Julia bitterly opposed Lincoln and the Union, and was probably the cause of her husband's resignation from the army in wartime. The two were separated at the time of Dickerson's death in a mental hospital in 1872.

The next year Gilpin resumed his courtship as the two enjoyed many of the parties in St. Louis' winter season of 1873–1874.[47] On January 18, 1874, William in his formal fashion (he was now aged 59, Julia 37, and General Pratte 71) wrote to Pratte at his farm near Jonesboro:

[45] *Boulder News* (Boulder, Colo.), November 29, 1872.
[46] *Colorado Chieftain* (Pueblo), October 30, 1873.
[47] *St. Louis Post Dispatch*, January 9, February 5 and 13, 1874.

Your charming daughter, Julia and myself have made the interesting discovery that we have long mutually and absolutely loved one another. Having no doubt of the entire fidelity of each to the other, we resolve to marry. We hope for and ask the parental consent and benediction of yourself and madame. We have discussed together very soberly, my ability and determination to take generous care, for life, of Julia and her good little children; and she expresses herself satisfied. It will be a great happiness to us to see you in person, if it is agreeable to you to visit St. Louis. We beg and hope for an early and an auspicious reply. You have accorded to me from early boyhood, a cordial and disinterested friendship. Accept my grateful appreciation of this and approve of my resolution now to make these agreeable relations complete and perpetual.

> Respectfully and cordially,
> William Gilpin.[48]

The general and madame gave their "auspicious reply," and on February 16 the wedding took place in the home of Julia's uncle, United States Senator Louis Bogy. The couple left that same evening for a honeymoon in Denver and California; they were accompanied by Julia's eldest, nine-year-old Louise, and a nurse, an ex-slave known as "One-Eyed" Julia Greeley.

By spring Gilpin had bought an attractive home in Denver, at 443 Champa Street, and had brought Julia's other children to live with them.[49] This ready-made family increased the next year with the birth of twins, William and Marie Louise (May 12, 1875), news of which prompted one waggish editor to remark that he had always believed "in Gilpin's theory of finding rich things 'in mass and position,' (if you sink deep enough)." On July 10, 1877, Louis "Bogy" Gilpin was born, the last of the Gilpin children.[50]

Denver papers indicate that the first dozen years of the Gilpins' marriage were filled by lavish and expensive entertaining, with the Gilpins at the center of western society. Julia's gowns and antique jewelry were obviously matters of much pride to her, and

[48] William Gilpin, letter to General Bernard Pratte, January 18, 1874, State Historical Society of Colorado.

[49] Most of my information about Julia is from Helen Cannon, "First Ladies of Colorado: Julia Pratte Gilpin," *Colorado Magazine*, XXXVIII (October, 1961), 267–274. *St. Louis Post Dispatch*, February 17, 1874; *Denver Tribune*, February 22, 1874.

[50] *Colorado Chieftain* (Pueblo), May 20, 1875.

William, who was often out of the city during the parties, complained frequently of the social expenses. The several parlors of their Champa Street home were regularly crowded with "groups of ladies and gentlemen upon whose lips flashed and sparkled epigram and repartee." The affairs were expensively catered, and bands were hired to add to the enjoyment; Gilpin's $1,200 Weber Grand was the most beautiful piano yet seen in Colorado.[51]

In family matters William's deepest concern was the education of the children. The Dickersons all received parochial schooling— Louise in an academy in Philadelphia, Sidney at Notre Dame, graduating in 1885, Julia and Elizabeth in Denver, with a European tour as a graduation present. His own three children he preferred to have educated in the Denver public school system; he hoped that young William could attend Annapolis.[52]

The activities of his wife, and the education of his children consumed some of William's time, but his business concerns were affected little. He had by the late 1870's achieved the position of elder statesman of the Rockies and was in attendance at most conventions, celebrations, and other public gatherings. No longer anxious for office he stood by and watched friends like Bela Hughes, Lafayette Head, John Routt, Henry Teller, Jerome Chaffee, and even old Albert Boone elbow one another for positions when statehood finally arrived in 1876.

He was guest of honor and speaker in Pueblo to toast the first Santa Fe railway cars and joined in "the biggest drunk of the century," an episode prolonged several days because a Kansas blizzard delayed the arrival of a special excursion group. Fireworks, billiards, and too much food added to the party, described by a reporter as "riotous."

When the abortive Denver and New Orleans completed its first seventy-two miles of track, another celebration was held. Speeches were made; Gilpin and Governor Routt were toasted, and the engine was pronounced a "daisy" by one and all. Spike by spike, William's dreams for the West materialized while his own public

---

51 *Rocky Mountain News* (Denver), February 14, 1879.

52 Sidney was an exceptional student, receiving many honors at Notre Dame (Letter to author from Notre Dame University, Alumni Association, May 20, 1966).

image became more secure.[53] When, in 1882, one editor (*Leadville Democrat*) asked if Colorado had any former officials to be proud of, two other editors agreed that "William Gilpin is the only one we know of. He kept the territory of Colorado in the Union and was bounced out of office because he would not sanction swindling the government on contracts."[54]

Unfortunately William's home life now began to deteriorate sadly. He and Julia increasingly found things to quarrel about—religion, politics, money, and child-rearing, according to Julia's biographer. Julia was a devoted Catholic, almost "obsessed" by her church, giving to it much effort and money (including the land for St. Joseph's Hospital). William, of course, was raised a Quaker, but church of any kind had long ceased to have much importance to him. Politics probably was only a minor irritant, twenty years now after the Civil War. But finances mattered too much; Julia took her role of society's leader very seriously, and William could not get accustomed to spending a fortune after too often knowing what he liked to call "secret hunger."

Doubtless methods of child-rearing caused problems in a home that included so many step-children and half-brothers and sisters. And in the troubled times which culminated in a separation in 1887, the Dickerson children quite naturally supported their mother against William. But so also did William's own three.

More likely these several factors brought to a head a personality clash that was nearly inevitable. Two intense, powerful personalities, accustomed to two separate homes and modes of life for their entire adulthood, simply could not adjust to one another. Examples of William's occasionally very odd behavior have been scattered throughout this narrative; when he and Julia had personal troubles, his enemies remembered them, while his friends countered with similar stories about Julia.

One descendant of the Prattes said that most of that St. Louis family was "handsome, brilliant, able—but difficult, and with violent tempers." Julia's sister was considered most eccentric—

[53] Fossett, *Colorado*, p. 591; L. L. Waters, *Steel Trails to Sante Fe* (Lawrence: University of Kansas Press, 1950), p. 51; *Colorado Chieftain* (Pueblo, Colo.), March 16, 1876 and March 11, 1882; Overton, *Gulf to Rockies*, p. 81.

[54] *Golden Transcript* (Golden, Colo.), January 25, 1882.

always wearing muddied, white clothes in St. Louis' winter slush and permitting her "uninhibited" children to soil family portraits with water guns.

Julia's brother exhibited something of the family temper in 1884 when William was a delegate to the first cattle convention in St. Louis. After an argument he allegedly attempted to kill Gilpin, who was saved only when Julia thrust herself between the men.

On another occasion William and Julia were in the home of Mrs. John T. Speer, discussing business of some sort. (Mrs. Speer was the children's teacher.) Julia became angry and attempted to stab her husband with a paper cutter. Mrs. Speer intervened and took the weapon safely away. Not unnaturally these accounts made it easy for William's friends to whisper that Julia had driven her first husband into the asylum where he had died.

In March, 1887, William initiated divorce proceedings, claiming extreme cruelty in the form of threats on his life, attempts to get his property, alienation of the affections of his children, and extravagance. Julia filed a cross-complaint, denying all of his charges as the creations of a disordered mind. Julia opposed divorce in principle, but wanted custody of the children.

The press and public of Denver reveled in the apparent end of the "high-life marriage" even though most proceedings of the divorce were secret—to the disappointment of large crowds. William's testimony made much of his fear for his life. He maintained two detectives on his payroll to watch over him, and, in their absence one day, he was assaulted in front of his home by his stepson, Sidney, and two accomplices. Sidney was arrested and fined for the action.

William won his case December 8, 1887, and received custody of his three children. Custody of the Dickerson children was, of course, not a consideration. Louise had married Frank Sherwin; the youngest girl, Elizabeth, was already sixteen years of age. Julia and Sidney, out of school, usually attended the divorce hearings with their mother.

Scandal-hungry Denverites were to receive more entertainment than that accompanying the divorce of a famous seventy-two-year-old. On the day of the decree William bought a house at 1321 South Fourteenth Street and moved in before the occupants could leave. Aided by a friend, three detectives, and four deputy sheriffs, William took two carriages to his Champa Street home and attempted to remove the children.

Little Louis armed himself with a stick which he used on the officers until he was subdued. Before a large neighborhood crowd the Governor and one of the men tore Marie from her mother's arms, the child's screams accompanying her mother's tears. Willie ran. More than an hour elapsed before he was found under a pile of straw, and taken off to his father's new house, without a good-by to his mother.

Julia told a reporter that she believed William was insane and, therefore, bore him no malice. All that she wanted was to keep the children with her. She promptly filed a writ of error to the Colorado Supreme Court.

Considering her writ, that Court reversed the case in April, 1889. The next year William appealed to the same court, the jury disagreed, and a new trial was called for, but never held. In May, 1891, Julia and William agreed to dismiss their complaints and they were shortly re-united at the Fourteenth Street home.

The Dickerson children now had homes of their own, but William had temporarily increased his household during the separation by bringing his sister, Mary Sophia, to live with him. She was some five years older than William and had never married, and he hoped that she could be responsible for the children. But according to one newspaper he ignored Mary entirely and would not eat or talk with her. They, too, quarreled when she tried to leave—she claiming that he held her prisoner for her money, he contending that she had been insane for over forty years and that a clergyman had written him to take her into his home because she had been living on an Indian reservation. The matter was never clarified because Mary Sophia died that year.

One final tragedy struck the Gilpins. In the summer of 1892 Willie Gilpin, age seventeen, was vacationing in the mountains when he fell from a slope in the Platte Canyon and was instantly killed.[55]

55 Cannon, "First Ladies of Colorado," pp. 267–274; unidentified newspaper clipping, Chicago Historical Society; General Bernard Pratte, Jr., "Reminiscences," *Missouri Historical Society Bulletin*, VI (October, 1949), 59–71; *Denver Republican*, June 19 and December 9, 1887; Dawson Scrapbooks, LXII, 23,

The period between 1887 and 1892 was thus a time of great personal trial for William and Julia, yet his creative energies were such that his writing continued undiminished. He had become a personal friend of Hubert Howe Bancroft, whose interest in the West had prompted him to interview William for a brief biographical sketch. About 1888 Bancroft evidently went to Denver where the two discussed Gilpin's career in great detail. The result was *The History of the Life of William Gilpin*, written by Bancroft but obviously the remembrances of William Gilpin. The book was a part of Bancroft's series known as *The Chronicles of the Kings*, in which almost every biography was subsidized by the subject. Gilpin paid $10,000 for this bit of vanity.

The Gilpin-Bancroft roles were reversed when in 1890 William published his last book *The Cosmopolitan Railway*. He is listed as the author and Bancroft's History Company as publisher, but Bancroft (or some staff member) did a considerable amount of the writing. This literary cooperation was evidently suggested by Bancroft during a visit of William and the children to Bancroft's San Francisco home. The Gilpins then completed an extended rail vacation visiting Portland and Victoria before savoring the delights of the new Canadian Pacific from Vancouver to Montreal, returning home by way of New York, Chicago, and Kansas City. In Denver Gilpin immediately wrote to Bancroft telling him of the public clamor for a railway network, and the information about it that Gilpin could give in the proposed book.[56]

On September 25 William sent Bancroft the first of several checks, each for a sum of one thousand dollars or more, presumably to defray publishing costs. In one letter Gilpin referred to the pro-

---

State Historical Society of Colorado; William to Mary Sophia Gilpin, June 20, 1875, Ms. in State Historical Society of Colorado. Mary was traveling in Greece when William wrote to her. She had previously seen an article about her brother while she was in Russia; *The Daily News* (Denver), August 5, 1888; an unidentified newspaper account of the divorce listed William's wealth at some $160,000. He appeared to be buying Denver real estate with the proceeds of his San Luis Valley lands on which the taxes were quite heavy (*The Colorado Sun* [Denver], July 20, 1892).

[56] John W. Caughey, *Hubert Howe Bancroft*, p. 322; Gilpin to H. B. Hambly, September 27, 1890, Gilpin to Hubert Howe Bancroft, September 7 and 25, October 15, November 12, 1890, and one undated, P–L330, Bancroft Library.

jected book as "our joint work" and he suggested chapters that Bancroft might "beat into . . . sounding shape." Not surprisingly William wanted most help on sections dealing with finance.[57]

Gilpin invited Bancroft to work with him in Denver on the manuscript and William repeatedly asked what help he could give the famed publisher. They consulted Lippincott's concerning the copying of material in William's *Mission of the North American People*; some of the same maps were used, and some of William's same speeches appeared in the appendix of each work.

*The Cosmopolitan Railway* is not, however, a rehash except in small part, and that primarily William's comments on world geography. Bancroft's hand is discernible in large sections, possibly whole chapters, and much of William's bombast was toned down by Bancroft or some other editor. Another innovation is the use of long quotations, many unidentified, many from other books by Bancroft, but in neither instance typical of Gilpin construction. How much labor each man put into the study can not accurately be judged. Considering Bancroft's usual methods, however, it is curious that nowhere did he take credit for writing about *The Cosmopolitan Railway*.

Except for information on the reconciliation with Julia, the last Gilpin manuscripts written were his letters to Bancroft about the book. Approximately seventy-five years of age, William had lost none of the enthusiasm so contagious in his letters to his mother fifty years before. He thought that the book was "likely to magnetize mankind in the way they have long been wishing and waiting to be roused."[58] He was "assuming hope that it will appear and be worthy of our country, and of the *fathers of our country*."[59]

Even before publication Gilpin claimed that he had received a thousand letters of favorable response to his volume. As usual William was caught up in a cause, puzzling though that cause might be. "We must give our time in *our* generation, to continue— to purify—and to exalt free from retrogression what has so gloriously come down to us: and what the splendid fidelity of our People 'to the practice of virtue, always in exercise' has so con-

[57] Gilpin to Bancroft, September 25, 1890, P–L330, Bancroft Library.
[58] Gilpin to Bancroft, September 25, 1890, P–L330, Bancroft Library.
[59] Gilpin to Bancroft, October 15, 1890, P–L330, Bancroft Library.

tinuously prolonged and promise to keep enduring and make perpetual."[60]

Evidently the Redcoat menace had not disappeared, for he had just seen "six splendid iron clads, *in war trim* . . . British ambassadors to Alaska. . . . England is preparing this time [the pelagic seal controversy] to unite all the world against *us*. Our Pacific coast is very long and very full of gaps. May we not wake up inside and look out through them?"[61]

But the people "are calm, moderate and severely inspired to speak out. Vox populi, vox Dei." Soon "we may with *moderation* and wisely, march and fire to the front."[62]

In this fashion William Gilpin thought and spoke and wrote, grandly and vaguely, to his last days. A neighbor remembered that Gilpin visited his home every Sunday. He would talk of the olden times to his impatient audience, then put forth again his pet hobby, a railroad from Vancouver to Alaska: "There's Russia facing us—only forty miles away—and Russia will one day be a country next in greatness to the United States. Why can't they see the importance of connecting Alaska by rail with California."

Then he would thump his cane, courteously and gravely take his leave, and trudge homeward.[63]

The newspaper evidence is contradictory, but apparently William was run over by a horse and buggy some time in 1893. He had been still active in his business affairs, but the shock of the accident evidently lingered with him. On January 19, 1894, he walked around town and visited the state house as usual. He said that he was feeling better than he had in some weeks, and friends hoped that he had about recovered from his accident. That evening he spent quietly with his reunited family in their Fourteenth Street home. He played backgammon with Marie, then went to bed.

The following morning Julia attempted to awaken him and

---

[60] *Ibid.*

[61] Gilpin to Bancroft, September 25, 1890, P–L330, Bancroft Library.

[62] Gilpin to Bancroft, November 12, 1890, P–L330, Bancroft Library.

[63] Clarence L. Jackson, "My Recollections of William Gilpin," *Colorado Magazine*, XXVI (July, 1949), 236–237. Jackson, son of the famous western photographer, William H. Jackson, thought that Gilpin was "sweet on" Clarence Jackson's grandmother, who would say, "I hope he confines his talk to that old railroad scheme and doesn't bother me." But they all respected him.

found that he had died in his sleep. The coroner's certificate listed the cause of death as "thrombosis left," coming at the age of seventy-nine. He was buried in Mt. Olivet cemetery in Denver next to his son, Willie, almost but not quite, in his mountains.

William left no will but some comprehension of the large extent of his remaining business interests can be gained from Julia's activities and will. In 1900 she sold their home and made St. Louis her residence although continuing to spend much time in Denver. Her children by Captain Dickerson had all established their homes before William's death, and Julia evidently visited with these families in Denver and St. Louis. She died in St. Louis on December 21, 1912, at seventy-six years of age.

From the three Gilpin children there were no descendants: Willie was killed by his fall; his twin, Marie, married John Dodson, a New Jersey actor, but had no children; Louis never married.[64]

And so William Gilpin's line ran out.

[64] *Creede Candle* (Creede, Colo.), January 26, 1894; *Colorado Chieftain* (Pueblo), January 25, 1894; Dawson Scrapbooks, LXII, 23, State Historical Society of Colorado; *St. Louis Globe Democrat*, December 22, 1912; copy of the will of Julia P. Gilpin, Record Office, City and County of Denver, Colorado. At her request Julia was buried in the same plot with William and their son, Willie, in Denver. Incredibly, William's marker has the wrong year of his death, showing 1893 instead of 1894.

# Epilogue

William Gilpin was a man of action, but he also was a literary man with a unique position in American letters. His books and articles have been given casual treatment in a number of studies, but four present-day commentators on American writing have made careful analyses that should be noted in any Gilpin biography. The first of these writers was the late Bernard De Voto, who unquestionably "discovered" Gilpin and evidently prompted the work of the other three critics.

In *Harper's Magazine* for March, 1944, De Voto wrote an article entitled "Geopolitics with the Dew on It," an examination of two of Gilpin's books, *The Mission of the North American People* and *The Cosmopolitan Railway*. De Voto said that while the works included "much sheer fantasy" they did contain "remarkable intuitions," and in his opinion established Gilpin as the first American geopolitician.

Drawing upon Humboldt's *Cosmos*, which Bancroft said Gilpin carried in his knapsack, Gilpin delineated the "Isothermal Zodiac," a belt thirty degrees in average width across the Northern Hemisphere, passing through the oceans at their narrowest, and the continents between at their widest points. More or less centered in the zone is the "Axis of Intensity," an isothermal line of 53 degrees F., mean annual temperature. This line can be moved by altitude and other geographical factors, but it clings rather closely to the fortieth parallel, according to Gilpin.

In the isothermal zodiac live 95 per cent of the white race, and within it have sprung up the greatest cities and the highest cultures, as world migration and military movements converged upon the Axis. To De Voto, Gilpin's major intellectual achievement was the discovery that a larger portion of North America lies in this zodiac than does any other continent, a promise of greatness for the people who occupied that land. Furthermore, North America is concave, a huge bowl with coherent river systems and orderly communications that result in a "centripetal amalgamated" people with one language, one outlook, a truly continental nation, intensifying the momentum of superiority.

Gilpin thought of Europe and Asia, on the other hand, as inverted bowls, convex, with the Alps and Himalayas in the respective centers. Rivers are not interconnected, communications are jumbled, and the result is many diverse peoples, suspicious and afraid of one another, lacking all unity. (Africa and South America are written off by Gilpin as "'feeders" because they are completely outside the Isothermal Zodiac.)[1]

De Voto, writing during World War II, when geopolitics rode a wave of popularity, compared these premises and conclusions of Gilpin with those of Sir Halford Mackinder. Mackinder visualized a world island or land mass made up of Europe and Asia with Russia and Siberia composing the heartland, and the two American continents forming a single island outside the land mass. But, De Voto declared, the writers independently reached the same conclusion that history is the defense of the best land from the attacks of outsiders.

De Voto also contrasted Gilpin's geopolitics with that of Henry and Brooks Adams, who felt that Christianity held Europe together against the disruptive and centrifugal effects of mechanical power. De Voto concluded that Gilpin would disagree markedly; Europe to him was chaos, and such unity as did exist was the result of mechanical power. But Europe was old and did not concern Gilpin,

[1] Bernard De Voto, "Geopolitics with the Dew on It," *Harper's Magazine*, CLXXXVIII (March, 1944), 313–323. Gilpin could have made a case for Sydney, Melbourne, Johannesburg, Cape Town, Montevideo, Buenos Aires, and Santiago as evidence that great cities grew along the 40th parallel in the southern hemisphere also, but he generally ignored them because the resources for their growth did not move along the axis of intensity, but came from the northern hemisphere.

who preached that a Cosmopolitan Railway must be built by Americans and Russians because they would get the most from it; the United States would find vast new markets in Asia and India, while Russian-Asian disharmony would once and for all be transcended by the unifying force of the railway.

According to De Voto, Gilpin believed that nature had decreed that North America (or the United States, almost identical to Gilpin) would extend its democracy, its harmony, and its progress to the rest of the world, a geopolitics of peace contrasting sharply with the geopolitics of war taught by Karl Haushofer and the German general staff of the 1930's and 1940's. Curiously, however, Gilpin's "dew-covered" geopolitics of peace required an American understanding with Russia, just as General Haushofer's geopolitics of war required a German understanding with that same state.

De Voto concluded his essay with the observation that the Adamses, Mackinder, and Gilpin could all agree upon Russia's momentous role for the future, but he felt that the fresh, naive geopolitics of Gilpin was the most logical of the four practitioners of that era—that the agriculture and commerce of the United States would, in short, subdue the barbarism, ignorance, and tyranny of the world.

A second serious study of the writings of William Gilpin was made by Henry Nash Smith, who devoted a chapter to Gilpin in his *Virgin Land: The American West as Symbol and Myth*.[2] In this work Gilpin shares "Book I: Passage to India" with Jefferson, Benton, Asa Whitney, and Walt Whitman; Gilpin's chapter is called "The Untransacted Destiny."

Smith assumes that among these men is held one basic theme— that the American West was primarily a road to the Orient. Jefferson's interest in farmers caused him to stress the need for exploring and building roads through the West primarily to secure the land for the American people. But he did send John Ledyard to Russia, and he told Meriwether Lewis to give consideration to transcontinental commerce, as he searched for his highway to the Pacific.

The heir to Jefferson, according to Smith, was Thomas Hart Benton, who sought for his nation the "fabulous wealth" of India

[2] New York: Vintage Books, 1957. This persuasive gem was the book that first suggested to me that Gilpin was more than just a Colorado politician and worth further investigation.

just as Europe had always done. Now a great United States could secure that commerce, shipping the luxuries of Asia to Europe and the manufactured and farm goods of Europe *and* America to Asia. For the commerce passing through America might be more valuable to the United States than the sale of her own commodities.

Asa Whitney built upon Benton by offering his proposal to solve the enormous question of financing the project; Smith, however, thinks of Whitney as more than just a railroad promoter; Whitney had spent two years in the China trade and he considered it the "foundation of all commerce since the earliest ages." More, Whitney felt that a railroad was absolutely essential for the passage to India, not only as the carrier of the treasured goods, but as a "creative power" that would transform the farmer from demi-savagery to a useful position in society. Smith concludes that Whitney's proposals were at odds with the planless squatter movement favored by Stephen A. Douglas, and probably most other American statesmen, as the traditional method of expansion.

When treating of Gilpin, Smith (like De Voto) has to rely on Bancroft for biographical material and, therefore, reproduces some errors of fact. They played little part in Smith's analysis, however, and can be ignored.

Smith opens this small chapter with the declaration that Gilpin's writings give him claim to being considered "the most ambitious student of the Far West during the second half of the nineteenth century," then goes on to summarize the joint influences of Benton and Humboldt (in that sequence) upon Gilpin.[3] Gilpin believed that science verified and predetermined the rise of empires, each more westerly than the one before; when man found the Mississippi Valley, he "was inaugurating the greatest of them all," in Smith's language.

[3] Smith found similarities in the language of Benton and Gilpin—"the headlong rhythms, the hyperboles, the devices of ornamentation—but there is one important difference. Where Benton's oratory is in the polemic mode of Congressional debates and reaches its full development only when it can take the form of an attack on an adversary (the East, the Past, the British Empire, antiexpansionists, and so on), Gilpin is too much a bardic seer to argue with anyone. He is a mystic, burning with certainty, striving to convey to his audience the contagion of his own ecstatic vision" (*Virgin Land*, p. 39–40). This is true of most of Gilpin's writings, but in a few of his editorials, speeches, and letters he easily held his own as a rabble-rouser, particularly in his younger days.

Professor Smith traces the development of Gilpin's reasoning about the theories of expansion due to the force of empire, the importance of Asiatic trade, and even the power of the frontier farmer, all of which Gilpin accepted. Supplementing these assumptions, Smith contends, was the Humboldt-Gilpin doctrine that

Physical nature . . . governs the development of human communities . . . mountain ranges and river systems group themselves into a system having a supreme and unbreakable order which is at the same time absolutely good. This order will ultimately determine the condition of the civilizations of the earth, elevating the United States above all other nations.[4]

Smith then suggests that the same science which saw all of the parts of the earth in a single, harmonious pattern also nourished Gilpin's western sectionalism.

Walt Whitman is the last speaker studied by Smith in "Passage to India." In a very brief treatment Smith sees Whitman arrayed with Benton and Gilpin looking upon the eastern seaboard as a relic of feudalism and turning to the West, dominated by nature, as the place where the true America would grow. To Smith, Whitman was gradually drawn to the prairies, the Rockies, and ultimately, to the Pacific slope which led to Asia. In "Facing West from California Shores," Whitman suggested that the course of empire was circling the globe and that when America stretched its destiny across the Pacific, man would be home again.

Concludes Smith on Whitman: "The new era begun with the closing of the cycle of history meant even more than the mingling of peoples: it was to restore man's lost harmony with nature."[5]

When Whitman wrote of the pioneer army, he sounded phrases which Smith found very suggestive of William Gilpin. "Years of the Unperformed," he thought, might echo Gilpin's frequently expressed "untransacted destiny of the American people," and "Pioneers! O Pioneers!" seemed to resemble Gilpin's experiences as well as his description of the pioneer army.

The evidence that Whitman borrowed from Gilpin may not be undeniable but the similarities are so numerous and often so strik-

[4] *Ibid.*, p. 43.
[5] *Ibid.*, pp. 47–51.

ing that Smith's proposition should be examined in a greater detail
than Smith presented.

That Gilpin and Whitman would share attitudes toward the
West was in itself not surprising. Whitman in his days on the
*Eagle* spoke very clearly the Locofoco language; he was a Jacksonian and a Bentonian; he favored hard money, Manifest Destiny,
low tariffs, and the absence of monopoly; and, like Gilpin, he spoke
for the mass of American people.

But reference to specific passages by the two men are more revealing (in each example cited, the Gilpin expression came into
print a few or many years before the Whitman counterpart).

In the *Central Gold Region* Gilpin wrote that the pioneer "column is about to *debouch* to the front and occupy" the Great Plains,
California, and Oregon. In "Pioneers! O Pioneers!" Whitman's
detachments of labor and Western youths "debouch upon a newer,
mightier world."

Other examples from "Pioneers" that typify Gilpin's language
would include "Have the elder races halted?"; "Colorado men are
we . . . from the great sierras and the high plateaus"; "Central
inland race are we from Missouri"; "By those swarms upon our
rear we must never yield or falter, ages back in ghostly millions
frowning there behind us urging."

Gilpin's phrase "Untransacted Destiny," which he first used in
Congress in 1846, is reflected, as Smith mentioned, in Whitman's
"Years of the Modern" (also called "Years of the Unperformed"),
which concludes with "The performed America and Europe grow
dim. . . ./The unperform'd . . . advance upon me."

In "A Broadway Pageant" Whitman sees the arrival of two
Japanese diplomats in New York; in Gilpin-like tones he writes of
Asia, the "Originatress," bequeathing its heritage to the West
which now in the "new empire grander than any before . . . I chant
America the mistress." Where Gilpin in 1846 told Congress that
America would "cause stagnant people to be re-born," Whitman
has "Commerce opening, the sleep of ages having done its work,
races re-born refresh'd."

Other coincidental references can be related extensively. They
can be found in "Song of the Redwood Tree," "Unnamed Lands,"
"The Prairie States," "Thou Mother with Thy Equal Brood,"
("venerable priestly Asia" and "royal feudal Europe" sail on the

ship of democracy), "Election Day"—even the preface to the 1855 edition of *Leaves of Grass* speaks the theme of the contribution of continents.

"Passage to India" incorporates a greater variety of Gilpin thought than any other Whitman poem. The usual language—the greatness of the ancient East re-awakened by America's commerce —permeates the poem; but Whitman is now interested in the cable and the Pacific railroad, the networks spanning the earth and welding lands together, precisely Gilpin's dream.

In 1879 Whitman took his "Long Jaunt West," which he recorded in "Specimen Days." The borrowing from Gilpin is even more apparent in Whitman's prose than in his poetry. The list of geographical sites is shorter and less tedious than in some of the poetry, but some of the facts appropriated are more exact.

Like Gilpin, the poet places Missouri in the "front rank of the Union." He is impressed with Denver and its "delicious atmosphere" (Gilpin's favorite adjective for a good climate); each man finds the Mississippi Valley the earth's most important region and, in particular, compares it with the Mediterranean basin. This is the heart of the Union; its men are America's best (especially the *average* men); the capital of the United States will one day be located between St. Louis and Denver, and if a clincher is needed, Whitman lists the Yazoo and the St. Francis among the most important tributaries of the Mississippi, two sources surely never cited by anyone except Gilpin.[6]

None of the studies of Whitman that I have consulted gives any clue to these apparent copyings; the two men evidently never met. Whitman could easily—especially in his newspaper days—have read Gilpin's books or printed speeches. The best guess is that the poet was introduced to Gilpin's ideas in one of the printed versions of the 1846 report to the Senate.

---

[6] For purposes of these comparisons I have used Gilpin, *Mission of the North American People* (Philadelphia: J. B. Lippincott, 1873), which includes several of his speeches in the appendix; Gilpin's 1846 report to the United States Senate; Walt Whitman, *Leaves of Grass*, and *The Complete Poetry and Prose of Walt Whitman*. I have given consideration to Cowley's thesis that Whitman tried to identify homosexuality with the expansive democracy of America; I can not see that it bears any relevance to my contention that Gilpin's writings were studied by Whitman.

The third writer taking more than a passing interest in Gilpin's publications is James Malin in *The Grassland of North America*. Malin has some concern with Gilpin's theories on the history of civilization and with a comparison of Gilpin's geopolitics to those of Turner, Mahan, and Mackinder. Malin would agree with De Voto that Gilpin exaggerated too frequently but that his theory of the North American landmass, while less publicized than the sea-power, climate, frontier, or pivot of history schools, was no more visionary or quaint than any of them.[7] "All such thinking is subject to the limitations placed upon geographical determinism in any form, and upon single factor interpretation," assumes Malin.

His chief interest in Gilpin, however, is in the latter's study of the Great Plains. Malin believes that Gilpin was essentially correct in his appraisal of the value of that region, and concludes:

Gilpin was constructive and positive, not negative, in his estimate of the grassland. He did not use deficiency terminology; his mind was remarkably free from the perverted estimates derived from the mental limitations of man conditioned by maritime climates—the grasses and animals were products of natural equilibrium in a continental climate, and he emphasized that such environment had been the homes of great civilizations in Asia, Africa, and in pre-Columbus North and South America. . . . in any case [Gilpin's writings] constitute the most provocative and significant estimate of the North American grassland interior written during the middle period of the nineteenth century.[8]

The last author who has made any serious appraisal of Gilpin is Wallace Stegner in his study of the work of John Wesley Powell, *Beyond the Hundredth Meridian*. Stegner places Gilpin as Powell's antagonist, the spokesman for those forces who could see no American desert, who encouraged the reckless settlement of the arid regions, and who did not understand—and who resisted—the new dry land policies that Powell tried to get a politics-minded Congress to adopt. The Gilpin vs. Powell theme predominates throughout the *Hundredth Meridian*; the book literally starts with Gilpin and ends with an appraisal of Powell that declares that the myths and objections of the Gilpins are still with us.[9]

[7] James C. Malin, *The Grassland of North America*, pp. 177–192.

[8] *Ibid.*, p. 192. Reprinted by permission of the author.

[9] Wallace Stegner, *Beyond the Hundredth Meridian*; William C. Darrah,

Using considerable literary license, Stegner implies that Gilpin originated the myths about the boundless future of the Mississippi Valley and the plateau country beyond. "He [Powell] would know enough to correct Gilpin in all his major assumptions and most of his minor ones," challenges Stegner. Gilpin represented fiction, fantasy, the homesteaders' dreams; Powell represented science, research, unpopular facts. In short, to Professor Stegner, Gilpin is the symbol of all of Powell's problems.

The result is some error of fact and some lifting of Gilpin out of his admittedly bewildering context. Gilpin never said, for example, that rain follows the plow. He, on the contrary, opposed that dangerous conclusion and frequently lectured his readers on "Pastoral America" because as he said, the characteristic was "novel to our people." Gilpin wrote (*Mission of the North American People*, p. 72) that the Great Plains were rainless, not arable, "resisting the plow"; but they were pastoral, and could support millions of head of livestock once the American people understood that their westward movement had at last led them into unfamiliar resources.

Nor did Gilpin ever insist that the 160 acre farm was sacred. His own real estate promotions in Colorado necessitated specific Congressional approval of that vast, undemocratic tract. When Gilpin thought about land sales, it was in terms of what *he* could sell, not what the United States government should do, and his homesteads were large.

Stegner accurately records some of Gilpin's nonsense—such as settlers not really needing housing on the American plateau, and all Indians looking alike. But the real issue between Gilpin and Powell (and I see no evidence that they ever met or recognized the existence of one another) is still unsettled, and perhaps Stegner is correct in calling it a semantic one. Much time can be wasted defining the word "desert"; Gilpin (*Mission*, p. 49) seems to mean that it is land completely lacking in fertility, irrespective of the availability of water. Powell prefers "arid region" to desert (he was enough of a politician to use "semihumid" in preference to "semiarid" for the lands between the ninety-seventh and the one hundredth meridian), and his great contribution rests not upon de-

---

*Powell of the Colorado.* The latter author includes Gilpin in his bibliography but otherwise does not mention him.

ciding exactly how many square miles of America are desert, but in forcing public recognition of the fact that entirely new land policies were essential in many portions of the American West.

The dust storms, the dust bowls, the abandoned farms are all too familiar in the western plains; yet there are green spots and some men still become wealthy from the grass in this same region. Meanwhile, as Gilpin predicted, the population of the valley grows, and who will wager today that the land between the Alleghenies and the Rockies will not support Gilpin's estimated 180,000,000 people?

Modern critics have thus examined the writings of William Gilpin. They have found a premier geopolitician, the most ambitious student of the Far West, an authority on the grasslands, and the creator of popular mythology about the Great American Desert. All of these analyses are at least partly correct, for in Gilpin were combined unusual elements of intellectual endeavor and bold action which puzzled his contemporaries as much as his twentieth-century critics.

Appropriately, William died in the same decade that the American frontier was permanently closed and the West that he loved and served disappeared forever. He was a product of that age, of course, and he spoke for a vast segment of it in his speeches, his writings, and his life. Through him we can know that West a little better, and, more important, perhaps we can recapture for our generation some of his confidence in America, his faith in her institutions, and his positive assurance of her greatness.

# BIBLIOGRAPHY

### Manuscripts

Church of Jesus Christ of Latter Day Saints. Historian's Office, Journal History, 1863. E K 2678, 2679. Salt Lake City, Utah.

Colorado Governor's Papers. Ralph Carr, 1939–1943. Mexican Land Grant Series, Colorado State Archives, Denver.

Crosby, Harry H. "So Deep a Trail: A Biography of Clarence King." Unpublished Ph.D. dissertation, Stanford University, 1953.

Dawson, T. F. Scrapbooks. State Historical Society of Colorado. Denver.

Eaton, Miles W. "A History of the Hemp Industry in Missouri." Unpublished M.A. thesis, University of Missouri, 1938.

Field, Jennie. "The Story of Kentmere." Edward Gilpin Papers, Historical Society of Delaware, Wilmington.

Gilpin, Elizabeth. "Journal to Johnstown, N. Y." 1830. Historical Society of Delaware.

Gilpin, Julia P. Copy of will. Record Office, City and County of Denver, Colorado.

Gilpin's Battalion. Record of Events, 1847–1848. Adjutant General's Office, National Archives.

Gilpin, William.

> "Biographical Sketch of William Gilpin, adapted from a dictation [c. 1880]." Typescript. P-L330, Bancroft Library. University of California, Berkeley.

> Collection. Chicago Historical Society, Chicago.

> Collection. Historical Society of Pennsylvania, Philadelphia.

> Gilpin File.

>> Letters Received, 1836–1837. Adjutant General's Office, National Archives, Washington, D.C.

>> Mexican War Records, National Archives, Washington, D.C.

Auditor's Certificates, 1861–1862. Fiscal Branch, National Archives, Washington, D.C.

Letters of Auditor to William Gilpin, 1861–1862. Fiscal Branch, National Archives, Washington, D.C.

Letters and Applications, no date, Foreign Affairs, National Archives, Washington, D.C.

Letter Book, 1861–1862. Indian Bureau, National Archives, Washington, D.C.

Letters Received, 1861–1862. Office of Indian Affairs, National Archives, Washington, D.C.

Gilpin Folder. Historical Society of Delaware.

Letter to General Bernard Pratte, January 18, 1874. State Historical Society of Colorado.

Letter to Mary Sophia Gilpin, June 20, 1875. State Historical Society of Colorado.

Letters to H. H. Bancroft, 1899–1890. P-L330, Bancroft Library.

Manuscript, 1889–1890. P-L330, Bancroft Library.

Gilpin Papers. Missouri Historical Society, St. Louis.

"A Pioneer of 1842," October 18, 1884. P-L28, Bancroft Library.

Glenn, H. W. Letter to author, December 14, 1965.

Hensley, Orlana. "The Thomas Hart Benton Faction in Missouri Politics," Unpublished M.A. thesis, University of Missouri, 1937.

Howell, J. V. Letter to author, December 16, 1965.

Ladd, W. S. to M. P. Deady. Papers. Oregon Historical Society, Portland.

Lazarus, Myron L. "Joshua Gilpin, Esq." Unpublished M.A. thesis, University of Delaware, 1959.

Lincoln, Abraham. Papers, 1861. Manuscript Division, Library of Congress. Washington, D.C.

Medill, W. Letters to William Gilpin, 1861. Comptroller, Fiscal Branch, National Archives.

Miller, Nyle H. Letter to author, April 6, 1965.

Missouri Circuit Court Records, 1865, 1866. Volumes O and P. Independence, Jackson County, Missouri.

National Archives and Records Service. Letter to author, June 19, 1961.

Natrona County, Wyoming, Historical Society. Letter to author, October 15, 1964.

Newsclipping about William Gilpin, 1873 (unidentified source). Chicago Historical Society.

Notre Dame University. Alumni Association. Letter to author, May 20, 1966.

Pamphlet Box, 183, 1862–1871. State Historical Society of Colorado.

Parrish, J. L. Manuscript, 1839. P–A60, Bancroft Library.

Paulus, Lena. "Problem of the Private Land Grant of New Mexico." Unpublished M.A. thesis, University of Pittsburgh, 1933.

Pennsylvania, University of. Alumni Records. Letter to author, July 7, 1964.

Pennsylvania, University of. Records Center. Letter to author, September 21, 1960.

Pettygrove, F. W. Manuscript, 1878. P–A60, Bancroft Library.

Post Returns, Fort Leavenworth, 1847–1848, Adjutant General's Office, National Archives.

Potter, John Mason. Letter to author, May 4, 1965.

Pratt, Orville C. Unpublished Diary, 1848. Coe Collection, Yale University Library. New Haven, Connecticut.

Sibley, George. Collection, 1844. Missouri Historical Society.

Stanchfield, E. E. Manuscript of an Interview. No date. State Historical Society of Colorado.

Sublette, William. Papers. Missouri Historical Society.

Tabor, Horace A. W. Scrapbooks. State Historical Society of Colorado.

Ulbricht, John H. "Frank P. Blair, Jr. and Missouri Politics, 1856–1860." Unpublished M.A. thesis, University of Missouri, 1936.

United States Military Academy. Letter to author, July 31, 1958.

United States War Department, Record Group 94, 1848–1849. Adjutant General's Office. National Archives.

Van Buren, Martin. Papers. Manuscript Division, Library of Congress.

Waldo, Daniel. "Critiques," 1878. P–A74, Bancroft Library.

Waldo, David. Manuscript Collection, 1851–1852. Missouri Historical Society.

"Why President Lincoln Made Gilpin Governor of Colorado," Unidentified clipping. State Historical Society of Colorado.

Wildman, Augustus and Thomas G. Papers, 1858–1865. Coe Collection, Yale University Library.

Zweig, Sheldon S. "William Gilpin: First Territorial Governor of Colorado." Unpublished M.A. thesis, University of Colorado, 1953.

### Legal Citation

*Tameling v. United States Freehold Land and Emigration Company*, 93 U.S. 644 (1877), Reports of the Supreme Court of the United States.

UNITED STATES PUBLIC DOCUMENTS (PRINTED)

*Congressional Globe.* 25th Cong. 1837–1838; 29th Cong. 1845–1846; 36th Cong. 1860–1861.

House of Representatives.

*Executive Document No. 327.* 25th Cong., 2nd Sess., 1838.

*Executive Document No. 225.* 25th Cong., 3rd Sess., 1839.

*Executive Document No. 72.* 28th Cong., 2nd Sess., 1845.

*Executive Document No. 3.* 29th Cong., 1st Sess., 1845.

*Executive Documents Nos. 8, 41, 56, 60, 70.* 30th Cong., 1st Sess., 1848.

*Executive Document No. 1.* 30th Cong., 2nd Sess., 1848.

*Executive Document No. 14.* 36th Cong., 1st Sess., 1860.

*Executive Document No. 56.* 37th Cong., 2nd Sess., 1861–1862.

*House Committee Report on Purchase of Army Supplies.* 37th Cong., 2nd Sess., 1862.

*Miscellaneous Document No. 81.* 39th Cong., 2nd Sess., 1867.

Senate.

*Executive Document No. 1.* 30th Cong., 1st Sess.:, 1848.

*Executive Document No. 15.* 36th Cong., 1st Sess., 1860.

*Journal.* 36th Cong., 1st Sess., 1860.

*Reports Nos. 178, 306.* 29th Cong., 1st Sess., 1846.

Interior Department.

*Report of Secretary of Interior.* November 30, 1861.

State Department.

*Territorial Papers, Colorado Series.* Vol. I, Incoming Letters, 1859–1874; Vol. II, Executive Proceedings of Governor Gilpin and printed documents, 1861.

War Department.

Record Group 94, 1848–1849. Adjutant General's Office. National Archives.

NEWSPAPERS

Baltimore, Maryland. *Niles' National Register,* 1840–1845.

Black Hawk, Colorado. *Daily Mining Journal,* 1865.

Boulder, Colorado. *Boulder News,* 1872.

Central City, Colorado.

*Daily Central City Register,* 1871.

*Miner's Register,* 1862.

Creede, Colorado. *Creede Candle,* 1894.

Denver, Colorado.

*Colorado Republican,* 1862.

*The Colorado Sun,* 1892.
*The Colorado Tribune,* 1869–1870.
*Commonwealth and Republican,* 1862–1863.
*The Daily News,* 1888.
*The Denver Daily Tribune,* 1872, 1874, 1878.
*The Denver Post,* 1919, 1960.
*Denver Republican,* 1887.
*Denver Tribune,* 1872.
*Denver Tribune Republican,* 1886.
*Illustrated Rocky Mountain Globe,* 1900.
*Rocky Mountain Herald,* 1913.
*Rocky Mountain News,* 1861, 1862, 1873, 1879.
Fayette, Missouri. *Missouri Democrat,* 1845, 1858.
Fowler, Colorado. *Fowler Tribune,* 1939.
Golden, Colorado. *Transcript,* 1882.
Gunnison, Colorado. *Gunnison Review,* 1880.
Independence, Missouri. *Independence Examiner,* 1842.
Jefferson City, Missouri. *Jefferson Inquirer,* 1847–1854.
Kansas City, Missouri.
*Kansas City Post,* 1924.
*Kansas City Star,* 1900, 1901, 1905, 1913, 1915, 1937, 1950.
*Western Journal of Commerce,* 1857–1860.
Liberty, Missouri. *Weekly Tribune,* 1846–1853.
Matamoros, Mexico. *The American Flag,* 1846–1848.
New Orleans, Louisiana. *Daily Picayune,* 1843, 1846.
New York, New York.
*New York Daily Tribune,* 1879.
*New York Times,* 1862.
Ouray, Colorado. *Ouray Times,* 1879.
Pueblo, Colorado.
*Colorado Chieftain,* 1873–1899.
*Daily Chieftain,* 1872–1873.
*Weekly Colorado Chieftain,* 1868–1877, 1882.
Randolph, Missouri. *Randolph Citizen,* 1858.
Saguache, Colorado. *Saguache Chronicle,* 1879.
St. Louis, Missouri.
*Daily Missouri Democrat,* 1861.
*Missouri Argus,* 1835–1839.
*Missouri Daily Argus,* 1839–1840.
*St. Louis Democrat,* 1843–1844.
*St. Louis Evening News,* 1853.
*St. Louis Globe Democrat,* 1912.

*St. Louis Post Dispatch,* 1874.
*St. Louis Reveille,* 1844, 1848, 1849.
*Tri-Weekly Missouri Republican,* 1860–1861.
*Weekly Missouri Democrat,* 1861.
Salt Lake City, Utah. *Deseret News,* 1863, 1868.
Washington, D.C.
   *Army and Navy Chronicle,* 1836–1839.
   *National Intelligencer,* 1853–1854.
   *National Republican,* 1861.
Wilmington, Delaware. *Journal Every Evening,* 1914.

## ARTICLES

Armstrong, Andrew. "The Brazito Battlefield," *New Mexico Historical Review,* XXXV (January, 1960), 63–74.

Ashley, Susan R. "Reminiscences of Colorado in the Early Sixties," *Colorado Magazine,* XIII (November, 1936), 219–230.

Barnes, Gertrude. "Following Frémont's Trail through Northern Colorado," *Colorado Magazine,* XIX (September, 1942), 185–189.

Barry, J. Neilson. "The Champoeg Meeting of March 4, 1844," *Oregon Historical Quarterly,* XXXVIII (December, 1937), 425–432.

Boardman, John. "The Journal of John Boardman," *Utah Historical Quarterly,* II (October, 1929), 99–121.

Boyd, Mark F. "The Seminole War: Its Background and Onset," *Florida Historical Quarterly,* XXX (July, 1951), 1–115.

Brown, Margaret L. "Asa Whitney and His Pacific Railroad Publicity Campaign," *Mississippi Valley Historical Review,* XX (September, 1933), 209–224.

Cannon, Helen. "First Ladies of Colorado: Julia Pratte Gilpin," *Colorado Magazine,* XXXVIII (October, 1961), 267–274.

Clark, Robert C. "How British and American Subjects Unite in a Common Government for Oregon in 1844," *Oregon Historical Quarterly,* XIII (June, 1912), 140–159.

"Colonel Grimsley's Proposed Expedition to Oregon in 1841," *Oregon Historical Quarterly,* XXIV (December, 1923), 434–447.

Cotterill, R. S. "National Railroad Convention in St. Louis, 1849," *Missouri Historical Review,* XII (July, 1918), 203–215.

Dale, Harrison C. "A Fragmentary Journal of William L. Sublette," *Mississippi Valley Historical Review,* VI (June, 1919), 99–110.

Davidson, Levette J. "Books Concerning Colorado, 1858–69," *Colorado Magazine,* V (April, 1928), 64–75.

De Voto, Bernard, "Geopolitics with the Dew on It," *Harper's Magazine*, CLXXXVIII (March, 1944), 313–323.

Dunham, Harold H. "New Mexican Land Grants with Special Reference to the Title Papers of the Maxwell Grant," *New Mexico Historical Review*, XXX (January, 1955), 1–22.

Gates, Paul W. "The Railroads of Missouri, 1850–1870," *Missouri Historical Review*, XXVI (January, 1932), 126–141.

Georges, Maurice O. "A Suggested Revision of the Role of a Pioneer Political Scientist," *Reed College Bulletin*, XXV (April, 1947), 67–84.

Gilpin, Joshua. "Journey to Bethlehem," *Pennsylvania Magazine of History and Biography*, XLVI (1922), 122–153.

Gilpin, Thomas. "Memoirs of Thomas Sr.," *Pennsylvania Magazine of History and Biography*, XLIX (1925), 289–328.

Gilpin, William. "The Cities of Missouri," *The Western Journal and Civilian*, XI (October, 1853), 31–40.

———. "The Mountain Formation of North America," *Mining Magazine* (August, 1857), 154–160.

Glaab, Charles N. "Visions of Metropolis: William Gilpin and Theories of City Growth in the American West," *Wisconsin Magazine of History*, XLV (Autumn, 1961), 21–31.

"The Great Basin of the Mississippi," *De Bow's Review*, XXIV (February, 1858), 159–165.

Hafen, LeRoy R. "Lewis Ledyard Weld and Old Camp Weld," *Colorado Magazine*, XIX (November, 1942), 201–208.

———. "Mexican Land Grants in Colorado," *Colorado Magazine*, IV (May, 1927), 81–93.

Hall, Mrs. Frank. "Seventy Years Ago: Recollections of a Trip through the Colorado Mountains with the Colfax Party in 1868," *Colorado Magazine*, XV (September, 1938), 161–168.

"The Hemp Growing Region of the United States," *De Bow's Review*, XXIV (January, 1858), 56–58.

Hodder, Frank H. "Genesis of the Kansas-Nebraska Act," *Proceedings of the State Historical Society of Wisconsin, 1912* (1913), 69–86.

Hougland, D. P. "Voting for Lincoln in Missouri in 1860," *Kansas State Historical Society Transactions, 1905–1906*, pp. 509–520.

Jackson, Clarence S. "My Recollections of William Gilpin," *Colorado Magazine*, XXVI (July, 1949), 236–237.

Judson, Katherine B. "Letter of Dr. John McLoughlin to Sir George Simpson, March 20, 1844," *Oregon Historical Quarterly*, XVII (September, 1916), 215–239.

Julian, George W. "Land Stealing in New Mexico," *North American Review*, CXLV (July, 1887), 17–31.

"Kansas History as Published in the Press," *Kansas Historical Quarterly*, XV (August, 1947), 329–330.

Karnes, Thomas L. "Gilpin's Volunteers on the Santa Fé Trail," *Kansas Historical Quarterly*, XXX (Spring, 1964), 1–14.

Lewis, G. Malcolm. "William Gilpin and the Concept of the Great Plains Region," *Annals of the Association of American Geographers*, LVI (March, 1966), 33–51.

Loomis, Nelson H. "Asa Whitney: Father of Pacific Railroads," *Proceedings of Mississippi Valley Historical Association*, VI (1913), 166–175.

Luckingham, Brad. "A Note on the Significance of the Merchant in the Development of St. Louis Society as Expressed in the Philosophy of the Mercantile Library Association," *Missouri Historical Review*, LVII (January, 1963), 184–198.

Marshall, Thomas Maitland. "The Miners' Laws of Colorado," *American Historical Review*, XXV (April, 1920), 426–439.

McGee, L. A. "Colorado Pioneers in the Civil War," *Southwestern Social Science Quarterly*, XXV (June, 1944), 31–42.

"Nathaniel P. Hill Inspects Colorado," *Colorado Magazine*, XXXIII (October, 1956), 241–276.

Nichols, Roy F. "The Kansas-Nebraska Act: A Century of Historiography," *Mississippi Valley Historical Review*, XLIII (September, 1956), 187–212.

*Oregon Historical Quarterly*, II (June, 1901), 192; IV (September, 1903), 271–272 [newspaper extracts].

Parish, William J. "The German Jew and the Commercial Revolution in Territorial New Mexico, 1850–1900," *New Mexico Historical Review*, XXXV (January, 1960), 1–29.

Pitcock, Cynthia De Haven. "The Darnes-Davis Case, 1840," *Missouri Historical Review*, LVIII (October, 1964), 31–45.

Porter, Kenneth W. "William Gilpin: Sinophile and Eccentric," *Colorado Magazine*, XXXVII (October, 1960), 245–253.

Pratte, General Bernard, Jr. "Reminiscences," *Missouri Historical Society Bulletin*, VI (October, 1949), 59–71.

Sanford, Albert B. "Camp Weld, Colorado," *Colorado Magazine*, XI (March, 1934), 46–50.

Schenck, Robert C. "Major-General David Hunter," *Magazine of American History*, XVII (February, 1887), 138–152.

"Slopes and Valleys of the Rocky Mountains," *The Western Journal and Civilian*, X (April, 1853), 1–11.

Tegeder, Vincent G. "Lincoln and the Territorial Patronage: The Ascendancy of the Radicals in the West," *Mississippi Valley Historical Review*, XXXV (June, 1948), 77–90.

Vevier, Charles. "American Continentalism: An Idea of Expansionism, 1845–1910," *American Historical Review*, LXV (January, 1960), 323–335.

Wood, William A. "Daniel Webster's Visit to Missouri," *Magazine of American History*, XIX (June, 1888), 513–516.

Wright, Arthur A. "Colonel John P. Slough and the New Mexico Campaign," *Colorado Magazine*, XXXIX (April, 1962), 89–105.

Wroten, William H., Jr. "Colorado and the Advent of the Civil War," *Colorado Magazine*, XXXVI (June, 1959), 174–186.

Zweig, Sheldon S. "The Civil Administration of Governor William Gilpin," *Colorado Magazine*, XXXI (July, 1954), 179–193.

## Books

Allen, [Miss] A. J. *Ten Years in Oregon*. Ithaca, N.Y.: Mack, Andersen, 1848.

Allen, Opal S. *Narcissa Whitman*. Portland, Ore.: Binfords and Mort, 1959.

Alter, J. Cecil. *Jim Bridger*. Norman: University of Oklahoma Press, 1962.

American Guide Series. *Colorado*. New York: Hastings House, 1941.

Anderson, George L. *General William J. Palmer*. Colorado Springs: Colorado College Press, 1936.

Athearn, Robert G. *Rebel of the Rockies*. New Haven, Conn.: Yale University Press, 1962.

Audubon, Maria R. *Audubon and His Journals*. 2 vols. New York: Charles Scribner's Sons, 1897.

Bancroft, Hubert Howe. *History of the Life of William Gilpin*. San Francisco: The History Co., 1889.

———. *History of Nevada, Colorado, and Wyoming*. San Francisco: The History Co., 1890.

———. *History of Oregon*. San Francisco: The History Co., 1886.

———. *The Works*. 39 vols. San Francisco: The History Co., 1883–1890.

Barrows, William. *Oregon: The Struggle for Possession*. Boston: Houghton Mifflin, 1889.

Bartlett, Ruhl J. *John C. Frémont and the Republican Party*. Columbus: Ohio State University Press, 1930.

Bates, Edward. *The Diary of Edward Bates*. Howard K. Beale (ed.). Washington, D.C.: Government Printing Office, 1933.

Benton, Thomas H. *Thirty Years' View.* 2 vols. New York: D. Appleton & Co., 1854–1856.

Bieber, Ralph P. (ed.). *Southern Trails to California in 1849.* Glendale, Calif.: Arthur H. Clark, 1937.

Bigland, Eileen. *The Indomitable Mrs. Trollope.* Philadelphia: J. B. Lippincott, 1954.

Binkley, William C. *The Expansionist Movement in Texas, 1836–1850.* Berkeley: University of California Press, 1925.

Blackmore, William. *Colorado: Its Resources, Parks and Prospects.* London: Sampson, Low, Son, and Marston, 1869.

Bonner, T. D. *Life and Adventures of James P. Beckwourth.* New York: Harper & Brothers, 1856.

Bowles, Samuel. *The Pacific Railroad—Open.* Boston: Fields, Osgood, 1869.

Brackett, Albert G. *History of the United States Cavalry.* New York: Harper & Brothers, 1865.

Brayer, Herbert O. *William Blackmore.* 2 vols. Denver: Bradford Robinson, 1949.

Bridenbaugh, Carl and Jessica. *Rebels and Gentlemen.* New York: Oxford University Press, 1962.

Brockett, Linus. *Our Western Empire.* Philadelphia: Bradley, Garretson, 1882.

Brooks, Van Wyck. *The Confident Years.* New York: E. P. Dutton & Co., 1952.

Brown, A. Theodore. *Frontier Community: Kansas City to 1870.* Columbia: University of Missouri Press, 1963.

Broyles, C. E., and John W. Hamm. *The Beaubien-Gilpin Grant; The Fraud of the Kellogg Survey Exposed.* Alamosa, Colo.: Independent Book and Printing, 1882.

Burnett, Peter H. *Recollections and Opinions of an Old Pioneer.* New York: D. Appleton, 1880.

Byers, William N. *Encyclopedia of Biography of Colorado.* Chicago: Century Publishing and Engraving, 1901.

Cable, John R. *The Bank of the State of Missouri.* New York: Columbia University Press, 1923.

Carman, Harry J., and Reinhard Luthin. *Lincoln and the Patronage.* New York: Columbia University Press, 1943.

Catterall, Ralph C. H. *The Second Bank of the United States.* Chicago: University of Chicago Press, 1903.

Caughey, John W. *Hubert Howe Bancroft.* Berkeley: University of California Press, 1946.

Chambers, J. S. *The Conquest of Cholera.* New York: Macmillan Co., 1938.

Chambers, William N. *Old Bullion Benton.* Boston: Little, Brown & Co., 1956.

Chester County Historical Society. *Lafayette at Brandywine.* West Chester, Pa.: Chester County Historical Society, 1896.

Chittenden, Hiram M., and Albert T. Richardson. *Life, Letters and Travels of Father Pierre-Jean de Smet, S.J.* 4 vols. New York: F. P. Harper, 1905.

Clyman, James. *James Clyman.* Charles L. Camp (ed.). San Francisco: California Historical Society, 1928.

Collins, Charles. *The Rocky Mountain Gold Regions and Emigrants' Guide.* Denver: Rocky Mountain News, 1861.

Colton, Ray C. *The Civil War in the Western Territories.* Norman: University of Oklahoma Press, 1959.

Connelley, William E. *Doniphan's Expedition.* Topeka, Kans.: By author, 1907.

―――― (ed.). *The Provisional Government of Nebraska Territory and the Journals of William Walker.* Lincoln, Neb.: State Journal, 1899.

Cooke, Philip St. George. *The Conquest of New Mexico and California.* Oakland, Calif.: Biobooks, 1942.

Corliss, Carlton J. *Main Line of Mid-America.* New York: Creative Age, 1950.

Dalton, William J. *The Life of Father Bernard Donnelly.* Kansas City, Mo.: Grimes-Joyce, 1921.

Darby, John F. *Personal Recollections.* St. Louis: G. I. Jones, 1880.

Darrah, William C. *Powell of the Colorado.* Princeton, N.J.: Princeton University Press, 1951.

Davis, Walter, and Daniel S. Durrie. *History of Missouri.* St. Louis: Robert Clarke, 1876.

Deatherage, Charles P. *Early History of Greater Kansas City, Missouri and Kansas.* Kansas City, Mo.: 1927.

Denver Pacific Railway. *First Annual Report.* Chicago: Rand McNally & Co., 1869.

De Terra, Helmut. *Humboldt.* New York: Alfred A. Knopf, 1955.

De Voto, Bernard. *The Year of Decision: 1846.* Boston: Houghton Mifflin, 1961.

Dilke, Charles W. *Greater Britain.* New York: Harper & Brothers, 1869.

Dixon, William Hepworth. *New America*. London: Hurst and Blackett, 1867.

Drake, Benjamin. *The Life and Adventures of Black Hawk*. Cincinnati: George Conclin, 1838.

Duffus, R. L. *The Santa Fé Trail*. New York: Longmans, Green & Co., 1930.

Edwards, Frank S. *A Campaign in New Mexico with Colonel Doniphan*. Philadelphia: Carey and Hart, 1847.

Edwards, Marcellus. *The Journal of Marcellus Edwards*. Ralph P. Bieber (ed.). Glendale, Calif.: Arthur H. Clark, 1936.

Edwards, Richard, and M. Hopewell. *The Great West*. St. Louis: Edwards' Monthly, 1860.

Elliott, Richard S. *Notes Taken in Sixty Years*. St. Louis: R. P. Studley, 1883.

Ellis, Elmer. *Henry Moore Teller*. Caldwell, Idaho: Caxton, 1941.

Ellison, Robert S. *Independence Rock*. Casper, Wyo.: Natrona County Historical Society, 1930.

Emory, William H. *Notes of a Military Reconnaissance*. Washington, D.C.: Wendell and Van Benthuysen, 1848.

Ewan, Joseph. *Rocky Mountain Naturalists*. Denver: University of Denver Press, 1950.

Farnham, Thomas J. *Thomas J. Farnham's Travels in the Great Western Prairies*. Reuben G. Thwaites (ed.). 2 vols. Cleveland: Arthur H. Clark, 1906.

Ferguson, Philip. *The Diary of Philip Ferguson*. Ralph P. Bieber (ed.). Glendale, Calif.: Arthur H. Clark, 1936.

Fergusson, Erna. *New Mexico*. New York: Alfred A. Knopf, 1955.

Ferril, Will C. *Sketches of Colorado*. Denver: Western Press Bureau, 1911.

Field, Mathew C. *Prairie and Mountain Sketches*. John F. McDermott (ed.), with Kate Gregg. Norman: University of Oklahoma Press, 1957.

Fisher, John S. *A Builder of the West*. Caldwell, Idaho: Caxton, 1939.

Foreman, Grant. *Indian Removal*. Norman: University of Oklahoma Press, 1932.

Fossett, Frank. *Colorado*. New York: C. G. Crawford, 1880.

Frederick, J. V. *Ben Holladay*. Glendale, Calif.: Arthur H. Clark, 1940.

Frémont, John Charles. *Memoirs of my Life*. Chicago: Belford, Clarke and Co., 1887.

Fritz, Percy. *Colorado: The Centennial State*. New York: Prentice-Hall, 1941.

Froebel, Julius. *Seven Years' Travel in Central America*. London: Richard Bentley, 1859.

Fuess, Claude M. *Daniel Webster*. 2 vols. Boston: Little, Brown & Co., 1930.

Galbraith, John S. *The Hudson's Bay Company as an Imperial Factor, 1821–1869*. Berkeley: University of California Press, 1957.

Gardner, Charles K. *A Dictionary of All Officers in the Army of the United States*. New York: G. P. Putnam's Sons, 1853.

Garrard, Lewis H. *Wah-to-Yah and the Taos Trail*. Ralph P. Bieber (ed.). Glendale, Calif.: Arthur H. Clark, 1938.

Gates, Paul W. *The Illinois Central Railroad and its Colonization Work*. Cambridge, Mass.: Harvard University Press, 1934.

George, Isaac. *Heroes and Incidents of the Mexican War*. Greensburg, Pa.: Review Publishing, 1903.

Ghent, W. J. *The Road to Oregon*. New York: Longman's, Green & Co., 1929.

Gibson, George R. *The Diary of George R. Gibson*. Ralph P. Bieber (ed.). Glendale, Calif.: Arthur H. Clark, 1935.

Gilpin, William. *The Cosmopolitan Railway*. San Francisco: The History Co., 1890.

———. *Mission of the North American People*. Philadelphia: J. B. Lippincott, 1873. (Published in 1860 as *The Central Gold Region*.)

———. *Notes on Colorado*. London: Witherby, 1870.

Glaab, Charles N. *Kansas City and the Railroads*. Madison: State Historical Society of Wisconsin, 1962.

Goddard, Frederick B. *Where to Emigrate and Why*. Philadelphia: People's Publishing, 1869.

Goetzmann, William H. *Army Exploration in the American West*. New Haven, Conn.: Yale University Press, 1959.

Govan, Thomas P. *Nicholas Biddle*. Chicago: University of Chicago Press, 1959.

Graebner, Norman. *Empire on the Pacific*. New York: Ronald Press, 1955.

Gray, William Henry. *A History of Oregon*. Portland, Ore.: Harris and Holman, 1870.

Greeley, Horace. *An Overland Journey*. New York: Alfred A. Knopf, 1964.

Greenhow, Robert. *The History of Oregon and California*. Boston: Little, 1845.

Gregg, Josiah. *Commerce of the Prairies*. Reuben G. Thwaites (ed.). Cleveland: Arthur H. Clark, 1905.

Grinnell, George Bird. *The Fighting Cheyennes.* Norman: University of Oklahoma Press, 1956.

Gwynn, Stephen, and Gertrude Tuckwell. *The Life of the Rt. Hon. Sir Charles W. Dilke.* London: J. Murray, 1917.

Hafen, Le Roy R. *Colorado: The Story of a Western Commonwealth.* Denver: Peerless Publishing, 1933.

————. (ed.). *Colorado Gold Rush.* Glendale, Calif.: Arthur H. Clark, 1941.

————. (ed.). *Pike's Peak Gold Rush Guidebooks of 1859.* Glendale, Calif.: Arthur H. Clark, 1941.

————, and W. J. Ghent. *Broken Hand.* Denver: The Old West, 1931.

————, and Carl Coke Rister. *Western America.* Englewood Cliffs, N.J.: Prentice-Hall, 1957.

Hagan, William T. *American Indians.* Chicago: University of Chicago Press, 1961.

Hall, Frank. *History of the State of Colorado.* 4 vols. Chicago: Blakely, 1889–1895.

Hall, Martin H. *Sibley's New Mexico Campaign.* Austin: University of Texas Press, 1960.

Hannay, David. *Life of Frederick Marryat.* London: W. J. Gage, 1889.

Harpending, Asbury. *The Great Diamond Hoax.* Norman: University of Oklahoma Press, 1958.

Harris, Edward. *Up the Missouri with Audubon: The Journal of Edward Harris.* John F. McDermott (ed.). Norman: University of Oklahoma Press, 1951.

Haskell, Henry C., and Richard B. Fowler. *City of the Future.* Kansas City, Mo.: Glenn Publishing, 1950.

Hayes, A. A., Jr. *New Colorado and the Santa Fé Trail.* New York: Harper & Brothers, 1880.

Herr, John K., and Edward S. Wallace. *The Story of the United States Cavalry.* Boston: Little, Brown & Co., 1953.

*History of the City of Denver, Arapahoe County, and Colorado.* Chicago: O. L. Baskin, 1880.

Hoig, Stan. *The Sand Creek Massacre.* Norman: University of Oklahoma Press, 1961.

Howbert, Irving. *Memories of a Lifetime in the Pike's Peak Region.* New York: G. P. Putnam's Sons, 1925.

Hughes, John T. *Doniphan's Expedition.* Cincinnati: By author, 1847.

Hunt, Elvid. *History of Fort Leavenworth.* Fort Leavenworth, Kans.: Command and General Staff School, 1937.

Hunter, Dard. *Papermaking in Pioneer America.* Philadelphia: University of Pennsylvania Press, 1952.

Irving, Washington. *The Adventures of Captain Bonneville, U.S.A.* Norman: University of Oklahoma Press, 1961.

Johnson, Allen, and Dumas Malone (eds.). *Dictionary of American Biography.* New York: Charles Scribner's Sons, 1928–1958.

Johnston, Abraham Robinson. *The Journal of Abraham Robinson Johnston.* Ralph P. Bieber (ed.). Glendale, Calif.: Arthur H. Clark, 1936.

Johnston, William Preston. *The Johnstons of Salisbury.* New Orleans: L. Graham and Son, 1897.

Kennerly, William Clark. *Persimmon Hill.* Norman: University of Oklahoma Press, 1948.

Kerby, Robert L. *The Confederate Invasion of New Mexico and Arizona.* Los Angeles: Westernlore, 1958.

Kerr, John K. *The Story of the United States Cavalry.* Boston: Little, Brown & Co., 1953.

King, Clyde L. *The History of the Government of Denver.* Denver: Fisher, 1911.

Larimer, General William. *Reminiscences of General William Larimer.* Lancaster, Pa.: New Era Printing, 1918.

Lavender, David. *Bent's Fort.* Garden City, N.Y.: Doubleday & Co., 1954.

———. *The Big Divide.* Garden City, N.Y.: Doubleday & Co., 1949.

———. *Westward Vision.* New York: McGraw-Hill Book Co., 1963.

Levin, Bernard (ed.). *Guide to the Manuscript Collections of the Historical Society of Pennsylvania.* Philadelphia: Historical Society of Pennsylvania, 1949.

Lewis, Walker. *Without Fear or Favor: A Biography of Chief Justice Roger Brooke Taney.* Boston: Houghton Mifflin, 1965.

Lincoln, Abraham. *The Collected Works of Abraham Lincoln.* Roy P. Basler (ed.). 8 vols. New Brunswick, N.J.: Rutgers University Press, 1953.

Linn, Elizabeth A. *The Life and Public Services of Dr. Lewis F. Linn.* New York: D. Appleton, 1857.

Lyon, William H. *The Pioneer Editor in Missouri, 1808–1860.* Columbia: University of Missouri Press, 1965.

Magoffin, Susan S. *Down the Santa Fé Trail and into Mexico: The Diary of Susan Shelby Magoffin.* Stella M. Drumm (ed.). New Haven, Conn.: Yale University Press, 1926.

Malin, James C. *The Grassland of North America.* Lawrence, Kans.: By author, 1947.

———. *The Nebraska Question, 1852–1854.* Lawrence, Kans.: By author, 1953.

McClure, A. K. *Three Thousand Miles through the Rocky Mountains.*
Philadelphia: J. B. Lippincott, 1869.

McClure, Clarence H. *Opposition in Missouri to Thomas Hart Benton.*
Nashville, Tenn.: George Peabody College, 1927.

McDermott, John F. (ed.). *Travels in Search of the Elephant.* St.
Louis: Missouri Historical Society, 1951.

McElroy, John. *The Struggle for Missouri.* Washington, D.C.: The
National Tribune, 1913.

McMechen, Edgar. *Life of Governor Evans.* Denver: Wahlgreen, 1924.

McReynolds, Edwin C. *Missouri: A History of the Crossroads State.*
Norman: University of Oklahoma Press, 1962.

———. *The Seminoles.* Norman: University of Oklahoma Press, 1957.

Meigs, William M. *The Life of Thomas Hart Benton.* Philadelphia:
J. B. Lippincott, 1904.

———. *The Life of Charles Jared Ingersoll.* Philadelphia: J. B. Lippincott, 1897.

Miller, Marion M. (ed.). *Great Debates in American History.* 14 vols.
New York: Current Literature Publishing, 1913.

Miller, William H. *The History of Kansas City.* Kansas City, Mo.:
Birdsall and Miller, 1881.

Million, John W. *State Aid in Railways in Missouri.* Chicago: University of Chicago Press, 1896.

Montgomery, Elizabeth. *Reminiscences of Wilmington.* Philadelphia:
T. K. Collins, 1851.

Montgomery, Richard G. *The White-Headed Eagle.* New York: Macmillan Co., 1934.

Moorhead, Max L. (ed.). *Commerce of the Prairies.* Norman: University of Oklahoma Press, 1954.

———. *New Mexico's Royal Road.* Norman: University of Oklahoma
Press, 1958.

Munroe, John A. *Federalist Delaware.* New Brunswick, N.J.: Rutgers
University Press, 1954.

*The National Cyclopaedia of American Biography,* VI. New York:
James L. White, 1896.

Nesmith, J. W. *Transactions of the Oregon Pioneer Association.* Salem,
Ore.: E. M. Waite, 1874–1886.

Nevins, Allan (ed.). *Narratives of Exploration and Adventure.* New
York: Longmans, Green & Co., 1956.

Newell, Robert. *Robert Newell's Memoranda.* Dorothy O. Johansen
(ed.). Portland, Ore.: Champoeg Press, 1959.

Nolan, J. Bennett. *Lafayette in America Day by Day.* Baltimore: The
Johns Hopkins University Press, 1934.

Overton, Richard C. *Gulf to Rockies*. Austin: University of Texas Press, 1953.

Palmer, Joel. *Joel Palmer's Journal*. Reuben G. Thwaites (ed.). Cleveland: Arthur H. Clark, 1906.

Parrish, William E. *David Rice Atchison of Missouri*. Columbia: University of Missouri Press, 1961.

————. *Turbulent Partnership: Missouri and the Union, 1861–1865*. Columbia: University of Missouri Press, 1963.

Pearson, Jim Berry. *The Maxwell Land Grant*. Norman: University of Oklahoma Press, 1960.

Pennsylvania, Historical Society of. See Levin, Bernard.

Perkins, George Gilpin. *The Kentucky Gilpins*. Washington, D.C.: W. F. Roberts, 1927.

Peters, De Witt. *Kit Carson's Life and Adventures*. Hartford, Conn.: Dustin, Gilman, 1874.

Pierson, George Wilson. *Tocqueville and Beaumont in America*. New York: Oxford University Press, 1938.

Polk, James K. *The Diary of James K. Polk*. Milo M. Quaife (ed.). 4 vols. Chicago: A. C. McClurg & Co., 1910.

Porter, Mae Reed, and Odessa Davenport. *Scotsman in Buckskin*. New York: Hastings House, 1963.

Potter, John Mason. *Thirteen Desperate Days*. New York: Ivan Obolensky, 1964.

Potter, Woodburne. *The War in Florida*. Baltimore: Lewis and Coleman, 1836.

Preuss, Charles. *Exploring with Frémont*. Norman: University of Oklahoma Press, 1958.

Primm, James N. *Economic Policy in the Development of a Western State, Missouri*. Cambridge, Mass.: Harvard University Press, 1954.

Prucha, Francis P. (ed.). *Army Life on the Western Frontier*. Norman: University of Oklahoma Press, 1958.

Pulszky, Francis and Theresa. *White, Red, Black*. 3 vols. New York: Redfield, 1853.

Ray, P. Orman. *The Repeal of the Missouri Compromise*. Cleveland: Arthur H. Clark, 1909.

Reavis, Logan V. *The National Capital Is Movable*. St. Louis: Missouri Democrat Book and Job Printing, 1871.

————. *A Pamphlet for the People Containing Facts and Arguments in Favor of the Removal of the National Capital to the Mississippi Valley*. St. Louis: E. P. Gray, 1869.

Redpath, James, and Richard J. Hinton. *Handbook to Kansas Territory and the Rocky Mountain Gold Regions.* New York: J. H. Colton, 1859.

Rich, E. E. *The Hudson's Bay Company, 1670–1870.* 3 vols. London: The Hudson's Bay Record Society, 1959.

Richardson, Albert D. *Beyond the Mississippi.* Hartford, Conn.: American Publishing, 1867.

Richardson, James D. (ed.). *A Compilation of the Messages and Papers of the Presidents, 1789–1897.* 9 vols. Washington, D.C.: U.S. Government Printing Office, 1896–1897.

Richardson, Rupert N. *The Comanche Barrier to South Plains Settlement.* Glendale, Calif.: Arthur H. Clark, 1933.

Richardson, William H. *Journal of William H. Richardson.* New York: By author, 1849.

Robinson, Jacob S. *A Journal of the Santa Fé Expedition under Colonel Doniphan.* Princeton: Princeton University Press, 1932.

Rodenbough, Theo. F. *From Everglades to Cañon with the Second Dragoons.* New York: D. Van Nostrand Co., 1875.

Rucker, Maude A. *The Oregon Trail and Some of Its Blazers.* New York: Walter Neale, 1930.

Ruxton, George A. F. *Ruxton of the Rockies.* Clyde and Mae Reed Porter and Le Roy Hafen (eds.). Norman: University of Oklahoma Press, 1950.

Sabin, Edwin L. *Kit Carson Days.* Chicago: A. C. McClurg, 1914.

Sanford, Mollie D. *Mollie: The Journal of Mollie Dorsey Sanford in Nebraska and Colorado Territories, 1857–1866.* Donald F. Danker (ed.). Lincoln: University of Nebraska Press, 1959.

Scharf, John Thomas. *History of St. Louis City and County.* 2 vols. Philadelphia: Louis H. Everts, 1883.

Schlesinger, Arthur M., Jr. *The Age of Jackson.* Boston: Little, Brown and Co., 1945.

Shepard, Edward. *Martin Van Buren.* Boston: Houghton Mifflin, 1894.

Shinn, Charles H. *Mining Camps.* New York: Alfred A. Knopf, 1948.

Simpson, Henry. *The Lives of Eminent Philadelphians.* Philadelphia: William Brotherhead, 1859.

Simpson, James H. *Navaho Expedition: Journal of Lt. James H. Simpson,* Frank McNitt (ed.). Norman: University of Oklahoma Press, 1964.

Smiley, Jerome C. *History of Denver.* Denver: J. H. Williamson, 1903.

Smith, Elbert B. *Magnificent Missourian.* Philadelphia: J. B. Lippincott, 1958.

Smith, Henry Nash. *Virgin Land: The American West as Symbol and Myth.* New York: Vintage Books, 1957.

Smith, Justin H. *The War with Mexico.* 2 vols. New York: Macmillan Co., 1919.

Smith, Willard H. *Schuyler Colfax.* Indianapolis: Indiana Historical Bureau, 1952.

Smith, William E. *The Francis Preston Blair Family in Politics.* 2 vols. New York: Macmillan Co., 1933.

Spalding, Charles C. *Annals of the City of Kansas.* Kansas City: Van Horn and Abeel, 1858.

Spicer, Edward H. *Cycles of Conquest.* Tucson: University of Arizona Press, 1962.

Sprague, John T. *The Origin, Progress and Conclusion of the Florida War.* New York: D. Appleton, 1848.

Sprague, Marshal. *Newport in the Rockies.* Denver: Sage Books, 1961.

Stearns, Charles. *The Black Man of the South and the Rebels.* New York: American News, 1872.

Stegner, Wallace. *Beyond the Hundredth Meridian.* Boston: Houghton Mifflin, 1962.

Steinel, Alvin T. *History of Agriculture in Colorado, 1856–1926.* Fort Collins, Colo.: State Agricultural College, 1926.

Stone, Wilbur Fisk (ed.). *History of Colorado.* 4 vols. Chicago: S. J. Clarke, 1918–1919.

Streeter, Floyd B. *The Kaw.* New York: Farrar & Rinehart, 1941.

Sunder, John E. *Bill Sublette, Mountain Man.* Norman: University of Oklahoma Press, 1959.

Swisher, Carl Brent. *Roger B. Taney.* New York: Macmillan Co., 1935.

Talbot, Theodore. *The Journals of Theodore Talbot.* Charles H. Carey (ed.). Portland, Oregon: Metropolitan, 1931.

Tocqueville, Alexis de. *Journey to America.* J. P. Mayer (ed.). New Haven, Conn.: Yale University Press, 1960.

Tomlinson, William P. *Kansas in 1858.* New York: H. Dayton, 1859.

Tyler, Samuel. *Memoir of Roger Brooke Taney.* Baltimore: John Murphy, 1872.

Underhill, Ruth. *The Navajos.* Norman: University of Oklahoma Press, 1956.

United States Government. *The War of the Rebellion: A Compilation of the Official Records of the Union and Confederate Armies.* 127 vols. Washington, D.C.: Government Printing Office, 1880–1902.

United States Government, Works Progress Administration. *Guide to Manuscript Collections of the Oregon Historical Society.* Portland: University of Oregon Press, 1940.

Victor, Frances Fuller. *The River of the West.* Hartford, Conn.: R. W. Bliss, 1870.

Wagner, Henry R. *The Plains and the Rockies*. Revised by Charles C. Camp. Columbus, Ohio: Long's College Book Co., 1953.

Ward, Christopher L. *The Delaware Continentals*. Wilmington: Historical Society of Delaware, 1941.

Waters, L. L. *Steel Trails to Santa Fe*. Lawrence: University of Kansas Press, 1950.

Webb, James J. *Adventures in the Santa Fe Trade: The Journal of James J. Webb*. Ralph P. Bieber (ed.). Glendale, Calif.: Arthur H. Clark, 1931.

Webb, William L. *The Centennial History of Independence, Missouri*. Independence, Mo.: By author, 1927.

West, Elizabeth. *Calendar of the Papers of Martin Van Buren*. Washington, D.C.: U.S. Government Printing Office, 1910.

White, Leonard D. *The Jacksonians*. New York: Macmillan Co., 1954.

Whitford, William C. *Colorado Volunteers in the Civil War*. Denver: State Historical and Natural History Society, 1906.

Whitman, Walt. *The Complete Poetry and Prose of Walt Whitman*. Malcolm Cowley (ed.), 2 vols. New York: Pellegrini and Cudahy, 1948.

———. *Leaves of Grass*. Sculley Bradley (ed.), New York: Rinehart and Co., 1949.

Whitney, Asa. *A Project for a Railroad to the Pacific*. New York: George W. Wood, 1849.

Whitney, Carrie W. *Kansas City, Missouri: Its History and Its People, 1808–1908*. 3 vols. Chicago: S. J. Clarke, 1908.

Wilcox, General Cadmus. *History of the Mexican War*. Washington, D.C.: Church News Publishing, 1892.

Winther, Oscar. *The Trans-Mississippi West: A Guide to Its Periodical Literature*. Bloomington: Indiana University Press, 1942.

Wislizenus, Adolph. *Memoirs of a Tour to Northern Mexico*. Washington, D.C.: Tippin and Streeper, 1848.

Withington, Mary (comp). *A Catalogue of Manuscripts in the Collection of Western Americana*. New Haven, Conn: Yale University Press, 1952.

Woolsey, Theodore D. *Divorce and Divorce Legislation*. New York: Charles Scribner's Sons, 1882.

Yarnes, Thomas D. *A History of Oregon Methodism*. Nashville, Tenn.: Parthenon, 1961.

Young, Otis. *The West of Philip St. George Cooke*. Glendale, Calif.: Arthur H. Clark, 1955.

# INDEX